A Reader's Companion to the Novels and Short Stories of Evelyn Waugh

A READER'S COMPANION TO THE NOVELS AND SHORT STORIES OF EVELYN WAUGH

AN ANNOTATED GLOSSARY OF THE NARRATIVES, A WHO'S WHO AMONG THE CHARACTERS, A GAZETTEER OF THE PRINCIPAL PLACES, A DESCRIPTION OF THE IMPORTANT PROPER NAMES, AND AN EXPLANATION OF ABBREVIATIONS USED IN THE STORIES

By

Paul A. Doyle

with an Appendix by

Donald Greene

PILGRIM BOOKS
Norman, Oklahoma

Doyle, Paul A.
　　A reader's companion to the novels and short stories of Evelyn Waugh : an annotated glossary of the narratives, a who's who among the characters, a gazetteer of the principal places, a description of the important proper names, and an explanation of abbreviations used in the stories / by Paul A. Doyle.
　　　p.　cm.
　Bibliography: p.
　Includes index.
　ISBN 0-937664-78-2
　1. Waugh, Evelyn, 1903-1966—Criticism and interpretation.
2. Waugh, Evelyn, 1903-1966—Dictionaries, indexes, etc.　I. Title
PR6045.A97Z682　1988
　　823'.912—dc19　　　　　　　　　　　　　　　　88-2407
　　　　　　　　　　　　　　　　　　　　　　　　　　　CIP

To my son, Rob,
who took an interest

CONTENTS

Preface	ix
Abbreviations Used for Waugh's Novels and Stories	xv
I. The Glossary	1

The Novels

Decline and Fall (1928)	3
Vile Bodies (1930)	15
Black Mischief (1932)	23
A Handful of Dust (1934)	27
Scoop (1938)	31
Put Out More Flags (1942)	35
Work Suspended (1942)	43
Brideshead Revisited (1945)	47
Scott-King's Modern Europe (1947)	59
The Loved One (1948)	61
Helena (1950)	67
Men at Arms (1952)	73
Love Among the Ruins (1953)	81
Officers and Gentlemen (1955)	83
The Ordeal of Gilbert Pinfold (1957)	91
End of the Battle / Unconditional Surrender (1961)	95

The Short Stories

	105
A House of Gentlefolks	105
An Englishman's Home	105
Basil Seal Rides Again	105

CONTENTS

    Bella Fleace Gave a Party   106
    By Special Request   106
    Charles Ryder's Schooldays   106
    Consequences   108
    Cruise: Letters from a Young Lady of Leisure   108
    Excursion in Reality   108
    Incident in Azania   108
    Love in the Slump   109
    Mr. Loveday's Little Outing   109
    On Guard   109
    Out of Depth   109
    Period Piece   109
    Tactical Exercise   109
    The Balance   109
    The Major Intervenes   111
    The Manager of the Kremlin   111
    Winner Takes All   111

II. The Dictionary   113

III. Appendices   205

    1. Frequent Abbreviations Used in Waugh's Fiction   207
    2. Common References in Waugh's Fiction   208
    3. Evelyn Waugh's Hollywood, by Donald Greene   209
    4. Map of Azania   213

Bibliography   215

Index to the Glossary   217

PREFACE

While teaching several of Evelyn Waugh's novels and some of his short stories in various college and university classes for many years, I became keenly aware that a considerable number of his allusions and references were unidentified. This situation was particularly distressing because it meant that the full satiric, comic, and thematic implications of many words, phrases, and passages were consequently not perceived. This omission also meant that Waugh's writings, which are exceedingly rich in allusion (in "undertones and innuendoes," to use his own words), did not receive the comprehensive understanding and analysis they merited.

Ignorance of historical, literary, and cultural information and even rather ordinary allusions increased drastically in the 1960s and in the early 1970s, when suddenly—for many—history came to mean only the present and the future, and learning in general was frequently belittled. Not only were countless students and others programmed not to trust anyone over thirty, but also fundamental data and past cultural knowledge were scorned. While more balanced times have arrived, and a return to basics is being stressed, there are vast knowledge gaps in considerable numbers of today's students, graduates, and general readers.

It is always surprising too how quickly people forget. Although many of Waugh's contemporaries fought in various branches of British military service in World War II, correspondence revealed that the meanings of many military terms and usages had faded from memory, and even specialized military manuals did not include various terms that were common in the 1920s, 1930s, and 1940s. Thus it would appear that, although this volume is intended primarily for American readers, it will also be of help to students and readers outside the United States and Canada.

Among Roman Catholics the Second Vatican Council (1962–1965) produced a similar outcome. Today it is rare to find even older Catholics who remember the meaning of Latin words and rituals which were for centuries basic to the liturgies and practices of the Roman church. Ask a member of that body to explain the practice of *toties quoties* or the meaning of the Exultet prayer, and he or she will very likely not recall. Even English-language terms such as

PREFACE

the "Seven Dolours of the Virgin Mary" or the "morning's new fire" will usually draw a puzzled expression.

Apart from providing help to the college and university student and the general reader, this book includes sundry allusions and references that even the scholar or advanced reader will not be able to decipher, words and phrases that puzzled reputable dictionary compilers and language experts. Let me cite some examples: "a handkerchief at Downside," "chub fuddler," "eighteenth in the Crick at Rugby" (which, surprisingly, has nothing to do with cricket), "shari," "Carthusian tie," "Chindits," "tukals," "Keatings," "call out the marker," "Burton's stucco tent," "G1098," "third E in Bee Garden," "OZNA," "Bedfordshire for you," "Sedobrol," "small pieces of coal in his dripping," "slap up," "Randall Cantuar," and "Homoiousion... Homoousion." This is just a sampling. Waugh's vocabulary is decidedly extensive, and his learning is much more comprehensive than has been granted by some critics. His books are geared for a widely read, cultured audience that is expected to recognize his allusions and their meanings. References to art, history, literature, and political, religious, and social aspects abound. The more a reader's mind is stocked with such information, the more he or she will fully appreciate the depth and richness of Waugh's novels and stories.

Furthermore, Waugh is a master of dialogue, and it is disappointing to discover that numerous words and phrases he uses are not found in the *OED*, in Webster's various dictionaries, or in Partridge — to mention just three vital sources of word meaning. Indeed, Waugh has often not been given proper semantic acknowledgment for recording the language of the Bright Young People. It is upsetting that the *OED*, for instance, does not credit him in this regard. Even in the area of abbreviations, none of the standard reference books (both British and American) in this category lists even half the abbreviations Waugh uses.

There are other gaps. For example, the most respected biographical reference authority could not furnish data on Yuan T'se. Other figures, such as Pussy Gresham, had to be researched beyond the knowledge readily available in libraries. The scholarly reader and researcher thus also needs assistance with certain references, which this volume furnishes.

As most serious readers are aware, many of Waugh's characters are based on real-life individuals, some of whom were quite willing to claim the resemblance (Lady Diana Cooper as Julia Stitch, for example), while others obviously were less willing to be identified. I have in numerous instances indicated the probable real-life prototypes for the fictional characters. I have deliberately limited these identifications to the most obvious and/or widely agreed-upon prototypes.

While working on the Glossary, I realized that a Dictionary unit, combining a Who's Who and a Gazetteer, would be immensely useful. Accordingly, this book is divided into two major parts, Glossary and Dictionary. In the earliest stages of this eight-year project, this volume was called "A Glossary, Who's Who, Gazetteer, and Listing of Proper Names." Such a title was obviously unwieldy, and the present encyclopedia term came to be substituted as a more concise description.

The glossary entries are arranged in alphabetical order under each novel or story. Since in every novel there is more than one word or phrase that requires clarification, the present arrangement makes it handy for the reader without too much page turning. The material of the particular novel under study can be consulted quickly. It would be profitable to read over the Glossary before reading a particular novel or story.

The Dictionary is arranged alphabetically, again for speedy reference. In some instances there are necessary cross references linking the Glossary and the Dictionary.

To avoid considerable repetition, I have listed in the Appendices words and abbreviations that Waugh uses with frequency. In some instances, further data have had to be presented in the Glossary. For example, although "Lloyd George" and "QM" are identified in the appendices, additional elaboration had to be given when they appear in a somewhat different form in a novel, say, in such expressions as "Lloyd George creation" or "the Q side." The various references to "House" have been reserved for the Glossary since, depending on the context, the word can indicate not only the Parliament but also a unit of a public school, or even a reference to Oxford's Christ Church.

I have annotated all of Waugh's short stories that appeared in collected editions of his fiction plus several that were scattered until Robert Murray Davis helpfully gathered them into his *Evelyn Waugh, Apprentice* (Norman, Okla., 1985). These stories are "The Balance," "A House of Gentlefolks," "The Manager of the Kremlin," "Too Much Tolerance," and "The Sympathetic Passenger." I also examined "Consequences," a narrative reprinted in Donat Gallagher's *The Essays, Articles and Reviews of Evelyn Waugh* (Boston, 1984). Except for the often reprinted "The Curse of the Horse Race," I have not included any of the juvenilia or college work because it was simply apprenticeship before the literary career commenced in earnest.

At times it was difficult to know what should or should not be placed in the Glossary (a problem with any Glossary), since some references will be widely known, while others are more complex and unknown or will be recognized by fewer readers. I, therefore, based decisions on American college and university testing while teaching the novels. Such words as "posh," or abbreviations such as "P.M." or "U.K." were familiar and thus have been omitted. On the other hand, most students did not understand the expression "in the soup" or, amazingly, an abbreviation like "R.A.F." Some names, such as Paddington, Euston, Victoria, and Charing Cross, were not listed because students recognized these in context as London railway stations. I also did not list references to the *Times* of London, which is mentioned in many novels.

At some future time a definitive variorum text of Waugh's novels will have to be produced, for the stories are filled with editorial misreadings and careless proofreading. I have attempted to give an impetus in this direction by indicating several of the textual errors and giving their correct form. To list just a few examples here: "the 1920 Committee" should read "the 1922 Committee"; "When we get over 1098" is properly "When we get our 1098"; "thimble and pen men" should read "thimble and pea men"; and "four months' solitary" should read "four weeks' solitary."

Another aspect is Waugh's considerable use of parody of other literary works. Shakespeare's "What a piece of work is man!" is parodied by Otto Silenus's "What an immature, self-destructive, antiquated mischief is man!" Edward C. McAleer ("*Decline and Fall* as Imitation,"

PREFACE

EWN [Winter, 1973]: 1–4) has given many examples of parody in *Decline and Fall*, but Waugh makes use of such allusions throughout his writings, and I have pointed out several that previously have not been recorded but have not attempted to exhaust this phase of his work.

The overall aim of this volume is to present a compendium of data and information which will be of considerable aid to anyone who reads or studies Waugh's fiction. It should be noted further that supplementary data or addenda may be sent for publication to the *Evelyn Waugh Newsletter*.

All quotations from Waugh's works have been reprinted by permission of the Peters Fraser & Dunlop Group, Ltd.

I am indebted to the Harry Ransom Humanities Research Center, the University of Texas at Austin, for allowing me to quote from unpublished manuscripts in their possession.

I thank the Board of Trustees of Nassau College, State University of New York, and the College Sabbatical Committee for granting me a sabbatical to do research for this volume.

I express deep gratitude to Robert Murray Davis, who read the typescript and offered many suggestions which helped improve the book.

I thank Donald Greene, Michael Richards, and Jacqueline McDonnell for granting me permission to quote directly from their correspondence.

The Lorette Wilmot Library, Nazareth College of Rochester, furnished me with photostats that were difficult to obtain elsewhere.

I also wish to acknowledge the help of many friends and correspondents who have shared knowledge and helped me in various ways to identify and explicate the meaning of various allusions and references. I must record my thanks to the following: Sir Harold Acton, Mark Amory, Neville Braybrooke, the Honorable Penelope Betjeman, Winnifred Bogaards, Stephen Brooks, Alan Brown, Sir Robert W. Burchfield, Mrs. M. Jay Byam, Frank Cavallo, Alan Clodd, Lady Diana Cooper, Edward Coyne, Ellen T. Crowley, Michael Davie, William Deedes, Ralph De Sola, Helen Fenwick, R. Fish, Roger Fulford, Donat Gallagher, Thomas A. Gribble, B. W. T. Handford, Peg Haskel, Jeffrey Heath, Philip Howard, Jeanne Hunter, Stanley Kallaur, Charles E. Linck, Jr., Richard A. Matzek, Sir Fitzroy MacLean, Jacqueline McDonnell, the Reverend Robert F. McNamara, Rosamund E. Moon, Malcolm Muggeridge, Mrs. Betty Patterson, John Paxton, Joanna Poletti, Anthony Powell, Alan Pryce-Jones, Peter Quennell, Sandra Raphael, the Reverend Michael Richards, John St. John, Martin Stannard, Peter Stansky, Richard Streeton, A. J. P. Taylor, archivist Ruth F. Vyse, the late Alec Waugh, Auberon Waugh, and the Honorable Marie I. A. Woodruff.

I must especially thank Donald J. Greene, of the University of Southern California, who used his very considerable knowledge to help me bring this volume to completion. It was Greene who discovered the meaning of many of the most difficult allusions, e.g., Burton's stucco tent, Pussy Gresham, and the poem in *The Loved One* beginning "O God who set her brave eyes wide apart." Furthermore, as a member of the Canadian army in World War II, he identified a countless number of the more obscure or outdated military terms which even several former members of the English military establishment seemed to have forgotten. I also

PREFACE

thank him for allowing me to reprint, as Appendix 3, his illuminating and invaluable map of and accompanying essay on Waugh's Hollywood. My depth of gratitude to Greene is truly immense, and I most happily acknowledge his help and encouragement.

Garden City, New York   PAUL A. DOYLE

ABBREVIATIONS USED FOR WAUGH'S NOVELS AND STORIES

BFGP	"Bella Fleace Gave a Party"	MA	Men at Arms
BM	Black Mischief	MCLO	"Mr. Crutwell's Little Outing"
BR	Brideshead Revisited	MCO	"Mr. Crutwell's Outing"
BSR	"By Special Request" (the alternate ending for HD)	MK	"The Manager of the Kremlin"
		MLLO	"Mr. Loveday's Little Outing"
BSRA	Basil Seal Rides Again	OD	"Out of Depth"
C	"Compassion"	OG	Officers and Gentlemen
CHR	"The Curse of the Horse Race"	OGP	The Ordeal of Gilbert Pinfold
Co	"Consequences"	OGu	"On Guard"
Cr	"Cruise"	POMF	Put Out More Flags
CRS	Charles Ryder's Schooldays	PP	"Period Piece"
DF	Decline and Fall	Sc	Scoop
EB	The End of the Battle (the American title for Unconditional Surrender)	SKME	Scott-King's Modern Europe
		SOH	Sword of Honour
EH	"An Englishman's Home"	SP	"The Sympathetic Passenger"
ER	"Excursion in Reality"	TB	"The Balance"
H	Helena	TE	"Tactical Exercise"
HD	A Handful of Dust	TMI	"The Major Intervenes"
HG	"A House of Gentlefolks"	TMWLD	"The Man Who Liked Dickens"
IA	"Incident in Azania"	US	Unconditional Surrender (British title for The End of the Battle)
LAR	Love Among the Ruins	VB	Vile Bodies
LITS	"Love in the Slump"	WS	Work Suspended
LO	The Loved One	WTA	"Winner Takes All"

THE GLOSSARY

DECLINE AND FALL (1928)

In choosing this title, Waugh parodies Edward Gibbon's history, *The Decline and Fall of the Roman Empire*, which appeared in six volumes (1776–1788). In concise, satiric form, *Decline and Fall*, like *Vile Bodies*, portrays several aspects of England's loss of power and influence after World War I.

Dedicatee

Harold Acton (1904–) became a friend of Waugh's at Oxford and was a famous aesthete there. Acton and Waugh remained friends, and Acton himself wrote several novels and numerous works of nonfiction. Some of the qualities illustrated by Anthony Blanche in *Brideshead Revisited* were based on the character of Acton.

"above stairs" — In the family's, not the servants', part of the house. "Upstairs" as contrasted with "downstairs," as in the TV series.
Achilles statue — The impressive statue of the Greek warrior Achilles in Hyde Park.
across the river — South of the Thames River in London. Lambeth and other south London districts are generally "rougher" than those north of the Thames.
all beer and skittles — Pleasure. Skittles is an easy form of indoor bowling.
Annamese — A person from Annam, now Vietnam.
the Apostolic Claims of the Church of Abyssinia — The Christian (Monophysite) Church of Ethiopia is the object of much satire in *BM*. Its origins are shrouded in some mystery. It maintains that it was founded by the evangelist Saint Mark and hence insists that it has an equal claim to apostolic descent with the Roman Catholic and other Christian churches. See Glossary under *BM, Nestorian*.
Arcady — Arcadia, a section of ancient Greece which was noted for rural happiness and tranquillity (see *BR*, book 1, "Et in Arcadia ego").
Mr. Arlen — Michael Arlen (1895–1956), the author of several popular, witty, gossipy novels describing the doings of wealthy sophisticates. Among his works are *The Green Hat* (1924) and *Mayfair* (1925).
art nouveau — From the French; literally "new art"; a late-nineteenth- and early-twentieth-century art movement that attempted to present ordinary objects in a fresh, decorative, ornamental fashion. It applied not only to painting but to furniture, glass, carpets, tapestries, etc. Some of its practitioners were Aubrey Beardsley, Victor Horta, and Louis Tiffany.
Ascot — A village in Berkshire noted for its horse races and the fashionable attire of those who attend them.
at the Bar — was a barrister, or legal counsel.
at the shop — The house of prostitution managed by Grimes.
Athenæum Club — A prestigious London club for men in all fields of learning.
"Avez-vous les jeunes filles de Madame Beste-Chetwynde?" — French for "Do you have Mrs. Beste-Chetwynde's girls?"

Babylonian captivity — In the Bible, the period of time (seventy years) in which the Jewish people were held in captivity in Babylon.
Bacchic — A reference to Bacchus, the god of wine in Roman classical mythology. Bacchus's followers indulged in drinking and abandoned behavior.
Basque district — An area in northern Spain and the nearby border area in France, the homeland of the Basques.

THE GLOSSARY

battels — The payments made by Oxford students for room and board.

Bauhaus at Dessau — A school established in Dessau, Germany, by a group interested mainly in architecture. Among its adherents were Walter Gropius, Marcel Breuer, Laszlo Moholy-Nagy, and Mies van der Rohe. They were especially interested in housing for workers and also took much interest in straight and rectangular construction, catering to the machine age. Gropius eventually came to America and was associated with the Harvard School of Architecture. Many of the glass-dominated, boxlike office buildings which came to dominate the Manhattan skyline reflect Bauhaus thinking. Tom Wolfe's *From Bauhaus to Our House* (New York, 1981) gives an account of this group. See also Reyner Banham, *A Concrete Atlantis* (Cambridge, Mass., 1986).

beano — A party; an English slang contraction of "bean feast."

the beaver — The beard.

Beckley — A village near Oxford.

Sir Bedivere — One of the Arthurian knights of the Round Table. He transports King Arthur's corpse to the three ladies on the boat and watches as the Avalon-bound vessel slowly disappears.

Belgrave Square — Belgravia, probably the most expensive and fashionable residential district in London.

Benares — Cheap brassware from the city of Benares, India, famous for its brass products.

Arnold Bennett — Enoch Arnold Bennett (1867–1931), popular English novelist and journalist, best remembered for his novel *The Old Wives' Tale* (1908). Coming from a working-class background, he had the reputation of being a social climber.

Bithynia — A country of Asia Minor, today part of Turkey.

blaspheming against the beauties of sixteenth-century diction — Reading the services in the Book of Common Prayer in a way that failed to show sensitivity to their beautiful English.

Bloody Mary — Mary Tudor, Roman Catholic Queen of England (1553–58), so called because many Protestants were executed during her reign.

Bloomsbury — An area of London, northeast of Hyde Park, noted as a residential area for many writers and intellectuals. Both the British Museum and the headquarters of the University of London are in Bloomsbury.

Boar's Hill, North Oxford — An outlying area of the city of Oxford, favored as a place of residence by college dons and intellectuals generally.

bob — A shilling.

bobby — A policeman, so called after Sir Robert Peel, who, as Home Secretary, founded the London metropolitan police force.

Bodleian — The principal library at Oxford University.

Boller blind — The drinking party held by the Bollinger Club which resulted in Paul Pennyfeather's expulsion from Oxford. See next entry.

Bollinger Club — A fictional club modeled on the Bullingdon Club, an Oxford social group founded in the nineteenth century. It has a very small and exclusive membership and has no regular meeting place. Its members include undergraduates as well as older members who attended the university.

Bond Street and Park Lane — A corner in the very fashionable, wealthy Mayfair section of London, east of Hyde Park.

bonhommous — Friendly, good-natured; from the French *bon homme*. The kind of French that Dr. Fagan deplores in Grimes.

Boulanger — A fashionable dress designer of the time.

Boulestin's — A famous London restaurant.

Boxer rising — A revolt in China in 1900 against foreign influence and imperialism. The Boxers were a secret society prominent in the rebellion. They emphasized athletic training, especially fist fighting.

Briggs . . . Brolly — Briggs were London outfitters who sold canes and umbrellas. "Brolly" is British slang for "umbrella."

Broadmoor — An institution for the criminally insane.

Buda-Pesth — In earlier English spelling, Budapest, Hungary. Budapest was formed in 1873 when the communities of Buda, on the right bank of the Danube River, and Pest, on the left bank, were united.

Cain's wife — Since the Bible records that Adam and Eve had, at the time of Cain's exile, only two children, Cain and Abel, skeptics have often tried to cast doubt on the truth of the Bible by asking how Cain could have acquired a wife.

DECLINE AND FALL

Camberwell Green — An attractive residential area in south London.

campaigns on the Afghan frontier — A reference to the several wars the British had fought on the border between Afghanistan and India in the nineteenth century.

Cannes — A very fashionable city and beach on the French Riviera.

Cardiff — One of the principal cities in Wales.

Carlton House Terrace — Situated near Saint James's Park, a very wealthy section of London.

Cartier — An expensive jeweler; the company has stores in both Europe and America, with headquarters on the Rue de la Paix, in Paris.

certificates — A reference to the School Certificate, an examination conducted by the Oxford and Cambridge Examination Board. Success in this exam exempted one from taking entrance exams to these universities.

Champs Élysées — One of the grand boulevards in Paris.

Chanel diamonds — A reference to Gabrielle ("Coco") Chanel (1883–1973), a famous French couturier, who used artificial jewelry with many of her clothing designs.

Charing Cross Road — A London street best known for its many theaters and secondhand bookstores.

Charvet — An expensive and fashionable men's-wear shop on the Place Vendôme, in Paris.

Chelsea — The section of London south of Hyde Park. It is bordered by Kensington on the west and Victoria on the east.

Cheltenham Spa — A pleasant resort in Gloucestershire.

Cheyne Walk — A well-to-do area in Chelsea especially distinguished by impressive red-brick Georgian houses.

churchings — Church prayer services of thanksgiving after women have given birth.

combinations — Old-fashioned long underwear.

common — In England "common" often means "lower class."

commoner's gown — A gown worn by a student who is not attending on a scholarship. It is shorter than a scholar's gown.

Common Room — Here the social room for the teachers of the school.

consecration of Archbishop Parker — Matthew Parker (1504–75) was appointed Archbishop of Canterbury by Queen Elizabeth I. His consecration in 1559 caused considerable controversy because it was argued that the ritual used was illegal. There was also a scurrilous legend that Parker was consecrated indecently in a London tavern.

cop it hot — Be punished.

Corbusier — Le Corbusier, the name used by Charles-Edouard Jeanneret (1887–1965), a French architect who emphasized nonornamental, boxlike designs. He believed that houses were "machines to live in." Otto Silenus seems to hold the same concept and is satirized for this attitude.

Corfu — One of the most attractive of the Greek islands.

corner turned up — Signifying a desire to meet a person.

cotton famine in the 'sixties — During the American Civil War, when the North placed a blockade on cotton shipments from the South, textile factories in northern England were unable to operate at full capacity.

county families — The older rural aristocracy of England, who tended to avoid the "high life" of London and looked down their noses at the *nouveaux riches*.

Country House Rag — A wild party usually involving considerable damage to furniture, etc.

crêpe de chine — Silk material.

the Crick at Rugby — At this time the Crick was a running event at Rugby School. Crick is a village in Northamptonshire about six miles east of Rugby. The village was the turning point in an out-and-back cross-country race, which was considered to be one of the most arduous events for boys at any public school. To finish the race as eighteenth was, therefore, a commendable performance.

Crikey! — Epithet, euphemism for "Christ!"

Croydon — A suburb of London best known at that time for its airport.

curate's wife — The wife of a clergyman, assistant to the rector or vicar of a parish.

cushy — Easy. The origin of the word is uncertain; possibly a form of cushiony, i.e., easy.

cut — Deliberately ignored.

Daily News — One of the cheaper and more popular London daily newspapers.

Dardanelles — A narrow waterway connecting the Aegean Sea with the Sea of Marmara. Nearby Brit-

THE GLOSSARY

ish forces fought an unsuccessful campaign against the Turks in World War I.

Davy Jones' locker — The bottom of the ocean. Davy Jones was a legendary evil spirit of the sea who caused ships to sink.

Dean Stanley's *Eastern Church* — A history of early Christianity by Arthur Penrhyn Stanley (1815–81), an Anglican clergyman. The full title of the book is *Lectures on the History of the Eastern Church* (1861).

debate with Jesus — A debate with students from Jesus College, one of the Oxford colleges. Jesus College had historical connections with Wales, and a number of its students came from there.

D.4.12 — In an early verson of *DF*, Waugh explains that this means "Block D, on the fourth landing and the twelfth cell." (See Robert Murray Davis, *Evelyn Waugh, Writer*, p. 47).

dippy — Insane.

doings — Money.

Domestic Bursar — The administrative officer of the college charged with the business management of its internal affairs.

domestic Tudor — The style of architecture during the monarchy of the Tudor family (King Henry VII to and including Queen Elizabeth I).

done in — Killed.

dotty — Insane.

Dover Street — A street in the heart of the wealthy Mayfair district.

dressed up to the nines — Dressed to perfection, referring to one who is dressed elegantly. The origin is uncertain; nines came to be considered a mystic number signifying perfection.

D.T.'s — Delirium tremens, that is, shaking accompanied by bizarre hallucinations (e.g., seeing pink elephants). D.T.'s were caused by excessive drinking.

Ebionites — A group of early Christians who advocated tenets contrary to orthodox belief; for example, they tended to deemphasize Christ's divine aspects, and they rejected the Epistles and used only one of the four Gospels.

Edgware Road — A long, wide London thoroughfare extending northwest from the Marble Arch.

Edmonton — A semiindustrial district of northern London.

Edward of Carnarvon, the first Prince of Wales — King Edward II (1284–1327). His conduct was often improper, and he was finally assassinated.

Edward Prince of Wales — Edward VII (1841–1910), king of Great Britain and Ireland, 1901–10.

Egdon Heath Penal Settlement — The Egdon Heath area plays a prominent role in Thomas Hardy's novel *The Return of the Native*, but the location of the prison Waugh is describing here is Dartmoor.

Eisteddfod — An annual Welsh festival in which participants compete for awards in singing, poetry, recitation, and other contests.

electric brougham — A small automobile (rather like a large, enclosed golf cart) operated by an electric motor.

Havelock Ellis — English author (1859–1939) who was best known for his writings on sexual psychology. His six-volume *Studies in the Psychology of Sex* (1900–10) was widely read and quoted. At the age of eighteen, Waugh wrote that he had read all six volumes.

emblazoned with the Royal Arms — The hatter was "by appointment" to the royal family.

"empress" ". . . Christian slave" — A reference to W. E. Henley's poem "To W.A." (the poem no. 37 in his "Echoes" series) in which occur the lines "I was a King in Babylon / And you were a Christian slave." The positions here are reversed; Margot is the dominant one.

Eton suits — Outfits consisting of short black jacket, black waistcoat, stiff white collar, and black or striped trousers. Until recently this was the uniform of the younger students at Eton.

Evensong — The Order of Evening Prayer sung or spoken in the Anglican church. The form of service is found in the Book of Common Prayer.

fast — Daring, excessive.

feel the wind a bit — That is, are hurt or suffer financially.

fifth form — Classes in a British public school may run from the third form (youngest boys) to the sixth form (oldest). Fifth-form boys would normally be about fifteen years old.

first Crusade — The Crusades were military expeditions from England and Europe to regain the Holy Land of Palestine from the Saracens. The first Crusade lasted four years, 1096–1100.

five-and-sixpence — Five shillings and sixpence; a shilling was 1/20 of a pound, and a penny 1/12 of a shilling (shillings and pence have now been replaced by "new pence," each 1/100 of a pound). At that time, equivalent to about $1.25. Throughout the 1920s the pound sterling was worth about $5.00.

Five per cent of ninety pounds—In personal correspondence to me, Donald Greene observes that there is a miscalculation of fee: "Mr. Levy is right in saying that five per cent of ninety pounds (1,800 shillings) is four pounds ten shillings (90 shillings). Then a 15% discount for cash is to be taken off that. 85% of 90 shillings, however, comes to 76.5 shillings (i.e. 76 shillings and 6 pence), which is equal to three pounds, *sixteen* shillings, and sixpence, not, as the text has it, three pounds *six* shillings, and sixpence. No doubt just a printer's error, leaving the 'teen' off 'sixteen.'"

flag day—One of the days on which charitable donations are solicited in the streets; those who give are presented with small flags or other tokens to place in their lapels.

Flanders—A region in Belgium where several bloody World War I battles were fought.

Flint and Denbigh Herald—The local newspaper. Flint and Denbigh were northern counties of Wales, where Llanabba Castle was situated. Arnold House, Llandulas, where Waugh taught—the original of Llanabba Castle—was in Denbighshire. The counties were later renamed Clwyd and Dyfed.

formation of the Coalition—In 1915, shortly after the outbreak of World War I, the Liberal government under Prime Minister H. H. Asquith entered into a coalition with the Conservatives under Andrew Bonar Law. The Coalition caused much political controversy.

Forsyte Saga—A series of novels by John Galsworthy (1867–1933) about the Forsyte family.

Founder's port—Wine kept to commemorate the founding of the college. Most older Oxford and Cambridge colleges were founded in the Middle Ages by important churchmen, noblemen, or members of royalty.

four months' solitary—An error common to many editions. It should read "four weeks' solitary."

frisson—French for "thrill," a tremor of excitement.

Fuzzy-Wuzzy in the Soudan—Black tribesmen in the Sudan whom the British fought and who were noted for their valor and fighting ability. They were nicknamed "Fuzzy-Wuzzies" because of their fluffy hair style. They occasioned Rudyard Kipling's famous poetic tribute "Fuzzy-Wuzzy." Presumably Colonel Sidebotham served under Lord Kitchener at the Battle of Omdurman (1896), in which the British avenged the death of Gordon at Khartoum in 1885.

game leg—A disabled leg; here a wooden leg.

gave me the slip—Got away from me.

General Strike—The strike in England in 1926, when many workers throughout the country went on strike to support striking coal miners. Since the government was able to keep essential services in operation and many other workers refused to stay away from their jobs, the General Strike was unsuccessful. See *BR*, book 1, chap. 8, where Charles Ryder returns to England to support the antistrike movement.

Geneva—A prominent city in Switzerland, the headquarters of the League of Nations.

gets gay—Becomes carefree and exuberant.

gets sniffy—Acts superior.

Gilbert and Sullivan—A reference to the popular light operas, such as *H.M.S. Pinafore*, *The Pirates of Penzance*, and *The Mikado*, with books by Sir William Schwenck Gilbert and music by Sir Arthur Sullivan.

gives me the pip—Causes me severe annoyance. Pip is a disease affecting various birds and poultry; hence the hyperbolic phrase means to cause a disease.

God's in His heaven; all's right with the world"—An allusion to lines from Robert Browning's poem "Pippa Passes."

The Golden Bough—A monumental twelve-volume study of comparative folklore and religion (1890–1915) by the English anthropologist Sir James Frazer (1854–1941).

General Charles George Gordon (1833–85). This British military figure was known as "Chinese" Gordon for his successful expedition to China in 1860 during which he captured Peking. Many years later the garrison at Khartoum, in the Sudan, which he commanded was besieged and overwhelmed by superior numbers. Gordon was killed in the slaughter.

got the push—Was expelled.

grease-caked Channel swimmer—Swimming the English Channel between England and France has

THE GLOSSARY

been a popular feat for many years. The grease helps reduce the effect of the cold water.

"Had he not moved unseen when darkness covered the waters?" — Cf. Genesis 1:2. Paul Pennyfeather acknowledges the undying presence and spirit of Grimes despite adversity and a seeming death in the swamp.

Hamburg — A German seaport.

Hanse ghetto — One of the areas restricted to Jewish inhabitants of the Hanseatic League, a group of towns in the northern part of Germany linked both politically and commercially.

Thomas Hardy — English novelist and poet (1840–1928).

Harrovian — A student who attended Harrow, one of the best-known and most prestigious English public schools.

Hertford — A college at Oxford, the college Waugh himself attended.

the High — One of the principal streets in Oxford.

historic Liberal campaign of 1906 — In the general election of 1906 the Liberal party administered a severe defeat to the Conservatives, who had been in power for many years.

holding the sponge — Serving as a prizefighter's second.

Holywell Press — A press in Oxford, which began as the partnership of Burrows and Doe in 1890 and became the Holywell Press, Ltd., in 1921, when it moved from its premises on Holywell Street to Alfred Street, where it is still situated.

House — British public schools are organized into individual units or "houses," which include their own dormitories.

the House — The House of Commons.

huîtres — French for "oysters."

Hyde Park — A large park in the western part of London. It features a lake, a bridle path, the Marble Arch, and the Albert Memorial.

in the box — In the witness box at the trial.

incense — The use of incense in Anglican services (a "High Church" practice) caused much controversy in the nineteenth and early twentieth centuries.

in the soup — In trouble.

"In Thy courts no more are needed" — A quotation from the anthem "Where Thou Reignest. Anthem for Quinquagesima or General Use." The words were written by the Reverend Benjamin Webb (1819–85) and adapted by F. A. W. Docker. The music was composed by Franz Schubert. The text begins: "Where Thou reignest, King of Glory, / Throned in everlasting light, / In Thy courts no more is needed, / Sun by day nor moon by night." The music is Des Tages Weihe, op. 146, Deutsche no. 763. It is also known as the "Birthday Hymn" and is included in the anthology *Choral Music*, edited by Ray Robinson, with a translation of the original German rather than the Webb/Docker text. See Donald Greene, "Reality into Art: Some Detective Notes on Waugh," *EWN* (Spring, 1986): 1–2.

"I smote the Philistine" — An allusion to the killing of Goliath by David; cf. 1 Samuel 17:49. The Philistines were enemies of the Israelites, the chosen people.

the itch — The desire to get married.

"I told him what was the matter with her" — Presumably that she was having her menstrual period. One scholar suggests that Peter may have mentioned that Margot was drugged on veronal.

"It was for a sign in Israel" — Quoted almost exactly from Ezekiel 4:3.

J.C.R. — See Appendix 1. Some editions have incorrectly F.C.R.

Je ne sais quoi — French for "I know not what," that is, an indefinable feeling or quality.

Jereboam — A large bottle.

jeune premier — French for "young first player," that is, the leading actor in a performance.

Dr. Johnson — Samuel Johnson (1709–84), essayist, poet, lexicographer, and conversationalist par excellence. Among his many accomplishments was his *Dictionary of the English Language* (1755).

jugged — Imprisoned.

League of Nations — An international organization of countries founded after World War I. It had its headquarters in Geneva, Switzerland, and worked to achieve peace, as well as to help solve problems with refugees and public health. The league went out of existence when World War II broke out. In many ways the United Nations is its successor.

League of Nations Committee — A committee formed to stop the transport of prostitutes from one country to another.

DECLINE AND FALL

League of Nations Union — A group organized to support the goals of the League of Nations, bringing about international peace, improved economy, the suppression of "white slavery" (international trade in prostitution), and similar altruistic accomplishments.

"Liberty's new building" — An addition built on Liberty's Department Store in London.

Longfellow — Henry Wadsworth Longfellow (1807–82), whose poems were often highly moralistic.

loopy — Insane, crazy.

Low Church — The branch of the Anglican Church that deemphasizes ritual and the authority of the clergy. "Low Church" adherents attempt to remove themselves from Roman Catholic associations such as stained-glass windows and emphasis on individual saints.

Luna Park — A large amusement park in Paris.

Ramsay MacDonald — MacDonald (1866–1937) was Britain's first Labour Party Prime Minister; he was elected to office in 1924.

mal soigné — French for "poorly groomed."

Manchester school utilitarian — In the manner of the Manchester school of economists, such as David Ricardo, who extended Adam Smith's laissez-faire economic theories.

Marseilles — A French seaport often associated with criminal activity.

Matisse — Henri Matisse (1869–1954), an influential French Impressionist painter, regarded in the 1920s as highly *avant-garde*.

Mayfair — A well-to-do, very fashionable section of London east of Hyde Park.

Mendelssohn — The composer Felix Mendelssohn (1809–47), whose "Wedding March," from the incidental music to *A Midsummer Night's Dream*, is very popular in the Western world.

Men of Harlech — A rousing march, often regarded as the national anthem of Wales.

"Merci, Monsieur! Gardez bien votre chapeau" — French for "Thank you sir. Guard your hat well." As Paul discovers, prostitutes would grab hats of passersby to lure them into their rooms.

Mesopotamia — A pleasant walking and relaxing area east of Oxford's University Parks, surrounded by two branches of the River Cherwell.

mewses — Originally streets or courts, especially in London, with stables for horses. Later many of the stables were converted into lodgings and garages which became quite fashionable.

Moabite — A member of a people living in the wilderness of Moab who were not in union with the Israelites; cf. Deuteronomy 2.

"Modern Churchman" — A clergyman who holds an "advanced," that is, unorthodox, theology.

Monte — Monte Carlo.

William Morris — Morris (1834–96), in addition to being a poet and art enthusiast, was also a founder of the firm of Morris, Marshall, Faulkner and Company. The company's purpose was to improve Victorian taste by manufacturing artistic furniture, tapestries, and similar household products. Morris was also a pioneer Socialist, and his utopian works *A Dream of John Bull* and *News from Nowhere* give a picture of an ideal society such as Paul Pennyfeather imagines here.

Mother Wales — A play on a book entitled *Mother India*, by Katherine Mayo, an exposé of the shocking conditions of life in India, a bestseller of 1927.

M.P. — Member of Parliament, i.e., of the House of Commons.

Mumm — A brand of champagne.

my heart just stood still — A reference to the love song "My Heart Stood Still," written by Richard Rodgers and Lorenz Hart. It was first sung in 1927 in a London revue and later the same year was one of the songs in the Broadway musical *A Connecticut Yankee*, based on Mark Twain's *A Connecticut Yankee in King Arthur's Court*.

Napoleon III — (1808–73), Emperor of France (1852–70), nephew of Napoleon I.

Newdigate Prize Poem — The principal Oxford prize for English poetry, awarded each year to an undergraduate for the best poem on an assigned topic.

Newmarket — An English town noted for its horse races.

"Nor iron bars a cage" — Line 26 from Lovelace's poem "To Althea, from Prison." It follows the line "Stone walls do not a prison make," used by Waugh as the title of part 3, chap. 1.

not on the end of a barge pole — Not for any reason. Compare "I wouldn't touch it with a ten-foot pole."

"O God, our help in ages past" — The first line of a hymn by Isaac Watts (1674–1748) which is a rendering of Psalm 90. It was published in Watts's

THE GLOSSARY

Psalms of David (1719) and entitled "Man Frail, and God Eternal."

Office of Works — The government department responsible for the construction and maintenance of public buildings.

"Oh, death, where is thy sting-a-ling-a-ling?" — From a popular soldier's song of World War I making fun of religious exhortations. Part of it goes: "Oh, death, where is thy sting-a-ling-a-ling, / Oh, grave, thy victory? / The bells of hell go ding-a-ling-a-ling / For you, but not for me." The first two lines are parodied from 1 Corinthians 15:55, part of the Anglican burial service.

Old Bailey — The Central Criminal Court in London.

Old Marston — A village near Oxford.

one-and-six — One shilling and sixpence, then about 35 cents.

one-over-the-eight — Intoxicated. The phrase, said to have originated in the English army and navy services, was based on the concept that eight glasses of beer were considered an acceptable limit.

Oppenheim — E. Phillips Oppenheim (1866–1946), famous for his spy stories.

O.S.C.U. — Oxford Students' Christian Union.

the other House — The House of Lords.

the other two advantages — Of marriage, besides "the avoidance of fornication." In the older form of the Marriage Service in the Book of Common Prayer, these are "the procreation of children" and the "mutual support" of man and wife.

panatrope — A gramophone.

"per Christum Dominum nostrum" — Latin for "Through Christ Our Lord."

Pervigilium Veneris — An anonymous Latin poem ("The Vigil of Venus"). The poem treats of a spring festival at which figures of classical myth await the appearance of the goddess of love. Margot is ironically a modern version of Venus bringing spring and love to Pennyfeather.

picture house — Movie theater.

play boxes — Receptacles in which boys kept their personal possessions.

Podger's — Grimes's house at Harrow School. Podger's is a fictional name. Houses at public schools are named after housemasters — here a Mr. Podger.

Pompeii — An Italian city destroyed by the eruption of Mount Vesuvius in A.D. 79. Remnants of the town, including the red-light district, can be seen by tourists.

Pompeiian sentry...the Citadels of the Plain — A reference to a famous painting (1865) by Edward Poynter depicting a Roman guard faithful to his post even though Mount Vesuvius is burying most of Pompeii in a volcanic eruption. Donald Greene writes in personal correspondence: "Interesting that Waugh calls the background the Citadels of the Plain, i.e., the Cities of the Plain, i.e. Sodom and Gomorrah (Scott-Moncreiff, to whom Waugh nearly got a job as secretary, translated Proust's *Sodome et Gomorrhe* as The Cities of the Plain). Very appropriate to Grimes, of course."

popped it — Pawned it.

prefects — Senior boys appointed to maintain discipline among the juniors.

Prep — The school period when students do homework for the next day's classes, somewhat similar to the American school study period.

presented to a living — Became the rector or vicar of an Anglican church.

priest hole — A secret room or small, closetlike space in a large house or in an estate where Roman Catholic priests were hidden during times of religious persecution in England, particularly during the sixteenth century.

Proust — Marcel Proust (1871–1922), French author whose *À la Recherche du temps perdu* (Remembrance of Things Past), a novel in seven books (1913–28), is regarded as one of the particularly memorable works of the twentieth century.

Provence — A province of France along the Mediterranean.

"public or secondary education?" — "Secondary school" in Britain refers primarily to a state-supported school, not to a private (and socially much superior) "public school."

public-school man — In England, a graduate of a private school, e.g., Eton or Harrow. English life has traditionally given special privileges to those who attend such institutions. Graduates usually attend Oxford or Cambridge and become leaders in government, banking, business, and other prominent fields and form the Establishment, or "old-boy" system of advantageous social and economic connections.

put it over on one of his girls — Had sexual relations

with one of the prostitutes in Toby's stable without paying.

quad — Short for *quadrangle*; most older English colleges are built in the form of a square surrounding an inner grassed or paved courtyard.

Quominus and Quin — The Latin *quominus* has several meanings, depending on its use with the subjunctive and imperative moods. *Quin* also has several meanings, "Why not?" "That now," "But come," etc., depending on whether it is used in main clauses, in subordinate clauses, in commands, or with negative verbs. Waugh uses the two words to indicate extremely troublesome and difficult Latin constructions.

Randal Cantuar — A signature used by the archbishop of Canterbury, Randall Thomas Davidson, who held this prestigious Church of England office from 1903 to 1928. Cantuar is the Latin abbreviation for Canterbury (Cantuarensis). It is the custom of Anglican bishops to sign their names with their Christian name and the Latin form of their religious see.

the reason she left you — It is implied that Bessy had venereal disease.

Reigate — A pleasant residential town south of London.

Reign of Terror — The time of the French Revolution in the latter part of the eighteenth century when killings were numerous, and anarchy tended to be dominant.

Reservation in the Lady Chapel — Keeping the consecrated elements (bread and wine) of Holy Communion in a chapel dedicated to the Blessed Virgin Mary. The practice (which is not authorized in the Anglican Prayer Book) was regarded as "High Church."

a rip — A wild young fellow.

rood screen — A screen separating the choir area from the main part of the church.

sacring bell — The bell rung to signal the Consecration of the Host during Holy Communion.

Salisbury — The Anglican cathedral at Salisbury, England, one of the most impressive churches in the British Isles. It is especially noted for its magnificent spire.

sat . . . for Smalls and Matriculation — Smalls (responsions) was the first university examination which had to be passed; matriculation is the process of being admitted to the university. What, therefore, is referred to here is taking the first examination and being admitted.

savoir faire — French for to "know how and what to do," that is, to behave with social propriety and expertise.

St. James's — A very well-to-do and fashionable street in London. The famous hat store Lock and Company is on Saint James's Street.

St. Peter and St. Paul in prison — Episodes related in Acts of the Apostles in the New Testament.

St. Sepulchre's, Egg Street — There is no London church at this address; the Church of Saint Sepulchre is on Newgate Street, near Holborn Viaduct. Egg Street is also fictional.

Schools — The Final Schools examination, the last exam for the B.A. degree at Oxford.

Scone College — A fictional college modeled on one of the numerous separately administered colleges comprising Oxford University. Because Scone, a district in Scotland, was for several centuries the seat of the Scottish kings, Scone College is identified by some critics with Oxford's Balliol College, which had Scottish associations. The Stone of Scone, on which Scottish kings sat during their coronation, was later placed beneath the coronation throne in Westminster Abbey. Jeffrey Heath, in *The Picturesque Prison: Evelyn Waugh and His Writing*, p. 294, observes that Scone was also the name of a Perthshire abbey destroyed during the Reformation.

Second Coming — The Judgment Day at the end of the world; the reference is to the Second Coming of Christ described in the Bible in Revelation.

Shaftesbury Avenue — A street running northeast from Picadilly Circus containing many theaters and other places of entertainment.

Skindle's — A popular hotel and restaurant at Maidenhead.

Sloane Square — A square on the western edge of Belgravia.

small pieces of coal in his dripping — pâté de foie gras. Dripping is the juices and fat from cooked meat.

small public school of ecclesiastical temper on the South Downs — An accurate description of Waugh's public school, Lancing, which had an An-

THE GLOSSARY

glican "High Church" tradition, near Worthing, Sussex, on the South Downs—a low range of hills.

Smiles' *Self-Help*—Samuel Smiles' book of that title. Smiles (1812–1904) was a popular Victorian writer who (along the lines of Horatio Alger) emphasized hard work and personal initiative to achieve rags to riches. See also "Jackson" in *BM*.

Southgate—A section in the northern suburbs of London. It became a borough in 1933.

South Kensington—The South Kensington Museum, now the Victoria and Albert Museum.

spliced—Married.

Standing Orders—The permanent regulations for conduct in prison.

Stoke-on-Trent—An industrial city in the Midlands of England.

"Stone Walls Do Not a Prison Make"—A line from Richard Lovelace's famous lyric poem "To Althea from Prison."

Sunday Express—The Sunday edition of the *London Daily Express*, owned by Lord Beaverbrook (which employed Waugh for a short time). See Dictionary, Lord Copper.

Sunday Mail—The Sunday edition of the *London Daily Mail*, a popular newspaper (for which Waugh reported in Abyssinia in 1935; see *Sc*).

a Swiss firm—That is, the League of Nations, whose headquarters were in Geneva, Switzerland.

Teneat Bene Beste-Chetwynde—Latin for "May Beste-Chetwynde Hold It Well."

"That's an odd thing to ask me in a totally strange house"—Presumably what Pennyfeather asked was the location of Mrs. Beste-Chetwynde's bedroom.

...this is your number—Prisoners in British and other jails are designated by serial numbers; thus Pennyfeather becomes D.4.12; see *D.4.12* above.

Three Miles (or, in some editions, Three Miles Open)—Donald Greene writes in personal communication that this distance must be a mistake: "It consists of six laps around the track, and when Clutterbuck 'wins' by going only five laps, he is said to have won the 'five furlongs.' A furlong is one-eighth of a mile. Therefore the race must have been a Three-Quarters Mile one—which in any case makes more sense for fifteen-year-old boys."

toff—A member of the "upper classes."

ton—French for "tone," applied to the world of high fashion.

took him to Dr. Peterfield and—Presumably had him castrated.

top hole—Just fine.

Tower of Babel—A confusion of languages and noise. The allusion is to the biblical tower that men attempted to build to heaven. Jehovah, to thwart their plan, caused them to speak in different languages and thus not to understand one another; see Genesis 11.

tram—A trolley car.

Tranby Croft cut—Totally ignored. Tranby Croft was a large English country house where, during a card game in which Albert Edward, prince of Wales (later King Edward VII) was participating, one of the players cheated. The cheater was henceforth ignored, or cut, by high-class society.

trunk calls—Long-distance telephone calls.

the Tudors and the dissolution of the Church—King Henry VIII of the (Welsh) Tudor dynasty ruled England 1509–47. He separated England from the Roman Catholic Church when the pope refused to grant him an annulment to marry Anne Boleyn; monasteries were destroyed or confiscated, and Henry was made the temporal head of the Church in England by an act of Parliament.

Turkish delight—A candy made of sugar, gelatin, and fruit juice.

Up Jenkins—A team game in which a small object is handed from one player to another. At the request of one team all hands are placed on a table, and the other team has to guess which hand is holding the object.

veronal—A drug popular at the time, often used as a sleeping potion.

village post-office—In Great Britain the telephone system is run by the government as part of the post-office service. A public pay telephone would have been available at the local post office.

Von Hügel—Baron Friedrich Von Hügel (1852–1925), Roman Catholic theologian who was widely read and studied in non-Catholic circles. He was related to the Plunket Greenes. Olivia Plunket Greene was influential in Waugh's conversion to Catholicism.

vox humana—A stop on an organ which when activated helps produce vibrating tones supposed to sound like a human voice.

DECLINE AND FALL

War Memorial Fund — A fund to construct a memorial for boys from the school killed in World War I. A guinea is one shilling more than a pound.

What did Dr. Johnson say about fortitude? — A reference to James Boswell's *Life of Samuel Johnson* (New York: Modern Library, n.d., p. 29). Johnson, when he was an Oxford undergraduate, flagrantly "cut" sessions with his tutor:

    Johnson: "I had no notion that I was wrong or irreverent to my tutor."

    Boswell: "That, Sir, shows great fortitude of mind."

    Johnson: "No, Sir, stark insensibility."

"What price the coon?" — "What do you think about the black fellow?"

when I was up — When I was attending the university.

white-aproned as Mrs. Noah — A reference to children's toy models of Noah's ark and its inhabitants.

whore of Babylon — In Revelation 17:1–6, Saint John sees a vision of a whore sitting on a scarlet-colored beast with seven heads and ten horns. Some Protestants have interpreted the whore of Babylon to be the Roman Catholic church.

William and Mary — King and queen of England, 1689–1702.

The Wind in the Willows — A famous children's fantasy by the English author Kenneth Grahame (1859–1932), published in 1908.

Virginia Wolf — Several of the editions of *DF* contain this misprint of Virginia Woolf (1882–1941), best known for her novels and essays and her association with the Hogarth Press.

York Minster — The architecturally magnificent Anglican cathedral in the city of York.

your standard — That is, your "form," or grade, in school.

VILE BODIES (1930)

The title is derived from Philippians 3:20–21 (also quoted in the service for the Burial of the Dead in the Book of Common Prayer): "For our conversation is in heaven; from whence also we look for the Saviour, the Lord Jesus Christ, Who shall change our vile body, that it may be fashioned like unto his glorious body, according to the working whereby he is able even to subdue all things unto himself." In chap. 8 of this novel, Waugh writes his own passage about "those vile bodies."

Dedicatees

Bryan and Diana Guinness were friends of Waugh's with whom he enjoyed much of the high-society scene of the time. Bryan Guinness succeeded his father as second Lord Moyne in 1944, after his father, the first Lord Moyne, British minister to Egypt, was assassinated by Israeli terrorists. Diana Mitford, the younger sister of Nancy Mitford, after a divorce from Guinness, married Sir Oswald Mosley, the British Fascist leader. Both she and her husband were imprisoned for subversive activity during World War II. Lady Mosley's imprisonment was thought unjust by many. Waugh's friendship with her became remote for many years, although, as two of his letters written in 1966 testify, it never completely terminated. See *Letters of Evelyn Waugh*, pp. 638–39. Waugh was opposed to Oswald Mosley's movement.

Author's Note:

Christmas is observed by the Western Church on December 25th — In the Eastern Church (e.g., the Greek and Russian Orthodox churches), which uses the Julian instead of the Gregorian calendar, the date is thirteen days later.

A.A. — Automobile Association.
Acre — A city in Palestine conquered during the Crusades.
Agincourt — The scene of a famous battle in France in which King Henry V of England won a stunning victory over a numerically superior French army. The battle occurred on October 25, 1415.
Albert Hall — The Royal Albert Hall, the largest public auditorium in London.
Almanak [sic] de Gotha — The *Almanach de Gotha*, an almanac which gives data on European nobility and royalty.
"And twopence for the cheque" — Until recently English checks had to have a twopenny stamp affixed to them to validate them.
"Aristotle, Works of (Illustrated)" — A notorious pornographic work of the nineteenth century bore this misleading name
Arlenish — Referring to the novels of Michael Arlen, who wrote about glittering London high society and its favorite living and playing locations. In *DF* (part 2, chap. 5) there is a reference to Arlen and Mayfair.
Armistice Day — November 11, commemorating the end of World War I.
artificial poppies — Poppies given in acknowledgement of charitable donations to help veterans' organizations. Wild poppies grew in the battlefields of Flanders, and the flowers became symbolic of World War I.
Aylesbury — A town in Buckinghamshire.

Bad hats every one of them — The phrase comes from the old Duke of Wellington's remark on surveying the members of a newly elected Parliament (who at that time wore their hats when they were seated in the House of Commons): "I never saw such

THE GLOSSARY

a lot of bad hats." Metaphorically, "bad hats" means untrustworthy people.

Bart. — Abbreviation of *baronet*, hereditary holder of the title "sir."

Beau Brummel — The popular name of George Bryan Brummel (1778–1840), who was the fashion plate of London society in his day.

Blast — A magazine, edited by Wyndham Lewis, designed to propagate modernist views in art, literature, etc. Its material and typography were designed to shock the reader and propagate Vorticism in the arts. Only two issues of the periodical appeared — one in June, 1914, the other in July, 1915.

Blue Books — Official reports of parliamentary or ministerial investigative committees.

Bond Street — A street of very elegant stores in Mayfair.

bonnet — The hood of a car.

"books...in my list" — Waugh is satirizing the practices of British censorship. Often books were smuggled in from Paris since many works, e.g., James Joyce's *Ulysses*, could not legally be brought into England at that time. Waugh himself was forced to delete several passages from *Decline and Fall* before it was thought decorous enough for publication.

both Archbishops — The two Archbishops of the Church of England, those of Canterbury and York.

bottles under the board — Lord Throbbing had been addicted to drugs.

A Brand from the Burning — John Wesley's rescue as a child from a fire in Epworth rectory became a symbol to him of God's providence, and he often quoted the text from Zechariah 3:2, "a brand plucked from the fire," which provided the title for the film (hence the scene in the film of "A Clergyman [Wesley's father] handing out a succession of children with feverish rapidity of action"). Epworth rectory was in Lincolnshire, and Wesley's father was rector there.

Bright Young People — Wealthy young British men and women who lived wild and recklessly in the 1920s — in many ways the British equivalent of the wild, partygoing, sexually promiscuous youth in America described by F. Scott Fitzgerald. The Bright Young People had their own popular expressions, e.g., "too, too shaming," and "sick-making." Waugh was the first writer to popularize their language in print.

Bude — A resort in north Devonshire.

Burberry — A raincoat made by the London firm of Burberry's or an imitation thereof.

Burke — Edmund Burke (1729–97), lawyer, political figure, and author. He was noted for his speeches and his writings championing various causes of emancipation.

Butcher Cumberland — William, Duke of Cumberland (1721–65), the younger son of King George II. He was commander of the British army which defeated the Jacobite uprising in Scotland in 1745–46 — with, it was charged, unnecessary severity toward the losers.

cachet Faivre — An aspirinlike preparation used to relieve headaches and hangovers.

Canning Town — A poor working-class district in east London.

Casanova Hotel — An ironic name for what turns out to be a "temperance hotel."

Chesham Bois — A village in Buckinghamshire, near Aylesbury.

Chief Constable — The head of the police in an English county.

chloral — A drug taken to induce sleep.

Christie's — A famous London auction establishment.

chub fuddler — A chub is a fish of the carp family; the verb *fuddle* means "to intoxicate." Grain was steeped in alcohol and then scattered on the surface of the water so that the fish would eat it, become intoxicated, and be caught with ease. Thus a chub fuddler is one who catches fish in this manner. There is an account of chub fuddling in Nancy Mitford's *Love in a Cold Climate*. The chub are caught in the above-described manner. They damage the trout fishing by eating the baby trout and their food. A chub fuddler with large ears would presumably risk getting a large amount of the alcoholic water in his ears and become intoxicated.

Cincinnatus — A Roman hero supposed to have lived in the fifth century B.C. He retired from his office as a consul to live the quiet life of a farmer. When Rome was in danger from invading enemies, he was recalled and made dictator. After he led the Romans to victory and the country was safe, he again gave up his governmental powers and returned to farm life.

Colombo — The principal city of Ceylon (now Sri Lanka).

VILE BODIES

Coo — Mild slang roughly equivalent to "gosh" or "golly."

Creative Endeavour — A puzzling term in this context. Donald Greene suggests it could be an editor's bowdlerization of the more appropriate Christian Endeavour — "a world-wide 'youth movement' of the Evangelical churches."

cutting — Newspaper clipping.

Dante's *Purgatorio* — One of the three sections which, together with the *Inferno* and the *Paradiso*, form *The Divine Comedy* of Dante Alighieri (1265–1321). The customs inspector possibly associates the word with "purgative," a laxative.

Debrett — Short for the bible of English nobility, Debrett's *Peerage, Baronetage, Knightage and Companionage*. It is issued annually. John Debrett was its original publisher.

Derby day — The day of the famous horse race at Epsom, in Surrey. It is held near Whitsunday (Pentecost), the seventh Sunday after Easter.

dicky — The rumble seat of an old-fashioned car.

Divine Discontent — This phrase seems to have been first used by the Reverend Charles Kingsley (1819–75).

Doubting 'All — Possibly an allusion to Doubting Castle in John Bunyan's *Pilgrim's Progress*, the home of the fearful Giant Despair. The reference is certainly symbolic of spiritual doubt in post–World War I Britain.

dun — A bill collector.

dye the carnation for his buttonhole — Green carnations were supposed to be the symbol of Oscar Wilde and the "aesthetic" movement in the 1890s. They were popularized in the satiric novel *The Green Carnation* by Robert Hichens (1894).

eau de Nil — A fashionable greenish color (like that of the River Nile).

Edwardian era — The period of outward gentility and tranquillity and dissipated living on high levels of society during the reign of King Edward VII (1901–10).

episcopal lawn sleeves — Very full sleeves of fine white linen worn by Anglican bishops.

Eton-cropped — Describing hair cut short and boyish like that of a student at Eton public school.

ex-Emperor of Germany — Kaiser Wilhelm II (1859–1941), grandson of Queen Victoria and nephew of King Edward VII, Britain's enemy in World War I. After the war he lived in exile in the Netherlands, where, after the death of his first wife, Empress Augusta, he married morganatically a woman of much lower social status, Princess Hermine.

flageolet — A type of flute.

"For East is East and West is West" — Part of the opening of Rudyard Kipling's poem "The Ballad of East and West" (1889). The poem begins, "Oh, East is East, and West is West, and never the twain shall meet / Till Earth and Sky stand presently at God's great Judgment Seat."

forty aces and two-fifty for the rubber — The scoring comes from the older game auction bridge, which was beginning to be superseded by contract bridge.

Four Last Things — A theological expression, prominent in Christian doctrine, meaning death, judgment, hell, and heaven.

Fox — Charles James Fox (1749–1806), British statesman whose independent views frequently brought him into conflict with the younger Pitt, and his party.

gentleman's relish — The trade name of a popular anchovy paste spread on toast or biscuits.

Government House at Ottawa — The official residence and office of the Governor-General of Canada.

Great North Road — The old main highway from London to Scotland.

gymkhana — A local sports meet involving horse competitions in racing, jumping, etc.

Hansard — A record of the debates and activities of the English Houses of Parliament, corresponding to the *Congressional Record* in the United States. The work was originally published by the printer Luke Hansard.

Harley Street — The locale of many medical offices in London.

"Has he given all to his daughters?" — The precise quotation occurs in Shakespeare's *King Lear*, act 3, scene 4: "Hast thou given all to thy two daughters?"

he and an American sang the Eton Boating Song — A school song celebrating strenuous sporting cooperation. Waugh is satirizing British public school "patriotism" — which obviously appeals to the

THE GLOSSARY

American as well. The song begins: "Jolly boating weather, / And the hay-harvest breeze, / Blade on the feather, / Haze on the trees.... / Swing, swing together / With your body between your knees."

Henrietta Street — The location of both Chapman and Hall and Duckworth's, Waugh's publishers.

High Commissioner — The chief representative of the British government in a commonwealth dominion or colony or a commonwealth nation of Britain; the equivalent of an ambassador.

high fender of diamonds — A jeweled half tiara.

Home Secretary — Sir William Joynson-Hicks, later Viscount Brentford, Home Secretary in Baldwin's Conservative administration from 1924 to 1929, notorious for his ham-handed methods of trying to maintain "morality" in England. Among his feats were the banning of James Joyce's *Ulysses* and the seizure of D. H. Lawrence's paintings.

hot and strong, as nice as Mother makes it — An allusion to tea.

Huxdane-Halley bomb — A bomb named for the "left-wing" scientists Sir Julian Huxley (1887–1975) and J. B. S. Haldane (1860–1936).

Independent Labour Party — A small Socialist group that refused to amalgamate with the main Labour party.

Inns of Court — The four legal societies in England through which one is admitted to the practice of law. The name also refers to the buildings of these societies in London.

Dr. Johnson — Samuel Johnson, the famous lexicographer and conversationist; see Glossary under *DF*.

Killiecrankie — The scene of a fierce battle in Scotland in which Jacobites (supporters of the return of the house of Stuart to the English throne) defeated a Royalist army. The battle occurred in 1689. The Stuart King James II had been deposed in 1688.

Kümmel — A strong German alcoholic drink made from various herbs.

Lady Hamilton — Emma, Lady Hamilton (ca. 1761–1815), probably best remembered for her adulterous affair with naval hero Horatio, Lord Nelson (1758–1805).

"laissez-passer" — French for a permit to pass through customs without inspection, normally granted only to international diplomats.

Last Trump — The Judgment Day at the end of the world when the trumpets of the Lord's angels will sound. See I Corinthians 15:51–52.

The Laurels — Donald Greene observes that many members of the English middle class believe that it adds social prestige to give their suburban homes a name such as this, instead of using a mere street number.

Laurencin eyes — A reference to the French painter Marie Laurencin (1885–1956), a modernist artist who also designed costumes and settings for ballet and the stage.

La Vie Parisienne — A French periodical featuring, among other material, pictures of women in sexy clothing and settings.

Lecky — William Edward Hartpole Lecky (1838–1903), British historian best known for his *History of England in the Eighteenth Century*, published in eight volumes (1878–90).

Little Lord Fauntleroy — A reference to the novel of that title by Frances Hodgson Burnett (1849–1924), published in 1886. It was made into a popular film in the 1920s, with Mary Pickford in the title role. The young protagonist, who grew up in the United States, is heir to the earldom of his grandfather, who at first rejects him because his mother is an American. But the boy's sweetness at last wins over his crusty grandfather. The allusion has come to mean a well-dressed but rather sissified young boy.

live, as Jehovah was said to have done, on the savour of burnt offerings — An allusion to many places in the Old Testament (e.g., Genesis 8:21) where the Lord is said to rejoice in the "sweet savour" of burnt offerings.

Lotti — A fashionable hotel in Paris.

made one big bomb — He was making a bombe, a frozen dessert.

Mag — Short for *magneto*, the apparatus which generated electricity in older cars.

Marinetti's *Futurist Manifesto* — Filippo Marinetti (1876–1944) was an Italian poet who initiated the futurist movement. This movement, launched with a "manifesto" in 1909, was to stimulate forceful, aggressive work in writing with particular emphasis on machines and speed.

market cross — A large stone cross erected in the

central market square or area of a town. Many English villages have these stone monuments in their marketplaces.

Marylebone — The London railway station serving Buckinghamshire.

Merc — A Mercedes car.

middle-day dinner — For a long time in both Britain and America the custom of having the main meal of the day at around noon instead of in the evening distinguished "lower" or "working" class from the "middle" or "upper" class.

"Midnight Orgies at No. 10" — No. 10 Downing Street is the official residence of the Prime Minister.

Millais — Sir John Everett Millais (1829–96), English painter who was one of the founders of the Pre-Raphaelite movement.

Mr. Outrage has IT — The capitalized "it" refers to "sex appeal" and potency. Elinor Glyn (1864–1943) wrote a story called *It* (1927), and actress Clara Bow was publicized by Hollywood as the "It Girl."

"Montparnasse in Belgravia" — The bohemian left-bank section of Paris, very unlike Belgravia.

Nancy — A slang term indicating that Lottie's waiter was very effeminate.

N.B.G. — No bloody good.

New Statesman — See Dictionary, *New Nation*.

Notre Dame — The famous cathedral in Paris.

nuit de Noël — Christmas Eve, the name of a perfume.

numéro mille soixante dix-huit — French for "Number 1,078." Prostitutes who were associated with armies were frequently given numbers by the military authorities, medically examined, and kept track of.

Oberammergau — A village in Germany in which the townspeople perform, usually every ten years, a famous Passion play portraying Christ's crucifixion.

Oh for the Wings of a dove — An allusion to the English translation of Mendelssohn's "Oh Könnt ich fliegen wie tauben dahin" by W. Bartholomew, from Psalm 55:6. It was one of the most popular songs for boy sopranos.

Omega — Waugh apparently has in mind the O.M., a successful Italian-made racing car of the late 1920s, but changes it to Omega to make the reference less awkward-sounding. The Omega was a luxurious French car showing the influence of, and attempting to compete with, the Hispano-Suiza. The O.M. stood for the Officine Meccaniche Company, which made cars in Brescia, Italy.

order of St. Michael and St. George — One of the orders of knighthood bestowed by the English monarch for public service. It originated in 1818.

Palladian — A revived classical Roman style in architecture, named for the Italian architect Andrea di Pietro (1508–80), called Palladio, who had considerable influence on English architecture.

panto — Slang for pantomime.

"Parlez anglais?" — French for "Do you speak English?"

penitential psalms — In the church liturgy, Psalms 6, 32, 38, 51, 102, 130, and 143.

Pitt — William Pitt the Younger (1759–1806), British Prime Minister under King George III, or, less likely, considering the dates, his father, William Pitt the Elder (1708–78), Prime Minister under King George II.

Plunket-Bowse — No auto by this name was ever made. Waugh is probably playing a joke on Olivia Plunket Greene, a girl to whom he was much attracted. Bowse was an early type of portable gun. When I mentioned this possibility to Robert Murray Davis, he suggested that Olivia's brother Richard might have been the playful target since Richard had bought a new car that made much noise but was very fast. See the *Diaries of Evelyn Waugh*, pp. 215, 223–24.

the Presence of Royalty — The reception was honored by members of the royal family — perhaps King George V and Queen Mary themselves.

Princess Elizabeth — A reference to the future queen, now Queen Elizabeth II. She was born in 1926 and became Queen in 1952. Her coronation took place in 1953.

procureuse — A female who procures women for purposes of prostitution.

Punch — A popular British humor magazine.

R.A.C. — Royal Automobile Club.

The real aristocracy, the younger members of those two or three great brewing families which rule London — The most famous of these families was the Guinness family, headed by the Earl of Iveagh. See *Dedicatees* above.

ribbon of the Garter — A dark-blue velvet ribbon which signifies that the wearer has achieved the highest order of English knighthood. The Order of

THE GLOSSARY

the Garter was founded by King Edward III in the fourteenth century. In English editions of *VB*, Waugh writes "Order of Merit" instead of "ribbon of the Garter." (Waugh realized that he had made a slip. If Outrage had been a knight of the Garter, he would have been "Sir Walter Outrage," not "Mr. Outrage," as the novel has him. This is perhaps evidence that the American editions were set from earlier, uncorrected copy of the British edition. The Order of Merit is the most distinguished of British honors which do not carry a title. It is restricted to twenty-four members.

Right Honourable Rape—The clever analogy between "Outrage" and "Rape" appears in this context to have more a political than a sexual connotation.

Father Rothschild—Rothschild is the name of the far-flung Jewish European banking family; thus Waugh links the wealth, intrigue, and mystery often associated with both the Rothschilds and the Jesuits.

saloons—Not, as in the United States, taverns, but "salons," large rooms for social gatherings.

sal volatile—Smelling salts.

saving your cloth, Rothschild—With apologies to your position as a clergyman.

sheepish house—Several writers have pointed out that Waugh promised to immortalize the youthful Jessica Mitford's pet sheep. He used the word "sheepish" as a substitute for "divine," so this word became part of the vocabulary of the Bright Young People. See Robert Murray Davis, "*Vile Bodies* in Typescript," *EWN*, Winter, 1977, pp. 7–8.

shirty—Angry.

"Si la jeunesse savait.... Si la vieillesse pouvait"—French for "If the young knew how.... If the old were able."

S.J.—Society of Jesus; that is, a member of the Jesuit order in the Roman Catholic church.

spanner—Wrench.

Speed Kings—Racing-car drivers.

"Spy"—A pseudonym used by Sir Leslie Ward (1851–1922). Most of his caricatures appeared in *Vanity Fair*.

strawberry leaves—A reference to the figures of the leaf on the coronet and coat of arms of a duke or marquess. They can be seen in Waugh's drawing in *BM* on the coronets adorning the luggage of General Connolly, duke of Ukaka.

stubborn Jew—The quotation from *Richard II* continues: "Renowed for their deeds as far from home, / For Christian service and true chivalry / As is the sepulchre in stubborn Jewry, / Of the world's ransom, blessed Mary's son." Jewry in this context means Palestine or Judea. John of Gaunt's famous speech continues with a denunciation of the present degenerate state of the country—"That England that was wont to conquer others / Hath made a shameful conquest of itself"—appropriate to the scene viewed from the airplane, and, indeed, to the theme of the novel. The "rediscovery" of Christ's sepulchre in Jerusalem is related in chap. 10 of *Helena*.

stylographic pen—Fountain pen.

super—Short for *supernumerary*; here a movie extra.

Tales from the Mist—The title appears to be nonexistent, but Waugh's irony is evident. Jacqueline McDonnell has written to me from Scotland: "There are plenty of such legends such as *Tales of the Glens* by Joseph Grant (1869) and *Tales of the Heather* by Emma Rose Mackenzie (1894). It is likely however that if Waugh had a definite book in mind, he was gently mocking Sir Walter Scott whose tales were adapted for elementary schools. Such titles exist as *A Collection for the Use of Schools Compiled from the Writing of Sir Scott* (1916) and *English Literature for Secondary Schools—Tales of a Grandfather—First Series—Sir Walter Scott* (1910). The actual tale told by Waugh is not mentioned but, as I say, I believe he was mocking at the Scott-and-tartan industry as it is known here."

tart—British slang for whore.

temperance hotels—Hotels catering to supporters of the temperance movement by refusing to sell alcohol on their premises.

"That's the King with the beard.... No, deary, the King of Ruritania"—Agatha mistakes the king for the then king of England, George V, conspicuous for his old-fashioned beard.

theosophy—A religious philosophy seeking involvement with, and knowledge of, God through personal intuition and attitudes.

thimble-and-pen men—Misprinted in many editions—it should read *thimble-and-pea men*. A kind of con game in which wagers were placed to guess under which of three or four thimbles a pea was located. The con man would often palm the pea so that people would lose their bets and he would profit by the deception.

"This scepter'd isle..."—A quotation from Shakespeare's play *King Richard II*, act 2, scene 1. It is part of John of Gaunt's inspiring speech about England.

toper—A heavy drinker.

two men with bowler hats—The two detective sergeants of the police mentioned elsewhere in the chapter. Their function is to ensure the safety of the leader of the opposition.

two minutes silence at eleven o'clock—A custom on Armistice Day honoring those who were killed in World War I.

undergraduate "rags"—Wild, comic pranks by college students.

Underground—The English subway.

Upper House—The House of Lords.

V.A.D.—Voluntary Aid Detachment—A group of volunteers trained in first aid and nursing.

valet-de-chambre—French for "valet, manservant."

waits—Christmas carolers.

Wendover—A town five miles southeast of Aylesbury.

Wesleyan—A follower of Methodism, founded by John and Charles Wesley in England in the eighteenth century.

Whitaker—Joseph Whitaker (1820–95), English publisher who is best known for his *Almanack*. This work has been published annually since 1868. It gives statistics and data on government, legal, commercial, and other topics. It originally was devoted to just English factual material but in recent years has included statistics on many other countries.

Whitehall—The central area of government offices in London and a name given to government offices in general.

"Without shedding of blood is no remission of sin"—Hebrews 9:22.

BLACK MISCHIEF (1932)

Dedicatees

Lady Mary Lygon and Lady Dorothy Lygon were children of the seventh Earl Beauchamp. Waugh became friendly with their brother Hugh Lygon (one of the models for Sebastian Flyte) at Oxford and later with the family. He developed a gossiping, fun-filled relationship with Lady Mary and Lady Dorothy.

abbatoirs—Slaughterhouses.

ambulatory—In a church the aisle around the choir and usually behind the altar. The term may also refer to a covered arcade.

Angelus—A prayer honoring the Blessed Virgin Mary said three times daily—morning, noon, and night. A church bell rings to indicate the time for the prayer.

animal-snap—A game played with cards showing pictures of animals. When two of the same pictures appear, a player quickly makes the noise appropriate to the animal (e.g., "Bow-wow" or "Moo") and takes the card played by his opponent. When one player has won all the cards, the game is over. Tony Last and Mrs. Rattery play it in *HD*.

Annamite boy—See Glossary under *DF*.

Arlen—See Glossary under *DF*.

askar—A native Moroccan infantryman.

azan—The Muslim call to prayer. The call is usually chanted by a muezzin who stands in the tower of a mosque.

Barchester Towers—The most famous of a series of six novels by Anthony Trollope (1815–82). The stories are set in and about the imaginary English cathedral town of Barchester. *Barchester Towers* was published in 1857.

Barren Fig Tree—The story is related in Luke 13:6–9.

Black and Tans—British soldiers sent to Ireland to thwart the Irish rebellion in 1919–21. They had a notorious reputation in Ireland for unusually cruel and oppressive terrorism. The name derives from their khaki uniforms worn with black belts.

blackwater—A severe malarial fever.

boodle—Money from graft.

brook Kedron—In the Bible, the brook where the ravens fed Elijah; see 1 Kings 17:5–6. The brook is also often called Cherith.

Chancery—The secretariat and records office of an embassy.

chemist—Pharmacist.

Chief Conservative Whip—A member of the Conservative party in Parliament whose duty it is to see that other members are present when votes are taken.

chota peg—A drink of whiskey. *Chota* is derived from a Hindi word for "small."

cleft staff—A long piece of wood hollowed out to carry messages written on paper. William Boot in *Sc* brings a batch of such sticks to Ishmaelia.

clock golf—A lawn game based on sinking a ball in a single cup placed within a circle of twelve tees.

consequences—A game in which each player takes a blank sheet of paper and at the top writes an adjective describing a male. Then each player folds the paper over so that the word cannot be seen, and hands it to the player on the left or right. Then everyone next writes, below the fold, the name of a male and then folds it over and passes the paper on. Then, in the same way, an adjective for a female, the name of a female, the place where the two meet,

THE GLOSSARY

what he says and what she says on the occasion, and, finally, what the "consequences" of the meeting are. Each entry is made independently and at random. At the end the sheets of paper are unfolded, and the narratives thereon are read. If the players are witty, the game can be fun.

constituency — A parliamentary district which elects a representative or representatives to a lawmaking group (here the House of Commons).

Coo — See glossary under *VB*.

coprophagists — Eaters of dung.

Croydon, le Bouget, Lyons, Marseilles — Towns in England and France with important airfields.

Cunarder — An English Cunard Line passenger ship.

cypher book — A book containing cyphers, or codes used for decrypting messages.

D.B.S. — "Distressed British Subject." See the account of this category (discontinued since World War II) in *SKME*, where the British council, Smudge, tells Scott-King what has happened to Whitemaid.

dons — A title given to tutors, fellows, and heads in English universities.

doyen — The senior member of a group who is its chief spokesman.

Dreyfus' innocence — Capt. Alfred Dreyfus (1859–1935), a French army officer, was imprisoned on Devil's Island for selling military secrets to Germany. The evidence was circumstantial, and much of the animosity against Dreyfus stemmed from the fact that he was Jewish. Eventually it was discovered that a Major Marie Charles Esterhazy was the guilty individual, but the French military command attempted to conceal this information. In 1889, through the efforts of the French novelist Emile Zola and others, Dreyfus was pardoned, and his commission was restored.

dry clinkers — Sun-dried bricks which make up the pavements of Aden. Aden, in southern Arabia, was for many years a British protectorate and an important seaport and naval base.

Durban — A seaport in South Africa. Dame Mildred Porch had used the flea powder (see *Keatings*, below) when she and Miss Tin stayed in South Africa.

dust up — a fight.

"Ecce ancilla Domini: fiat mihi secundum verbum tuum" — Latin phrases from the Angelus: "Behold the handmaid of the Lord; be it done unto me according to your word." The Angelus begins with the words "The Angel of the Lord announced unto Mary / And she conceived of the Holy Spirit."

Eno's — A reference to Eno's "Fruit Salts," a popular laxative and antacid of the time produced by John F. Eno, Ltd. Here quoted in a song.

Eritrea — A part of ancient Ethiopia which came under the control of Italy in the late nineteenth century. After World War II it again became federated with Ethiopia and in 1962 became a province of that country.

Esperanto — Pseudonym of L. L. Zamenhof, inventor of an artificial language intended to be understood internationally, or at least throughout Europe. It was organized on word bases shared by the principal languages of Europe.

Evian — A mineral water from Evian-les-Bain, a French spa.

"Floreat Azania" — "May Azania Flourish!"

F.O. — Foreign Office.

Galla — A member of a Cushite-speaking people who settled mainly in southern Ethiopia and in what was formerly British East Africa.

Goan — A native of Goa, a onetime Portuguese enclave in India. It was seized by India in 1962.

Grand chemin de Fer d'Azanie — The great railroad of Azania.

"gratia plena..." — Latin for "full of grace," part of the prayer to the Blessed Virgin Mary: "Hail, Mary! full of grace; the Lord is with you; Blessed are you among women." Luke 1:27–28.

Great Panjandrum — A title for a pompous busybody originated by Samuel Foote, an eighteenth-century British actor, while he was composing a nonsense speech designed to test another actor's memory.

great tattoo of Aldershot — An elaborate military parade and exhibition performed at Aldershot, England, the location of a major British army base.

gymkhana — See Glossary under *VB*. The word derives from gymnasium and the Hindi word for racquet court.

halma — A game, somewhat similar to Chinese checkers, in which the pieces are jumped over one another and moved about. The board contains 256 black and white squares.

happy families — A card game; see *Miss Chipps, the Carpenter's daughter* below.

Haroun al-Raschid — The Caliph in the *Arabian Nights* who wandered about at night looking for adventure.

H.I.M. — His Imperial Majesty.

hubble-bubble — A water pipe for smoking. The smoke is drawn through water in a long tube which is placed in the mouth.

"Imperator Immortalis" — Latin for Immortal Emperor.

Inns of Court — The lawyers' colleges; see Glossary under *VB*.

juju — An African magical charm or curse.

Keatings — A brand of flea powder.

kedgeree — a dish of rice mixed with fish, eggs, and other ingredients.

Kenya Game Reserves — Protected areas for wild animals in the former British African colony of Kenya.

khat — Leaves of a shrub used by Arabs as a narcotic. The leaves are chewed or boiled as a tea. Usually spelled *kat*.

Krafft-Ebing — Baron Richard von Krafft-Ebing (1840–1902), German physician famous for his book *Psychopathia Sexualis* (1886), which contains numerous case studies of odd or deviant sexual behavior. The book was especially popular in the first part of the twentieth century.

Lee-Enfield rifles — Standard rifles used by the British army after the Boer War. The rifle was developed by James Lee, and in 1895 it was modified at the Royal Small Arms Factory at Enfield, England and named Lee-Enfield.

Leviticus — The third book of the Old Testament, written for the Levites and recording ceremonial rules and practices.

levy — Conscripted troops.

Lottie Crump's — Lottie, the owner of Shepheard's Hotel, appears more prominently in *VB*. See Dictionary.

Marie Therese [sic] thalers — Silver coins depicting Maria Theresa (1717–80), Queen of Hungary and Bohemia, and Archduchess of Austria.

Mekka — Mecca, the Muslim Holy City, in western Saudi Arabia.

Messrs. Mappin and Webb of London — British silversmiths.

Metropolitan — An archbishop who has authority over other bishops in his area.

Michaelmas — September 29, the Feast of Saint Michael and All Angels.

"Mine eyes have seen the glory of the coming of the Lord..." — Lyrics from "The Battle Hymn of the Republic," composed by Julia Ward Howe in 1862. The lyrics are sung to the tune of "John Brown's Body." The British edition of *BM* mentions "John Brown's Body" in the text.

Miss Chipps, the Carpenter's daughter — A card in the "Happy Families" game. The cards have pictures of members of families with various occupations. The object of the game is to complete as many families as possible.

"Mon bon homme...il vous fait..." — "My good man, you must understand we do not drink anything at all. never."

Montessori — A system stressing self-education of children through emphasis on play and the training of hands and eyes. A minimum amount of teacher control is stressed. It was named for its innovator, educator Maria Montessori (1870–1952).

Mudies — A reference to Mudie's Library, a book-circulating enterprise with headquarters in London, founded by a bookseller and stationer named Charles Mudie.

Muezzin — A Muslim crier who calls the faithful to prayer from a minaret (tower) of a mosque.

Nacktkultur — Nudism; the theory that nudity emancipates a person's spirit.

navvies — Laborers.

Nestorian — A follower of Nestorius (ca. A.U. ?–451), patriarch of Constantinople. Nestorius was declared a heretic by the Pope because he insisted that the divine and the human were two separate aspects in Jesus Christ. According to orthodox belief, the human and the divine natures are united in Christ. In *BM*, Waugh refers to the established church of Azania as Nestorian, which differs from Ethiopian Monophysitism (Monophysites accepted only one nature in Christ). Donald Greene writes in personal correspondence: "I checked through Waugh's travel journals to see whether he actually thought the

Ethiopian church to be Nestorian and discovered he never in fact so describes it. So it must have been a deliberate novelistic device on Waugh's part to call the Azanian church Nestorian, perhaps to disarm charges that he was slandering the Ethiopian church."

O.C. — Officer commanding.

Oedipus — In psychology the Oedipus complex is a manifestation of infantile sexuality centering mainly on the attraction of a male child for his mother. The complex is named for the ancient Greek hero who married his mother, Jocasta.

Oxford Union — The debating society at Oxford University.

P. & O. — The Peninsular and Oriental Steamship Company, the principal British line serving Africa and the East.

packets — A lot (of money).

Parsee death house — An institution for Parsees in the stage of terminal illness. Parsees were members of an old Persian religious sect, most of whom fled from India during a period of Moslem persecution.

Pegity — A board game in which players put pegs in holes on the board. The first player who obtains a row of five pegs wins. Often spelled *peggity*.

picket — A small group of soldiers assigned to guard a position.

President of the Union — President of the debating society at Oxford.

Priestley — J. B. Priestly (1894–1984), English man of letters best known for his novel *The Good Companions* (1929). Waugh is, of course, satirizing him here.

racket — A drinking spree.

Seth, Emperor of Azania, Chief of the Chiefs of Sakyu... — The list of titles after Seth's name is an amusing satire on Emperor Haile Selassie's custom of using "King of Kings," "Conquering Lion of Judah," and similar designations after his name. Haile Selassie ruled Abyssinia (Ethiopia) from 1930 to 1974.

Shari — A heated debate or discussion.

shari of all the Wanda and Sakuyu chiefs — Conference between the two groups.

Shaw — George Bernard Shaw (1856–1950), great British Nobel Prize–winning playwright.

Six Weeks Passed — In some editions this phrase appears as a heading; in other editions it commences a new paragraph.

sowars — Members of an Indian cavalry regiment; here guards and troops working for the British legation in Azania.

stand down — Not run, or withdraw from running for political office.

Marie Stopes — English biologist and author (1880–1958). She was especially known for her activities in behalf of contraception.

sundowner — A drink taken near the end of the day, at or near sundown.

Surréalism — A modern movement, mainly in art, in which the artist portrays disconnected objects or images in a dreamlike state.

syce — A groom or attendant, usually in India.

"Taisez-vous, officier. Je désire de l'eau..." — "Be quiet, officer. I want some water. Please, where can you find that?"

"Three little maids from school are we..." — Lyrics from Gilbert and Sullivan's light opera *The Mikado* (1885).

topee — A pith helmet, a lightweight helmetlike hat.

Vicar Apostolic — A Roman Catholic bishop of an area not yet organized as a diocese.

"wallah" — A person who is connected with a particular type of work. Thus a "latrine wallah" would be a worker who cleans latrines. *Wallah*, from a Hindi word, was British army slang in India.

w.c. — a water closet, that is, a toilet.

White Fathers — A French Roman Catholic missionary order in Africa.

wog — A derogatory British slang term for a dark-skinned foreigner. The origin is uncertain; it probably derives from *golliwog*.

A HANDFUL OF DUST (1934)

Waugh takes the title from T. S. Eliot's *The Waste Land* (1922), four lines of which are quoted at the beginning of the novel.

A.B.C.—Railroad timetable.
Agadir—A seaport city in southwestern Morocco.
Aintree—The scene of the racetrack where the Grand National steeplechase is run each year.
amphoras—Clay pots with handles used in ancient times for storing wine and other liquids.
"Analogies"—A game in which the players write down descriptions that relate to particular set categories, e.g., listing a particular jewel, flower, animal, food, scent, etc., that they associate with the person being analyzed or described. There is a description of the game in Waugh's biography of *Monsignor Ronald Knox*, pp. 223–24.
Atlas caids—Berber chiefs in the Atlas Mountains, in northwest Africa.

badders—Bad news.
ballata station—A timber plantation on which balata trees are grown. The gum of these trees is used as a substitute for gutta-percha. *Ballata* is a less common spelling variation of *balata*.
Barnardo case—Down and out. Dr. Thomas J. Barnardo (1845–1905) ran homes for destitute children.
Bedivere—One of King Arthur's most devoted knights; see Glossary under *DF*.
Bevis—A novel (1882) by Richard Jefferies (1848–87).
Biarritz—A fashionable resort in southwestern France.
Bimetallism—A theory that a country's monetary system should be based on the circulation of both gold and silver. The gold and silver would be coined by the country's mint and would circulate at a fixed ratio. This doctrine is opposed to the single standard based on gold.
bone-setting—Treatment by an osteopath or chiropractor.

caid—A Moslem chief among the Berber tribes in northern Africa.
cassava—A plant noted for fleshy tuberous roots used as food.
cat—Vomit.
chantry—A chapel in which masses for a dead person's soul (here Tony Last's) are sung.
charabancs—Sight-seeing buses.
chucked—Avoided keeping a date or going to a party or meeting after accepting an invitation.
Chums—A British adventure magazine for boys.
"Cin no Djinñ how?"—This quotation causes confusion in many editions because punctuation is frequently omitted. Brenda is having trouble spelling the dog's name. She first writes "Cin"; then she thinks, no, it must be spelled "Djinñ." She finally questions how it should be spelled. In the English editions I have examined, "Cin" (obviously a misprint) is written "Gin."
circus factions—In ancient Rome and Constantinople the circus was an area used for games, chariot races, and similar events. Factions were groups who supported the various contestants (like modern "fan clubs," only more violent than most).
Ciudad Bolivar—A city on the Orinoco River in central Venezuela.
Coldstream Guards—One of the oldest and most famous regiments in the British army.
constituency—See Glossary under *BM*.

THE GLOSSARY

Cook's offices—Offices of Thomas Cook & Son, a famous travel agency.
Cottesmore—A town in Leicestershire, a popular fox-hunting region.
Courantyne—A river that flows into the Atlantic Ocean, the boundary between Guyana and Surinam.
crabbing—Complaining about.

dado—A band of paint around the lower wooden panels of the walls of a room.
death duties—Inheritance taxes.
Dedlock—Sir Leicester Dedlock, the excessively proud aristocrat in Charles Dickens's novel *Bleak House* (1852–53).
Demerara—A river basin in British Guiana (now Guyana).
demobilized—Discharged from military service.
"Du Côté de Chez Beaver"—French for "In the Direction of Beaver's Place," that is, where Beaver lives. The French phrase is a reference to Marcel Proust's title "Du Côté de Chez Swann." It should be noted that the title of chap. 6 uses the same words but with Mr. Todd's name. In the earliest editions the error "À Côté" appears in the first and sixth chapters instead of "Du Côté."
"Du Côté De Chez Todd"—French for "Where Mr. Todd Lives."

Elaine—Although there are several women with this name in the Arthurian sagas, the most prominent was the daughter of King Pelles. In one version she was the mother of Galahad by Lancelot. The room here was probably named after the Elaine in Alfred, Lord Tennyson's *Idylls of the King* (1859–85).

Farewell to Arms—A novel (1929) by Ernest Hemingway (1889–1961) about World War I.

Galahad—The most honorable of King Arthur's knights. He finally found the Holy Grail.
Gawaine—The nephew of King Arthur and one of his knights.
gêne—French for "uneasiness."
Georgetown—A city at the mouth of the Demerara River, the capital of the former crown colony of British Guiana (now Guyana).
golliwog—A doll dressed to represent a small black man.

Great Western—An English railway.
grog tray—A tray of alcoholic beverages, mixes, glasses, etc.
Guinevere—The adulterous wife of King Arthur and, therefore, a particularly appropriate name for Brenda Last's bedroom.

hard cheese—Tough luck, bad fortune.

Jelalabad—A reference to the siege of Jelalabad, in which the British defeated the army of Akbar Khan during the first Afghan War (1842). In many editions the word is misspelled "Jalalabad."
Mrs. Jellyby—In Charles Dickens's novel *Bleak House* (1852–53) a woman who neglected her family, devoting her attention to a plan to colonize a section of Africa.
Jimmy-o-goblins—Sovereigns, English gold coins no longer circulated.
jockeys—Bottles of male scent.

King's Proctor—A court official who watches over divorce cases to prevent unlawful collusion between the parties. At the time of *HD* adultery was the only grounds for divorce in England; thus fake adulteries were sometimes staged so that a couple could be divorced. About 1938 desertion and insanity were added as acceptable legal reasons for the termination of marriage.

Labour fellows—Members of the British Labour Party, implying a Socialist outlook.
Lancelot—The most talented warrior among King Arthur's knights. He committed adultery with Arthur's wife, Guinevere.
lascar—A sailor from the East Indies.
lawner—A lawn or garden party.

Malory—Sir Thomas Malory (fl. 1470), author of the great Arthurian saga *Le Morte d'Arthur* (ca. 1469–70), popularized in Victorian times in Alfred, Lord Tennyson's *Idylls of the King* (1859–85).
Manáos—A city on the bank of the Rio Negro in western Brazil. Usually spelled Manaus.
Matto Grosso—A town and a state in southwest Brazil; now spelled Mato Grosso.
Merlin—The famous magician associated with the Arthurian legends.

Mogador — A city on the southwestern coast of Morocco; now called Essaouira.
Mordred — Both the son and the nephew of King Arthur. Both he and Arthur died in a final combat with each other.
Morgan le Fay — King Arthur's fairy sister, one of the principal mischief-makers in the Arthurian romances.

ostlers — People who tend to horses.
oxer — A railing.

paper games — Games like "consequences" played with pencil and paper. A simple game would be choosing a list of subjects, e.g., rivers or birds, and then writing down as many as one can remember in each category beginning with a chosen letter. The person producing the longest number of names in a given time would be the winner.
Para — A state in northern Brazil; also the name given to the eastern mouth of the Amazon River.
Mr. Pecksniff — The famous hypocrite who appears in Charles Dickens's novel *Martin Chuzzlewit* (1843-44). Pecksniff was an architect and a surveyor.
Perceval — One of the Arthurian knights who sought the Holy Grail. In some versions of the saga he manages to gain sight of it.
Pig Scheme — A scheme to reduce the layer of fat on the bellies of pigs from a thickness of 2½ inches to 2 inches so as to reduce the amount of fat in bacon. See *HD*, chap. 5, sec. 2, where Jock discusses this issue with the Minister of Agriculture in Parliament.
put the kybosh on it — Put an end to it.

Queen Empress — Queen Victoria, who reigned from 1837 to 1901, was proclaimed Empress of India in 1876.

rat-catcher — Rather casual hunting attire consisting of knickerbocker trousers and a Norfolk jacket.
R.G.S. — Royal Geographical Society.
"Roll up the map — you will not need it again for how many years, said William Pitt" — An allusion to a statement made by Prime Minister William Pitt (1759–1806) about a map of Europe upon hearing of Napoleon's victory in the Battle of Austerlitz (1805). The actual quotation was, "Roll up that map; it will not be wanted these ten years."

Sedobrol — The trademark of a sedative drink. The trademark was registered in 1913 by John Henry Land, of Coalville, Leicestershire.
shingle — Gravel.
slap-up — High class, elegant.
Sloane number — A London telephone exchange.
the slump — The economic depression of the 1930s.
sock — Treat, e.g., pay for another's meal.
standing on the Clydeside — Being a candidate for election to Parliament representing the Clydeside district in Scotland. British candidates "stand" for election, whereas American candidates "run."
stinkeries — Slang for cages in which silver foxes were kept on breeding farms. Silver-fox farms were especially popular in England between World War I and World War II.

tabulae execrationum — Latin for ancient "tablets of curses."
Takutu — A river in Guyana and Brazil; it eventually unites with the Uraricuera River to form the Rio Branco.
Thiers — Louis Thiers (1797–1877), a French political figure and historian. In the English editions Brenda is reading a book on Nelson.
three-line whip — An order given by the various political party leaders to the members of Parliament notifying them how they must vote on an issue. To emphasize its importance, the order is underlined three times. Members who do not follow the order are regarded as disloyal to their party.
"Tom-all-alone's" — A hideous London slum in Charles Dickens's novel *Bleak House* (1852–53).
tombola — A bingo game.
Tours — A city in France.
Tristram — One of King Arthur's knights; he became involved in a tragic love affair with Iseult.

Uraricuera — A river in northern Brazil; also spelled Uraricoeia. It eventually joins the Tacutu River to form the Rio Branco.

Vanburgh [or Vanbrugh] — Sir John Vanbrugh (1664–1726), English dramatist and architect. His most famous play was *The Relapse* (1697). Among the buildings he designed were Blenheim Palace and Castle Howard (the mansion representing Brideshead Castle in the television production of *BR*).

THE GLOSSARY

walk out — Romantic affair among high society. Partridge cites Waugh's use of the words in *HD*.

Watt's *Physical Energy* — An equestrian statue entitled *Physical Energy*, in London's Kensington Gardens, sculptured by George Watts (1817–1904).

Wipers — Anglicization of Ypres, the name of a town in Belgium, the scene of several especially destructive battles in World War I.

Yarmouth Castle — An English passenger ship. The Union Castle Line was a noted British shipping company whose ships sailed chiefly between England and South Africa. All the ships' names ended in *Castle*.

yashmak — A veil worn by some Muslim women.

The Young Visiters — A novel (1919) by Daisy Ashford, allegedly written when she was nine years old.

Yseult — Better known as Iseult or Isolde, the wife of King Mark of Cornwall. As a result of a magic potion she and Tristram (Tristan) fell in love, and their relationship proved tragic.

SCOOP (1938)

Dedicatee

Laura Herbert, Waugh's second wife, married him in April, 1937. In some respects *Scoop* was a kind of late wedding present to her since he was working on this novel during the first year of their marriage. Later he dedicated *Brideshead Revisited* to her.

"a rivederci" — Italian for "until we meet again."
"**Attention, je vous en prie**" — French for "Attention, if you please."

Banja — A member of an African tribe.
"**beaucoup**" — French for "very much."
Benares trays — See Glossary under *DF*.
Bergner — Elisabeth Bergner (1900–86), Viennese film actress, also popular on the American and English stage. The playwright Sir James Barrie left her $10,000 in his will because she performed so brilliantly in his play *The Boy David*.
Blakewell — A country house; this fact was established by correspondence with Lady Diana Cooper.

capitulations — An agreement which permits a foreigner to remain under his own country's laws while living in another country.
"**Change and decay in all around I see**" — A line from the hymn "Eventide," by Henry Francis Lyte (1793–1847). The hymn begins with the words "Abide with me."
chota pegs... chota mallet — See Glossary under *BM*.
churchwarden — A long clay pipe.
cleft sticks — Wooden sticks hollowed out to hold messages written on paper. Mentioned in *BM*, chap. 7.
coat — A coat of arms.

"**comme ça**" — French for "like this."
"**Comment dit-on humidor...**" — French for "How does one say 'humidor' in French? It is a case to preserve cigars while I'm sailing in the Red Sea — and inside this are hospital instruments for amputating arms and legs, do you understand? And that is for killing snakes, and this is a boat which folds up, and these branches of mistletoe are for Christmas, for kissing underneath, you know."
"Sir, you must not make fun of the customs officials."
"They are to carry messages."
"It is a sport?"
"Yes, yes, certainly — sport."
[Most editions have the ludicrous misprint *Commons* for *Comment*.]
"**comprenez**" — French for "understand?"
Côte d'Azur — The fashionable, resort-oriented coast of France along the Mediterranean.
crazy pavements — Stones of different shapes fitted together to form a sidewalk.
cubbing — Hunting fox cubs.

Distressed Area... Model Madhouse — Names of events held to raise money for charity. Wealthy individuals sponsored plays, ballets, and parties to raise money for their favorite charities. These events were often given unusual or clever names to attract attention. This information was established by correspondence with Lady Diana Cooper, the original model for Mrs. Stitch.
Dizzy — The nickname of Benjamin Disraeli (later earl of Beaconsfield), prime minister of England, 1874–80. He was noted for an aggressive foreign policy.
go down — Defeat, overcome.

THE GLOSSARY

douanier — A customs official.

dragoman — A translator and guide in the Middle East and the Near East. He specialized in Arabic, Persian, and Turkish.

East Finchley — A district in north London near Golders Green, where Waugh grew up.

Elgin marble — One of a group of ancient sculptures which Lord Elgin arranged to have shipped to England early in the nineteenth century. They were bought by the British government and placed in the British Museum.

Ethelred the Unready — Ethelred (ca. 968–1016) was king of England during a disastrous period when the country was under continual attack by Danish invaders.

floater — Mistake, blunder.

"Floribus Austrum..." — A passage from Virgil's *Eclogues*, 2.1.58.

F.R.G.S. — Fellow of the Royal Geographical Society.

Garbo — Greta Garbo (1906–), Swedish-born film actress often associated with the words "I want to be alone."

Garge — A facetious dialectal pronunciation of "George," a common name for a farmer. Salter is congratulating William on his rejection of cider.

"Pussy" Gresham — This is one of the most difficult allusions in the Waugh corpus. Donald Greene writes in personal communication: "The historical nineteenth century figure who was most widely known to be nicknamed 'Pussy'—indeed, the only one I've so far encountered—was Granville George Leveson-Gower (died 1891), 2nd Earl Granville, Gladstone's Foreign Secretary (and many other things—Queen Victoria even offered him the Prime Ministership in preference to Gladstone).

"Granville was well known as a hedonist and a lover of easy living—the type of person who might well have appealed to Uncle Theodore Boot....

"Why 'Pussy' Gresham rather than 'Pussy' Granville? Could it be a typo? A mistake on Waugh's part? Interestingly, Granville's first wife was the widowed mother of Lord Acton the historian. Granville, with his wide diplomatic connections, did much to help his stepson in his education and career as a scholar. As we know Waugh became intimate with Acton's successor as Lord Acton and with his wife Daphne (much about them particularly in the *Life of Ronald Knox*). One of their children was named Pelline, after the Countess Granville. Could it be that Waugh really had this type of lazy epicureanism in mind, but wanted to spare his friends the Actons the embarrassment of naming their ancestor, and so changed 'Granville' to 'Gresham'?"

Hawksmoor — Nicholas Hawksmoor (1661–1736), English architect who worked with Christopher Wren on the designs of several buildings. He was also associated with Sir John Vanbrugh in the construction of Blenheim Palace and Castle Howard (the latter building was used for the Marchmain home in the television version of *BR*).

Heliogabalus — Varius Avitus Bassianus, Emperor of Rome, under the name Marcus Aurelius Antoninus, A.D. 218–22. His rule was extremely decadent. Heliogabalus was an adopted name.

"Il faut manger..." — French for "It is necessary to eat; it is necessary to live. What is the matter with the meat?"

"In Thy courts no more are needed..." — See Glossary under *DF*.

Irish Sweepstake — A lottery conducted by the Irish Republic to aid nursing facilities. The betting takes place on three horse races in Ireland every year.

jackal — A servant, or one who does drudgery for another.

jobbery — The practice of using a public office for personal gain.

K.C.B.'s — Knights Commanders of the Order of the Bath.

Kingsley Wood — Sir Kingsley Wood (1881–1943), holder of various cabinet offices (postmastergeneral, minister of health) in the 1930s. A member of the Conservative party, he was regarded by some (including Waugh) as ineffectual.

Latin Alcaics — An intricate verse form mixing iambics and other meters, named for the Greek poet Alcaeus (fl. ca. 600 B.C.).

Lawrence — T. E. Lawrence (1888–1935), British soldier and author. In World War I he was assigned by the British military as an adviser to the sharif of

Mecca. He became a powerful figure among the Arabs, had many military successes, and earned the sobriquet "Lawrence of Arabia."

Lido — A luxurious resort area on an island near Venice.

lifts — elevators.

loofah — A kind of sponge used in the bathtub. Also spelled *luffa*.

Mangelwurzels — Fleshy roots, large beets grown to feed cattle.

"Mauvais poisson..." — French for "bad fish — fearful odor — take away — and bring whiskey quickly."

More birthdayers — Each year in June selected people are given noble titles and honors on a day designed as the official birthday of the Queen; hence the term "Birthday Honors." In some editions the confusing misprint "more birthdays" occurs.

Munera — Latin for "gifts," "presents."

"Nay not so much as out of bed? / When all the birds have Matins said" — Lines from the poem "Corinna's Going a-Maying," by Robert Herrick (1591–1674).

"Notre condition professionnelle..." — French for "our professional rank. We welcome all free and fair competition."

Pam — The nickname of Lord Henry Palmerston (1784–1865), a powerful political figure who was Prime Minister of England, 1855–57 and 1859–65. He was noted for an aggressive foreign policy.

P. and O. — See Glossary under *BM*.

Parsee — See Glossary under *BM*.

Pernod — A trademark for a French liquer.

"Peut-être — French for "Perhaps."

"piacere" — Italian for "please." In various editions it is misprinted *piacene*.

"pied à terre" — French for, literally, "foot to the earth"; a small apartment or house used as a temporary or second home.

"poste restante" — Italian for "general delivery," i.e., mail held in a post office until someone calls for it.

"The Prime Minister is nuts on rural England" — A satiric hit at Prime Minister Stanley Baldwin, who was known as an enthusiast for the English countryside.

Punch-and-Judy — A popular puppet play with much violence.

R.A.C. — Royal Automobile Club; also mentioned in *VB*.

Reach-me-downs — Secondhand clothing of poor quality.

Rhodes — Cecil J. Rhodes (1853–1902), British financier who became a power in the South African diamond-mining industry. He established the Rhodes scholarships to enable students from the British Empire, the United States, and Germany to study at Oxford.

Romano's — A well-known bar and restaurant in London's Strand in the 1890s and the early part of the twentieth century. It particularly attracted figures from the world of sports, as well as journalism and the theater.

Rousseau — Henry Rousseau (1844–1910), French painter particularly known for his colorful jungle scenes with animals and lush foliage. Rousseau was called "Le Douanier" (which means "the Customs Official") because he had served in that occupation for a time.

St. Bride's — An Anglican church in Fleet Street, the heart of London's newspaper district.

Saint James's Palace — A brick mansion near Buckingham Palace which serves as one of the residences of English royalty.

saltire — In heraldry, an ×-shaped symbol.

Sassanian lounge — A reference to decoration done in the style of Sassanian, a form of Iranian art that originated in the Sassanid Dynasty in the third century A.D. Its murals depicted battles as well as animals and other figures.

slag — The waste material left after minerals have been separated from surrounding dirt or rock.

Spahi capes — Decorative and impressive capes worn by Spahi cavalry, the native Algerian force under the French. See Glossary under *WS*.

squiffy — Intoxicated.

tiffin gun — *Tiffin* is an Indian term for a midday meal. In British communities in India a gun was sometimes fired at noon or thereabouts to indicate that tiffin was ready. The misssionary, being a newcomer, assumed that tiffin was some kind of weapon.

"Tous sont des effets..." — French for "All are personal property — very useful."

"tout-de-suite" — French for "immediately."

THE GLOSSARY

Tutankhamen — An Egyptian pharaoh who ruled about 1340 B.C. His tomb was discovered in 1922 and opened by the English archaeologist Howard Carter the following year. It yielded jewels and many objects of historical interest.

two guineas — A guinea is 21 shillings (a pound and one shilling); hence 42 shillings (two pounds and two shillings).

U.N. — Universal News, a fictional news agency.

vetted — Medically examined.

Willis's rooms — Formerly called the Assembly Rooms, a London nightclub for dancing, dining, and gambling. Situated on King Street, it was especially popular in the 1890s.

"the Mary Selena Wilmark of Britain" — An imaginary figure, a fact which explains why no one has ever heard of her. Waugh might have conceived of the name from Mary Hawes Wilmarth, an American social worker prominent in the Legal Aid Society and in the Woman's Trade Union League during the first two decades of the twentieth century. She was reputed to be exceedingly intellectual and well informed.

PUT OUT MORE FLAGS (1942)

Dedicatee

Randolph Churchill (1911–68), the son of Winston Churchill, was a journalist and author who had a close friendship with Waugh for many years. Occasionally the friendship would cool, but they would gradually renew cordial relations.

ADDIS—Assistant Deputy Director Internal Security, a fictional appointment.

A.F.V.'s—Armored Fighting Vehicles (tanks, armored cars, etc.)

Alcibiades—A famous Greek general (450–404 B.C.). He was banished by the senate at Athens but gathered a military force and attacked and briefly conquered the city.

Angelica Kauffmann—Swiss-born painter (1741–1807). She traveled to England and studied with Sir Joshua Reynolds. She had a very successful career as a portrait painter and decorator.

Aphrodite of Melos—The Venus de Milo, the famous statue of Aphrodite, discovered on Melos, a Greek island in the Aegean Sea, in 1820.

Apuleius's ass—A reference to the Latin story *The Golden Ass*, by Lucius Apuleius (second century A.D.). It is the story of a protagonist who is transformed into a donkey and has many interesting experiences before returning to his human form.

A.R.P.—Air Raid Precautions. An organization whose members were similar to American air raid wardens.

"Ars longa"—Latin for "Art is lasting." The quotation, from Hippocrates, concludes: "vita brevis" ("life is short.")

Ascot—The promenade area for the Ascot horse races; see Glossary under *DF*.

Asquith—Herbert Henry Asquith (1852–1928), British political figure, later created the first Earl of Oxford and Asquith. He served as prime minister from 1908 to 1916. Waugh was a close friend of his daughter-in-law Katharine (Mrs. Raymond Asquith) and other members of the family.

"À tes beaux yeux"—French for "to your beautiful eyes."

Athenia—A British passenger liner which was sunk by a submarine in the Atlantic on September 3, 1939, while bound for Canada. The casualties were extremely severe.

A.T.S.—Auxiliary Territorial Service; that is, the women's army auxiliary corps.

Bakerloo railway—A line on the London Underground. It runs through the Baker Street and Waterloo stations, hence the name combination. It is popular with commuters.

Bassett-Lowkes—A London toy store specializing in scale models of locomotives, airplanes, etc.

batman—An officer's servant, an orderly.

Aubrey Beardsley (1872–98)—English illustrator whose famous drawings involve erotic and bizarre material. He was a prominent figure in the aesthetic movement of the 1890s.

Beddoes—Thomas Lowell Beddoes (1803–49), homosexual English dramatist.

béguin—French for infatuation.

Bench—A judicial post, here as a local justice of the peace or magistrate.

Blücher—Gebhard von Blücher (1742–1819), Prussian general whose army helped defeat Napoleon at the Battle of Waterloo.

Botany Bay—A convict settlement in Australia to which many English prisoners were sent, especially in the eighteenth and nineteenth centuries.

THE GLOSSARY

Boundaries inclusive and exclusive — Boundaries between one formation and those on either side of it.

Brancusi — Constantin Brancusi (1876–1957), Rumanian sculptor whose work, mostly painted in Paris, is modernistic and abstract. He has had considerable influence on modern sculpture, especially in metal and stone.

Bren gun — A light machine gun used by the British army in World War II. Brens were invented and made in Czechoslovakia.

Rupert Brooke — British poet (1887–1915) who reflected the patriotism of the early World War I period. A naval officer, he died of septicemia on a ship near Skyros and was buried on that Greek island.

Brown House — A dwelling in Munich, Bavaria (in what is now West Germany), which in 1931 became the headquarters of the Nazi party.

Brown Shirt — A member of the Nazi Storm Troopers.

Carpaccio — Vittore Carpaccio (before 1460–before 1526), Italian painter who gave dramatic effects to religious subject matter.

Cervantes — Miguel de Cervantes Saavedra (1547–1616), Spanish author best known for his novel *Don Quixote*.

Cézanne — Paul Cézanne (1839–1906), influential French painter who led the postimpressionists.

Charles I — British king (1600–49) who engaged in numerous conflicts with Parliament. He was tried by the House of Commons and was beheaded.

Chief Whip — See Glossary under *BM*.

Christ Church Grind — A point-to-point horse race organized by Christ Church College at Oxford.

Chums — See Glossary under *HD*.

Cochran — Sir Charles Blake Cochran (1872–1951), British promoter who sponsored money-making events ranging from sports to the Diaghilev ballet.

Jean Cocteau — French writer (1891–1963). Of considerable versatility, he was best known for his plays and films and was also proficient in developing ballets.

Compton Mackenzie — British novelist (1883–1972), perhaps best known for *Sinister Street*, published in two volumes in 1913 and 1914.

"Cor chase my Aunt Fanny..." — A slang phrase expressing incredulity.

Crécy — A town in France, the scene of a battle in 1346 in which English forces under King Edward III defeated the French army.

Crosse and Blackwell's regiment... General Service List — Crosse and Blackwell are British manufacturers of a wide variety of preserved foods — jams, pickles, etc. General Service List officers were officers insufficiently specialized to be posted to one of the recognized groups, e.g., engineers, infantry, artillery, or signals.

Dali — Salvador Dali (1904–), Spanish surrealistic painter. See *surréaliste*, below.

Dar-es-Salaam — A seaport city in former German East Africa. In 1916 it was captured by the British. In 1964 it became the capital of the Republic of Tanzania. Misprinted in some editions as Dar-as-Salaam.

deal — Cheap wood, usually pine or fir.

Diaghilev — Sergei Diaghilev (1872–1929), Russian ballet producer whose modernist ideas had considerable influence on Western art and theater.

Disraeli — See Glossary under *Sc, Dizzy*.

Doctor Ley — Robert Ley (1890–1945), Nazi leader particularly charged with controlling German labor.

"The dog it was that died" — A line from Oliver Goldsmith's poem "Elegy on the Death of a Mad Dog." The line preceding it is, "The man recovered from the bite."

Bulldog Drummond — Captain Hugh Drummond, the hero of several detective stories by H. C. McNeile (1888–1937), who wrote under the pseudonym Sapper. Gerard Fairlie wrote further stories about Drummond after McNeile's death.

ducks — Trousers of strong, usually cotton, cloth.

Erchman — Apparently a fictional name, suitably Germanic since the popularity of psychoanalysis and Freudianism in the early part of this century was frequently associated with German practitioners. (Patrick Balfour, in his *Society Racket* (London, 1933), reports that an Oxford undergraduate carried on a successful hoax by advertising and giving a lecture as the famous German psychologist Dr. Emil Busch. The lecture was deliberate gibberish, being filled with popular psychological jargon.) A less likely possibility is that Erchman may allude to Frank Buchman, an American minister who founded a movement to emphasize "healthy" aspects by combining a practical, robust Christianity with a mystical search for God's guidance.

PUT OUT MORE FLAGS

Eton—Probably the most prestigious public school in England.

farouche—French for "wild," "disorderly."

F.D.L.'s—Foremost Defended Localities; that is, the most advanced positions which a military formation is supposed to hold against enemy attack.

Flaxman Greeks—John Flaxman (1755–1826) was an English painter and sculptor. He made drawings of various scenes in Homer's *Iliad* and *Odyssey* and became a professor in the Royal Academy of Art.

von Fritsch—Baron Werner von Fritsch (1880–1939), German general who lost his position as army commander in 1938 because he was not sympathetic to Nazism.

General Strike—See Glossary under *DF*.

George IV—British king (1762–1830) who succeeded his father, George III, to the throne in 1820.

geyser—Gas hot-water heater.

Goebbels—Joseph Goebbels (1897–1945), a prominent Nazi official; he was in charge of Nazi propaganda.

Goering—Hermann Goering (1893–1946), powerful Nazi official who founded the Gestapo. He held several government positions under Hitler and was head of the German air force.

Goodwood week—The week-long horse races held at Goodwood Park, in Sussex. The races begin on the last Tuesday in July, and the week is a festive occasion known as "Glorious Goodwood."

General Gordon—See Glossary under *DF*.

"A green thought in a green place"—A line from "An Horatian Ode upon Cromwell's Return From Ireland," by Andrew Marvell (1621–1678). The line actually reads: "To a green thought in a green shade."

Grinling Gibbons—A Dutch, later English, sculptor and woodcarver (1648–1720). His carvings are found in Saint Paul's Cathedral and other churches, and he also worked on various houses and public buildings. His woodwork was highly decorative.

Grosvenor Square—One of the most fashionable areas in London.

Hogarthian—In the manner of William Hogarth (1697–1764), British painter and engraver. Many of his pictures are satirical caricatures illustrating defects and unsavory conditions in English life.

Horace—Quintus Horatius Flaccus (65–8 B.C.), one of the greatest of the Roman poets.

Hore-Belisha—Leslie Hore-Belisha (1893–1957), British political and government figure. He was secretary for war from 1937 to 1940. As a Jewish "outsider," he held views on army administration that were considered radical, and he soon lost the post.

How support batteries—Howitzer artillery units.

Humber Snipe—A small British-made passenger car.

Hypatia—A Greek philosopher of Alexandria (370–415 A.D.). She was accused of being an enchantress and was attacked and killed by a Christian mob. She was the subject of a popular novel of that name by Charles Kingsley.

"Il faut en finir..."—French for "It is necessary to finish [win]; we will win because we are the strongest."

In Memoriam—A series of poetic elegies (1850) by Alfred, Lord Tennyson (1809–1892), in memory of Tennyson's friend Arthur Henry Hallam, who died in 1833.

ironmongery—Metal and iron materials.

"It is an evil thing we are fighting"—Words spoken by British Prime Minister Neville Chamberlain (1869–1940) in his radio broadcast to the nation at the outbreak of war against Germany. The declaration of war by England occurred on September 3, 1939. Chamberlain continued as prime minister during the lull (called the "Phoney War" or the "Great Bore War") in 1939 and until May 10, 1940, when he was succeeded by Winston Churchill.

Jerries—Slang for Germans.

John—Augustus John, English painter (1878–1961) best known for his portraits.

Sir William Joynson-Hicks—(later Viscount Brentford) British Conservative political figure (1865–1932). He served in various government capacities; as Home Secretary, 1924–29, he was noted for his policy of enforcing "morality." His name was often abbreviated "Jix." His policies are satirized in *VB*.

Lord Kitchener—Horatio Herbert, first Earl Kitchener, English statesman and military figure (1850–1916). He served with great military success in Africa and was also later commander-in-chief in India. He became secretary of war and was especially known for his World War I recruiting achievements.

Knights Templar—Members of a military-religious order founded in the twelfth century. They were famous for their participation in the Crusades. The order was abolished in the fourteenth century, after accusations of homosexuality.

Knuckledusters—Brass knuckles.

Kümmel—See Glossary under *VB*.

Batty Langley—English architect (1696–1751) known particularly for a school of architectural drawing he established with his brother in London and for his many books on architecture.

Lares et Penates—Roman household gods who guarded the home and supposedly brought success. "Lares et Penates" is used as a general expression for a home and the possessions in the home.

T. E. Lawrence—See Glossary under *Sc*.

Leech—John Leech (1817–64), British caricaturist. He did many drawings for books and for many years did drawings for *Punch*. Mistakenly spelled Leach in some editions.

Leonardo—Leonardo da Vinci (1452–1519), Italian Renaissance artist, a man of talent in many professions. He is probably best remembered today for his portrait *Mona Lisa*.

Lepanto—The Italian name of the Greek seaport Návpaktos, the scene of a famous sea battle fought on October 7, 1571. A Christian fleet under the command of Don John of Austria, the brother of King Philip II of Spain, soundly defeated powerful Turkish naval forces and ended the Turks' advance in the eastern Mediterranean.

Limbo—Oblivion. In Roman Catholic theology it is the place of rest for unbaptized infants and for honorable people who died before the coming of Christ.

"The Lion Has Wings"—A British film used for propaganda purposes. In the movie German bombers do not carry out their mission over England because they are afraid of the barrage balloons.

Lloyd George—See Appendix 2, "Common References in Waugh's Fiction." The Lloyd George fund was used to support any political need of which Lloyd George approved. The money was collected from the sale of titles of nobility and honors.

Loamshires—An imaginary English rural county frequently used in fiction. It also refers to a fictional army regiment from that county. Loam is good agricultural soil.

Lovat-Fraser—Claud Lovat-Fraser (1890–1921), British artist best known for his book illustrations. He also did stage designing.

Lytton report—A report (1932) to the League of Nations, headquartered in Geneva, Switzerland, which deplored the invasion of Manchuria, a region of China, by the Japanese and urged that they be obliged to leave. The report was named for British diplomat Victor Alexander George Robert Lytton, the second earl of Lytton (1876–1947), who headed the commission that drafted the document.

MacDonald—See Glossary under *DF*.

Maginot line—A series of fortifications built by France in the 1930s as protection against a possible German invasion. In World War II the Germans overran the line with relative ease. It was named in honor of André Maginot, who served as the French minister of war between the world wars.

Maida Vale—A fashionable street in an upper-middle-class residential area of London.

man who used to dress as an Arab and then went into the air force—Lawrence of Arabia; see Glossary under *Sc*.

march tactically—Before World War II a company of soldiers marched in neat columns, three abreast, in step, and to cadence. About the time of World War II it was realized that this procedure made the group highly conspicuous to enemy air observation, and in military exercises where there was pretense of danger from air attack, the order was given to "march tactically," which meant that everyone moved along on his own and was supposed to shelter himself under trees, etc.

matelots—French sailors.

Mein Kampf—English translation, *My Struggle*, a book (1924) by Adolf Hitler describing his political views and goals.

"memento mori"—A reminder of death, such as a skull.

Milton—John Milton (1608–74), English poet best known for his poem *Paradise Lost*.

M.I.9—In the English editions I have seen, Basil says he is, inexplicably, M.I.13 whenever he uses this identification ruse. In Chapman Pincher's *Too Secret Too Long* (New York, 1984), Pincher points out that M.I.8c and M.I.14 were secret English intelligence organizations. Each of these numbers is just one figure away from M.I.9 and M.I.13 of *POMF*, and both organizations were set up about the time Waugh was writing the novel. Could the M.I.5 section have become alarmed by the publicity and similarity of the numbers and demanded number changes?

money for old rope — Something that is obtained for no cost or very little cost.

Lord Monmouth — The fictional Marquess of Monmouth who appears in Benjamin Disraeli's novel *Coningsby* (1844). The quotation appears in book 4, chap. 6.

William Morris — See Glossary under *DF*.

Mosley — Sir Oswald Mosley (1896–1980), the leader of the British Fascists (Blackshirts). He was imprisoned for a time during World War II. *VB* is dedicated to his wife, Diana Mitford, then Mrs. Bryan Guinness.

"**Nature I loved, and next to Nature, Art**" — A line from the poem "Finis," by Walter Savage Landor (1775–1864).

Nelson — Horatio, Lord Nelson (1758–1805), British admiral and naval hero who was killed during the battle of Trafalgar, in which the French fleet was destroyed.

"**nocturnes**" — Paintings of night scenes popularized by the American painter James McNeill Whistler (1834–1903).

Nollekens — Joseph Nollekens (1737–1823), a very popular British portrait sculptor. He did acclaimed busts of famous people, such as King George III, and also sculptured many statues in marble. Misspelled as Nollekins or Nolleykins in some editions.

O group — Orders group. The officers commanding the various companies of an infantry battalion assemble at a rendezvous to be given orders by the battalion commander for a military maneuver (for a description of such a maneuver see *BR*, "Prologue"). Afterward the company commanders similarly summon their platoon commanders for an O group meeting.

Old Bill — The central character in the popular cartoons of Bruce Bairnsfather during World War I. Old Bill represents a veteran military campaigner, a symbol of the British fighting man, a tough, cynical, competent, and reliable old soldier.

Oscar and Aubrey — Oscar Wilde and Aubrey Beardsley; see Wilde and Beardsley in the Glossary of this novel.

Palais de Danse — French for "dance hall."

peckish — Hungry.

Petain — See Glossary under *OG*, *Vichy French*.

pierrots — Figures in French pantomimes. Pierrot played the role of a fool or clown.

platoon schemes and company schemes — Tactical exercises carried out by a platoon and by a company.

Pompeian — Decorated in the style of the ancient paintings, particularly frescoes, of Pompeii. Pompeii was buried in ash in the eruption of Vesuvius in A.D. 79, but archeologists have unearthed much of the city, and its wall decorations and architecture have been much imitated.

prie-dieu — A bench with a supporting shelf at which one can kneel upright to pray.

J. B. Priestley — See Glossary under *BM*.

P.T. — Physical Training.

put down smoke — Discharge a smoke screen to conceal an area and troop movements and confuse the enemy.

Quadragesimo Anno — Latin for *In the Fortieth Year*, the title of an encyclical issued in 1931 by Pope Pius XI. In 1891, Pope Leo XIII published the encyclical *Rerum Novarum* on labor relations. *Quadragesimo Anno* commemorated the fortieth anniversary of this papal essay. It reinforced the principles of Pope Leo's encyclical and updated the material, condemning communism, socialism, and materialistic individualism which disregarded fundamental human rights.

R.A.P. — Regimental Aid Post, where wounded soldiers are taken for first aid by regimental medical corpsmen before being taken off to a central Casualty Clearing Center.

R.D.F. — Radio Direction Finder, much later called radar.

recce — Reconnaissance.

Red Square — A large central square in Moscow, synonymous with the center or heart of communism.

Ribbentrop — Joachim von Ribbentrop (1893–1946), German Nazi official. He was foreign minister under Hitler from 1938 to 1945 and had served as ambassador to England.

rifles to be pulled through — A cord or piece of oiled cloth is pulled through the barrel of a gun to clean it.

ring contour — Contour lines on a contour map connect all points of equal height above sea level. A line in the form of a ring indicates the top of a hill or smaller protuberance.

rocket — Reprimand.

Saladin — The Sultan of Egypt and Syria (1138–93), a powerful ruler and successful military leader. Like Leonardo da Vinci, he was allegedly homosexual.

Sam Browne belt — A leather belt worn with an army dress uniform. The belt, named for Sir Samuel J. Browne, had a strap attached to it which went over the right shoulder.

Saturnalia — A wild celebration; originally the festival honoring the Roman god Saturn.

Scapa — See Glossary, under *OG, Scapa Flow*.

Schleswig-Holstein — Two adjoining duchies once held by the king of Denmark, the control of which caused considerable international contention. Both duchies were annexed by Prussia in the 1860s. They are now part of Denmark and West Germany.

Scottsboro trials — The trials, in Scottsboro, Alabama, of a group of blacks found in a railroad freight car with white prostitutes. The prostitutes charged rape, and at the trials (1931–32) the men were convicted and sentenced to death. After much public protest they were eventually freed.

Mrs. Siddons — Sarah Kemble Siddons (1755–1831), famous English actress, especially well known for her roles in Shakespearean plays. Sir Joshua Reynolds painted a portrait of her called *The Tragic Muse*.

Sidney — Sir Philip Sidney (1554–86), English poet, courtier, and soldier.

Siegfried Sassoon — British poet (1886–1967) and author of memoirs and biographies. He is best known for his poems relating to World War I. He served in that war and was decorated for bravery.

slump — The economic depression beginning in 1929 and continuing until the outbreak of World War II (1939).

Soapy Sponge . . . Jawleyford Court — Soapy Sponge is the protagonist of Robert S. Surtees's hunting novel *Mr. Sponge's Sporting Tour* (1853). As his name implies he sponges off people, and among his victims is the squire of a splendid country estate called Jawleyford Court. See *Surtees*, below.

Socrates — Greek philosopher (ca. 469–399 B.C.), the teacher of Plato. The latter recorded much of his thought.

soldier manqué — Soldier disappointed in his goal.

Spartans — Greeks from the city-state of Sparta noted for their toughness, stoicism, and brevity of speech (the word *laconic* originated from Laconia, Sparta's district).

"spoilt priest" — A person who has had a vocation to the priesthood but has failed to attain it. Such a person has usually failed in his subsequent career and often drinks excessively.

Spread Eagle at Thame — A famous restaurant and inn in the village of Thame. John Fothergill, the eccentric owner, chained a copy of *Decline and Fall* in the main lavatory.

Squadron Lawn at Cowes — The premises, on the Isle of Wight, of the Royal Yacht Squadron, the most exclusive yachting club in Britain. Cowes was the scene of lavish social gatherings, promenades, and yachting races.

start line — The position where the soldiers of the battalion line up to await the order to begin an attack.

Gertrude Stein — American-born expatriate (1874–1946) who settled in Paris and established a writing and art salon that supported and encouraged promising artists, including Ernest Hemingway. Her own writing is marked by startling stylistic experiments.

Stilton — A famous British cheese.

subaltern — A subordinate; a commissioned officer below the rank of captain.

Sucks to you — The rough equivalent of American "Nuts to you." It connotes the triumph of the speaker at the discomfiture or defeat of the hearer.

surréaliste — An artistic and literary movement, popular in the 1920s and 1930s, emphasizing fantasy, dreams, and images of the subconscious mind. It was much influenced by Freudianism.

Surtees — Robert Smith Surtees (1803–64), British novelist and writer about fox hunting and other sports. His novels were generally filled with humor. Waugh was especially familiar with Surtees's *Mr. Sponge's Sporting Tour* (1853) and *Jorrocks's Jaunts and Jollities* (1838).

tell your beads — Say the Rosary, a Roman Catholic devotion of saying prayers while counting them on a string of beads. The devotion honors the Blessed Virgin Mary and asks her to intercede with Christ to help the person who is praying.

1098 stores — Military supplies; see *When we got over 1098*, below.

Thermopylae — A narrow pass in Greece where the Spartans, severely outnumbered, fought the Persians in 480 B.C. Leonidas, the Spartan king, and his men fought heroically to the last man.

third E in Bee Garden . . . B in Bee . . . E in Garden — The letters BEE GARDEN are printed across the map and form points of reference.

Thornton — Robert John Thornton (1768–1807), a physician and botanist. He published several books, including *The Temple of Flora* (1799–1807). One of the most famous plates in the book is that of the night-blooming cereus. Although Thornton wrote the text of the book, the artists were Peter Henderson; Philip Reinagle, who drew the cereus; and Abraham Pether.

Toulon — A French seaport on the Mediterranean, the site of an important naval base.

track junction — The point on the map where two paths or roads join.

Trotskyism — The rapid, extreme, worldwide revolutionary communism espoused by Leon Trotsky (1877–1940). He fell into disfavor with Stalin, was banished from Russia, and was eventually assassinated in Mexico, where he had taken refuge.

Troubles — The period of civil war in the southern counties of Ireland lasting roughly from 1919 to 1923. Irish Republican groups fought the British occupying forces, and then there was warfare between those supporting the Irish Free State and those who wanted England separated from Ireland, including Ulster (the six northern counties).

Trust House — One of a large chain of hotels (now Trust Houses Forte).

the Turf in London — A men's club (founded in 1868) whose members were prominent individuals especially interested in horse racing and other sports.

2300 hrs. — 11:00 P.M.

twig — Catch on to, understand.

Utrillo — Maurice Utrillo (1883–1955), French post-impressionist artist famous for his paintings of Paris, especially the Montmartre section.

Vickers — A type of machine gun used by the British army.

Virgil — Publius Vergilius Maro (70–19 B.C.), Roman epic poet whose most famous work is *The Aeneid*.

Waterloo — A village in Belgium near the site of the famous battle in which Napoleon was defeated by British and Prussian forces on June 18, 1815.

W.D. — War Department.

Wellington — The first Duke of Wellington (1769–1852), the English military commander who led the allied British and Prussian forces in the defeat of Napoleon at Waterloo in 1815.

"What a sell!" — What a deception!

"when we got over 1098" — G1098 was a War Office form which listed the equipment each unit was to be issued. "Over" in some editions is very likely a misprint for "our."

white feathers — During World War I women often gave white feathers to men in civilian clothes as a symbol of their supposed cowardice in not being in the military.

Wilde — Oscar Wilde (1856–1900), Irish-born English poet and playwright. He was the leader of the English aesthetes, but his involvement in a homosexual scandal eventually brought imprisonment and ruin.

Godfrey Winn — British journalist and author (1908–71).

Wolfe — James Wolfe (1727–59), English general who defeated the French forces on the Plains of Abraham, in Quebec, and was killed there.

Xenophon — Greek soldier and author (431–355 B.C.). He wrote on a wide variety of topics, including history, philosophy, and politics.

Yellow Book — An English quarterly periodical published from 1894 to 1897. It was a vehicle for the aesthetes and featured work by, among others, Aubrey Beardsley, Max Beerbohm, and Oscar Wilde.

Yuan Tse tsung — A reference to Yuan Tsi (A.D. 210–63), one of the first "romanticists" in China. He is listed in Lin Yutang's *The Importance of Living* (1937). Two epigrams from Lin Yutang's book are printed at the beginning of *POMF*.

zero hour — The hour in which a military operation is scheduled to begin.

WORK SUSPENDED (1942)

Dedicatee

Alexander Woollcott (1887–1943) was a well-known American journalist who also wrote books and plays and compiled several anthologies. He achieved considerable attention for his "Town Crier" radio broadcasts. Woollcott had been supportive of Waugh's writing, having given particularly high praise to *Decline and Fall* and *A Handful of Dust*.

Academy—Royal Academy of Art, London.
Alhambra—A group of buildings in Granada, Spain, especially noted as impressive examples of Moorish architecture.
Arundel prints—The Arundel Society, named for Thomas Howard, earl of Arundel, a patron and collector of art, reproduced colored prints of famous artworks to increase public awareness of and involvement with culture.
Athenaeum—A London club; see Glossary under *DF*.
August 25th, 1939—The birth date of Lucy's child is not mentioned in the 1942 edition.

Bartolozzi prints—Prints by Francesco Bartolozzi (1727–1815), Italian engraver. He went to England, became a member of the Royal Academy, and continued his work in prints and engravings.
beak—A judge or magistrate.
Max Beerbohm—Max Beerbohm (1872–1956), widely admired English satirist, essayist, and caricaturist. He won much fame for his novel *Zuleika Dobson* (1911).
Belisha crossing—The flashing amber light used in Britain to indicate a pedestrian crossing. The idea was inaugurated by Leslie Hore-Belisha, Minister of Transport, 1934–37.

Clive Bell—English art critic (1881–1964) who was married to Vanessa Bell, Virginia Woolf's sister. He published several books on art.
Berber—A member of a people of northern Africa.
Ford Madox Brown—English romantic painter (1821–93) who had an inspiring effect on the Pre-Raphaelites. The reference to Brown is omitted from the 1948 edition of *WS* and later printings.

capitulations—See Glossary under *Sc*.
Cézanne—See Glossary under *POMF*.
copper—Policeman.

don—See Glossary under *BM*.
"done out"—Redecorated.
Dreyfus—See Glossary under *BM*.
dumb crambo—A game in which one group names a word rhyming with another word which has to be guessed by the opposite side. The opposite group must act out the correct word in pantomime.

Flaxman—See Glossary under *POMF, Flaxman Greeks*.
fou rire—French for "uncontrollable laughter."
freehold—Title to and ownership of real estate.
Frith—William Powell Frith (1819–1909), English artist who painted both historical and contemporary scenes.

Gauguin—Paul Gauguin (1848–1903), French painter best known for his lush and colorful paintings of people and scenes in the Pacific South Seas.
Greats—The final B.A. examination at Oxford University, especially the honors course in classical literature, philosophy, and history.

THE GLOSSARY

William Halfpenny — English architect (d. 1755) best remembered for the many books he wrote on a wide range of architectural styles.

Humboldt's Gibbon — Humboldt's woolly monkey *Lagothrix humboldtii*. This spider monkey was named for Friedrich H. A. von Humboldt, who first described it in a zoological book he wrote with Aimé Bonplan in 1811. Such a monkey was exhibited at the London Zoo in the late 1930s.

I.C.I. — Imperial Chemical Industries, a gigantic British firm which manufactures chemicals, paints, plastics, etc.

Jacobite — Derived from Jacobus, the Latin form for James, it refers to supporters of King James II, who was deposed from the English throne in 1688, and his son, James Stuart (called the "Old Pretender"). Jacobite followers also supported Charles Edward Stuart (called "Bonnie Prince Charlie" and the "Young Pretender"). Bonnie Prince Charlie led a rebellion from Scotland in 1745, but his armies were defeated by the English at the Battle of Culloden in 1746.

Kensington Gardens — A large park adjoining Hyde Park in a very fashionable section of London.

Kipling's *Light That Failed* — Rudyard Kipling's novel *The Light That Failed* (1890) deals with an artist who gradually goes blind from a wound he received while fighting in the British army.

Knight of Malta — A member of an order founded in Jerusalem near the end of the eleventh century. It originally consisted of monks who guided pilgrims through Europe to the holy shrines in Palestine. In the sixteenth century the order moved to the island of Malta but finally settled in Rome. It is a distinguished Roman Catholic order whose chief function today is to run free clinics in hospitals.

kulak — A wealthy Russian peasant, of a group frowned upon by the Russian Communists.

Batty Langley — See Glossary under *POMF*.

Lely — Sir Peter Lely (1618–1680), an artist who was born in Holland but made his fortune in England, where he became the principal painter of the royal court.

life-preserver — A blackjack.

Manuelo style — A very ornate architectural style developed in Portugal in the sixteenth century and named for King Manuel I (1469–1521). It used nautical motifs such as stone cables, buoys, and other decorations found in or related to ships. This allusion is omitted from the 1948 edition of *WS* and later printings.

marriage dot — Dowry.

Millais — See Glossary under *VB*.

Mods — Short for "moderations," intermediate examinations in various subjects as a preliminary to the final honours examinations for the B.A.

Morris papers — Wallpapers made in the factory established by William Morris.

Morris tapestry — Tapestry manufactured by the William Morris firm, founded in the Victorian period. See Glossary under *DF*.

Moulay Abdullah — The walled quarter of Fez between the old city and the ghetto area, so called in honor of a sixteenth-century ruler of the town.

New College Essay Society — An undergraduate organization at New College, Oxford.

pas-devant — French for "not in front of," i.e., not to converse on certain matters when the servants or children (who are not supposed to understand French) are present.

penny dreadfuls — Cheap magazines containing stories of imaginative adventure, emphasizing melodramatic events with an emphasis on violence. These magazines originally sold for one penny.

quartier toléré — French for "tolerated area," that is, the red-light district.

Rubenses — Paintings by Peter Paul Rubens (1577–1640), Flemish artist who traveled widely and painted subjects in several countries. He had particularly effective ability with colors.

St. John's Wood — A well-to-do section of London west of Regent's Park.

Senegalese — Persons from the Senegal section of West Africa, long controlled by the French.

shakedown — Improvised lodging and accommodations.

Song of Solomon — A book in the Old Testament that

describes an idyllic love between a man and a woman.

Spahi officers—Members of the Algerian native cavalry who were part of the French army. The Spahis originated in Turkey. See also *Sc.*

Spode—Josiah Spode (1754–1827) British pottery maker, famous for the bone porcelain named for him.

Stanhope Gate—A strolling area in the southeastern section of Hyde Park.

Subs—Short for *subscriptions*.

Tweedledum—Tweedledum and Tweedledee are opinions that are essentially the same. John Byrom (1692–1763) created the two characters to satirize two quarreling musical groups who really held the same opinions. Lewis Carroll gave these names to two characters in *Through the Looking Glass*.

Whistlerian—A reference to James McNeill Whistler (1834–1903), American painter who was widely accepted in both British and French artistic circles.

Winterhalter—Franz Winterhalter (1806–73), German artist especially remembered for his portrait painting.

BRIDESHEAD REVISITED (1945)

Dedicatee

Laura Waugh, Evelyn's wife.

Abdul Krim — Abd-el-Krim, or Abdel Krim (1881–1963), who led the Rif tribesmen in Morocco and fought against both French and Spanish armies.

Acre — See Glossary under *VB*.

Adam room — A room decorated in the late-eighteenth-century style popularized by Robert and James Adam. Adam style shaped Roman and Greek classical designs into lighter proportions and added a delicate elegance.

Agincourt — See Glossary under *VB*.

Aladdin's treasury — A reference to the story of Aladdin and his magic lamp in the *Arabian Nights*. This allusion was omitted from the 1960 revised edition of *BR*.

Aleppo — A city in northern Syria.

All Souls — An Oxford College which has no undergraduates but is reserved for postgraduate scholars and researchers.

Ampleforth — An English Roman Catholic school run by the Benedictine order.

Anglo-Catholics — Members of the Anglican church who in their beliefs and practices are close to Roman Catholics. They regard themselves as a national Catholic church independent of Roman (Vatican) control.

Antic Hay — A popular satiric novel (1923) by Aldous Huxley.

apaches — Parisian rowdies and "toughs," after the southwestern American Indian tribe.

Arundel prints — Reproductions of famous paintings; see Glossary, *WS*.

Ashmolean Museum — A museum at Oxford University, founded by Elias Ashmole. It contains coins and many other antiquarian treasures.

Atlas — A range of mountains in northwest Africa.

Augustus John — An artist who painted Angela Lyne's portrait. See *POMF*, chap. 3.

Balaclava — A village in the Crimea, the scene of a battle during the Crimean War in which British and French cavalry unsuccessfully attacked opposing Russian forces. A brigade of British cavalry, which made a suicidal attack on the Russians on October 25, 1854, was immortalized in Tennyson's poem "The Charge of the Light Brigade."

Baldachino at St. Peter's — A large ornamental canopylike covering over an altar (here that of Saint Peter's Basilica in Rome).

Baldwin — Stanley Baldwin (1867–1947) prominent British political and government figure. He served three separate terms as Prime Minister, in 1923, from 1924 to 1929, and from 1936 to 1937. Waugh was friendly with his son Arthur ("Bloggs"). See Dictionary, "Sir James Brown."

Bannockburn — A town in central Scotland, the scene of a famous battle (June 24, 1314) in which Scottish forces led by Robert Bruce defeated a British army under the direction of Edward II.

Barbizon — A French village associated with Jean François Millet, Théodore Rousseau, and other artists of the Barbizon school of landscape painters. In some editions it is misprinted "Barbison."

battels — See Glossary under *DF*.

Battle in the West where Arthur fell — The legendary Battle of Camlan in Wales in A.D. 537 in which King Arthur was mortally wounded by his nephew Modred. Modred was also killed in the combat.

Batum — A city on the Black Sea.

THE GLOSSARY

Bayswater — A residential area on the northern fringe of Hyde Park, London.

Beatific Vision — The vision of God in heaven.

bedder — Bedroom. In the 1960 revised edition of *Brideshead Revisited*, "bedder" is changed to "next door."

Belgian Futurist — A style in painting and other arts that sought to express the energy and violence associated with the new age of machinery.

Clive Bell — See Glossary under *WS*.

Bellini — In the 1960 revised edition of *BR*, Charles Ryder tells Lord Marchmain that he likes the paintings of Bellini. Charles, however, is surprised to learn that there were three Venetian painters named Bellini — the father, Iacopo (ca. 1400–ca. 70), and his two sons, Gentile (ca. 1429–1507) and Giovanni (ca. 1430–1516). The Bellini allusion is not given in the standard 1945 edition.

bêtise — French for "foolish mistake."

Black Birds — A famous black musical group that was especially popular in Europe in the late 1920s and early 1930s.

Blackwell's — The largest and most famous bookstore in Oxford.

Blessed Sacrament — In Holy Communion, the consecrated Host, representing the Body and Blood of Christ.

BNC — Brasenose College at Oxford.

Boar's Hill — See Glossary under *DF*. During the period in which *BR*'s events occur, the area was supposedly rather stuffy, and Jasper is emphasizing that one should not be tainted with such stuffy intellectualism.

bob — See Glossary under *DF*.

Boeuf sur le Toit — A bar in Paris.

bondieuserie — Religious ornaments.

Bordighera — A seaport resort community in northwest Italy.

bosh — Foolishness.

Brancusi — See Glossary under *POMF*.

Bricktop's and the Bal Nègre — Parisian night clubs where black entertainers were regular attractions.

"Brother Grandee" — The club Waugh is describing is Ye Sette of Odde Volumes. Each member has a special name preceded by the term "Brother." Alec Waugh discusses this club in *My Brother Evelyn and Other Portraits*, pp. 248–50.

"Bubbles" — A portrait by Sir John Millais of a child blowing soap bubbles. It became very well known because it was used to advertise Pears soap.

Bullingdon — See Glossary under *DF*.

bunked — Expelled.

buskers — Itinerant street performers.

Byron — George Gordon, Lord Byron (1788–1824), noted English poet of the romantic period, who lived in Italy for several years and wrote about Venice.

Canning — An undergraduate Conservative political club, named after the early-nineteenth-century prime minister George Canning.

Cap Ferrat — A wealthy area on the southern coast of France.

Captain Morvin's Riding Academy — Waugh appears to be thinking of the school where he learned to ride horseback, Captain Hance's Riding Academy at Malvern. Morvin may have been derived from free association with Malvern.

Carlton — The Oxford University New Tory (i.e., Conservative) Association, a political club.

Carpentier — Georges Carpentier (1894–1975), French prizefighter. At one time he was the world's light-heavyweight champion; he was defeated by Jack Dempsey in 1921 when he fought for the heavyweight title.

catechism — A question-and-answer religious instruction book for beginners used in many churches.

Cézanne — See Glossary under *POMF*.

Chamberlain — See Glossary under *POMF*, *"It is an evil thing we are fighting."*

"The Charge of the Light Brigade" — A reference to Alfred, Lord Tennyson's poem of that title about a famous British cavalry charge at Balaclava in the Crimean War.

Charlus — Baron de Charlus, one of the main characters in Marcel Proust's *Remembrance of Things Past*.

Chatham — An undergraduate Conservative political club.

Chippendale — Thomas Chippendale (ca. 1718–79), especially known for his elegant furniture designs.

chucka — See Glossary under *HD*.

Clive — Robert Clive (1725–74), British military and political figure in India. He won great acclaim for a military victory at Plassey in 1757.

Close de Bère — In many editions a misprint for "Clos de Bèze."

Clovis's army — The army of Clovis I (A.D. 481–511),

a king of the Franks who conquered most of Germany and France. He was converted to Christianity and had all his followers converted.

Cocteau — See Glossary under *POMF*.

Collections papers — Examinations based on reading assignments done over the vacation. The papers are checked by the tutors who gave the reading assignments.

Colleoni — Bartolomeo Colleoni (1400–75), Italian military figure. Andrea del Verrocchio sculptured an equestrian statue of Colleoni which is on view in Venice.

come a cropper — Fail completely; literally, fall backward over the crupper of the horse one is riding.

coming up — Entering Oxford or being readmitted to a college.

Commem. — Short for "Commemoration." During the weeks of late June and early July once every three years commemoration balls are held by most of Oxford's thirty-five colleges. Tents are erected on the quadrangles, and dinners, orchestras, games, and prizes are provided for the students and their guests. The commems. originally honored the founders of the colleges.

Cook's — See Glossary under *HD*.

Corporate Communion — A Sunday when students receive Holy Communion as a group.

Cressid — Or Cressida, a beauteous young Trojan woman, the daughter of Calchas. She promised her love to Troilus but proved unfaithful. Many writers have told the story of this medieval romance, *Troilus and Cressida*.

crocodile — A procession, usually of children, walking two and two.

Grace Darling — The daughter of a lighthouse keeper who with her father managed to save survivors from a shipwreck off the Farne Islands in 1838. She was the subject of a sentimental Victorian painting.

Daumier — Honoré Daumier (1808–79), French caricaturist and painter.

Debrett — See Glossary under *VB*.

Defence Corps — Volunteers supporting the police, the army, and the government during the General Strike in 1926. The General Strike was officially called off on May 12, 1926.

Delacroix — Eugène Delacroix (1798–1862), French artist. His general motif was romanticism, but he also involved himself in avant-garde experiments.

Deuxième service — The second service of a meal in a French railroad dining car.

Diaghilev — See Glossary under *POMF*.

The Diary of a Nobody — An amusing novel of Victorian life (1894) by George and Weedon Grossmith.

Dominican — A Roman Catholic priest of the Order of Saint Dominic.

Doric temple — A temple constructed in the simplest style of Greek columnar architecture.

Douro — A river in Spain and Portugal; it flows through a wine-making center.

Drake — Sir Francis Drake (ca. 1540–96), British sea dog and naval hero. He was especially acclaimed for his part in the defeat of the Spanish Armada.

Duchess of Malfi — An English tragic play by John Webster (ca. 1580–ca. 1625). In a famous scene she is tormented by her evil brothers, being forced to endure the disturbing and menacing behavior of insane individuals both within and outside her home.

"Ecco ci siamo, signori" — Italian for "Here we are, gentlemen."

Ego te absolvo in nomine Patris — Latin for "I absolve you in the name of the Father . . . ." spoken by the priest during the administration of the sacrament of extreme unction in traditional pre–Vatican II Roman Catholic practice. Extreme unction is the anointing with holy oils of one who is believed to be near death.

Eights Week — A week in the summer when boat races (with eight oarsmen in each boat) were held among the various Oxford colleges.

Eminent Victorians — A collection of four biographical essays (1917) by Lytton Strachey. Their subjects are Cardinal Manning, Dr. Thomas Arnold, Florence Nightingale, and General Charles George Gordon.

entail — A legal requirement that an estate pass at death from father to son or other male heir, so that the father is unable to will it to someone else.

epergne — A decorative dish or ornament placed in the center of a dinner table. It may have branches that hold candles and small-size dishes for condiments or desserts.

Ephesus — An ancient city in Asia Minor near the Aegean Sea.

epitaph at Thermopylae — See Glossary under *POMF*.

THE GLOSSARY

Et in Arcadia Ego — Latin for "I, too, in Arcadia." Arcadia was a region of Greece inhabited by shepherds. A famous essay by Erwin and Gerda Panofsky ("The 'Tomb in Arcady' at the 'Fin-de-Siècle,'" in *Wallraf-Richartz-Jahrbuch*, Vol 30 [Köln, 1968], pp. 287–304) traces the history of this phrase, which appeared in many paintings from the Renaissance onward. At first such paintings showed a skull in the middle of a quiet, happy pastoral landscape, indicating that the phrase meant "Even in Arcadia, I, Death, am there." Later the skull disappeared, and the phrase was read as "I [the painter or viewer] too once lived in Arcadia." The skull in Charles Ryder's study bearing the phrase indicates that Waugh was aware of this dual significance.

Farm Street — The Farm Street Church, in London's Mayfair section. It is the Jesuit Church of the Immaculate Conception and also the headquarters of the Jesuits in England.

Father Brown — G. K. Chesterton's detective hero, who appears in many stories. The quote beginning "I caught him..." appears in the story "The Queer Feet," one of the narratives in *The Innocence of Father Brown* (1911).

Father Christmas — The English name for Santa Claus.

la fatigue du Nord — The boredom of the North, meaning that there is more excitement and joy in the Mediterranean countries, such as Italy and Greece.

"F.E." — F. E. Smith (1872–1930), the first Earl of Birkenhead. He was deeply involved in British political issues (serving, e.g., as Lord Chancellor from 1919 to 1922) and was especially famous for his caustic wit.

fête champêtre — French for "rural festival."

Firbank — Ronald Firbank, English novelist (1886–1926). His witty style and fresh, clever use of dialogue had considerable influence on Waugh.

flap — A needless fuss.

Florentine Quattrocento — The fifteenth century, a flourishing period in art and literature, especially in Italian cities like Florence.

Flying Scotsman — A speedy passenger train running between London and Edinburgh.

footer — Rugby football.

four last things — See Glossary under *VB*.

Franco — Francisco Franco (1892–1975), Spanish military figure who led the revolt against the Republican government in the Spanish Civil War. With the victory of his forces in 1939, he became dictator of the country.

French novels of the second empire — Novels written during the time of Napoleon III (1852–70). This period in France produced fiction by such famous writers as Victor Hugo and Alexandre Dumas the younger.

Roger Fry — English painter and art expert (1866–1934). He wrote several notable books of art criticism and gave much support to Paul Cézanne and other postimpressionist painters.

Gallipoli — A Turkish peninsula where the British and their Allies fought the Turks in 1915 to gain control of the Dardanelles. After heroic fighting on both sides the Allies were forced to withdraw early in 1916.

garçonnière — A bachelor's apartment.

Garsington — Garsington Manor, the country estate of Lady Ottoline Morrell, in Oxfordshire. Lady Ottoline entertained artists, writers, and other intellectuals at the estate, especially Lytton Strachey and other members of the Bloomsbury group. In one of the illustrations ("All the Street Seemed to Be Laughing at Him") that he did for *DF*, Waugh satirized the promiscuous Lady Ottoline by naming one of the brothels "Chez Aux Nymphes Otoline." The character Hermione in D. H. Lawrence's *Women in Love* is based in part on Lady Ottoline.

gated — Confined to one's college for a specific period of time depending on the severity of the offense against decorum or college regulations.

Gauguin — See Glossary under *WS*.

George — A restaurant (formerly also a hotel) in the city of Oxford.

the larger honours came with the Georges — That is, the marquessate and earldom were granted under the various British kings who ruled in the eighteenth and nineteenth centuries. King George I of England assumed the throne in 1714. The Flyte family was Protestant until Lord Marchmain was converted when he married.

Georgian Poetry — A series of poetry anthologies introduced by Edward Marsh and continued by Mrs. Harold Monro in an attempt to introduce new poetry to a larger public. The first anthology, covering 1911–12, was published in 1914 by Monro's

Poetry Bookshop in London. Later anthologies covered the following years: 1913–15, 1916–17, 1918, and 1920–22.

"Gertie" Lawrence — Gertrude Lawrence (1901–52), English actress best known for her roles in musical comedies.

Gethsemane — A place of suffering; specifically, a reference to Christ's suffering in the Garden of Gethsemane, on the Mount of Olives.

Gide — André Gide (1869–1951), French novelist and playwright. He also wrote a considerable amount of literary criticism. He was awarded the Nobel Prize for Literature in 1947.

Gilbert-and-Sullivan — See Glossary under *DF*.

La Gioconda — The famous portrait of Mona Lisa by Leonardo da Vinci.

given a dose — Acquired a venereal disease, specifically gonorrhea. In the revised edition of 1960 this is changed to "infected."

Goebbels — See Glossary under *POMF*.

Goering — See Glossary under *POMF*.

Gorbals — A notorious slum district in Glasgow, Scotland.

grandmother's steps — A correspondent who has played this game describes it thus: "The kid who is 'It' stands with his face against a wall and counts to ten (or recites some rhyme). The other players begin on a common start line, and while 'It' is counting, move forward with short but cautious steps. The 'It' suddenly turns round, and if he sees anyone still moving, he orders everyone back to the start line.... This is repeated until somebody at last reaches the wall without being caught. Then he becomes 'It' for the next repetition." The game has variations; e.g., in some versions only the player who is caught moving has to return to the start line; the other players can retain their positions. This game has many different names. In Pennsylvania it is called "red light."

Greats — See Glossary under *WS*.

great sucks — A great "put-down."

Grenadier — A member of the Grenadier Guards; the members of this regiment are designated to guard the English monarch.

Grid — Short for Gridiron, a social club for undergraduates formed in 1883.

Halifax — Edward Frederick Lindley Wood, first Earl of Halifax (1881–1959). In the early 1930s, as Viscount Irwin, he was Viceroy of India, where he supported the movement for Indian independence. Later, as Foreign Secretary, he supported Prime Minister Neville Chamberlain's policy of appeasing Hitler. In 1940, he was Winston Churchill's chief competitor for the prime ministership. Still later he was ambassador to the United States. He was a member of the Conservative party.

halma — See Glossary under *BM*.

Hansard — See Glossary under *VB*.

Hatton Garden — A district on the north side of Holborn Circus, in London. It is the principal district for diamond merchants.

Hawkins — Sir John Hawkins (1532–95), British naval commander who won many notable victories, particularly against the Spaniards.

Hegel — Georg Wilhelm Friedrich Hegel (1790–1831), famous German philosopher. His very abstruse theories had a wide influence on many nineteenth- and twentieth-century movements such as Marxism and existentialism.

Henley Regatta — A traditional series of July boat races on the Thames River at Henley.

Henry's speech on St. Crispin's Day — King Henry V of England won a decisive victory over a vastly superior French force near the village of Agincourt on October 25, 1415. In Shakespeare's *Henry V* the king gives a stirring speech (cf. act 4, scene 3). Crispin was martyred in the third century, and his feast day was October 25.

History Previous — An examination at Oxford that came at the end of the second term. It was intended to check to see that students were making proper progress in their studies so that they could continue further.

Sir Samuel Hoare — English political figure (1880–1959) who held many government positions, such as Secretary of State for Home Affairs from 1937 to 1939. He belonged to the Conservative party.

Hogarthian page-boy — See Glossary under *POMF*.

Holman Hunt's ... "The Awakened Conscience" — William Holman Hunt (1827–1910), one of the founders of the Pre-Raphaelite art movement in England. *The Awakened Conscience*, one of his most popular paintings, depicts a girl who is living in sin remembering the innocence of her childhood. In his study of Rossetti, Waugh applauds this work.

Holywell — One of the principal streets in Oxford.

Home Secretary — The senior British Secretary of

THE GLOSSARY

State who deals with domestic affairs. Among his duties he is to maintain peace and order, and he is the ultimate overseer of the criminal-justice system, which embraces not only police and prisons but also industrial schools and asylums. See Glossary under *VB*.

"Home they brought her warrior dead" — One of the most famous lyrics in Alfred, Lord Tennyson's poem *The Princess* (1847).

Horthy — Admiral Miklos von Nagybanya Horthy (1868–1957), Hungarian government and military figure. He commanded the Austro-Hungarian fleet in World War I and led the anti-Bolshevik troops when the monarchy fell. In effect he was head of state in Hungary from the end of World War I until near the end of World War II.

Hotted — Tricked.

House — A popular name for Christ Church College at Oxford.

"in extremis" — Latin for "at the point of death."

Ingres — Jean Auguste Ingres (1780–1867), French classical painter.

Inigo Jones — British architect (1573–1652). His studies in Italy led him to introduce into England the classical style of the later Renaissance. In addition to his architectural work he designed sets for court masques.

Irwin — See Glossary above under *Halifax*.

Isis — The Oxford University undergraduate magazine.

Jesuitical — Relating to the Jesuit religious order in the Roman Catholic church. The term is usually derogatory and means tricky, deceptive, hair-splitting.

Jorrocks — See Glossary under *POMF, Surtees*.

Kaiser — Kaiser Wilhelm II (1859–1941), German emperor from 1888 to 1918. On the outbreak of World War I, Lottie Crump relegated his photograph to the lavatory. See Glossary under *VB, ex-emperor of Germany*.

McKnight Kauffer — Edward McKnight Kauffer (1890–1954), American artist who lived in England from 1914 to 1941 and was known for his posters and book illustrations.

Keble — One of the Oxford colleges, founded in 1870 and named in honor of the Reverend John Keble (1792–1866), a leader of the Anglican "High Church" Oxford Movement.

"Kelly's eye — number one, legs, eleven, and we'll Shake the Bag" — Terms used in the game housey-housey. There was an old song about one-eyed Kelly: "legs" would represent the number eleven, and "Shake the Bag" means to reshuffle and mix up the numbers more thoroughly before they are drawn.

Kemal's army — The army of Kemal Ataturk (1881–1938), a celebrated Turkish military leader and statesman.

Knight of Malta — See Glossary under *WS*.

knocking-shops — Brothels.

Krak-des-chevaliers — A castle built for military defense by the Knights Hospitalers in 1131, during the Crusades, at the town of Krak, in Jordan. The Knights Hospitalers were a military and religious organization originally called the Order of St. John of Jerusalem. In the sixteenth century they came to be called the Knights of Malta; see Glossary under *WS*.

Kurds — Sumni Moslems who live near Mount Ararat. They are most populous in Iraq and Iran.

Lady into Fox — A novel (1922) by David Garnett. The story concerns a wife who turns into a fox.

Landseer — Sir Edwin Henry Landseer (1802–73), English painter who became well known for his paintings of dogs and other animals.

Last Trump — See Glossary under *VB*.

League of Nations Union — A society supportive of the League of Nations and its goals for peace and international social and economic development. See also Glossary under *DF*.

Lear, Kent, Fool — Three important characters in Shakespeare's *King Lear*.

Lear on the heath — In Shakespeare's play *King Lear* (ca. 1606), his vicious daughters turn Lear out on a heath in the midst of a violent rainstorm. His mind becomes deranged by the combination of his daughters' cruelty and the severity of the weather.

legitimist — One who supports legitimate authority, here particularly in regard to a title claimed because of direct descent.

Lepanto — See Glossary under *POMF*.

Levant — The region from western Greece to western Egypt that borders the eastern shore of the Mediterranean Sea.

Lido — See Glossary under *Sc*.

Limbo — See Glossary under *POMF*.
L of C — Lines of Communication.
long vac — **Long vacation** — The long Oxford summer vacation from June to October.
Lotti — See Glossary under *VB*.
louche — French for "shady."
Luna — A fashionable restaurant in Venice.
Lyonnesse — An undefined area off the southwest of England, the land from which King Arthur reputedly came.

Maeterlinck — Maurice Maeterlinck (1862–1949), a Belgian playwright whose symbolist poetic style sought to evoke moods. Although he was also an essayist, it was his plays, like *Pelléas et Mélisande* (1892) and *L'Oiseau bleu* (*The Blue Bird*, 1909) which helped win him the Nobel Prize for Literature in 1911.
Magdalen — One of the colleges at Oxford.
Magyar — Hungarian.
"Maison Japonaise" — A brothel done in the flamboyant style of Japanese decoration of the time.
Marathon — A battle near the ancient Greek town Marathon in which an army of Athenians routed a vastly superior Persian force in 490 B.C. Miltiades, the Athenian general, won considerable acclaim for this victory.
marchese — Marquis.
Mare Nostrum — Literally, "Our Sea," meaning the Mediterranean, a slogan much used by Mussolini and his supporters, who were seeking domination over the Mediterranean.
Maritain — Jacques Maritain (1882–1973), French Catholic philosopher and author noted for his modern exposition of Thomistic philosophy.
Maronites — Members of a Christian sect that ultimately joined the Roman Catholic Church. They are particularly numerous in Lebanon.
Maundy Thursday — The day before Good Friday. "Maundy" derives from the first words of a hymn sung on that day, "Mandatum novum do vobis," that is, "A new commandment I give unto you" (John 13:34). Christ instituted the Eurcharist on Maundy Thursday.
"Max" — A reference to William Maxwell Aitken, the first Baron Beaverbrook, a powerful British newspaper magnate. See also Glossary under *OG*.
Medici Press — The press of the Medici Society of London, which published books on literature and art, usually limited editions on fine paper. The society issued, for example, Sir Thomas Malory's *Le Morte d'Arthur*, the *Meditations* of Marcus Aurelius, and selections from William Blake and Rupert Brooke. It also published prints.
Mercury — A small ornamental fountain in Tom Quad, the main quadrangle of Christ Church College. A statue of Mercury stands in the water.
Merton — One of the colleges at Oxford.
Mesopotamia — See Glossary under *DF*.
Michaelmas term — The autumn term at Oxford beginning after September 29, the Feast of Saint Michael and All Angels. It continues until early December.
Florence Mills — The very appealing singing star of the "Black Birds" (see Glossary above).
Miss Mitford — Mary Russell Mitford (1787–1855), author of *Our Village* (5 vols, 1824–32) and other stories of quiet rural life in England.
Modern Greats — A familiar name for PPE (philosophy, politics, and economics).
Morris stuffs — Cloth and materials from the firm founded by Victorian poet and artist William Morris (1834–96). He hoped to raise artistic sensibilities and was involved in the manufacture of furniture, tapestry, carpets, etc. He also founded a printing firm, Kelmscott Press.
mostica — Although from the context the word means "mosquito," the Italian word for "mosquito" is *zanzara*. Joanna Poletti has found no such word even in the Venetian dialect. She has observed that before iceboxes were in general use there were boxes with screened doors that were kept in a cool place and were used for storing food. Such a box was called a *mosticario*. There are many dialect variations, and *mostica* could originate in one of these, or typing and proofreading errors could be involved, or Waugh may have made up the word because it sounded right, basing it on the French word for "mosquito," *moustique*.
mug — A fool.
muniment-rooms — Rooms containing title deeds and similar documents which support a person's or a family's claim to an estate or other rights.

"National Service" — Service in support of the government during the General Strike of 1926.
N.C.O.'s — Noncommissioned officers.
Nelson — See Glossary under *POMF*.

Newman — A Roman Catholic club and group at Oxford named after Cardinal John Henry Newman.

Newman's day — The time of John Henry Newman (1801–90), English author and Anglican clergyman, who converted to Roman Catholicism. He was the most important figure of the Oxford Movement.

1920 Committee — Some editions of *BR* contain this typesetting error. It should read "1922 Committee." The 1922 Committee was a group of Conservative members of Parliament who revolted against Lloyd George's coalition government.

Nissen hut — A tunnel-shaped building made of corrugated iron. Such huts could be assembled quickly and thus were popular for wartime uses.

"Oh God, make me good, but not yet" — A form of "Da mihi castitatem et continentiam, sed noli modo" (Saint Augustine, *Confessions* 8.7).

oleograph of the Sacred Heart — A colored print of Christ showing his exposed heart, a symbol of Christ's love for humanity.

Omega workshops — Studio schools begun by Roger Fry in 1913. Fry, whose most notable associates in this venture were Vanessa Bell and Duncan Grant, believed that painters should have the opportunity to create in other mediums; thus the Omega artists produced furniture, dishware, rugs, and curtains and engaged in many other arts and crafts. The workshops closed in 1919.

0915 hours — 9:15 A.M.

Order Group — See Glossary under *POMF*.

O.S.C.U. — See Glossary under *DF*.

0730 hours — 7:30 A.M.

O.U.D.S. — Oxford University Dramatic Society.

Palazzo. Pronto — "Palace. At once."

Palladian — See Glossary under *VB*.

Palmerston — See Glossary under *Sc, Pam*.

P. and O. — See Glossary under *BM*.

Pantelleria — An Italian island in the Mediterranean. During World War II it was a heavily fortified military base which was battered by Allied forces.

Parks — The University Parks, a section of Oxford which was originally the gun park of the royalist artillery in the Civil War (1642–46).

Partagas — Handmade Havana cigars noted for quality and expensiveness.

Pathetic Fallacy — The technique, especially common in poetry, of giving human qualities or emotions to inanimate objects, e.g., the "angry wind." John Ruskin first used the term "pathetic fallacy," denouncing this metaphorical technique as false and irrational.

Polly Peachum — The heroine of *The Beggar's Opera* (1728), by John Gay, which had a famous revival in London in the 1920s often attended by Waugh.

Peckwater — Peckwater Quadrangle, one of the main components of Christ Church, the largest Oxford college.

peg out — Die, a metaphor from the card game cribbage.

Peke — Short for "Pekinese."

Penelope — The wife of Ulysses in Homer's *Odyssey*. She was beset by suitors when it was presumed that Ulysses had died.

a penny at the church door — Roman Catholic catechisms outlining basic Roman Catholic belief were sold for a penny from book racks at the back of churches.

piano nobile — The principal floor, the one above the ground floor.

Picabia — Francis Picabia (1878–1953), French painter associated with the cubist and dadaist movements.

Pindar's Orphism — Pindar (ca. 522–442 B.C.) was a Greek poet, and Orphism was one of the mystical religious cults of his time.

Piranesi — Giovanni Battista Piranesi (1720–78), Italian architect and engraver, chiefly noted for his drawings of classical ruins.

plenary indulgences — In Roman Catholic doctrine, the granting of pardon for the temporal punishment caused by sin even after the sin has been confessed in the sacrament of penance.

Pompeian figures — See Glossary under *POMF*.

Pont Street — An upper-class residential street in Belgravia, London. In *WS*, Roger and Lucy Simmonds first met at a dance in Pont Street.

Pontus — An ancient country in Asia Minor bordering the Black Sea.

pop — A social club and debating society at Eton.

poppet — A child or animal that brings pleasure and joy.

potin — A row or disagreement.

Pre-Raphaelitism — A book by John Ruskin about a mid-nineteenth-century English artistic and literary movement associated with writers and painters like Dante Gabriel Rossetti and Holman Hunt, who

54

attempted to paint in the manner of the Italian artists before Raphael. They used bright colors and gave an ethereal quality to their work. They were the subject of Waugh's first book.

proctors — Officials of Oxford University whose function is to maintain discipline. Their assistants are called "bulldogs."

prosciutto — Italian for "ham."

Proust — See Glossary under *DF*.

putative parentage — A supposed parentage.

Quattrocento — The fifteenth century, a term used in reference to the flourishing, glorious period of Italian art and literature.

Quebec — City in Quebec Province, Canada, the scene of a notable battle (1759) between English forces led by General James Wolfe and French defenders led by Marshal Louis Joseph de Montcalm. The English gained access to the Plains of Abraham, defeated the French, and captured Quebec, although the heroic Wolfe was killed.

Queen Alexandra's Day — A day in June when roses are sold to obtain money to help hospitals. The practice was inaugurated in 1912 by Alexandra (1844–1925), the Queen consort of King Edward II. The day was commonly called "Alexandra Rose Day."

Quis? — Latin for "Who?"

"Quomodo sedet sola civitas" — Latin for "How doth this city sit solitary that was full of people." Lamentations 1:1.

Raphael — Rafaello Santior Sanzio (1483–1520), Italian painter, one of the most significant figures in the history of art.

Ravenna — Italian city famous for Byzantine churches and mosaics.

R.C. — Roman Catholic.

reading History — In American terms, majoring in history.

Madame Récamier — Jeanne Récamier, Frenchwoman of fashion and wit (1777–1849). She was a popular figure among the wealthy and famous people of the nineteenth century and entertained royally in her salon.

Reinhart nun — Very proper, reserved, and saintly. Max Reinhart (1873–1943) was an Austrian producer and director of plays geared to scenic effects. His best-known work was his pageant play *The Miracle*, which was very successful both in England and in the United States. Lady Diana Cooper played the leading role in the English production, and Waugh frequently visited her while she was touring in this spectacle.

remittance man — A man living in a foreign country on money regularly sent to him from home on condition that he stay there and not return.

Rhyme Sheets from the Poetry Bookshop — The Poetry Bookshop, directed by Harold Monro, was not only a bookstore but also a publishing center at 35 Devonshire Street, near the British Museum. The Rhyme Sheet poems, suitable for hanging on a wall, were short and decorated by various artists. Claud Lovat Fraser decorated several.

Ribbentrop — See Glossary under *POMF*.

Rimbaud — Jean Rimbaud (1854–91) influential French symbolist poet. He spent many years in Africa, while Gauguin went to Tahiti.

Roncevales — A mountain pass in the Spanish Pyrenees, the scene of a legendary battle (A.D. 778) in which the famous French epic warrior Roland was treacherously attacked by Saracens while leading his men through a narrow pass. Roland and his men, considerably outnumbered, fought to the death. Spelled "Roncevalles" in some editions.

Rupert's horse — Prince Rupert (1619–82), a cavalry leader under King Charles I during the English Civil War in the seventeenth century. Rupert was famed for his bravery in battle.

Ruskin — John Ruskin (1819–1900), British author best known for his five-volume *Modern Painters*. He was one of the earliest defenders of the Pre-Raphaelites. He was a professor of art at Oxford for some years.

Ruskin School of Art — John Ruskin (1819–1900), British artist and author, who established a drawing school at Oxford. In addition to teaching students, Ruskin also worked to bring art to ordinary working people.

St. Anthony of Padua — Although born in Portugal, Anthony (1195–1231) is associated with the Italian city Padua. A member of the Franciscan order, he was noted for his preaching and biblical scholarship. He was canonized as a saint the year after his death. He is invoked by Roman Catholics especially to find lost objects, and countless Catholics over the years have testified to their success in recovering articles because of Saint Anthony's aid.

St. Mark's — The splendid Roman Catholic cathedral in Venice.

S. Nichodemus of Thyatira — A mythical saint.

Samothrace — A Greek island in the Aegean Sea.

Sappers'-demonstration — Activity by the Royal Engineers Unit who in their line of work blew up and destroyed things.

schools — See Glossary under *DF*.

scrimshankers — Military men who are shirking their duty.

scupper — Ruin.

Sebastian contra mundum — Literally, "Sebastian against the world," that is, standing more or less alone against all others. The phrase *contra mundum* was particularly associated with Athanasius (ca. A.D. 298–373) against the Arian heresy.

sent down — Expelled or suspended.

Seven Dolours — The seven sorrows of the Blessed Virgin Mary. They are subjects for prayer and meditation in Roman Catholicism. Specifically they are the prophecy of Simeon; the flight into Egypt; the three-day disappearance of Christ; the suffering of Christ on the way to Calvary; the Crucifixion; the taking down of Christ's body from the Cross; and the placement of the body in the tomb.

Sèvres — Porcelain made in Sèvres, France.

shooting stick — A canelike stool which when opened becomes a small chair.

A Shropshire Lad — A collection of poems (1896) by A. E. Housman.

"si, si, subito, signori" — Italian for "Yes, yes, quickly, gentlemen."

Mrs. Simpson — Mrs. Wallis Warfield Simpson (1896–1986), a twice-divorced American for whose love King Edward VIII of England abdicated his throne in 1936. The episode became one of the most sensational news stories in modern times. After the abdication they became the Duke and Duchess of Windsor.

Sinister Street — A novel (1913) by Compton Mackenzie which makes much use of Oxford as a setting; see Glossary under *POMF*.

snubs to her — A derisive comment on the order of the American slang expression "Nuts to her."

Soanesque — In the architectural style of Sir John Soane (1753–1837).

"the sound of lyres and flutes" — This phrase occurs in Walter Pater's discussion of the *Mona Lisa* in his essay "Leonardo da Vinci" (1869). This essay became part of Pater's *Studies in the History of the Renaissance* (1873).

South Wind — An immensely popular satirical novel by Norman Douglas.

Spezia — An Italian naval base near Genoa.

the stone — The limestone or sandstone of which many Oxford buildings are constructed.

Stonyhurst — A well-known English Roman Catholic public school.

strawberry leaves — See Glossary under *VB*.

stumer — A bad check.

subalterns — See Glossary under *POMF*.

subfusc — Clothing consisting of an academic robe, a black suit, and a white bow tie. It is worn during examinations and other special events.

Tatler — A magazine focusing on the doings of British fashionable society.

Tenebrae — The religious service of Matins and Lauds sung during Holy Week preceding Easter Sunday. The service commemorates the crucifixion of Christ.

1045 hours — 10:45 A.M.

Tennyson — The Honorable Lionel Hallam Tennyson (1889–1951), the grandson of the poet, who later became the third baron. He played cricket for Hampshire County. His full first-class cricket career stretched from 1913 to 1937. His main years were 1919 to 1933, when he was Hampshire's captain. He played nine test matches for England and was captain three times against Australia in 1921.

till Tom stops ringing — The impressive six-ton bell in the Tom Tower of Christ Church College at Oxford. When it completed ringing its 101 strokes at midnight, undergraduates were supposed to be in their rooms.

Tintoretto — An Italian artist (1518–94), whose real name was Jacopo Robusti.

Titian — Tiziano Vecelli or Vecellio (ca. 1477–1576), Italian painter. He painted many religious subjects as well as scenes from classical myths.

tombola — The English game housey-housey, similar to American bingo.

Tom Quad — The quadrangle near the great bell in Tom Tower of Christ Church.

Toulouse-Lautrec odalisque — Henri Marie Raymond de Toulouse-Lautrec, French artist (1864–

1901) famous for his posters and lithographs. He drew many prostitutes, dance-hall girls, and other women who were not members of respectable society.

Trafalgar — A cape on the coast of Spain where the British fleet under Lord Nelson won a famous naval battle in 1805.

Travellers' — A Parisian club.

Trebizond — A city in Turkey on the Black Sea. At one time it was part of the Roman Empire.

Trent or Tring — Trent, on the northern outskirts of London, was the location of the magnificent country seat of Philip Sassoon. Tring, in Buckinghamshire, was the seat of the splendid estate of one of the Rothschilds. No doubt the conservatories of both estates contained much hothouse tropical greenery.

Trilby — An artists' model in George du Maurier's novel *Trilby* (1894) who is mesmerized by Svengali into becoming a successful singer.

Trinity — One of the colleges at Oxford.

2315 hours — 11:15 P.M.

Union — The Oxford Union Society; the Union refers both to the debating society and to the hall where debating occurs.

using an instrument — Performing illegal abortions.

Van Gogh's "Sunflowers" — Vincent Van Gogh (1853–90), Dutch painter. Near the end of his life he painted a famous series of pictures of sunflowers.

Vanity of vanities, all is vanity — Words from Ecclesiastes 1:2 and passim.

vaporetto — A steam launch.

Wandering Jew — A legendary figure said to be doomed to wander about the world until the second coming of Christ because according to the legend he spoke harshly to Christ while the latter was carrying his cross to the place of crucifixion. The legend of the Wandering Jew has appeared in literary works by Goethe, Eugène Sue, and many others.

"Warning Shadows" — A popular silent film of the 1920s. Waugh saw it on November 29, 1924, and thought it "quite superb" (*Diaries*, p. 189).

The Waste Land — A classic modernistic poem (1922) by T. S. Eliot. It is regarded by many literary critics as the most significant twentieth-century English poem.

Whatman H.P. drawing paper — A very expensive fine-grain paper used especially for watercolor drawings.

The Wisdom of Father Brown — A volume of G. K. Chesterton's detective stories (1914) featuring a Roman Catholic priest as the sleuth.

Wykehamist — A graduate or member of Winchester College, nicknamed after its founder, William of Wykeham (1324–1404).

Xanthus-side — The ancient name for the Scamander River, which flowed near Troy; mentioned in Homer's *Iliad*. Some studies claim that these are two different rivers.

You want either a first or a fourth. There is no value in anything between — It is better to be brilliant or lazy than to be middling. A first class degree is the highest scholastic achievement, while a fourth class degree is the lowest graduating rank.

SCOTT-KING'S MODERN EUROPE (1947)

Dedicatee

The dedication is to "Mariae Immaculatae Antoniae," the Honorable Marie (Mia) Acton Woodruff, the wife of John Douglas Woodruff. The translation of the Latin inscription is "To Mary Immaculate Antonia, the bold spouse of a too cautious spouse." Douglas Woodruff refused to have the book dedicated to him because it might have offended his Spanish friends (he and Waugh had recently returned from Spain and parts of *SKME* are based on their experiences there). Mrs. Woodruff was baptized Marie Immaculée Antoinette. The name Antoinette came from her godfather, Count Anthony Arco Valle.

Alcazar — A fortress in Toledo, Spain, which in size and location dominates the city.
"Army Class" — Students whose aim was to go on to military academies to establish careers in the service.

bimetallists — Proponents of a double standard of money based on both gold and silver; see Glossary under *HD, bimetallsim*.
blackleg — A strikebreaker; a scab.
British Council — An organization designed to promote knowledge of British culture overseas.

"Ça" — French for "that."
"Ça c'est le hoquet" — French for "That is a hiccup."
cock-a-hoop — Slang for "very enthusiastic."
Comic Muse — Thalia, the Greek muse of comedy.
"Comment dit-on en français 'hiccup'?" — French for "How do you say 'hiccup' in French?"
Court of St. James's — The official name of the English court. Saint James's Palace is one of the official London residences of the ruling king or queen.

Danzig — The Free City of Danzig, a source of conflict between Germany and Poland before and during World War II. The Nazis seized the city, but after the war it became part of Poland.
Daumier's law courts — Honoré Daumier (1809–79), a French painter, drew many comic and satiric caricatures, including subjects connected with the judiciary, e.g., *In the Court of the Assizes*.
désoeuvré — French for having finished one piece of work and not yet begun another.

"Évidemment..." — French for "Obviously, professor. Cognac is necessary."

Mr. Will Hay — An English vaudeville comedian.

I.C.I. — A huge chemical corporation; see Glossary under *WS*.

"J'en ai affreusement" — French for "I have them severely."

Le Nôtre — André Le Nôtre (1613–1700), French landscaper. He developed the concept of formal gardens with wide vistas. The gardens surrounding the Palace of Versailles are his most famous design.
Like the immortal private of the Buffs he stood in Elgin's place — Lines alluding to the poem "The Private of the Buffs," by Sir Francis Hastings Doyle (1810–88). The Buffs is a nickname for the Royal East Kent Regiment, whose uniforms had buff-colored facings. The poem glorifies a young soldier

THE GLOSSARY

from Kent fighting and dying to preserve the British Empire.

Lord's — A famous cricket field in London, the headquarters of the Marylebone Cricket Club. Thomas Lord bought the ground for the club.

old Greats — Philosophy, Greek, and Roman history.

Pericles — A Greek political leader and orator (ca. 490–29 B.C.), one of the greatest statesmen of Athens.

Pétainist — A follower of Marshal Henri Pétain, the premier of unoccupied France in World War II. See Glossary under *POMF*.

"Plaît-il, mon professeur?" — French for "I don't understand, professor."

Poseidon — In Greek mythology, the god of the sea.

Priestley — See Glossary under *BM*. This is another satiric hit at the novelist and dramatist J. B. Priestley, whose "left-wing" tendencies Waugh did not approve of. Mentioning Priestley shortly after referring to Shakespeare, Dickens, Byron, and Galsworthy adds to the satiric amusement.

sitter — Candidate.

Slovene royalists — Slovenes who advocated a monarchy for Slovenia rather than union with the Serbs and Croats in what ultimately became modern Yugoslavia under Marshal Tito.

they were lighting a candle that day which by the Grace of God should never be put out — An allusion to the words spoken by Bishop Hugh Latimer to Bishop Nicholas Ridley when the two men were to be burned at the stake (hence the pun on "lighting a candle") for their Protestant beliefs in sixteenth-century England; cf. Thomas A. Gribble, "The Nature of a Trimmer," *EWN*, Autumn, 1981, p. 3. See also Glossary under *OG*, "I'm coming. Be of good comfort.... put out."

Tolpuddle martyrs — A group of agricultural workers who were prosecuted by the English government for their attempts to unionize workers. On account of public indignation the men became popular heroes and were ultimately freed. Their union was formed at Tolpuddle, in Dorset, in 1833.

Trevi — A famous fountain in Rome. Coins are tossed into the fountain to bring good luck.

***tricoteuse* of the Terror** — One of the Parisian women who knitted during guillotinings at the time of the French Revolution. Although engaged in the quiet practice of knitting, they vocally encouraged killings and other bloodthirsty acts of violence. The most famous (fictional) example is Dickens's Madame Defarge in *A Tale of Two Cities*, who uses a code in her knitting to keep track of the aristocrats whom she wants executed.

Trotskyites — Supporters of the Communist theories of Leon Trotsky (1877–1940); see Glossary under *POMF*.

Upsala — A city in Sweden, the site of a famous university.

Wal-Wal — A settlement in Ethiopia where Ethiopian and Italian armies fought on December 5, 1934.

THE LOVED ONE (1948) Subtitled "An Anglo-American Tragedy."

Dedicatee

Nancy Mitford (1904–73) was a close friend of Waugh's and one of his chief correspondents after World War II. She wrote several books, including the novels *The Pursuit of Love* (1945) and *Love in a Cold Climate* (1949).

Agamemnon—The king of Argos who, with his brother Menelaus, became the leader of the Greek army during the Trojan War.

"Aimée, thy beauty is to me / Like those Nicean barks of yore..."—An adaptation of Edgar Allan Poe's "To Helen." His poem begins, "Helen, thy beauty is to me / Like those Nicean barks of yore."

Alcestis—The wife of Admetis in Greek legend. She loved her husband so deeply that she was willing to go to Hades so that his life would be spared.

Anabaptists—Members of a religious sect founded in the sixteenth century during the Reformation. They did not believe in infant baptism. John of Leiden, one of its leaders, introduced polygamy and other excesses.

the immortal Anderson couple—Several lines here are taken from Robert Burns's poems "John Anderson, my Jo."

Antigone—The daughter of Oedipus who attempted to bury her brother Polyneices even though his burial was forbidden by King Creon of Thebes. She was immortalized in Sophocles' famous play.

Apollo—A monthly periodical published in London in the 1920s.

Arbuckle Avenue—The irony is underscored when one remembers that film comedian Fatty Arbuckle was involved in a notorious sex and death scandal in the 1920s.

Attic—Greek.

Bel Air—A very well-to-do-section of Los Angeles. See Appendix 3, "Evelyn Waugh's Hollywood."

Arnold Bennett—See Glossary under *DF*.

the Big Three—The Legal Branch, Labor Disputes, and Finance sections of studio management.

Bilbao—A seaport city in Spain.

Blunden—Edmund Blunden (1896–1974), English poet (writing usually about rural subject matter) and literary critic.

boater hat—Boating hat, a stiff straw hat.

Boeotian—Referring to Boeotia, a district in ancient Greece. Agamemnon, Menelaus, and other Greek chieftains sailed with their troops from a seaport there to launch their attack on Troy and commence the Trojan War. The goddess Artemis prevented the wind from blowing for a time, so the ships could not sail to Troy until Agamemnon appeased her by sacrificing his daughter Iphigenia.

Boots subscriber—Boots is a large chain of British drugstores (in England called "chemists"). One of their most popular departments was a rental service of recent books to which readers could subscribe.

Rupert Brooke—See Glossary under *POMF*.

"Bury the great Knight..."—A parody of Alfred, Lord Tennyson's "Ode on the Death of the Duke of Wellington," beginning "Bury the great Duke."

"the Heart of the Bruce"—Robert Bruce (1274–1329), Scottish military and political hero who became king of Scotland in 1306.

canty—Merry.

Coldstream blazer—A jacket bearing the crest of the Coldstream Guards, the second-oldest regiment in the British army.

Compton-Burnett—Ivy Compton-Burnett (1892–

THE GLOSSARY

1969), English novelist. Waugh admired her writing.

Connolly—Cyril Connolly (1903–74), English literary critic. He and Waugh were friends but were not above criticizing each other on occasion. See also other Connollys in Dictionary.

Cunarder—See Glossary under *BM*.

Deirdre—A heroine of ancient Irish legend, the subject of works by William Butler Yeats, John Millington Synge, and others.

"...Dowson, 'If you ever come to read it, you will understand'"—A reference to the English poet Ernest Dowson (1867–1900). The quotation originated in the "Preface: For Adelaide" to his *Verses*: "If you ever care to read them, you will understand."

Eton Rambler tie—A cricket-club tie worn by graduates of Eton. The tie has three stripes—green, lavender, and purple.

five-to-two—Rhyming British slang for "Jew." The origin of this usage is unknown.

Flecker—James Elroy Flecker (1884–1915), English poet and playwright whose most famous play, *Hassan*, was published posthumously in 1922.

"...For many a time / I have been half in love with easeful death."—Lines from John Keats's "Ode to a Nightingale."

Four Square Gospel—A religious sect founded by George Jeffreys in Ireland in 1915. The evangelist Aimée Semple MacPherson, whom Waugh satiried in *VB* as Mrs. Ape, founded the Pentecostal Fundamental International Church of the Four Square Gospel in Los Angeles. She acquired a large radio audience with her "Four Square Gospel Radio Broadcast," and her evangelical crusades attracted thousands of people.

Freud—Sigmund Freud (1856–1939), Austrian physician and founder of psychoanalysis.

"God set her brave eyes wide apart"—A line from the poem "Any Lover, Any Lass" by Richard Middleton (1882–1911). Since Waugh omits the first four lines of the poem, and since the poem is not included in *The Oxford Book of English Verse*, this verse has been extremely difficult to locate. Donald Greene (*EWN*, Winter, 1981, pp. 6–7) first discovered the source of this quotation, one of the most difficult to identify in all of Waugh's fiction.

Gosse—Sir Edmund Gosse (1849–1928), English poet, literary critic, and all-around man of letters. He was a distant cousin of Waugh, who detested his "middlebrow" influence on literature.

Grand Sanhedrin—The supreme governing board, a reference to the supreme council that governed Jewish affairs in ancient times.

Grenadiers—See Glossary under *BR*.

guichet—French for "ticket booth."

Handel—George Frederick Handel (1685–1759). German-born composer who became a British citizen. The "Dead March" from his oratorio *Saul* is probably the most familiar of funeral marches. Perhaps this, or the lugubrious adaptation of one of his arias called "Handel's Largo," was what was heard here.

Hanover Terrace—A fashionable, attractive street in London adjoining Regent's Park. Waugh's father sometimes visited Gosse there (see Waugh's autobiography *A Little Learning*, p. 65).

Hellas—Greece.

Henley—William Ernest Henley (1849–1903). British poet and literary critic, perhaps best known for his poem "Invictus."

Hesperides—In classical mythology, the nymphs who watched over a garden where golden apples grew.

"Hindu Love-song"—Probably, as Donald Greene has suggested in personal correspondence, Laurence Hope's *Indian Love Lyrics*, in particular No. 3, the "Kashmiri Love Song," beginning "Pale hands I loved, beside the Shalimar." Greene observes that this sentimental lyric "was wildly popular throughout the 1920s and '30s and is exactly the kind of thing Whispering Glades would love.... Of course, the highly sexual connotations of Laurence Hope's "poetry" go well with the sex-and-death theme of *LO*." Donat Gallagher observes that Waugh wrote an essay on Forest Lawn both for the *Tablet* and for *Life*. The *Life* article refers to the "Indian Love Call," while the *Tablet* uses "Hindu Lovesong." See *The Essays, Articles and Reviews of Evelyn Waugh*, ed. Donat Gallagher, p. 332.

hogmanay—New Year's Eve in Scotland with the accompanying parties and heavy drinking.

Hopkins—Gerard Manley Hopkins (1844–89), Jesuit poet whose first collected edition did not appear until 1918. He introduced many technical innovations and had considerable influence on twentieth-century poets.

Horizon — An important British journal devoted to the arts, founded by Cyril Connolly in 1939. It terminated in 1950. *The Loved One* was first published in *Horizon*.

in full ball rig — The English editions I have seen print "in full rig." Donald Greene suggests a typographical error and theorizes that "fig" (meaning dress, equipment, decoration) was probably intended here.

"I wither slowly in thine arms / Here at the quiet limit of the world" — Lines from Alfred, Lord Tennyson's poem "Tithonus."

I Zingari ribbon — The insignia of the chic I Zingari Cricket club, founded in 1845 by four Cambridge University men. "I Zingari" means "Gypsies."

Henry James — Celebrated American-born novelist and short-story writer (1843–1916) who became a British citizen.

Joyce — James Joyce (1882–1941), Irish writer of fiction best known for his experiments with the stream-of-consciousness technique. He achieved renown for *A Portrait of the Artist as a Young Man* (1916) and *Ulysses* (1921).

Kafka — Franz Kafka (1883–1924), Austrian novelist and short-story writer famous for such works as *The Trial* and "The Metamorphosis."

Kierkegaard — Sören Kierkegaard (1813–55), philosopher, considered by some to be the father of existentialism.

Knife and Fork Club — A social dinner club for business and professional people. The organization has clubs in numerous American cities.

"Know that death is common; all that live must die" — In an effort to console her son over his father's death, Queen Gertrude expresses this thought in act 1, scene 2, of Shakespeare's *Hamlet*. The actual phrasing is: "Thou know'st 'tis common—all that lives must die," which indicates that the hostess is poorly educated and has memorized an advertising spiel. The fact too that she thinks Hamlet is a writer is a further satire on her intellectual inadequacy as well as on those who run Whispering Glades.

Lake Island of Innisfree — "Lake Isle of Innisfree," one of William Butler Yeats's most popular poems, in which the poet has a honeybee hive and enjoys the buzzing of the bees.

Harry Lauder — Scottish comedian and songwriter (1870–1950).

Laudian — Referring to William Laud (1573–1645), an Anglican clergyman who eventually became Archbishop of Canterbury. He was beheaded by his Puritan opponents, who objected to his "High Church" policies.

limeys — Englishmen. In the eighteenth century British sailors were given lime juice to drink to prevent scurvy.

"Lloyd George creation" — A reference to titles of nobility, which could be purchased when Lloyd George was Prime Minister of England.

London Mercury — A popular literary magazine founded by John C. Squire in 1919. It was considered one of the most influential British periodicals in the 1920s.

Lorenzo Medici — Waugh is having playful fun here by using the name of Lorenzo de' Medici ("Lorenzo the Magnificent"), the fifteenth-century tyrannical ruler of Florence and patron of the arts.

Lovat-Fraser — See Glossary under *POMF*.

"The Lovers' Seat" — There is actually at Forest Lawn a stone ring through which lovers may grasp hands and swear loyalty in love.

Maenad — One of the female followers of Dionysus, the Greek god of wine drinking, merrymaking, and fertility. The Maenads danced wildly and behaved as though intoxicated.

mantle of Lear — A reference to Shakespeare's tragedy *King Lear*.

Marat — Jean Paul Marat (1743–93), French political figure assassinated in his bathtub by Charlotte Corday.

Maud — Maud Alice Burke, an American, who became Lady Cunard after marrying Sir Bache Cunard, who died in 1925. In the mid-1920s she changed "Maud" to "Emerald" because of the emeralds she wore. For many years Lady Cunard lived near Hyde Park at No. 9, Grosvenor Square, one of the most fashionable and wealthy sections of London. She loved gathering well-known people together for food and conversation. See also Dictionary, *Ruby*.

THE GLOSSARY

Maureen—there are two here already—References to Maureen O'Sullivan, who won notice as Jane in the Tarzan films, and Maureen O'Hara.

"memento mori"—See Glossary under *POMF*.

Metroland—The district around London served by the Metropolitan subway system. The name also recalls Lady and Lord Metroland; see Dictionary.

Minotaur—A monster—half man and half bull—in Greek legend. He dwelt in a labyrinth built by Daedalus at Knossos.

moke—Donkey.

Harold Monro...the Poetry Bookshop—Harold Monro (1879–1932), English poet and poetry enthusiast. He opened the Poetry Bookshop in London in 1912, and it quickly became a meeting and gathering place for poets and intellectuals.

nautch—Entertainment in India relying primarily on attractive and talented dancing girls.

Nissen huts—See Glossary under *BR*.

"Now sleeps the crimson petal, now the white"—A line from Alfred, Lord Tennyson's poem *The Princess*.

"Oh for the Wings of a Dove"—See Glossary under *VB*.

"On thy midnight pallet lying"—The first line of poem 11 in A. E. Housman's volume *A Shropshire Lad*.

Oona—The name Oona is probably most commonly associated with playwright Eugene O'Neill's daughter, who married comedian Charlie Chaplin.

Ouida—Pen name of Louise de la Ramée (1839–1908), who wrote many romantic melodramatic novels.

Oxford Book of English Verse—One of the most popular anthologies of poetry ever published. It was first issued by Oxford University Press in 1900, edited by Sir Arthur Quiller-Couch, and has been reprinted numerous times. Quiller-Couch edited a new revised and enlarged edition in 1939.

Paolos and Francescas—Paolo and Francesca were lovers who were put to death in Ravenna, Italy, in 1289 for adultery. Their story has been related by Dante and other authors.

Phoenix—A society and theater founded in 1919 with the goal of presenting the older English playwrights. It specialized in Elizabethan, Jacobean, and Restoration dramas.

Poems of Today—An anthology designed to give young people an awareness of "the newer poetry of their own day." The first collection was published in August, 1915, for the English Association by Sidgwick & Jackson, Ltd.

"Queen Elizabeth said to her Archbishop"—Queen Elizabeth I said to Sir Robert Cecil in March, 1603: "The word 'must' is not to be used to princes. Little man, little man . . . but ye know I must die and that makes you presumptuous." Cecil had recommended that she retire to bed; this episode occurred during the queen's last illness.

Robin de la Condamine—English actor whose stage name was Robert Farquharson. Harold Acton writes a short portrait of him in *Memoirs of an Aesthete, 1939–1969* (New York, 1971).

Rodin—François Auguste Rodin (1840–1917), French sculptor.

Rotarian...Knight of Pythias—Rotary and Knights of Phythias are fraternal organizations made up of business and professional men usually devoted to civic and humanitarian projects in the clubs' communities.

Sartre—Jean Paul Sartre (1905–80), influential French existentialist philosopher and author.

Shelley—Percy Bysshe Shelley (1792–1822), one of the great poets of the English romantic period.

"Shall I compare thee to a summer's day"—The first line of Shakespeare's Sonnet 18.

Gertrude Stein—See Glossary under *POMF*.

table-turning—Involvement in seances and similar practices.

Tents of Kedar Hotel—In British editions it is called the "Garden of Allah Hotel." As Robert Murray Davis reports in *Evelyn Waugh, Writer* (Norman, Okla., 1982), p. 195n, Waugh's American publisher, Little, Brown, prevailed on him to change the hotel name since the Garden of Allah was the actual name of a famous hotel on Sunset Boulevard, very prominent in the life of the movie colony. Tallulah Bankhead, Errol Flynn, W. C. Fields, John Barrymore, and Greta Garbo were some of the prominent stars associated with the Garden of Allah, which no longer exists.

Donald Greene observes in personal correspondence Waugh's "wonderfully witty feat" of using the "Tents of Kedar" as a name for "a very Hollywooden haunt of exiled Britishers." He notes the use of "Tents of Kedar" in Psalm 120, where the psalmist pleads to be delivered from "lying lips, from a deceitful tongue." The psalm proclaims, "Woe is me, that I sojourn in Meshech, that I dwell among the tents of Kedar!" Greene quotes the commentary of the *New Oxford Annotated Bible*: "An exile's prayer for deliverance from enemies (a lament)... Meshech... Kedar, remote regions in Asia Minor and north Arabia."

"**They told me, Francis Hinsley, they told me you were hung**" — A parody of William Johnson Cory's "Heraclitus," beginning "They told me, Heraclitus, they told me you were dead." The original is quoted in *OG*, part 2, chap. 1, by Field Marshal Lord Wavell, Commander-in-Chief, Middle East. The Greek that Cory was imitating is Callimachus, Epigram 2.

"**Till a' the Seas Gang Dry My Dear... While the sands of life shall run**" — Lines from Robert Burns's poem "A Red, Red Rose."

vestal virgin — In ancient times, a virgin consecrated to the service of the Roman goddess Vesta. The vestal virgins were in charge of keeping the sacred fire burning in Vesta's temple.

Wagner — Richard Wagner (1813–83), famed German operatic composer.

"**The Wearing of the Green**" — A traditional popular Irish melody denouncing British rule in Ireland; the author and the exact date of origin are uncertain. It is, of course, highly inappropriate for Francis Hinsley's funeral and demonstrates that attendance at the funeral is hypocritically intended for publicity purposes.

Wee Kirk o' Auld Lang Syne — Waugh is making fun of Whispering Glades' use of Robert Burns's Scottish dialect. Robert Burns (1759–96) achieved fame for his poems in that form. The phrase above means "The Little Church of Old Long Ago." Burns used the phrase "wee kirk" in some of his poems, and Forest Lawn, the real-life counterpart of Whispering Glades, has a church called Wee Kirk o' the Heather.

Where the Rainbow Ends — The play described, published in 1912, was written by Clifford Mills and John Ramsay.

"**Scottie Wilson**" — Wilson (1887–1972), British "primitive" painter who for a time had a considerable vogue in intellectual circles.

the Works — That is, the writings of Sir Francis Hinsley.

Zola — Emile Zola (1840–1902), French author and man of letters who developed the naturalistic novel.

HELENA (1950)

Dedicatee

Penelope Betjeman, the daughter of Field Marshal Sir Philip Chetwode, was the wife of Sir John Betjeman, poet laureate of England from 1972 until his death in 1984. Penelope Betjeman was a close friend of Waugh and a convert to Catholicism.

Actium — A promontory in Greece where the forces of Antony and Cleopatra were defeated by Emperor Octavian in 31 B.C.

Aelia Capitolina — Another name for Jerusalem.

Aeneas — The mythical hero of Virgil's *Aeneid*.

Aeons — Long periods of time. The Gnostics believed time was divided into aeons.

agape — A meal (love feast) celebrating love and community among the early Christians.

Ahriman — In Zoroastrian belief, the chief evil spirit.

Alban — An old name for England.

Allectus — A Roman ruler during the Roman occupation of England.

Antioch — An ancient city at one time under Greek rule and later controlled by the Romans, becoming an important Christian center. It is in present-day Turkey.

Arianizer — A follower of Arius, a member of the Arian heresy.

Arius — A priest (A.D. 256–336) who began the Arian heresy, which denied the full divinity of Christ.

Astarte — The Babylonian goddess of love.

Augustus — The first Caesar Augustus, Roman emperor who ruled from 27 B.C. to A.D. 14.

Aurelian — Emperor of Rome, A.D. 270–75.

"Ave atque vale" — Latin for "Hail and farewell."

beano — See Glossary under *DF*.

Bithynia — See Glossary under *DF*.

blow-out — Slang for a lavish, extravagant banquet or party.

Boadicea — A legendary woman in English history who rebelled against Roman rule.

Brutus — In myth, Brutus is often mentioned as the first king of the Britons. He was the great-grandson of Aeneas. It should be noted that he is not the Brutus associated with Julius Caesar.

bum-boats — Boats carrying goods and items for sale to a ship anchored close to shore.

"The Career Open to Talent" — From the phrase attributed to Napoleon: "La carrière ouverte aux talents," meaning that in a new, "democratic" age even the lowliest-born have the opportunity to use their talents to rise to high positions of power.

Carinus — Marcus Aurelius Carinus, Roman emperor, A.D. 283–85. He died in battle against Diocletian's forces, assassinated by one of his own men.

Carus — Marcus Aurelius Carus, Roman emperor, A.D. 282–83. He became emperor after the murder of Probus.

catechumen — One studying to become a Christian.

Catherine — An early Christian martyr who died during the rule of Emperor Maximus (A.D. 383–88).

Châlons — A city in northeastern France once occupied by the Romans.

Chlorus — Greenish. Constantius's face looks green from all the drinking and banqueting the night before.

Claudius — Claudius II (Marcus Aurelius Claudius), emperor of Rome, A.D. 268–70.

Coptic elder — An aged member of the Coptic sect. The Copts were descendants of Egyptians who had been converted to Christianity. The Coptic church,

THE GLOSSARY

stressing only one nature in Christ—the divine—was officially labeled heretical by the Council of Chalcedon in A.D. 451. A very small number of Copts remain in communion with Rome.

XP—Greek chi-rho, a symbol for Christ, the first two letters of the Greek name of Christ.

Ctesiphon—A city in present-day central Iraq, near Baghdad.

Cymbeline—A legendary English prince captured by Caesar when the Romans invaded Britain and taken to Rome. Later he was alleged to have returned to England as a ruler living in harmony with the Romans.

Dalmatia—A region in the Croatia area of Yugoslavia bordering the eastern side of the Adriatic Sea.

Deaths of the Persecutors—A treatise on God's denunciation of Roman emperors (from Nero to Diocletian) who persecuted the Christian church.

"Demiurge"—A Platonic term for the Creator of the world.

Diocletian—Gaius Aurelius Valerius Diocletianus, Roman emperor who was notorious for his persecution of Christians. He decided to divide the empire and as a result became joint ruler with Maximian (A.D. 286–305) and Constantius I (A.D. 305–306). Constantius succeeded him.

Donatus—A fourth-century heretical bishop in North Africa.

Dosithus—Correctly Dositheus, first-century A.D. Samaritan mystic and rival of Simon Magnus. He attempted to take over Simon's claim to be "the Standing One" but did not succeed. He did have his followers, however, and was one of the several Gnostic heretics of that era.

dower-house—A house on the same land as the family residence. The house was available for use by a widow after her husband's death.

Drepanum—An ancient seaport on the northeast coast of Sicily now called Trapani.

Flavian family—A leading Roman family. The Emperors Vespasian, Titus, and Domitian were all Flavians.

Gaius—Second-century A.D. Roman jurist and commentator on the law who wrote several treatises on law, including the *Institutiones* (ca. 161). This book had considerable influence on Emperor Justinian's sixth-century treatise of the same title.

Galerius—Gaius Galerius Valerius Maximianus, Roman emperor, A.D. 305–10. In 305–306 he was joint emperor with Constantius I.

Gallic—Relating to France.

Gallienus—Son of Valerian (d. ca. A.D. 269), he was co-emperor with his father. Later he ruled alone; his complete reign was A.D. 253–68.

Garden of Gethsemane—An area on the lower part of Olivet where Christ prayed. See *Olivet* below.

Gaul—France.

Gnostic—An adherent of Gnosticism, a potpourri of mystical beliefs developed from Greek, Oriental, and Christian influences. It involved knowledge passed on by experts who initiated new candidates into the mysteries and consisted of several sects. Much emphasis was placed on contemplation and self-discipline. Many different Gnostic groups developed in the second century A.D.

Golgotha—A small hill near Jerusalem where Jesus was crucified.

Gordian—There were three emperors of this name. Probably Gordian III (Marcus Antonius Gordianus, A.D. 238–44) is meant.

"grandmother's steps"—See Glossary under *BR*.

Helena . . . the partner of Simon, the Standing One—Simon Magnus, a Samaritan who lived in the first century A.D., was reputed to possess magical powers and was thought by many writers to be the founder of Gnosticism. Simon sometimes claimed that he was the Messiah, and he often designated himself as "the Standing One." He was worshiped as God by many followers. He traveled with a woman named Helena (Luna) whom he had rescued from a life of prostitution in Tyre. He claimed that she reincarnated in various forms (for example, she had been Helen of Troy). He also proclaimed her as Thought, a universal mother who gave him the idea of creating angels. He is assumed to be the Simon, from whose name the word *simony* originated, referred to in Acts 8:9–24.

"Helena's isle"—Saint Helena, an island in the South Atlantic Ocean controlled by the British. Napoleon was exiled there, 1815–21.

her twin brethren—Castor and Pollux.

Homoiousion . . . Homoousion—Homoousians (from Greek *homos*, "same") believed the three Persons of the Trinity to be of the same substance. Homoiousians (from Greek *homoios*, "similar") believed the three Persons to be of similar, but not identical, substance. The squabble over this seemingly minute point of theology was often satirized.

horologium — An instrument for telling time; here either a sundial or a water clock.

hypostatic — Having to do with substance. Here it refers to the doctrine of the Trinity — the union of three persons (Father, Son, and Holy Spirit) in one God. The term also signifies the union of the divine and the human in Christ.

Idaea — Relating to Mount Ida. There was a Mount Ida in Crete associated with the goddess Rhea, and another in Asia Minor connected with Cybele. As time went on, their identities were often interchanged.

Iliad of **Homer** — Marcias is reading from book 3 of the *Iliad*.

Ilium — Troy.

Illyrians — The people of Illyria, ancient name for the Adriatic coastal area of Albania, Yugoslavia, and part of Greece, At one time it was a Roman province.

"Invention of the Cross" — In a manuscript in the Harry Ransom Humanities Research Center, University of Texas at Austin, Waugh wrote, "Invention originally meant 'discovery'; in modern use it means 'contrivance' or 'fabrication.' Hence the lady's (Lady Astor) confusion."

Labarum — The banner or standard of some of the Roman emperors in the last years of the empire. It pictured a spear topped with an eagle. The cross staff comprised a gold-fringed purple streamer decorated with precious stones.

Lactantius — Lucius Caelius Firmianus, Christian writer (ca. A.D. 260–340). He wrote principally on history and religion, and was noted as a superb prose stylist.

Longinus — Greek philosopher who was killed in A.D. 273 by order of Emperor Aurelian because he helped Queen Zenobia of Palmyra, an enemy of Aurelian.

Maximian — Marcus Aurelius Valerius Maximianus, Roman co-emperor with Diocletian, A.D. 286–305. His daughter Fausta married Constantine, but he eventually became an opponent of his son-in-law. He committed suicide in 310.

Milvian Bridge — The scene of a battle during which a flaming cross allegedly appeared in the sky with the words "In hoc signo vinces" ("By this sign you will conquer"). This vision persuaded Constantine to accept Christianity.

Mithras — A Greek and Latin name for Mithra, a Persian sun god who was for a period a minor figure in Zoroastrian belief. The cult of Mithras-Mithraism was adapted by many Roman legionaries and spread throughout Europe and the middle East. Mithras was regarded as a warrior comrade who fought the forces of evil.

tale of Mithras — According to the tale, Mithras captured a sacred bull. He sacrificed the animal, and from that sacrificial animal came all good aspects of life.

Mithraum — A place, usually an underground cave, where Mithraic ceremonies and initiations took place.

Moesia — An area in southeastern Europe which was conquered and controlled by the Romans.

Moesian connection — Relatives and interrelated groups from Moesia.

Nicaea — The site in Asia Minor of a council of Christian clergy held in A.D. 325, presided over by Constantine the Great. It condemned the Arian heresy and affirmed the doctrine of the Trinity.

Nish — A city in present eastern Yugoslavia, the birthplace of Constantine the Great.

"None but My Foe to Be My Guide" — "Quotation from old Scottish ballad, 'I would I were where Helen lies.'" Waugh's note in manuscript in the Harry Ransom Humanities Research Center, University of Texas at Austin.

Nones of May — The ninth day before the Ides. The Nones is May 7 and the Ides is May 15 (the Romans counted inclusively).

Numerian — Numerianus (3rd century A.D.), a son of Emperor Carus who was put in charge of the eastern region of the Roman Empire while his father went on a military campaign. He was joint emperor with Carinus, 283–284, and was murdered in 284.

"Odi profanum vulgus et arceo" — Latin for "I hate the common people, and I ward them off," the first line of ode 1 of book 3 of Horace's *Odes*.

THE GLOSSARY

Olivet — The Mount of Olives, a ridge east of Jerusalem associated with Christ.

"Oremus" — Latin for "Let us pray," a common phrase in the traditional Roman Catholic Mass.

Ormazd — In Zoroastrian belief, the force of good, the spirit that created everything. Also called Ahura Mazdah.

Palatine — The hill in Rome on which stood the emperors' palaces.

pallium — A vestment bestowed by the Pope on an Archbishop or bishop to indicate official recognition of his authority. The bestowal on Macarius meant that he was no longer a suffragan bishop, subordinate to the Bishop of Caesarea, and that his diocese of Jerusalem was now an independent diocese in its own right.

"per Christum Dominum nostrum" — See Glossary under *DF*.

Pict — A pre-Celtic race in Scotland.

Pontifex Maximus — The chief official in Rome who oversaw religious principles and moral behavior.

Praetorian — Members of the palace guard of the Roman emperors.

Praxiteles — Greek sculptor (ca. 370–330 B.C.), one of the earliest masters of this art.

Priam — The King of Troy who in some legends was mentioned as a distant ancestor of Helen's family.

Probus — Marcus Aurelius Probus (third century A.D.), Roman general and emperor, A.D. 276–82.

Quintilius — Marcus Aurelius Claudius Quintillus, emperor briefly in A.D. 270, although some lists of Roman emperors do not include him. He was proclaimed emperor after the unexpected death of his brother (Claudius II) in a plague. He did not have his brother's talent and failed to travel to Rome. In the meantime, Aurelian won several battles and was proclaimed emperor by the troops. When Quintilius realized that Aurelian had more support, he committed suicide.

Ratisbon — A German city in Bavaria, now called Regensburg.

Raven — One of the seven steps or grades achieved by initiates into the Mithraic beliefs.

Scamander — A river near Troy. It is frequently referred to in accounts of the Trojan War.

sea-girt Kranae — Reechoes the phrase translated from Homer's *Iliad* in chap. 1: "the night on sea-girt Kranae when I first knew you."

Seleucia — A city in present-day central Iraq conquered by the Romans.

Silchester — A town in southern England occupied by the Romans in ancient times.

snaffle — A bit for a horse's mouth.

Souls — Believers in Gnosticism. Waugh writes, "It was the name given to a section of English society circa 1905 who specialized in poetry, paper-games... etc. *No* religious connotation." In manuscript in the Harry Ransom Humanities Research Center, University of Texas at Austin. In *Helena* Waugh is referring to the Gnostic Souls of the Roman era.

stabularia — A hostler, that is, a stable boy who handles horses.

stolen queen — Helen of Troy, the wife of King Menelaus.

Strasbourg — A city in northeastern France once occupied by the Romans. Spelled Strasburg in the English edition.

suppedaneum — A footrest.

Swabian — Of or from Swabia, a German duchy.

taurobolium — A ceremony which included sacrificing a bull to Cybele.

Te Deums — Renderings of a Latin hymn of thanksgiving that begins "Te Deum laudamus" ("We praise thee, O God") It dates from the fourth century and is believed to have been composed by Saint Ambrose.

Teucer — Son of Telamon and stepbrother of Ajax. He traveled with the Greek forces to fight in the Trojan War. After the war he returned to his native land but was banished by his father who thought, incorrectly, that Teucer had killed Ajax. Telamon was King of Salamis who assisted Hercules in his battle against the Amazons.

Thermopylae — See Glossary under *POMF*.

Titus — Emperor of Rome, A.D. 79–81. He was succeeded by Domitian.

ΤΟΥΤΩ ΝΙΚΑ — Greek for "By this sign you will conquer." In English editions I have seen the form **ΤΟΥΤΩΙ ΝΙΚΑ**. A more familiar version of the slogan is **ΕΝ ΤΟΥΤΩΙ ΝΙΚΑ** — EN meaning "in." It is often rendered in Latin as "In hoc signo vinces." On the night before the Battle of Saxa Rubra (A.D.

312), a town north of Rome, Constantine I received a vision telling him to inscribe the Cross and this motto on the shields of his soldiers. Constantine defeated Maxentius and his armies at the Battle of the Milvian Bridge and was later converted to Christianity.

Trajan — Roman emperor, A.D. 98–117.

Trèves — A city in western Germany near the Luxembourg border. It was occupied by the Romans for many years.

Trinovantes — According to various chronicles, the ancient name of London, the city of the Trinobantes.

Twelfth Night — The eve of the twelfth day after Christmas. The twelfth day, January 6, is celebrated as the Feast of the Epiphany (the arrival of the Magi at Christ's birthplace in Bethlehem).

Tyre — A city in Lebanon on the Mediterranean.

Valerian — Emperor of Rome, A.D. 253–260. He was known for his persecution of Christians. He was eventually captured by the Persians and died as a prisoner.

veil of Cryphius — One of the ceremonies evolving into fuller union with Mithras.

Virgil — See Glossary under *POMF*.

Vitruvian — Pertaining to Vitruvius, a Roman architect and engineer in the early part of the first century B.C., author of the ten-volume *De architectura*.

"what sucks" — British slang for "what an ironic joke."

"Zivio! Viva! Arriba! Heil!" — "Long live! Long live! Long live! Hail!" Waugh writes, "These verses, which refer of course to Napoleon... are written in the style of the popular songs of the negroes of the British West Indies." Waugh explains many of the terms that might be unfamiliar: *"chips*—gambling counters; *shook the bones*—shaking the dice; *a natural*—the winning score; *chop*—food; *baby*—lover; *snake's eyes*—the bottom score; *played for a sucker*—duped." In manuscript at the Harry Ransom Humanities Research Center, University of Texas at Austin.

MEN AT ARMS (1952)

Dedicatee

Christopher Sykes was a friend of Waugh's who also served in the British army in World War II. He is "Roger Stillingfleet" in *WS*. He wrote a biography of Waugh in 1975.

ack — Short for "acknowledge."

Ack-Ack — Anti-aircraft unit. "Ack" was the World War I voice code for the first letter of the alphabet — "Ack, Beer, Charlie, Don," etc. The code has been revised several times since.

Agincourt — A famous English victory; see Glossary under *VB*.

King Albert of the Belgians — Albert I (1875–1934), who led an army that bravely resisted the Germans in World War I

Alexander's visit to Siwa — Alexander the Great visited the oasis of Siwa (also spelled Siwah), where he was proclaimed a pharaoh by the sacred oracle of Amon (also spelled Ammon). In some versions, he was said to be designated a son of the god Amon.

Altar of the Repose — A side altar in a Roman Catholic Church. At the end of traditional Catholic services on Maundy Thursday the altar is stripped, and the tabernacle is emptied and left open. The Communion Host is transferred to a side altar (the Altar of Repose) and is surrounded with lighted candles and flowers. The Host remains there until Easter services.

Altmark — A German prison ship carrying almost three hundred captured British merchant seamen. On February 16, 1940, the British discovered the *Altmark* sailing along the Norwegian coast carrying almost three hundred captured British merchant seamen. A British destroyer pursued the *Altmark*, trapped it in a fjord, and rescued the prisoners, who were then returned to England.

Anzac — Australian and New Zealand Army Corps, troops from Australia and New Zealand who served in both world wars.

Arciprete — A priest who is a rural dean.

Ash Wednesday — The Wednesday that begins Lent.

ATM — Army Training Memorandum, one of the pamphlets on military matters periodically issued to officers, supposed to be kept confidential.

"Aves" — "Hail Marys."

balls-up — A mixup, in American a "snafu."

Barham — A British battleship that took part in the Dakar expedition. See Waugh's *Diaries*, p. 481.

batman — See Glossary under *POMF*.

Battle of Malplaquet — A battle in which British and allied troops, commanded by the first duke of Marlborough defeated the French in 1709 during the War of the Spanish Succession. In the battle the Royal Corps of Halberdiers drove away French marauders by pelting them with apples. This episode is fictional.

Battle Schools — Training schools for simulated battle experience, using live ammunition, for example.

Beau Brummel — When the eighteenth-century English dandy George ("Beau") Brummel's gambling debts became excessive, he fled to Calais and spent the remaining years of his life in France. See Glossary under *VB*.

Bechuanaland — An area in southern Africa once controlled by the British, now the Republic of Botswana.

Bechuana tummy — Apthorpe's euphemism for the effects of heavy drinking; that is, a hangover. Since Apthorpe had been in Bechuanaland in Africa, he,

THE GLOSSARY

in his officious and reticent way, blames his sickness on a mysterious jungle illness which sounds intriguing and romantic.

Bedfordshire for you—Bedfordshire is an English county abbreviated Beds. Ritchie-Hook is instructing the men to retire for the night.

Beds and Herts or the Black Watch—Names of two British regiments, i.e., the Bedfordshire and Hertfordshire Regiment and the Black Watch (the Royal Highland Regiment).

Belgravia—MA, SOH. A small ship supposedly carrying food for the French at Dakar. See Waugh's *Diaries*, p. 481.

"Benediteme padre, perche ho peccato"—Italian for "Bless me, father, because I have sinned." The first two words are misprinted "Beneditemi" in some editions.

biffing—Attacking.

black-shirt—A member of the Fascist party.

Blanco—Trademark for a cleaner used in the British army to whiten belts and other military equipment.

blood—Wine.

blot your copy book—Do something militarily improper.

blue funk—Terror.

blue-jobs—Sailors.

"Blues"—The Royal Horse Guards Regiment, in which Waugh was an officer after leaving the Royal Marines.

B.M.—Brigade Major, the senior staff officer in a brigade.

bob—A shilling, a twentieth of a pound; in modern British currency, fivepence.

Boche—German.

Bohemia—The older name of the western area of Czechoslovakia.

boil out—Clean out one's rifle with boiling water. After range practice or other use, rifles were held over a cauldron of boiling water, a funnel was put in the breech, and boiling water was poured through.

Bouchers—Works by François Boucher (1703–70), French artist remembered for his paintings of shepherds, Cupids, and similar bucolic classical subject matter.

Boulle—André Boulle (1642–1732), a French craftsman noted for his furniture inlaid with shells, ebony, metal, and similar decorations.

box-wallah—See Glossary under *BM*, *Wallah*.

Bren—See Glossary under *POMF*, *Bren gun*.

Brinkman ma.—The *ma.* is short for *major* and is used to distinguish the elder of two people with the same last name, usually brothers.

burgee—A flag or banner used, especially by ships, for identification or signaling.

Calais—A seaport in France across the English Channel from Dover.

called out the marker—It is a practice on drill parades to call forward the right-hand man, or marker, of the front rank of a unit. He (or "they" in a large parade) marches to a prearranged or standard position on the parade ground. The rest of the men of the unit then take up their positions relative to the marker.

canon—The most sacred part of the Roman Catholic Mass. It begins with the Preface and Sanctus and ends with the Minor Elevation (that is, just before the recitation of the Lord's Prayer).

Canon—This title, which is not used in the Catholic Church in the United States, has been explained in personal correspondence by the Reverend Michael Richards, who writes from England: "In the British Isles senior and well-established Catholic priests are given the title 'canon' and become members of the chapter of canons with the responsibility of advising the bishop in the conduct of the diocese.... So the clergy in question are not necessarily on the staff of a cathedral."

capitation grant—An allowance granted a priest based on the number of persons for whom he performed services.

Cesare armato...—Italian for "a falcon-eyed Caesar, armed." James J. Lynch has identified this reference as an allusion to canto 4 of Dante's *Inferno*, where Dante has a vision of Caesar among the great historical figures who reside in Limbo. See "An Allusion to Dante in *Men at Arms*," *EWN*, Winter, 1984, p. 7.

chaffing—Joking, bantering.

Neville Chamberlain—English prime minister, 1937–40; see Glossary under *POMF*.

chassés—Gliding steps in which one foot is moved along the floor.

chotá pegs—See Glossary under *BM*.

the City—The financial section of London.

clap—Venereal disease, specifically gonorrhea.

Coldstream—The Guards regiment of that name, see Glossary under *HD*.

company schemes — Training exercises for an infantry company.

cosseted — Pampered.

County Cork — A county in Ireland.

covered lines of approach — An approach made while protected by gunfire from one's own troops or by natural cover. Also, a route that gives protection from observation or gunfire by the enemy.

CSM — Company Sergeant Major.

Dakar — A seaport in West Africa which for many years was controlled by the French. It is now in the Republic of Senegal. The Dakar campaign occurred in September, 1940. For further details see Waugh's *Diaries*, pp. 481ff.

Dartmouth — An English seaport in southwest England, the site of the Royal Naval Cadet Training College.

day Churchill became Prime Minister — May 10, 1940.

dead ground — Concealed areas which are invisible to persons watching from a particular observation point.

General De Gaulle — Charles DeGaulle (1890–1970) was the leader of the Free French forces who fought against Hitler from headquarters in London after Hitler's armies conquered France.

dekko — A look or glance.

Dissent — A reference to those Protestants who refused to adhere to the Established Church of England.

"Domine non sum dignus" — Latin for "O Lord I am not worthy," words from the prayer in the mass where one begs pardon for sins to become worthy to receive communion.

doppelganger — A "double-walker," a supernatural apparition who looks just like the person who sees it.

Downside — An English Roman Catholic school for boys as well as a Benedictine monastic community with an impressive abbey church.

ducks and drakes — Treat something casually. Ducks and drakes is the pastime of skimming a stone along the surface of water and watching the stone bounce as the water ripples.

Duke of Wellington at St. Paul's — The Duke of Wellington, hero of the Battle of Waterloo, had an elaborate funeral and burial at Saint Paul's Cathedral, London.

Dunkirk — A French seaport from which the British evacuated thousands of their own and Allied soldiers after Hitler's armies had overrun most of western Europe. This mammoth operation occurred from May 26 to June 4, 1940.

Earl of Essex — Robert Devereux, second earl of Essex (1566–1601), a successful soldier and courtier and an especial favorite of Queen Elizabeth I. Ultimately he incurred her displeasure and was beheaded.

1800 hours — 6:00 P.M.

en brosse — French for "like a brush." In American, "crew-cut."

enfant terrible — French for "terrible infant," a person, usually youthful, who causes considerable difficulty by wild, rash actions.

Ensa — Acronym of Entertainments National Service Association. Similar to the American USO (United Service Organization); both groups gave performances and entertainments to cheer the morale of those in military service.

Farm Street — A reference to the Jesuit church there; see Glossary under *BR*.

Father Rank — The priest in Graham Greene's novel *The Heart of the Matter* (1948).

Februato Juno — The Romans established the practice of sending love greetings in honor of the goddess Juno on or about February 14. In Roman mythology Juno was the wife of Jupiter, the king of the gods.

Fiji **was torpedoed** — In his diaries Waugh records the date as September 1, 1940. The cruiser managed to reach port safely.

First Ashanti War — A war fought in what is now Ghana, Africa, in 1873–74. The British sent four expeditions against the Ashanti tribes before annexing their territory.

Fixed Lines — In personal correspondence Donald Greene has given a clear and thorough explanation of "firing on fixed lines." He writes: "The reference is to a procedure (like so many things in the training described by Waugh, more relevant to trench warfare in World War I than to the circumstances of W.W. II) whereby machine guns can engage enemy targets at night, when those targets are not visible. During the day, the target is sighted, and an 'aiming peg' within view of the gunner is placed in line with the target. Also, the distance of the objective is estimated, and the gunner instructed to set that elevation on his gun (in this case, 1,800 yards) so as to attain the right trajectory to hit the target. So at night the gunner aims his gun at the aiming peg (illuminated by the 'night lamp'), sets his gun at an elevation of 1,800 yards, and presumably hits the target. The absurdity of the incomprehension of the principle by the recruits is apparent. But that was very often the way such instruction by sergeant instructors went on—just rote directions with no attempt to explain the underlying principle."

fizzer—A person who is very strict and explosive.

flap—See Glossary under *BR*.

footer—See Glossary under *BR*.

1415—2:15 P.M.

Français de Dakar—The French of Dakar.

Freetown—A prominent seaport as well as the capital of Sierra Leone, in west Africa.

frightful wax—Very angry and upset.

froggy—A derogatory slang term for the French, short for "frog-eaters," referring to the fact, which the British thought perverse, that frogs' legs are part of French cuisine.

Furibundus—Raging, furious.

gaffes raisonnées—French for "intentional blunders."

gear—Equipment and possessions.

general dogsbody—An errand boy.

German Uhlans—Cavalry forces of Tartar origin, introduced into German armies in the nineteenth century; they were especially effective in using lances and sabers.

Goanese—A native of Goa; see Glossary under *BM*, *Goan*.

God of Kipling's *Recessional*—The poem "Recessional" is a warning to the British for all the boasting they have been doing at the time of Queen Victoria's diamond jubilee and a passionate plea for them to start behaving with some humility—if they do not, all their "pomp of yesterday" shall be "as one with Nineveh and Tyre." In this reference Churchillian boastings are immediately followed by retribution by God, who is prepared to put the British, or any other group with swollen heads, in their place.

goggling—Staring with wide eyes.

"going to Brighton . . . 'guilty party' "—Brighton is an English seaside resort. For many years adultery was the only allowable cause for divorce in England. Thus fake adulteries would be staged with one of the parties, usually the husband, going to Brighton for a night or two with someone other than the spouse. Evidence would be taken by detectives hired for the occasion, and these data would be presented in court to secure the divorce. In *HD*, Tony Last goes to Brighton for that purpose.

Goya—Francisco José de Goya Lucientes (1746–1828), Spanish artist whose paintings often emphasize dark, gloomy, and macabre material.

Grip—Control, take hold of a situation.

GS02 (Q)—General Staff Officer, grade 2 (quartermaster). In *SOH* the initials D.A.Q.M.G., for Deputy Assistant Quartermaster-General, are substituted. In *SOH*, Waugh realized that GS02 (Q) was a mistake. The four staff divisions of the British Army are G: General Staff, responsible for operations, training, and intelligence; A: Adjutant-General's branch, responsible for personnel; Q: Quartermaster-General's branch, responsible for supplies; and O: Master-General of the Ordnance branch, responsible for providing arms. Someone from the G branch could not be in charge of Q matters; hence the change to DAQMG (Deputy Assistant Quartermaster-General), an actual staff position at the divisional level.

G.1098—Military supplies.

G.2 Training—General Staff Officer, grade 2, in charge of training.

Halberdiers—A fictional name for the Royal Marines.

"Halte-la! Qui vive?"—French for "Halt there! Who is it?"

"handkerchief" at Downside—Being a prefect at Downside School; becoming a prefect was a mark of accomplishment.

Happy Families—A card game that involves asking many questions; see Glossary under *BM*, *Miss Chipps, the Carpenter's daughter*.

Harley Street man—A doctor. Many doctors had offices on Harley Street, in London; thus Harley Street is identified with physicians as Fleet Street is identified with newspapers.

Ian Hay—Scottish novelist and playwright (1876–1952) whose real name was John Hay Beith.

the Head's—*Head* is short for *headmaster*.

The Heart of the Matter—Graham Greene's best-selling and controversial novel (1948) about a Catholic police official in Africa.

heliograph — An instrument that sends messages by means of flashes of sunlight reflecting off a mirror.

Hera in the arms of Zeus — In Greek mythology Hera (Roman Juno) was the wife of Zeus (Roman Jupiter), the king of the gods.

Hittite tablets — The Hittites were an ancient people living in Asia Minor. They left many inscriptions and engravings on stone tablets which have considerable historical and archeological value.

high-church — A high-church Anglican; that is, Anglo-Catholic.

Holy Week — The week beginning on Palm Sunday and ending on the Saturday before Easter. During the week the passion of Christ is commemorated with many prayers and religious ceremonies.

Hore-Belisha — See Glossary under *POMF*.

Host — The wafer of bread that is, through the words of Consecration at the Mass, transformed into the Body of Christ. The wine in the chalice is consecrated after the bread. The Host on view in the monstrance is a consecrated wafer.

Housey-housey... Kelly's eye — A bingo game; see Glossary under *BR, Kelly's eye,... etc.*

Humber Snipe — See Glossary under *POMF*.

idée fixe — French for "obsession."

Immolatus — Latin for "killed as a sacrifice."

I.O. — Intelligence Officer.

Irish Guards — A well-known British infantry regiment, especially distinguished for its bravery and fighting ability in World War I.

General Ironside — General (later Field Marshal) William Ironside (1880–1959). He was chief of the British Imperial General Staff, 1939–40. After the debacle at Dunkirk, he was relieved of his post.

James II — Born in 1633, king of England, Scotland, and Ireland, 1685–88. His conversion to Roman Catholicism and his Catholic sympathies were important factors in his overthrow in the Revolution of 1688. Many of his supporters and their descendants believed that his forced departure from the throne was illegal. He died in 1701.

J.D. — Judging distance.

"Joignez-vous..." — French for "Join us to set France free."

junker — See Glossary under *LAR*.

Kaiser — See Glossary under *BR*.

Karonga — A town in southeast Africa, in a region at one time controlled by the British, today the independent country of Malawi.

"Kasanga... Makarikari" — Kasanga is a port city on Lake Tanganyika, Tanzania, in east Africa. Makarikari is in the northeastern part of the present-day Republic of Botswana.

kept *cave* — Kept guard.

King's Regulations — The official British red book containing military rules and procedures. It is colloquially called the "Army's bible."

Last Post — Final salute; see Glossary under *OGP*.

Lee-Enfield — See Glossary under *BM, Lee-Enfield rifles*.

Lent — The forty days preceding Easter, set aside as a period of prayer and fasting.

Lillehammer — A town near Oslo, Norway, where British and German armies fought during the British Norwegian campaign in World War II.

Limerick — A county in Ireland.

Lincoln's Inn — One of the lawyers' colleges in London where students are trained for their bar examinations.

lingua franca — A common language composed of Italian and words of several other languages whose general meaning can be understood; often spoken in Mediterranean ports.

LMG — Light Machine Gun.

Loamshires — A mythical regiment; see Glossary under *POMF*.

Loos — A village in northern France, the scene of heavy fighting between English and German troops in World War I.

Lourdes — See *Our Lady of Lourdes*, below.

made his recce — Made his reconnaissance; looked over the situation.

Maginot or the Siegfried Line — The Maginot Line, named for André Maginot (1877–1932) was a series of fortifications built along France's eastern border to ward off German attacks. The Siegfried Line, named for the mythic German hero, was a line of pillboxes and other military installations built by the Germans on their western frontier. Both lines of defense were constructed in the 1930s. At the beginning of World War II the Germans easily outflanked the Maginot Line in invading France.

Mannerheim — Baron Carl Mannerheim (1867–

1951), Finnish field marshal who inflicted several defeats on the Russian invaders in the early phase of World War II.

Mary Tudor — The daughter of King Henry VIII and Catherine of Aragon (1516–58). During her reign as queen of England (1553–58), Calais in France, the last English possession on the Continent, which had been under English control since the fourteenth century, was lost to French forces.

Matto Grosso — See Glossary under *HD*.

Maundy Thursday — See Glossary under *BR*.

Maynooth — The major seminary in Ireland which trained young men for the Roman Catholic priesthood.

mealies — Corn.

"Memento, homo,..." etc. — Latin for "Remember man that thou art dust and into dust thou shall return." These words are spoken by the priest in Roman Catholic services on Ash Wednesday while placing ashes on each person's forehead as a reminder of death, judgment, heaven, and hell.

Mende...Swahili — African dialects.

Meuse — A river rising in northeastern France and flowing into Belgium. It was the scene of fortifications and battles in both world wars.

Mikkeli Marshes — A swampy area near the Finnish city of Mikkeli where the Russian armies for a time suffered military setbacks.

Milwaukee accents — Perhaps a reference to the Americanized British accent of John Pick, professor of English for many years at Marquette University, in Milwaukee, Wisconsin. The scholar who suggested the meaning of this allusion is J. W. Scheideman; see *EWN*, Autumn, 1983, p. 3.

minute — A short official note.

monstrance — A metal receptacle with a small glass window in which the Host is displayed when carried in a procession or set on an altar.

Sir John Moore at Corunna — John Moore, an English general (1761–1809) defeated a French army at Corunna but was killed there. His death was portrayed in Charles Wolfe's famous poem "The Burial of Sir John Moore" (1817).

mot juste — French for "proper, precise word."

M.T. — Military transport.

Mussolini — Benito Mussolini (1883–1945), Italian dictator and ally of Hitler.

National Art Treasures — Famous paintings, sculptures, etc., were moved from London and other large English cities to rural areas to protect them from German air raids. Considerable numbers of women and children were also evacuated to less populous areas of England.

National Service — Military conscription. The conscripts served for a specified period of time.

no catch — Difficult.

OC D Coy to OC 2 pl. — Abbreviation for "Officer Commanding D Company to Officer Commanding second platoon."

0830 — 8:30 A.M.

off collar — Off-color, pale; that is, ill.

off-colour — Feeling sick.

"Oggi, sempre" — Italian for "Today, always."

Oratory — Brompton Oratory, near the Victoria and Albert Museum, in London. The formal name of this Roman Catholic chapel is the Oratory of Saint Philip Neri.

O.R.s — Other ranks; that is, for ranks other than commissioned officers. In American, "enlisted men."

0700 — 7:00 A.M.

0730 — 7:30 A.M.

Our Lady of Lourdes — Bernadette Soubirous, later canonized as Saint Bernadette, experienced apparitions of the Virgin Mary at Lourdes in France in 1858. A shrine was built there to honor the Virgin and is a popular goal of pilgrims. The waters of the springs at the shrine are said to have cured many ill people.

PAD — Passive Air Defense; that is, cover provided against air attacks.

padlocked — Wearing a chastity belt.

Papistry — Referring to the office of pope; a derogatory term for Roman Catholicism.

Paschendael — Correctly spelled Passchendaele, a village in northern Belgium and the locale of intense battles in 1917.

Pathans — Muslim tribes mainly in Afghanistan.

penal years — The years beginning with King Henry VIII's break with the Roman Catholic church in the sixteenth century. Harsh restrictions were imposed. People were obliged to acknowledge the English monarch as head of the church, attend Anglican services, etc. The Catholic mass was forbidden.

Severe civil penalties, imprisonment, and even, in some cases, death were imposed. The penal laws punished not only Roman Catholics but also, until the Toleration Act of 1689, Protestant Nonconformists. Catholic emancipation from various restrictions was not fully achieved in England until 1829.

At Philippi — Philippi was a city in Macedonia where the armies of Antony and Octavius defeated Brutus and his followers in 42 B.C. "At Philippi" is an effective recurrent phrase in Shakespeare's *Julius Caesar*. In the play the ghost of the murdered Caesar appears to Brutus and promises to meet him at Philippi.

piling arms — Stacking rifles upright, muzzle to muzzle. The drill takes two pages to relate in the traditional British *Manual of Elementary Drill (All Arms)*. In the next paragraph Apthorpe quotes part of it: "... the odd numbers of the front rank will seize the rifles of the even numbers...." More of the drill is quoted in *MA* and in *OG*. *OG* ends with Color-Sergeant Oldenshaw leading the exercise, a rather pointless one, given the fighting methods of World War II.

pips — Diamond-shaped insignia on the shoulders of an army officer's uniform designating his rank.

Podesta — During the Fascist period in Italy under Mussolini, the principal magistrate or mayor of a town or commune.

Pope Pius — Pope Pius IX, who reigned 1846–78.

Popular Front — An organization composed of left-wing political parties allied against fascism. In England the movement was espoused by Sir Stafford Cripps.

pounding the square — Drilling on the barracks square, or parade ground.

J. B. Priestley's novels — See Glossary under *BM, Priestley*.

Providence — Divine guidance in daily life.

pull through — See Glossary under *POMF, rifles to be pulled through*.

Q side — Quartermaster.

Quantocks ... Blackdown Hills — Regions in Somerset.

racé — Thoroughbred.

R.A.M.C. — Royal Army Medical Corps.

requiem — A Roman Catholic Mass said for the repose of the soul of a deceased person.

Richelieu — A French battleship based at Dakar. See Waugh's *Diaries*, p. 481.

Rising of '45 — Charles Edward Stuart (1720–88), popularly known as "Bonnie Prince Charlie," commenced a rebellion in Scotland in 1745, the goal of which was to return the Stuart family to the throne of England (his grandfather King James II had been deposed in 1688). After winning several victories, Bonnie Prince Charlie's armies were crushed at the Battle of Culloden on April 16, 1746. Charles eventually returned to the Continent, and his cause never again seriously revived.

R.N.V.R. — Royal Naval Volunteer Reserve.

rocket — See Glossary under *POMF*.

Rodin's Burghers — Auguste Rodin (1840–1917), French sculptor. One of his most artistic creations is *The Burghers of Calais*.

Rosslyn Park — A London amateur football club founded in Hampstead in 1879. Evelyn's brother, Alec, played for the team in the 1920s.

RT — Radio telephony.

a second Ruskin — John Ruskin (1819–1900), who taught classes in art and practical craftsmanship at Oxford, actually had his students do pick-and-shovel work on a road.

"il Santo Inglese" — Italian for "the English saint."

scamped — Stolen.

Scobie — The protagonist in Graham Greene's novel *The Heart of the Matter* (1948).

scrape — Go to confession; that is, in the Roman Catholic church, to relate one's sins to a priest in the Sacrament of Penance. The word derives from Old English, meaning 'to erase'; hence sins are erased through the Sacrament.

scratch — A substitute, makeshift.

send in my papers — Request a discharge.

1700 — 5:00 P.M.

Severn — A river which rises in Wales, flows westward, and then curves southwest until it empties into the Bristol Channel.

Sèvres — Porcelain; see Glossary under *BR*.

sham-Augustan prose — The Augustan period in England (imitative of the Augustan period in Rome, 27 B.C.–A.D. 14) occurred in the early half of the eighteenth century and featured such authors as Joseph Addison, Richard Steele, Jonathan Swift,

THE GLOSSARY

and Alexander Pope. The Augustans emphasized lucidity, precision, moderation, and polished urbanity. Waugh is satirizing Churchill by claiming that his prose is fake Augustan.

"shooting a line" — Slang for "exaggerating."

"Sia lodato Gesu Cristo" — Italian for "Jesus Christ be praised."

simpatico — Italian signifying in special harmony and friendship with another person.

643202 — An ordnance map is divided into squares and has numbers along the borders of all four sides. As Donald Greene has written to me: "In Waugh's time the square would have been in miles, not kilometres." The number 643202 "would indicate a point in the map square bounded by line 64 on the west and line 20 on the south, and $^3/_{10}$ of a mile east of line 64 and $^2/_{10}$ of a mile north of line 20."

Snap — See Glossary under *BM, animal snap*. The meaning here is that the medals match, demonstrating the identity of religious faith despite the disparity of condition and rank.

Somaliland — An area in east Africa. The British had established part of it, on the south shore of the Gulf of Aden, as a protectorate.

"start all over again from your beginnings and never breathe a word about your loss" — Lines from Rudyard Kipling's poem "If." The phrase actually begins, "start again at your beginnings..."

stone — Monument.

stony — Short for *stone-broke*, having no money.

sub judice — Under litigation in a court.

Sucking up — Playing up to, or being obsequious, to win favor and privilege.

Suora Tomasina — Italian for Sister Tomasina.

syndicates — Military groups working together to solve a military problem or to plan an action.

Tablet — A British Catholic weekly newspaper. Waugh often contributed to it after 1936.

TEWTS — Tactical Exercises Without Troops.

1300 — 1:00 P.M.

"'Tis Invercauld comes yonder..." — Lines spoken by characters in the film, the "Rising of '45," which Guy Crouchback had seen in his youth. There are several references to Prince Charles in the film.

Mr. Toad in the *Wind in the Willows* — In Kenneth Grahame's children's classic, published in 1908, Mr. Toad is a country squire who, although conceited, is essentially kindly.

Troy — An ancient city in Asia Minor, the scene of the famous war between the Trojans and the Greeks.

twelve hundred hours — 12:00 noon.

VADs — See Glossary under *VB*.

Vale — Latin for "Farewell"; that is, the last year in school.

valse — Waltz

Vincent de Paul Society — An organization, founded in Paris in 1833, whose function is to help the poor. It was named for Vincent de Paul (ca. 1581–1660), a Roman Catholic priest who devoted his life to charitable works among the needy and was later canonized.

Wallace Collection — Sir Richard Wallace (1818–90), a wealthy British art collector, willed his collection to England. It is now exhibited in Hertford House, in London.

War House — See *War Office*, below.

War Office — The central military headquarters in London.

wettest fellows — Most stupid and dullest individuals.

"Where is the best place to hide a leaf? In a tree" — An allusion to lines from G. K. Chesterton's story "The Broken Sword" in the collection entitled *The Innocence of Father Brown*. The precise quotation is: "Where does a wise man hide a leaf? In the forest."

White Man's Grave — Africa was often given this appellation because so many white colonizers, missionaries, etc., died there of malaria and other tropical diseases.

"Wipers" — A mispronunciation and misspelling of Ypres, a town in Belgium where several destructive battles were fought in World War I. British troops incorrectly pronounced Ypres as "Wipers"; hence the spelling.

"Would you like to sin..." — Verse about Elinor Glyn, English novelist, in whose novel *Three Weeks* (1907) a seduction takes place on a tiger skin. The author of this jingle is anonymous.

Xenophon — See Glossary under *POMF*.

Zionist — One who wished to set up an independent Jewish state in Palestine.

Zululand — A region in southern Africa, now part of Natal.

LOVE AMONG THE RUINS (1953)

The title is taken from Robert Browning's poem "Love Among the Ruins" (1855), in which a large and dominating city has been destroyed. Browning's narrator will meet a girl with "yellow hair" to illustrate that love is superior to wealth, power, and other aspects of life. The area is now rural, and in the second and third lines of the poem we learn that sheep graze over "Miles and miles / On the solitary pastures." Waugh very likely chose the name of his protagonist from these lines. Further, Miles's girl friend, Clara, has a blonde beard; but, unlike the situation in Browning's poem, love comes to ruin.

Dedicatee

John McDougall was a publisher and a close friend of Waugh's. The translation of the dedication is "a friend who sits in the place of a parent." Not only does this suggest the usual meaning of "takes the place of a parent for me," but also it literally refers to McDougall's filling the late Arthur Waugh's (Evelyn's father) editorial direction of Chapman and Hall. McDougall joined Chapman and Hall in 1946.

beak—Slang for magistrate.
Bevan-Eden Coalition—A reference to British political figures Aneurin Bevan (1897–1960) and Sir Anthony Eden (1897–). Bevan was a leader of the Labour party, and Eden (whom Waugh usually referred to as "Jerk") was a Conservative party leader and later Prime Minister (1955–57). Although of different parties, they became friendly. Waugh portrays their followers as uniting to impose on England the horrors of the "brave new world." It may seem strange to some casual readers of Waugh that Conservative Anthony Eden is treated unfavorably here. Contrary to the belief of such readers and even of some critics, Waugh was not a supporter of the Conservative party. He was especially distressed that both the Labourites and the Conservatives "sold out" Eastern Europe to communism. Eden's invitation to Marshal Tito, Yugoslavia's Communist dictator, to visit England understandably irritated Waugh.
birds—Persons; in British slang, women.

cribs—Burglaries, specifically, the safes that had been opened.
Crown Derby—An extremely expensive design of chinaware, often treasured as an heirloom.

done in—Killed.

fist in Barcelona—The clenched-fist sign indicating support of the Republican side in the Spanish Civil War. See Glossary under Short Stories, "The Major Intervenes" (also entitled "Compassion"), *Attlee Brigade*.

He had made a desert in his imagination which he might call peace—An allusion to Tacitus, *Agricola*, line 30: "Ubi solitudinem faciunt, pacem appellant," Latin for "Where they [the Romans] make a desert, they call it peace."
Horizon—See Glossary under *LO*.
Housewives' Union—A militant group of Englishwomen of the late 1940s and 1950s who protested vehemently against rigid controls of food and clothing by the Labour government. Leftist writers and speakers were very hostile to the union.
hymeneal—Referring to Hymen, the Roman god of marriage, represented by a torch (illustrated in the

hardcover edition) to ignite the fires of matrimonial love.

Janissary—A Turkish soldier of the sultan's guard, originally organized in the Middle Ages. They grew in power and became undisciplined until they were finally dispersed in the nineteenth century.

Junker—A member of the German army officer caste which originated in powerful Prussian landowning families. Junkers were known for their ruthless and rigid militaristic attitudes.

lag—Convict.

the Last Viceroy—Lord Louis Mountbatten (1900–79), formerly Prince Louis of Battenberg, later Earl Mountbatten of Burma. He was appointed by the Labour government of Clement Attlee as Viceroy of India to effect the independence of India from British rule in 1947 (an action which Waugh, like many others of conservative bent, deplored). Although a cousin of the sovereign and a leading military commander in World War II, Mountbatten was regarded by Conservatives with suspicion as a radical. In a bitter piece of irony he (and members of his family) were assassinated in 1979 by the Irish Republican army as symbols of British despotism.

Left Book Club—An organization for subscribers who had leftist or Socialist beliefs. It was started by publisher Victor Gollancz in 1936.

Moor—The prison in Devon's Dartmoor region, noted for its mists, bleakness, and eeriness. Arthur Conan Doyle used this setting for *The Hound of the Baskervilles*.

New Writing—An anthology published about twice a year from 1936 to 1940. It was edited by John Lehmann and encouraged avant-garde poems, stories, etc.

nineteen stone—One stone, the normal British unit of human weight, equals fourteen pounds.

nipper—Small child.

Nissen hut—See Glossary under *BR*.

"On such a night as this"—The romantic opening scene of act 5 of Shakespeare's *The Merchant of Venice*.

"post coitum tristis"—The full quotation is "Post coitum omne animal triste est," Latin for "After sexual intercourse every animal is sad." In *The Oxford Dictionary of Quotations*, the author of the line is listed as unknown. Waugh changes the neuter *triste*, agreeing with "animal," to the masculine *tristis*, agreeing with "Miles."

purposeless obstruction of stone—The Cenotaph, the national memorial to the British dead in World War I (and later World War II) which stands in the middle of Whitehall. It was the custom of men who passed it on the street to raise their hats in tribute to what it stands for.

put down—Killed.

quiversful of boys to Winchester and New College—From Psalm 127: "Lo, Children are an heritage of the Lord.... As arrows are in the hand of a mighty man, so are children of the youth. Happy is the man that hath his quiver full of them." Sometimes used half-ironically of the traditionally large families of nineteenth-century Anglican clergymen. Both New College and Winchester were founded by William of Wykeham, and boys going to Oxford from Winchester normally went to New College, where scholarships might be available for them.

Scrubs—Wormwood Scrubs Prison, in London.

sparklers—Diamonds.

Spender—Stephen Spender (1909–), English poet and literary critic. He was active in left-wing causes. Waugh published a savage review of his memoirs; see *The Essays, Articles and Reviews of Evelyn Waugh*, ed. Donat Gallagher, pp. 394–95.

Whitehall—See Glossary under *VB*.

OFFICERS AND GENTLEMEN (1955)

Dedicatee

Major-General Sir Robert Laycock (1907–68) was a military man whom Waugh greatly admired. Among other appointments Laycock was Chief of Combined Operations from 1943 to 1947. For a time Waugh served under him.

AA — Antiaircraft.

ACIGS — Assistant Chief of the Imperial General Staff.

"Accidenti! Porca miseria" — Italian for "Damn, the Devil take you."

act of *pietas* — An act of respect and duty.

ADS — Advanced Dressing Station.

Afridi — Mountaineering Pathans who lived in the Afghanistan-Pakistan border region.

AG — Adjutant General.

"Ah, chère madame..." — French for "Ah, dear lady, you do indeed look like a movie star today."

ALCs — Assault Landing Crafts.

Alex — Alexandria, Egypt.

AMGOT — Allied Military Government of Occupied Territory.

ARP — See Glossary under *POMF*.

A.T. — [Women's] Auxiliary Territorial Service. In World War I W.A.A.C. (Women's Army Auxiliary Corps) was used.

Ali Baba's lamp — Waugh appears to be confusing two stories in the *Arabian Nights*. Aladdin was involved with the magic lamp that would provide him with everything he wanted, while Ali Baba learned the magic words "Open Sesame" to obtain treasures from the forty thieves.

All Souls' Day — November 2. In Roman Catholic practice a day devoted to prayer for the souls in purgatory. Masses, prayers, and other pious practices are designed to release souls from their temporary stay in purgatory and send them to heaven.

Alpes-Maritimes — A department of southeastern France bordering Italy and Monaco.

Alsatian — A native of Alsace, in France.

"Anglais"... "Par-là" — French for "English... through there."

annexation of the Baltic republics — The Russians aggressively seized control of Latvia, Estonia, and Lithuania.

Anti-Comintern Pact — An agreement between Japan and Germany signed on November 25, 1936, allying them against the Communist nations included in the Comintern (the Third Communist International).

Armageddon — A final war between the forces of good and evil. Cf. Revelations 16.

Ayrshire — A county in southwestern Scotland.

back-benchers — Less influential members of the House of Commons, who sit in the rear.

Battle of Britain — A series of air battles (August to October, 1940) between the British and German air forces. In these encounters the effective achievements of the British prevented the Germans from ultimately invading England.

being fly — being shrewd, wily.

Benghazi — A port in Libya on the Mediterranean Sea.

BGS — Brigadier, General Staff.

Bisley — A village in Surrey, near the town of Woking. It has been the location of rifle shooting competition, the National Rifle Association having set up a range there in 1890. Winners of the annual international sharpshooting contests at Bisley have always received much acclaim. The point is that Hound's

THE GLOSSARY

failures at horsemanship at Sandhurst were compensated for, in the mind of the army, by his successes as a marksman.

blue jobs—See Glossary under *MA*.

B.M.—See Glossary under *MA*.

boiled—Got very angry.

Bonnet—See Glossary under *VB*.

Bonnie Prince Charlie—See Glossary under *MA*, *the rising of '45*.

Borghese gardens—An attractive park and leisure area in Rome. Among other things it features an impressive art gallery.

Boulestin's *Conduct of Kitchen*—A book on French cookery (1925) by Marcel Boulestin, who in addition to being a distinguished chef was also the proprietor of Boulestin's Restaurant, in London.

Jerome [Hieronymus] Bosch—A Flemish artist (ca. 1450–1516) who specialized in macabre and grotesque paintings.

Brazzaville—A port town on the Congo River, in Middle Congo (now the People's Republic of the Congo).

Brendan's—The reference is to Brendan Bracken (1901–58), who became Minister of Information in the British cabinet in 1941. In American editions of *OG* the word is misspelled Brendon's. The correct form, Brendan's, appears in the English editions I have examined.

broke his Lenten fast—For centuries it was customary for Roman Catholics to follow laws of fasting and abstinence (from meat) from Ash Wednesday to noon on Holy Saturday. Thus Mr. Crouchback ends his fast at lunchtime on the day before Easter. Since the Second Vatican Council, the rules on fast and abstinence in the Roman church have been considerably liberalized; e.g., there is no fast or abstinence on Holy Saturday.

Rupert Brooke—Poet-patriot of World War I; see Glossary under *POMF*.

"**Ça, madame, c'est génial**"—French for "Now, madame, that is inspired."

Canea—Seaport on the northern coast of Crete, the scene of heavy fighting and much destruction in May, 1941.

Cape Town—A South African port city on the Atlantic Ocean.

Catalan refugees—Soldiers from Catalonia, a region in northeastern Spain.

Cavafy—Constantine Cavafy (1863–1933), Greek poet who lived most of his life in Alexandria.

"**Cè scappato il capitano**"—Italian for "The captain has escaped."

"**Cè scappata la mucca**"—Italian for "The cow has got out." Various editions have errors in some Italian quotations. I have given the correct forms in this and subsequent references.

Challoner—Richard Challoner (1691–1781), prominent English Catholic bishop and author. He is best remembered for his devotional manual *Garden of the Soul*.

"**Charlie copped it**"—a reference to the wounded New Zealand brigade major in the commandeered car.

Chartreuse de Parme—One of Stendhal's greatest novels (1839).

"**Chère madame, quel...**"—French for "Dear lady, how droll your basket."

Child Roland to the dark tower—An allusion to Robert Browning's poem "Childe Roland to the Dark Tower Came" (1855). It is the story of a brave knight who reaches a tower although he has despaired of succeeding in his quest. *Child* is a misprint in many editions of *OG*.

chits—Notes or vouchers.

C.I.G.S.—Chief of the Imperial General Staff.

C-in-C—Commander-in-chief.

Circe—In Greek mythology, an enchantress who could turn men into swine.

clear as the horn of Roland—Roland was at first too proud to blow his horn to call for help; later when he decides to sound the horn, it is too late to save the rear guard. See allusion in chap. 4, "the gorge of Roncesvalles."

Commander-in-Chief—Field Marshal Archibald Percival Wavell, who was at this time commander-in-chief of the British forces in the Middle East.

Concorso Ippico—An arena in Rome for horse races and horse competitions.

conform—That is, agree that Henry VIII, not the Pope, was the head of the English church and accept the other doctrinal and liturgical changes introduced by the King and his supporters.

construe—Translate with an emphasis on knowing the syntax of each sentence.

CP oblique RX [CP/RX]—A military code file reference. It is not listed in any of the various dictionaries of abbreviations. Several correspondents were unable to agree about the precise meaning of the last two initials. The most probable meaning is "Command Post/Rush to X Commando unit."

Gordon Craig...Maeterlinck — Edward Gordon Craig (1872–1966), British theatrical figure. He introduced many new lighting and scenic effects to the British stage, using various stage levels, and stark Greek dramalike forms. His styles were perfectly adapted to the dreamy, symbolistic work of Maurice Maeterlinck (1862–1949), Belgian playwright and poet.

crofters — Small tenant farmers in the highlands of Scotland.

CSM — See Glossary under *MA*. In *SOH* the initials G.S.M. (Garrison Sergeant-Major) are substituted.

dekko — See Glossary under *OG*.

Deposition — The removal of Christ's body from the Cross.

D.L.F. — Director of Land Forces.

Don't, Mr. Disraeli — A comic novel (1940) by Caryl Brahms and S. J. Simon, set in the Victorian period. Caryl Brahms was a pseudonym of Doris Caroline Abrahams.

Downside...Abbey — See Glossary under *MA*.

DPS — Director of Personal Services.

DQMG — Deputy Quartermaster General. In *SOH* the initials DAQMG (Deputy Assistant Quartermaster General) are correctly used. THe DQMG is a highly placed staff officer at Army Headquarters in London.

DSD — Director of Staff Duties.

D.S.O. — Distinguished Service Order.

Duke of York's Steps — Granite steps leading up to the Duke of York's Column, which stands near London's Saint James's Park. The column is a memorial to King George III's son Frederick, Duke of York, long Commander-in-Chief of the British army.

Durban — See Glossary under *BM*.

"The earth is the Lord's and the emptiness thereof" — A parody of Psalm 24, which begins, "The earth is the Lord's and the fullness thereof."

Easter duties — A member of the Roman Catholic Church was required to go to confession and communion at least once a year between the first Sunday of Lent and Trinity Sunday.

"Et pour..." — French for "Now to begin...smoked salmon."

"Excusez-moi, mon père..." — French for "Pardon me, father, is there a priest who speaks English or Italian?"

Exultet — A Latin prayer said during the traditional Roman Catholic church services on Holy Saturday: "Exultet jam angelica turba caelorum: exultent divina mysteria; et pro tanti regis victoria, tuba insonet salutaris" ("Let now the heavenly troop of angels rejoice; let the divine mysteries be joyfully celebrated; and let a sacred trumpet proclaim the victory of so great a king").

factor — One who is paid to look after the land of the owner.

fender — A fencelike barrier in front of a fireplace.

"Fine Flower of the Nation" — The precise wording has not been identified, although the thought is not new. The *OED*, for example, records a quotation from the sixteenth-century schoolmaster Richard Mulcaster: "Noblemen, which be the flowre of gentilitie." Did Waugh perhaps pick Boy Mulcaster's name in *BR* with the contrasting irony in mind?

Fleet Street — The heart of the London newspaper district.

Forster...*Guide*" — E. M. Forster (1879–1970) wrote a classic guide to Alexandria.

"Français" — "French."

Gallipoli — See Glossary under *BR*.

Gestapo — The vicious and dreaded Nazi secret police.

GHQME — General Headquarters, Middle East.

Gib — Gibraltar.

G.O.C.s — General Officers Commanding.

Gorbals — See Glossary under *BR*.

gorge of Roncesvalles — Roncevales was a village in Spain where the rearguard of Charlemagne's army led by Roland was defeated. See Glossary below, *Roland*.

grand couturier — A high-class dress designer.

Great West Road — The main highway leading west from London.

Green Jackets — The King's Royal Rifle Corps and the Rifle Brigade.

Greswold major — The older of the two Greswold brothers at the school.

GSO I — General Staff Officer (grade I).

Gyppy — Egyptian.

THE GLOSSARY

Hamilton-Grand—A fictional name—a search of the British army lists failed to turn up this name. In English editions it is printed Hamilton-Brand.

Helen and Menelaus—Helen was the wife of King Menelaus. She was kidnapped by Paris and carried off to Troy. After the Greeks won the war, she returned to her husband.

"Here, my dear Watson"—An imitation of Sherlock Holmes addressing his associate, Dr. Watson.

HLI—Highland Light Infantry.

Holy Saturday—The day before Easter Sunday when the lengthy morning services were held in the traditional Roman Catholic ritual. After Vatican Council II (1962–65), the Saturday services were shifted to the evening and shortened.

H.O.O.—Hazardous Offensive Operations. Also at times called by Waugh Hostile Offensive Operations.

House—House of Commons.

Hubble-bubble—A water pipe; see Glossary under *BM*.

Hudor. Hydro. Dipsa—Greek root forms for "liquid."

Hussar—A member of a cavalry regiment.

Hypatia—See Glossary under *POMF*.

"I can do it in Greek," said the cabinet minster—In personal correspondence, Donald Greene remarks that the cabinet minister is probably Anthony Eden, who was quite accomplished in Greek, having received special instruction in the language at Eton. He was in Egypt at the time.

"I'm coming. Be of good comfort...put out"—Words spoken by Bishop Hugh Latimer to Bishop Nicholas Ridley—see Glossary under *SKME*, *they were lighting a candle*....

"Je crois bien..."—French for "I know very well you did not find that in Egypt."

"Je veux me confesser..."—French for "I wish to confess, in French if necessary. But I very much prefer English or Italian if possible."

Jerries—See Glossary under *POMF*.

Jocks—The Scotch.

Juno **copped it**—A reference to the British destroyer *Juno*, which was sunk by German warplanes off Crete on May 27, 1941.

Khartoum...Kitchener—Khartoum is a city in the Sudan where British general Horatio Kitchener (1850–1916) won an impressive victory over the Mahdi and recaptured the city.

Knightsbridge or Windsor—Locations of formal ceremonial military parades at Knightsbridge Barracks, in London, or at Windsor Castle, the royal residence twenty-five miles west of London.

"La vache souterraine? Ou la..."—French for "The underground cow? Or the cow on the Métro [subway]?"

Last Trump—The last trumpet, an allusion to the Day of Judgment; see Glossary under *VB*.

"La veuve?"—French for "The widow?"

Lido—See Glossary under *Sc*.

lighter—A boat or barge used for loading or unloading ships when the ships are anchored a distance away from piers.

Livy—An important Roman historian (59 B.C.–A.D. 17).

L of C—See Glossary under *BR*.

Harold Macmillan—English Conservative political and publishing figure (1894–1987). He served as Prime Minister of Great Britain from 1957 to 1963.

Madame Tussaud's—A museum in London which displays lifelike figures of famous people made from wax.

Mrs. Maisky—The wife of Ivan Maisky, the Russian ambassador to England during World War II.

John Martin—English painter (1789–1854), best remembered for his romantic landscapes.

Maundy Thursday—See Glossary under *BR*.

Max—Max Aitken, Lord Beaverbrook, the Canadian-born head of a vast English newspaper chain. His efforts as Minister of Aircraft Production and later as Minister of Supply in increasing the rate of production of war material contributed greatly to Britain's victory in World War II (though Waugh here disapproves of his support of Russia at the time).

"May his soul..."—A common Roman Catholic prayer for the dead.

ME—Middle East.

MEF—Middle East Forces.

MLC—Motor (vehicle) Landing Craft.

M.M.—Military Medal, awarded for gallantry in action to "other ranks" (enlisted men), not officers. Ludovic (*EB/US*) received the medal for his rescue of Guy and others from Crete and felt guilty about it.

Molotov pact — Vyacheslav Molotov, the Russian diplomat, signed the Soviet-German Nonaggression Pact with the German von Ribbentrop on August 23, 1939. The agreement made Germany and the Soviet Union allies.

mosky — A representation of the Egyptian guide's pronunciation of *mosque*. The guide presumably wishes to give a guided tour.

Nebi Daniel — A mosque in Alexandria.

"Night and day" — A phrase from "Night and Day," the title of one of the most famous songs of American composer Cole Porter (1893–1964). In the next few pages Trimmer sings several words from this song.

"No capitano oggi, signora, Tenente" — Italian for "Not captain now, lady, lieutenant."

No Orchids for Miss Blandish — A very popular tough-detective novel (1939) by James Hadley Chase, the pen name of René Raymond.

obliques of "Badger" — Photographs of the "Badger" Operation.

O.C. Transit Camp — Officer Commanding Transit Camp. See "Dictionary," *Number 6 Transit Camp*.

0500 hrs. — 5:00 A.M.

Old Man — Prime Minister Winston Churchill.

0900 hours — 9:00 A.M.

1000 hours — 10:00 A.M.

1000 to 1100 hours — 10:00 to 11:00 A.M.

Oran — A seaport in Algeria. The British navy attacked the French fleet based there so that the Germans could not make use of the ships.

0615 hours — 6:15 A.M.

0700 hours — 7:00 A.M.

0610 — 6:10 A.M.

packet — Wound.

Palace — St. James's Palace.

partition of Poland — The Molotov pact (see above) enabled the Germans to enter Poland and the Russians to claim the eastern part of that country.

passes of Thessaly — A brave, poetic, and heroic aura, recalling the magnificent efforts of Leonidas and his Spartans in defending the pass from Thessaly against an overwhelmingly superior force of Persians.

Pass of Glencoe — A pass in the highlands of Scotland.

Noel Paton — Sir Joseph Noel Paton (1821–1901), Scottish artist who painted a wide variety of subjects.

Pharaoh and Moses — In the Old Testament the plagues which descend upon the Egyptians force the Pharaoh to allow Moses to lead the Israelites out of Egypt and toward the Promised Land.

Philoctetes — The most celebrated archer in the Trojan War.

Picasso — Pablo Picasso (1881–1973), Spanish artist, best known for his avant-garde abstract paintings.

pigeon — Business, problem.

pig-skin Gladstone — A traveling bag named after British statesman William E. Gladstone.

pinching — Stealing.

pip — See Glossary under *MA*.

P.M. to Secretary of State for War — Prime Minister Winston Churchill to Sir Anthony Eden, then Secretary of State for War. Churchill actually did support an aggressive attack policy toward the Germans. Waugh has changed the wording and, of course, added the fictional Ritchie-Hook. See *EWN*, Autumn, 1975, p. 8.

pongoes — British navy slang for soldiers (from the name of an African ape).

Portsmouth — Important English naval base southwest of London.

putting you on the square — Drilling on the parade ground of the barracks.

Q fellows — The Quartermaster and his staff.

QMG — Quartermaster General.

RAMC — See Glossary under *MA*.

RASC — Royal Army Service Corps.

RDF — Radio direction finder, that is, radar.

Red Flag — A popular English Labour and Communist party song with the refrain "We'll keep the Red Flag flying yet," sung to the tune of "O Tannenbaum" (and "Maryland My Maryland").

resources of the Ukraine — The Ukraine, in the southwestern part of the Soviet Union, is one of the richest agricultural and mineral areas in the world.

Rift Valley — A valley in west Kenya.

Rommel — Erwin Rommel (1891–1944), German military leader known as "the Desert Fox." After winning many tank battles in North Africa, Rom-

THE GLOSSARY

mel's army was eventually defeated by British general Bernard Montgomery's forces at El Alamein.

rosary...three decades — See Glossary under *POMF, tell your beads*. The penance of saying three decades consists of three "Our Fathers," thirty "Hail Marys" and three "Glorias."

RSM — Regimental Sergeant Major.

St. Omers records — An English Catholic college established at Saint Omers, France. It was abolished in the middle of the eighteenth century.

Saint Roger of Waybroke defend us... — In his confusion Guy invokes the aid of Roger, who is not a saint, and recites part of the very popular prayer invoking the aid of Saint Michael the Archangel. This prayer was said in English at the end of the traditional Latin Roman Catholic Mass. This practice was eliminated by the Second Vatican Council.

"Sales Boches!" — French for "Filthy Germans!"

Sandhurst — The British Royal Military College, the English equivalent of West Point.

"*sauve qui peut*" — French for "every man for himself."

Scapa Flow — A sea basin in the Orkney Islands, off the northern coast of Scotland, the location of a large British naval base.

"the Senior" — The familiar name of the United Service Club (founded in 1815, now defunct), to distinguish it from the Junior Army and Navy Club, for regular officers. It was at the southeast corner of Waterloo Place and Pall Mall, very handy to the Admiralty and the War Office.

Simonstown — A town and former British naval base in South Africa.

Sitrep — See Glossary under *OGP*.

SNO — Senior Naval Officer, the naval officer in charge of all shipping in a port.

The Soma — The mausoleum of Alexander the Great.

"Son amant..." — French for "Her lover, without a doubt."

Sphakia — Cape Sphakia, on the northwest coast of Crete.

Spion Cop — A battle fought in Natal in 1900, during the Boer War.

Strand — One of the main streets in London.

Stukas — German dive bombers.

sub specie aeternitatis — See Glossary under *OGP*.

Suda — Suda Bay, on the north coast of Crete; the site of a British base captured by German paratroops in May, 1941.

Tanks for Russia Week — A special week which commenced in British factories on September 22, 1939, when English workers were informed that all their military production from September 22 to 29 would be sent to the Russian front. As a result production greatly increased.

tea was "off" — Tea was no longer being served.

that morning's new fire — In the traditional Roman Catholic service on Holy Saturday morning, a small fire is struck from a flint, and coals are kindled. The fire, emblematic of the light of Christ and His Resurrection, is then blessed. Several prayers are said, the first of which, translated from the Latin, reads, "O God, who through Thy Son, the cornerstone, has bestowed on the faithful the fire of Thy glory, sanctify this new fire produced from a flint that it may be profitable to us: and grant that by this paschal festival we may be so inflamed with heavenly desires, that with pure minds we may come to the feast of perpetual light. Through the same Christ our Lord, Amen."

"They told me, Heraclitus, they told me you were dead..." — See Glossary under *LO*.

Tilsit and Tolstoi — References to Leo Tolstoi's *War and Peace* (1866), in which the treaty of cooperation, signed at Tilsit, between Napoleon and Czar Alexander I — formerly deadly enemies — is shown to change the whole picture of European diplomacy, as did the Molotov-Ribbentrop pact of 1939 (see *Molotov pact* above).

Tipu Sultan's musket — A reference to an Indian ruler (1749–99) more commonly known as Tippoo Sahib. He fought several battles against British forces and was killed in one of these skirmishes.

Tobruk — A seaport in Libya, the scene of several intense battles between British and German forces in World War II. It was successfully defended by the British in 1941 but was captured by the Germans in June, 1942.

toties quoties — Latin for "as often as." On November 2, Roman Catholics could gain this plenary indulgence as often as they made a visit to a church and said the "Our Father," the "Hail Mary," and the "Gloria Patri" six times for the pope's intention. This indulgence also depended on whether the person had been to confession and Mass during a — usually — eight-day period before or after All Souls' Day. This indulgence was applied to the souls in Purgatory; thus a Catholic following the prescribed practices could benefit several souls during the course of November 2. This custom was eliminated by the Second Vatican Council.

Tsarkoe Seloe — The summer palace of the Russian czars outside Leningrad. Now the Pushkin Museum.

Turner — Joseph M. W. Turner (1775–1851), English painter noted for his landscapes.

28/6/41 — R. S. Martin observes that the date given here is in error. He points out that the date should read 28/5/41; cf. *EWN*, Spring, 1957, p. 7. In British practice (unlike American), the number of the day (here 28) precedes that of the month (5).

T/y — Temporary. Donald Greene writes in correspondence: "All wartime commissions were temporary, unlike commissions in the regular (permanent) army during peacetime. At the end of the war, a regular soldier who had reached the wartime rank of brigadier might revert to his permanent rank of major (Tommy Blackhouse, a regular, refers to this possibility). Commissions issued to those who, like Guy, were in the army only for the duration of the war simply lapsed when they were discharged (their holders could be carried for a while afterwards on a non-active reserve basis, subject to possible call-up for active service in case of emergency). Frequently, of course, former temporary officers continued unofficially to use their former titles in civilian life, such as Waugh's riding instructor Captain Hance."

"un peu..." — French for "a little disheveled, no?"

"Very flat Norfolk...Moonlight..." — Quotations from Noel Coward's comic play *Private Lives* (1931). Shortly thereafter the British edition reads: "I was quoting from my favorite play." The American edition reads: "I was quoting from Noel Coward."

Vichy French — The French who supported the German occupation. Marshal Henri Pétain, premier of Unoccupied France, was their leader, with headquarters in the city of Vichy.

ville lumière — French for "lighted city."

"When wilt thou save the people?..." — Lines from "The People's Anthem" by Ebenezer Elliott (1781–1849).

"the Widow Twankey" — A ludicrous figure in pantomime. She is the mother of Aladdin in pantomimes based on that story. The role was usually played by a man.

winkle the mortar out — Displace the mortar from its position.

wogs — See Glossary under *BM*.

W/T — Wireless telegraphy.

Zero plus fifty-two — Fifty-two minutes after zero hour.

zero plus sixty — The beginning of a military operation is scheduled for some particular time, e.g., 0700 hours (7:00 A.M.). This is designated the "zero hour" of the operation, and subsequent events scheduled to take place in the operation are timed from it. Thus "zero plus sixty" would mean "60 minutes after zero hour," which if zero hour were 7:00 A.M., would be 8:00 A.M.

THE ORDEAL OF GILBERT PINFOLD (1957)

Dedicatee

Daphne Fielding (née Vivian, then Viscountess Weymouth and Marchioness of Bath, later Mrs. Alexander Fielding) was a writer friend of Waugh's. Among her books was *The Duchess of Jermyn Street* (1964), a biography of Rosa Lewis, whom Waugh had portrayed as Lottie Crump in *VB*.

Albert Hall — A hall in London in which British fascists (blackshirts) held several meetings in the 1930s.

angst — Anxiety and anguish developed from pondering the tragedies afflicting humanity and the world.

Boucher — François Boucher (1703–70), French artist who was especially interested in subject matter from the Greek and Roman classical periods.

"The Box" — Some English faith-healers possess such boxes. Parts of a person, for example, hairs, are placed in the box; and electromagnetic waves are transmitted therein. It is hoped that cures can thus be produced. Christopher Sykes, in *Evelyn Waugh: A Biography*, p. 359, discusses this point. See also *Diaries*, February 29, 1956.

Brigade tie — Members and former members of the various British military units wear ties of different colors and designs with civilian clothes. This is the tie of the Household Brigade of Foot Guards. See *Guards tie* below.

"cave" — Latin for "Watch out."

Mr. Chadband — The hypocritical minister in Charles Dickens's novel *Bleak House*.

The Cocktail Party — A popular verse play (1949) by T. S. Eliot.

cop it — Receive trouble.

Corybantes — Followers of the goddess Cybele, the Roman mother of the gods, who danced wildly to very loud music.

"Dolce far niente" — Italian for "pleasant idleness."

18 B — The section of British wartime regulations about security whereby those suspected of subversive activity could be put in jail and kept there indefinitely without trial. It was under this section that Diana and Oswald Mosley were incarcerated. See Lady Mosley's autobiography *A Life of Contrasts* (New York, 1977); see also Glossary under *VB*.

Filbert — A nut. "Gilbert the Filbert, the Colonel of the Knuts" was a well-known British music-hall song originally sung by Basil Hallam and was popular before and after World War I.

Fragonard — Jean Fragonard (1732–1806), French artist best remembered for his works portraying romantic love.

Galleface in Colombo — At Galle near Colombo, Sri Lanka (formerly Ceylon) rocky headlands reach the water's edge. *Galleface* refers to the exposed surface of rock.

Goneril? Regan?...Cornwall — Characters in Shakespeare's *King Lear*. Goneril and Regan are the ungrateful and cruel daughters of the king; Cornwall is the husband of Regan.

Philip Henry Gosse — English naturalist (1810–88) who wrote several books on zoology. He was the father of Sir Edmund Gosse (see *LO*, Chap. 1),

THE GLOSSARY

whose autobiographical *Father and Son* gives a vivid picture of him.

gouache — A method of painting with opaque colors that have been mingled with water and gum.

Government Front Bench — The prominent governing party members and the most important opposition members sit on the front benches in the Houses of Parliament.

grazier — A person who oversees the feeding of cattle on the land on which they graze.

Guards tie — A blue-and-red-striped tie worn by three British military units: the Life Guards, the Royal Horse Guards, and the Foot Guards.

HMG — Her Majesty's Government.

Jenkins's ear — An ear of one Captain Jenkins allegedly cut off by Spanish officers while they were searching his ship. The incident caused a brief war between England and Spain in 1739. Misspelled "Jenkin's ear" in some editions.

shrine of Kandy — Kandy is a city in Ceylon (now Sri Lanka). Nearby is a Buddhist shrine (allegedly containing one of Buddha's teeth) which is popular with tourists and religious pilgrims.

knut — A fop.

Lady Day — A feast of the Blessed Virgin Mary; Annunciation Day, March 25.

Lascars — See Glossary under *HD*.

Last Post — A bugle call in the British army indicating the last posting of guards for the night; also used at military funerals, like the American "Taps."

leman — A mistress, or, ironically in this passage, a sweetheart.

Magnasco — Alessandro Magnasco (1667?–1749), Italian artist.

Michaelmas — See Glossary under *BR*.

moonstone — A milk-colored stone considered, and used as, a gem.

Mosley — See Glossary under *POMF*.

old Etonian — One who attended Eton College.
0930 hours — 9:30 A.M.
0312 hours — 3:12 A.M.

Parsee — See Glossary under *BM*.

"Ce Monsieur Pinfold essaie..." — French for "This Mr. Pinfold always attempts to get to see me, and he has tried to get himself introduced to me by several of his friends. Naturally I refused."

"Do you know one sole friend of his? It seems to be that his connections are very ordinary."

"At the beginning, one can always be mistaken about a stranger. We finally realized in Paris that he is not on our social level."

Mr. Pooter at the Mansion House — The likable but continually frustrated clerk who is the central character in *The Diary of a Nobody* (1894), a novel by George and Weedon Grossmith. One of the highlights of Pooter's life is an invitation to a ball at the Mansion House, the official residence of the Lord Mayor of London. He is unhappy when the newspaper account of it misspells his name as "Porter."

Private of the Buffs — See Glossary under *SKME*.

"Pull for the shore" — A phrase from the hymn "Light in the Darkness" ("Life-Boat"), by Philip P. Bliss.

Quisling — A traitor. Major Vidkun Quisling (1887–1945) was a Norwegian who became the puppet leader of Norway during the Nazi occupation during World War II.

rag — A session of teasing and playing jokes.

Raj — Regime, rule (here the British rule of India).

Rhinebeck — A scenic New York village near the Hudson River, in the foothills of the Berkshire Mountains. Many well-to-do people have homes there and use it particularly as a summer resort.

The Rock — Gibraltar.

Rouault — Georges Rouault (1871–1958), French expressionist painter well known for poignantly sad and bitter pictures of, among others, judges and clowns. One of his favorite subjects was Christ's sufferings.

sitrep — Situation report.

Osbert Sitwell — English man of letters (1892–1969), best known for his association with his sister Edith and his brother Sacheverell, as well as for his five-volume autobiography.

S.O.E. — Special Operation Executive, a World War II British organization created to sabotage enemy installations.

sub specie aeternitatis — Latin for "from the point of view of eternal values," that is, a belief in a spiritual purpose emphasizing Judgment and eternity in heaven or hell.

tea train — The early evening train.
tick — An unpleasant person.

Travancore — A region in southwestern Indian.

Up Jenkins — See Glossary under *DF*.

Westward Ho! — A long anti-Catholic historical novel (1855) by Charles Kingsley.
wet — Slang for "extremely foolish" or "amateurish."

THE END OF THE BATTLE (UNCONDITIONAL SURRENDER) (1961)

Dedicatee

Margaret Waugh (born 1942), one of Waugh's three daughters, was said to be his favorite child. In 1962 she married Giles FitzHerbert. She was the author of *The Man Who Was Greenmantle*, a biography of Laura Waugh's father, Aubrey Herbert. She was killed in January, 1986, when she was hit by a car in London.

Absolution — A pronouncement containing the words "absolution of sins" said at the beginning of the traditional mass.

Act of Emancipation — The act of Parliament of 1829 which lifted restrictions on Roman Catholics in England. Penalties against Catholics in England had commenced in the sixteenth century.

Aden — A seaport in Yemen, formerly an important British naval base.

affection for the horse — A liking for horses.

General Alexander — Sir Harold Alexander (1891–1969), prominent English military figure whose distinguished career included service as Commander-in-Chief of the Allied Forces in Italy from November, 1944. Because of his war exploits he was created Earl Alexander of Tunis. After the war he served as Minister of Defence and then as Governor-General of Canada.

All Souls — An Oxford college for scholars. It was not attended by undergraduates.

almoner — A social worker.

Hans Andersen — Danish writer (1805–75) who is best remembered for his fairy tales.

Anglo-Sephardi — English-Jewish. The Sephardim are descendants of Spanish and Portuguese Jews.

A.N. Other — That is, "another." An old British joke to provide anonymity. The superstitious Ludovic does not even want to pronounce Guy Crouchback's name.

Anzio — A seaport on the western coast of Italy. The Allies landed forces there against the Germans and Italians in World War II. Heavy fighting continued from January 22 to May 23, 1944, when the Allies were victorious.

A.O. — Administrative Officer.

Apulia — A region in southeastern Italy.

"Arrivederci" — Italian for "Till we meet again."

Asquith — Herbert Henry Asquith (1852–1928), prominent British Liberal political figure. He was Prime Minister from 1908 to 1916, when he was succeeded by Lloyd George.

A.T. — See Glossary under *OG*.

A/Ty — Acting temporary. Donald Greene observes in correspondence that "Acting" sounds like a redundancy along with "temporary" but is not: "Within the broad category of temporary (wartime) commissions, some were substantive (tenured, as we might say) and some acting (non-tenured). An officer could be reduced from his substantive rank only by action of a court martial trying him for some offence; acting rank, however, could be cancelled merely by administrative action (as happened to Guy, who reverted to lieutenant on occasion — and to Waugh)."

Auchinleck — Sir Claude Auchinleck (1884–1981), English general, Commander-in-Chief in the Middle East, 1941–42. He was succeeded by General Sir Harold Alexander.

awful cloud on Sinai — The smoke that rose from Mount Sinai when God gave Moses the Ten Commandments.

Balaclava helmets — Knitted woollen headgear that covers the neck and forehead as well as the upper part of the shoulders.

THE GLOSSARY

Balliol 1921–1924—That is, he attended Oxford's Balliol College during those years.

Banquo—A general in Shakespeare's play *Macbeth* whom Macbeth has killed because of a prophecy that Banquo's descendants will become kings of Scotland.

Sir James Barrie—Scottish novelist and playwright (1860–1937).

Sylvia Beach—An American patron of letters (1887–1962) who started the famous Shakespeare & Co. Bookshop in Paris. The store became a rendezvous for many famous writers. She was also the pioneer publisher of James Joyce's *Ulysses*.

Benares—See Glossary under *DF*.

Benedictus—Latin for "blessed"; the Canticle of Zachary beginning "Blessed be the Lord God of Israel; because He hath visited and wrought the redemption of His people." The prayer is found in Luke 1:68–79.

bibelots—Small curios, statues, trinkets, and objets d'art.

bloods—Wild, athletic men.

"blotted his copy-book"—See Glossary under *MA*.

Bluebell—Trademark of a polishing compound.

Blues—See Glossary under *MA*.

Bordighera—See Glossary under *BR*.

Borghese Gardens—See Glossary under *OG*.

bowler—Also called "derby," a felt hat with a turned-up brim and a domed top. Waugh himself in later years was partial to this hat and was frequently photographed wearing one.

"British warm"—A short overcoat worn by a British officer.

The bulrushes, the burning bush, the plagues of Egypt—Allusions to the biblical story of Moses. He was placed in a basket in bulrushes and was saved from death by the Pharaoh's daughter, who adopted him. He received a message as God's chosen when he beheld a fiery bush that did not burn. He was later able to have God send ten plagues to Egypt to force the Egyptians to allow the Israelites to leave Egypt. Moses' story is told in the Old Testament in Exodus, Leviticus, Numbers, and Deuteronomy.

Burton's stucco tent—Sir Richard Burton (1821–90), noted English traveler and Arabic specialist, was buried in the Mortlake cemetery. His marble tomb is shaped like an Arab tent. Donald Greene observes in personal correspondence that it is interesting that Waugh calls it "stucco"; it was actually made of marble. "Possibly this is because Burton, in spite of his wife's last minute efforts to convert him [she had a Roman Catholic priest give him the last rites while he was dying—similar to the Lord Marchmain episode], had no particular religion, except possibly an admiration for Islam, and Waugh resented the presence of his spectacular mausoleum in the Mortlake Catholic cemetery." See Donald Greene's "Reality Into Art: Some Detective Notes on Waugh," *EWN*, Spring, 1986, pp. 3–4.

Hall Caine—English novelist (1853–1931), several of whose turn-of-the-century books achieved popularity.

came out—Was presented to society as a debutante.

Canadians...Dieppe—A trial invasion of the European continent was staged in August, 1942, at Dieppe, the French seaport. Most of the attack forces, consisting mainly of Canadian and British troops, with about one hundred American Rangers, were either killed or captured.

Canvey Island—An urban district in Essex, about thirty miles from London.

"The captains and the kings depart"—A line from Rudyard Kipling's poem "Recessional."

Caroline—Of the seventeenth century, signifying the reign of English King Charles I (1625–49).

Boni de Castellane—Count Boniface de Castellane (1867–1932), an international celebrity before and after World War I. He married the heiress of Jay Gould—one of the first marriages of European nobility to American heiresses—and spent her money lavishly. There is a long obituary for him in the *New York Times*, October 20, 1932, p. 21, where he is called "the king of the boulevardiers."

Cathedral—London's Westminster Cathedral, the principal Roman Catholic church in England.

Cavour—Camillo Benso di Cavour (1810–61), Italian political figure and diplomat who achieved considerable success in bringing about a united Italy. The House of Savoy was at the heart of the Risorgimento movement.

censed—Perfumed with incense. Incense is used in Catholic funeral masses and in other rituals. The burning of the incense signifies religious fervor, the aroma symbolizes virtue, and the smoke signifies prayer rising to the throne of God.

Chiang—Chiang Kai-shek (1887–1975), leader of the Chinese Nationalist forces which eventually were driven out of China by Mao-tse-Tung's Communist forces. The Nationalists settled on the island of Taiwan.

Childern.as — December 28, the Feast of the Holy Innocents.

Chindits — The name given to his troops by General Orde Wingate in the British Burma Campaign against the Japanese in World War II. The name was derived from Chinthey, a mythical animal that is half-lion and half-griffin. It is supposed to guard the Burmese from evil spirits.

Churchill...Sphinx — At the Cairo Conference in November–December, 1943, the chief participants were Churchill, Roosevelt, and General Chiang Kai-shek.

Clausewitz — Karl von Clausewitz (1780–1831), a Prussian officer who wrote several books on the art and techniques of waging war.

Coimbra — A city in Portugal.

"Confiteor" — Latin for "I confess," a prayer said at the beginning of the traditional Roman Catholic mass in which one confesses one's sins and asks for forgiveness.

congress at Teheran — Churchill, Roosevelt, and Stalin met at Teheran, in Iran, in November–December, 1943, after the conference at Cairo.

cop one — Wounded or killed in military action.

"Cor...dekko" — Slang meaning roughly "By gosh, just take a look."

Côte d'Azur — See Glossary under Sc. In several editions a final e is incorrectly added to Azur.

Cowes — See Glossary under POMF, Squadron Lawn at Cowes.

"cracking form" — Lively and good-humored.

"Cras, Hora septem" — Latin for "Tomorrow. Seven o'clock."

crimson of a monsignor — A monsignor's robes were edged in crimson to designate his rank.

crossing the Red Sea — The Bible relates that God parted the sea to allow the fleeing Israelites to cross safely. When the pursuing Egyptians entered the channel, the sea closed over them, and they were drowned.

Lord Curzon and Elinor Glyn — The aristocratic first Marquess Curzon (1859–1925), who had, among other distinctions, served as viceroy of India and competed with Stanley Baldwin for the prime ministership, carried on a liaison with novelist Elinor Glyn for several years. He was the stepfather of Waugh's friends Alfred and Herbert Duggan and was Chancellor of Oxford University while Waugh was an undergraduate.

Dakota — The Douglas C-47 plane, the famous DC-3, used by the military to carry cargo or troops.

Dalmatia — See Glossary under H.

Darby and Joan — Two people who have been happily married for a long time. The names originated in an old English ballad.

De Profundis — Latin for "out of the depths"; a prayer (Psalm 129) commencing, "Out of the depths, I have cried unto Thee, O Lord."

"Dies Irae" — Latin for "Day of Wrath," a long medieval hymn forming the Sequence of the traditional Roman Catholic requiem Mass. It refers to the Day of Judgment, when God will appear to reward the just and punish the evildoers by sending them to hell.

Dispersal — The spread of the Jewish people to various countries outside Palestine after the Babylonian captivity.

"The dog it was that died" — See Glossary under POMF.

Dominican...Advent — The Dominicans, a religious order in the Roman Catholic Church, are especially known for their preaching. Advent is the period before Christmas, beginning on the fourth Sunday before the feast. It is common in the Roman Catholic Church and in some other churches to have special devotions, services, and sermons during Advent to prepare parishioners for the feast commemorating Christ's birth.

"douceur de vivre" — French for "sweetness of living."

drabs — Prostitutes.

"Major Dracula" — Dracula connoted "mysterious" and "scary" after the title character in Bram Stoker's novel *Dracula* (1897), about a vampire who thirsted for human blood and, of course, could not face sunlight.

D.T.'s — See Glossary under DF.

Eaton Terrace — A street in the fashionable Belgravia area of London.

1130 hours — 11:30 A.M.

"Entrate e s'accomode" — Italian for "Come in and make yourself comfortable." *Entrate* is plural and should correctly be *entra*. Waugh is satirizing the

THE GLOSSARY

language deficiencies of the officer, who is supposed to be an expert in Italian.

"Et uxor tua?"—Latin for "And your wife?"

"Facilius loqui latine..."—Latin for "It is easier to speak Latin. This is for a Mass. My wife is dead." It is a custom in Roman Catholicism to have masses said for the dead so that the soul may, through the prayers and the efficacy of the Eucharist, be soon released from Purgatory. Money or some other offering is made to the priest who says the masses. Some editions have an incorrect *latina*.

factotum—Latin for "do everything"; a servant who handles a wide variety of responsibilities.

F.A.N.Y.—First Aid Nursing Yeomanry service. In some editions it is misprinted with a second *N*.

Scott Fitzgerald—F. Scott Fitzgerald (1896–1940), American novelist and short-story writer. He portrayed the flappers and playboys of the roaring twenties, and his subject matter has several affinities with Waugh's.

"Fin de Ligne"—French for "End of the Line."

Flaxman—See Glossary under *POMF*.

floater—See Glossary under *Sc*.

Foggia—A city in southeastern Italy.

Fowler—Henry Fowler (1858–1933), English language expert whose *Modern English Usage* (first published in 1926) is a standard guide to correct style.

Fragonard—See Glossary under *OGP*.

Franco—Francisco Franco (1892–1975), Spanish dictator; see Glossary under *BR*.

Fuseli—Henry Fuseli (1741–1825), an artist. Although he was born in Switzerland, Fuseli did most of his painting in England.

G.S.O. 2—General Staff Officer, grade 2.

G. 2—That is, GSO2 (Coordination); Major Grace-Groundling-Marchpole, as it turns out.

Mrs. Gamp—A nurse in Charles Dickens's novel *Martin Chuzzlewit*. She always carried an umbrella and quoted a mythical Mrs. Harris, whose views supported hers.

Garden of the Soul—A popular book of prayers by Roman Catholic Bishop Richard Challoner (1691–1781), first published in 1740.

Garibaldi—Giuseppe Garibaldi (1807–82). Italian military figure who fought for the independence and unification of Italy. He won many battles as a guerrilla leader both in South America and in Italy. He was a soldier, not a political tactician.

gazetted—Said of one whose appointment is announced in the official *London Gazette*.

Gestapo—The vicious Nazi secret police.

give him socks—Eric Partridge's *Dictionary of Slang* explains that this expression means "beat or thrash soundly."

Mr. Gladstone—William E. Gladstone (1809–98), prominent Liberal British political figure who served as Prime Minister on four separate occasions.

"the Grace of God is in courtesy"—A line from Hilaire Belloc's poem "Courtesy."

Grand Hotel in Rome—There is a statue of Moses near the Grand Hotel.

"Gratias"—Latin for "Thanks."

"Gratias tibi. Dominus tecum"—Latin for "Thanks to you. The Lord be with you.

Grimm—Jacob Grimm (1785–1863) and Wilhelm Grimm (1786–1859), brothers who wrote fairy tales.

Habsburg Empire—A powerful dynasty of rulers of Austria-Hungary. Through intermarriage and other associations additional countries, such as Spain and Flanders, were at times allied. This dynasty began during the Renaissance and collapsed after World War I.

hatchment—A panel which holds the coat of arms of a dead person. The insignia is displayed only temporarily.

heart-to-hearter—A heart-to-heart, or confidential, talk.

Hemingway...Bret—Brett, Lady Ashley, was the unfulfilled and tragic heroine of Ernest Hemingway's novel *The Sun Also Rises* (1926), which depicted members of the so-called lost generation.

Cardinal Hinsley—Arthur Hinsley (1865–1943), the Roman Catholic cardinal of England during part of World War II.

"Ho visitato Sicilia, poi..."—Italian for "I have visited Sicily; then I have lived for a good while on the Ligurian coast. I have travelled in almost every part of Italy."

House—House of Commons.

House of Savoy—A dynasty that ruled parts of Italy and France from the Middle Ages to the end of

THE END OF THE BATTLE

World War II. The House of Savoy was at the heart of the Risorgimento movement.

"Ingemisco, tamquam reus..." — Latin for "Guilty, now I pour my moaning; / all my shame with anguish owning; / Spare, O God, Thy suppliant groaning."

"In memoria aeterna..." — Latin words from the Gradual of the traditional Roman Catholic requiem Mass: "The just shall be in everlasting remembrance; he shall not fear evil hearing." The words are taken from Psalm 111.

International Brigade — A Communist-organized volunteer army with members from Britain, the United States, France, and other countries who fought for the Republican side in the Spanish Civil War against Franco, who was aided by Hitler and Mussolini. The brigade was organized by the Comintern in Paris in 1936 and was disbanded in 1938.

Iris Storm — The declassée, ill-fated heroine of *The Green Hat* (1924), by Michael Arlen (1895-1956).

"It's a mad world, my masters" — A line from *Western Voyage*, by John Taylor (1580-1653).

Henry James — See Glossary under *LO*.

Jugs — Slang for Yugoslavians (often spelled Jugoslavians).

Kafka — See Glossary under *LO*.

Omar Khayyam — A Persian poet of the eleventh century. His *Rubaiyat* was popularized in a free translation by Edward Fitzgerald in 1859.

King-in-Exile — King Peter II of Yugoslavia (1923-70). When the Germans conquered the principal areas of Yugoslavia, the king set up headquarters in England. He never returned to power because after the war Yugoslavia was controlled by Tito and his Communist forces.

Klee — Paul Klee (1879-1940), Swiss artist whose paintings are extremely colorful and stress a dreamlike world of fantasy.

Knights of Malta — See Glossary under *WS*.

Kyrie — The prayer beginning with the Greek words "Kyrie eleison" ("Lord have mercy"). It is a brief litany said or sung shortly after the beginning of the Roman Catholic Mass.

Lady Cripps's Fund — Money raised to help the Chinese. The fund was named for Lady Cripps, wife of Sir Stafford Cripps (1889-1952), ambassador to the Soviet Union and later Chancellor of the Exchequer in the postwar British Labour government.

Lateran Treaty — An agreement between the Vatican and the Italian government signed on February 11, 1929, granting Vatican City the status of a sovereign state. Pope Pius XI was reigning at the time.

Léger — Fernand Léger (1881-1955), French artist involved in the cubist movement.

"like a beautiful and ineffectual angel beating in the void his luminous wings in vain" — The reference is to Shelley and occurs in Matthew Arnold's *Essays in Criticism, Second Series*.

"Lì per me..." — Italian for "There for me everything will go smoothly."

"locum refrigerii, lucis et pacis" — Latin for "a place of comfort, light and peace." This phrase is from the Memento of the Dead prayer of the traditional Roman Catholic Mass. It reads: "Memento etiam, Domine, famulorum famularumqae tuarum N. et N. [here the names of the people prayed for are inserted], qui nos praecesserunt cum signo fidei, et dormiunt in somno pacis. Ipsis, Domine, et omnibus in Christo quiescentibus, locum refrigerii, lucis et pacis, ut indulgeas, deprecamur. Per eumdem Christum Dominum nostrum. Amen" ("Be mindful, O Lord, also of Thy servants and handmaids N. and N., who have gone before us with the sign of faith, and rest in the sleep of peace. To these, O Lord, and to all who sleep in Christ, we beseech Thee to grant of Thy goodness, a place of comfort, light and peace. Through the same Christ our Lord. Amen." Guy is obviously remembering his father's recent death and the funeral service as he parachutes to earth and experiences "a foretaste of paradise," which his father is now enjoying in heaven.

"Locust Years" — "And I will restore to you the years that the locust hath eaten." Joel 2:25.

Logan Pearsall Smith — American-born English man of letters (1865-1946), especially known for his essay writing and concern for prose style.

magistras — The chiefs.

Marchesa Casati — Marchesa Luisa Casati, a wealthy Italian noblewoman who gave lavish and bizarre entertainments. She eventually fell on hard times and had to be supported by friends in a very modest style. Harold Acton describes her in *Memoirs of an Aesthete, 1939-1969* (New York, 1970), pp. 40-42.

Peter Quennell also furnishes some data in his *Customs and Characters* (Boston, 1982), pp. 78–80.

Mihajlovic — Draža Mihajlović (1893–1946), Yugoslavian leader of guerrilla troops (called Chetniks) against the Germans. His differences with Tito and the British preference for Tito's guerrillas over his forces led him into collaboration with the Axis powers. He was executed after the war.

"Miles Anglicus sum" — Latin for "I am an English soldier."

missal — A book containing the prayers and liturgy of the Mass. Missals often printed the Latin side by side with the English translation.

M.M. — See Glossary under *OG*, book 2, chap. 2.

Captain Montagu — English Captain James Montagu (1752–94), who was killed in a battle against French forces near the island of Ushant on June 1, 1794.

Montenegrin — A native of Montenegro, formerly a kingdom in southern Yugoslavia. In Tito's Communist arrangement after World War II, Montenegro became a federated part of Yugoslavia.

Monty — Field Marshal Bernard Montgomery, a leading English military commander in World War II.

Mortlake — The burial occurred in Saint Mary Magdalen Churchyard, a Catholic cemetery in the Mortlake section of London.

Mussolini — See Glossary under *MA*.

Mystical Body — In Roman Catholic teaching, the church is the Mystical Body of Christ. Christ is the head, and the members of the church constitute the body.

NBG — See Glossary under *VB*.

New College — A college at Oxford; the reference is to the ensign or armorial bearing associated with that particular college. Waugh's father, Arthur, went to New College.

Newport — The wealthy, fashionable resort island off the coast of Rhode Island.

"Night and Day" — See Glossary under *OG*.

Florence Nightingale — English nurse (1820–1910) whose bravery and competence were particularly notable in the Crimean War (1854–56). She was also the founder of the first professional school of nursing.

Nissen hut — See Glossary under *BR*.

no longer *persona grata* — No longer personally acceptable, that is, his presence in Yugoslavia was no longer acceptable to the partisan ruling group.

Nomen — Latin for "name." The name for whom the Mass is said is mentioned during the service.

"Non es partisan?" — Latin for "You are not a partisan?"

No Orchids for Miss Blandish — See Glossary under *OG*.

O.C. Troops — Officer commanding the troops.

on the rocks — In financial distress.

Order of St. John of Jerusalem — Another name for the Knights of Malta; see Glossary under *WS*.

"Other Ranks" — That is, ranks other than commissioned officers.

outré — Out of place, unconventional.

"Overlord" — The code name for the Allied Normandy invasion of German-occupied western Europe in June, 1944.

P.A.D. — See Glossary under *MA*.

Palazzo Corombona — See "Dictionary," *Corombona*.

Pan-Slavism — The concept of cultural and political ties among Slavic people. After 1917 it was associated with Russian dominance of the Balkans.

Paternoster — Latin for "Our Father," the first words of the Lord's Prayer, beginning, "Our Father, Who art in Heaven."

Pavlova — Anna Pavlova (1882–1931), Russian ballerina who achieved worldwide fame. She spent her last years in a house opposite the house where Waugh grew up in North End Road, Golders Green. See *A Little Learning* (Boston, 1964), p. 35.

penal times — Times of religious persecution against Roman Catholics beginning in the sixteenth century; see Glossary under *MA*.

People's Army — A term used by the Soviet Union and other Communist countries to give the impression that democracy is prominent in their institutions.

Per — Lady Perdita.

Peter Pan — A famous play by Sir James Barrie (1904) about a boy who did not want to grow up.

Piedmontese usurpation — In the nineteenth century Nationalist elements in Italy supported the concept of uniting the different sections of the country under the Piedmont-Sardinia group. In 1870, Rome was captured by the Piedmontese; the pope lost his territory and was confined to the Vatican. These issues were eventually settled by the Lateran Treaty.

THE END OF THE BATTLE

Pine's *Horace* — John Pine published a two-volume edition of Horace's collected works entitled *Quinti Horatii Flacci Opera*. The first volume was published in London in 1733, and the second in 1737. The books are distinguished not only by their rarity but also by their illustrations, engraved on copperplate by Pine.

place...coolness, light and peace — Waugh is remembering the English translation of "locum refrigerii, lucis et pacis," words from the traditional Roman Catholic Mass. The Latin is quoted later at the parachute training camp.

Posillipo — A promontory southwest of Naples. Correctly spelled Posilipo.

"praesente cadavere" — Latin for "in the presence of the corpse."

Praesidium — An executive committee supposedly representing a country or group democratically. In Communist countries such a group is standard and controls the populace dictatorially.

presbytery — The house where the priest lives; it is near or attached to the church. It is called "rectory" in the United States.

prie-dieu — See Glossary under *POMF*.

Providence — See Glossary under *DF*.

Puginesque — In the manner of Augustus Welby Pugin (1812–52), a devout English Catholic architect who was very influential in the Gothic revival movement.

purgatory — In Roman Catholic doctrine, a place for souls after death where they suffer temporarily until they are purified of all sins and are thus ready to enter heaven.

Queen Alexandra's nurses — the Imperial Military Nursing Service was founded by Queen Alexandra in 1902.

Quislings — Traitors; see Glossary under *OGP*.

rag is brewing — Stunts or tricks are being prepared.

R.A.M.C. — See Glossary under *MA*.

R.A.S.C. — See Glossary under *OG*.

R.C.H. — Royal Corps of Halberdiers.

Requiem — See Glossary under *MA*.

Herr von Ribbentrop — Hitler's minister of foreign affairs; see Glossary under *POMF*.

Risorgimento — A period of intense Italian nationalism from the early part of the nineteenth century to 1870.

Roget — Peter Roget (1779–1869), the compiler of the famous *Thesaurus* (1852) named for him. It has gone through many editions.

"Roman candles" — Fireworks rockets that rise and fall abruptly; here the meaning is parachutes that do not open.

Rossetti — Dante Gabriel Rossetti (1828–82). English Pre-Raphaelite artist and poet.

Royalist officers — Supporters of the monarchy of King Peter II. Tito had the officers executed because they would be opposed to his plans for a Yugoslavian Communist government.

Ruby at the Dorchester — See "Dictionary," *Ruby*.

Sacred Heart — A representation of Christ with his heart showing, signifying his love for humanity.

sacring place — Place of consecration. Here Westminster Abbey, in London, British monarchs are crowned.

St. Edward the Confessor — King of England who died in 1066. He was an extremely religious individual, and after his death he was canonized. He is buried in Westminster Abbey, which he founded.

St. Margaret's, Westminster — See "Dictionary."

St. Nicholas' Day — December 6.

St. Peter-in-chains — Michelangelo's famous sculpture of Moses is in St. Peter-in-Chains Church, Rome.

Salerno — Salerno, Italy, was invaded by Allied forces in 1943. The fighting was particularly ferocious with heavy casualties on both sides. The Germans were eventually forced to retreat.

Sandhurst — See Glossary under *OG*.

sang-froid — French for cold-bloodedness, calmness in the face of danger.

Dorothy Sayers — English writer (1893–1957), best known for her detective stories, especially those in which Lord Peter Wimsey is the principal figure. She composed religious works, as well as a verse translation of Dante's *Divine Comedy*.

"Siciliano lei?" — Italian for "Are you Sicilian?"

"slosh" — A game played on a billiard table. Only some of the balls are used, and no cue sticks are involved.

"Sono più abituato..." — Italian for "I am more accustomed to the Genoese dialect, but I can often understand and make myself understood everywhere in Italy except in Sicily."

Split — A Yugoslavian city on the Adriatic Sea.

THE GLOSSARY

"Spruce's veiled ladies" — Peter Quennell reports that Cyril Connolly (the real identity of Spruce) had barefoot girls attending and serving him; cf. Quennell's *The Wanton Chase* (New York, 1980), p. 22.

Stalin — Josef Vissarionovich Dzhugashvili (1879–1953), who took the name Stalin, meaning "steel." He was the virtual dictator of the Soviet Union from the late 1920s until his death. He was popularly called Joe by supporters and admirers in Western countries.

Sten guns — British short barreled, rapid-firing carbines which can be easily carried. The name is derived from the inventors, a Major Sheppard and a Mr. Turpin.

subfusc — See Glossary under *BR*.

subscription — Dues.

Sword of Stalingrad — Like so much else in Waugh's trilogy, this exhibit sword was based on fact; see David Wykes, "Evelyn Waugh's Sword of Volgograd," *DQR* 7 (1977): 82–99.

Te Deum — See Glossary under *H*.

"There's a special providence in the fall of a bomb" — This line calls to mind "There's a special providence in the fall of a sparrow," which occurs in Shakespeare's *Hamlet*, act 5, sc. 2, line 231.

They also served who only stood and waited — Guy Crouchback is referring to the last line of John Milton's sonnet on his blindness. The poem begins, "When I consider how my Light is Spent," and ends with the line "They also serve who only stand and wait."

Tito — Josip Broz (1892–1980), who took the name Tito. A Yugoslavian Communist guerrilla leader who harassed the German invaders in World War II. After the war he became the ruler of Yugoslavia.

tosh — Garbage.

Toulouse-Lautrec — Henri Raymonde de Toulouse-Lautrec (1864–1901), French artist perhaps best known for his colorful posters.

Trollope's *Can You Forgive Her?* — A novel by Anthony Trollope (1815–82).

"Tuis enim fidelibus..." — Latin for "To those who are faithful to you, O God, life is changed, not ended." This prayer is from the Preface in the traditional Roman Catholic Mass for the dead.

tukals and fanes — Huts and temples.

Ulysses — A landmark novel by James Joyce, first published in 1922, which successfully introduced the stream-of-consciousness technique into modern fiction.

Uncle Joe — Joseph Stalin. See *Stalin*, above.

unfrocked priest — A priest no longer canonically certified to perform the duties of his calling.

Uniate Abyssinians — Abyssinian Christians who followed the Eastern rite but were in union with the Roman Catholic church.

the Union — See Glossary under *BR*.

U.N.R.R.A. — The United Nations Relief and Rehabilitation Administration.

Vin d'Honneur — A wine-drinking party usually in honor of a distinguished guest.

Mrs. Viveash — Myra Viveash, a stylish, social-minded, but promiscuous character in Aldous Huxley's novel *Antic Hay* (1922).

W.A.A.F.s — members of the Women's Auxiliary Air Force.

walls of Diocletian at Split — Split was founded by the Roman emperor Diocletian in A.D. 300, and architectural remains from that period still exist. See *Split* above.

Hugh Walpole — Best-selling English novelist (1884–1941); many of his books were popular in the 1920s and 1930s.

Waste Land — T. S. Eliot's monumental poem; see Glossary under *BR*. In Eliot's poem the drowned Phoenician sailor Phlebas helps develop the year-god symbolism involving eventual rebirth and resurrection.

von Weich's — More accurately, "von Weichs." Baron Maximilian von Weichs (1882–1954) was a German general who commanded armies on the Western Front and in Russia. Later he was the principal commander of German forces in southeast Europe.

Wesleyan — See Glossary under *VB*.

windy — Scared.

"wings in vain" — The reference is to Shelley and occurs in Matthew Arnold's *Essays in Criticism, Second Series*.

Winston — Prime Minister Winston Churchill.

Wiseman Club — An organization of Catholics named for Cardinal Nicholas Wiseman (1802–65), who was appointed the first archbishop of Westminster in 1850.

THE END OF THE BATTLE

"A woman's only a woman..."—A quotation from Rudyard Kipling's "The Betrothed."

Zeitgeist — German for the prevailing spirit of a particular period.

Zion — Palestine. The subsequent quotation refers to Zionists, i.e., those urging a Jewish homeland in Palestine.

Zurbarán ascetic — Francisco de Zurbarán was a seventeenth-century Spanish artist who was noted for painting monks and saints in meditation and prayer. In the first British edition and in all the American editions except *SOH*, the name has been misspelled Zubarán.

THE SHORT STORIES (Only those stories requiring annotations are included.)

"A House of Gentlefolks" (1927)

bad hat—See Glossary under *VB*.
Bellini—Giovanni Bellini (1430?–1516); see Glossary under *BR*.
Brindisi—A port city in southeastern Italy.
Buda-Pest—See Glossary under *DF*.
Crillon—A fashionable hotel in Paris.
ducal house—A house owned by a duke.
Lloyd *Trestino*—The *Trestino* was a boat run by the Lloyd Steamship Line. The intention here is to sail on to Greece.

"An Englishman's Home" (1939)

cleft stick—See Glossary under *BM*. Cleft sticks are also prominent in William Boot's luggage in *Sc*.
Crown Derby—See Glossary under *LAR*.
flea in the ear—Scolded.
"God gave all men all earth to love..."—Lines from Rudyard Kipling's poem "Sussex."
ha-ha—A ditch containing a hidden sunken fence which divides property.
ha'p'orth—A halfpenny's worth of tar; that is, very little.
jumble sale—A sale of donated odds and ends held for charitable purposes.
the mark of Plague in the court of the Decameron—The *Decameron*, by Giovanni Boccaccio (1313–75), completed in 1353, presents ten characters telling stories to distract themselves and while away the time during the bubonic plague in Florence in 1348. The first sign of the plague on the body of a victim caused terror and flight.

Rotarians—See Glossary under *LO*.
Wolf Cub account—In England, Wolf Cubs are boys from eight to eleven years old, the younger division of the Boy Scouts.

"Basil Seal Rides Again" (1963)

Dedicatee

Mrs. Ian Fleming—Ann Charteris married Ian Fleming, who is best remembered as the author of the James Bond stories. Ann Fleming and Waugh particularly enjoyed gossip about high society and mutual friends.

American slump—The economic depression of the 1930s.
"belle époque"—French for "splendid era."
Bühl—A reference to Charles André Boulle; see Glossary under *MA*.
Gretna Green Romances—Gretna Green is a village in Scotland, just across the English border. Many runaway couples married there because parental consent was not required there above age sixteen, and a declaration of marriage could be made without clerical approval or license.
"His Aunt Jobiska made him drink..."—This and the following lines are from Edward Lear's poem "The Pobble Who Has No Toes."
H.R.H.—His Royal Highness. Arthur, Duke of Connaught (1850–1942) was the third son of Queen Victoria.
Ischia—An island off the western coast of Italy.
Lawrence of Arabia—See Glossary under *Sc*.
National Trust—An English organization dedicated

THE GLOSSARY

to preserving buildings and land of historical interest or beauty. It has purchased many country houses, parks, etc.

Peerage — *Debrett's*, a book listing aristocrats and members of the nobility.

PEN Club — An international organization of authors. The initials stand for "Poets, Playwrights, Essayists, Editors, and Novelists."

"rien ne va plus" — French for "No more stakes accepted." This phrase is called by the croupier of the roulette table when the wheel begins to spin.

Row — Rotten Row, the path in London's Hyde Park popular with horseback riders.

Serpentine — The lake in Hyde Park, London.

twenty-firster — A twenty-first birthday party.

"Bella Fleace Gave a Party" (1932)

Free State — The Republic of Ireland, as distinguished from the British-controlled six northern Irish counties (Northern Ireland, or Ulster).

Museum — The British Museum, in London.

Spectator — A weekly paper devoted to commentary on current news, literary topics, and similar material.

Strongbow — Richard Strongbow, the nickname of Richard de Clare, the second earl of Pembroke (d. 1176), who was one of the earliest English leaders to set about conquering Ireland.

transmontane pietists — People across the mountains from Rome, mainly Germans, who advocated a rather individualistic, evangelical Christianity as opposed to the more traditional, religiously orthodox rituals and practices of the church.

General Wilson — Sir Henry Hughes Wilson (1864–1922), British military leader who was Chief of the Imperial General Staff at the time of his assassination by the Irish Republican Army.

"By Special Request" (1934)

hard cheese — See Glossary under *HD*.

"Charles Ryder's Schooldays" (1982)

Note: B. W. T. Handford (*TLS*, April 9, 1982, p. 412) stresses the autobiographical nature of "Charles Ryder's Schooldays." Ryder is based on Waugh, while Curtis-Dunne is modeled on Lord Molson, and Wheatley on Roger Fulford. Handford believes that Jorkins is based on Max Mallowan and that Mercer is Dudley Carew. Handford also provides the identity of several of the masters, perhaps the most famous being J. F. Roxburgh, who is portrayed as A. A. Carmichael.

"Abou Ben Adhem, may his tribe increase" — The first line of "Abou Ben Adhem," a famous poem by Leigh Hunt (1784–1859).

Army Class B — Students who are gearing for study at military college.

bell for Hall — The bell announcing dinner.

"The Bells of Heaven" — A poem by Ralph Hodgson (1871–1962). Some lines from the poem are quoted near the end of the story. The poem is only ten lines and has as its theme kindness to animals.

blighter — Rascal, fellow.

bolshie — Rebellious and troublemaking, short for Bolshevik.

Broughton — The home village of Charles Ryder's family.

bye-term — A term which is not the main term for entering the school; for example, instead of entering in the fall, the student would have entered in the spring. There were three terms each year, mid-September to mid-December, mid-January to early April, and early May to late July. Most students entered in September; those who entered in January or May were said to have come in bye-term.

Bystander — An illustrated weekly devoted to art, literature, travel, and similar topics.

Carthusian [tie] — The black necktie with pinkish stripes of the Charterhouse School, in Surrey. The school was attached to a Carthusian monastery in the Middle Ages.

Certificates — See Glossary under *DF*.

The Choice at Wyndhams — A play at a London theater.

Choral Communion — A sung Eucharist service.

"Coming to the Graves?" — A misprint; should read Groves, the latrines at Lancing, which were at a distance from the main buildings.

THE SHORT STORIES

Corinthian tie—The white-and-navy-blue necktie of the Corinthian Football Club. The club was founded in 1882 and was composed principally of Oxford and Cambridge blues.

Walter Crane's *Bases of Design* —A text on design, first published in 1898, by Walter Crane (1845–1915). A second edition appeared in 1904. Crane was the Director of Art Design in Manchester Municipal School of Art.

Dartmouth—See Glossary under *MA*.

Daumier—See Glossary under *BR*.

dibs—Prayers.

d'Italie—A restaurant in the Soho section of London.

Double Greek—A double session (that is, class period) of Greek study.

fags—Younger students at English public schools who are obligated to perform menial tasks for the advanced, older students.

fly—Shrewd.

Hugh Walpole's *Fortitude* —See Glossary under *EB*. *Fortitude* (1913) was Walpole's first commercially successful novel.

Geohegan—The head of the House who beats Ryder and some of the other students for disobeying O'Malley's order.

Georgian Poetry—See Glossary under *BR*.

Golden Treasury—A famous anthology of poetry by Francis Turner Palgrave (1824–97). The full title of the volume was *The Golden Treasury of the Best Songs and Lyrical Poems in the English Language* (1861).

Gothic revival—A period of new interest in medieval Gothic architecture that flourished in the late eighteenth and early nineteenth centuries. Many buildings were constructed in that style during the period.

greased—Was a fawning sycophant.

Hall—The dinner meal in the dining hall.

Hassall's *History*—A popular textbook by Arthur Hassall (1853–1930). The full title is *British History Chronologically Arranged*.

Head's House—The home of the Headmaster.

house-captain—The boy (prefect) in charge of a particular house at the school.

House Room—The principal area of a house (unit of a school) occupied by forty boys. B. W. T. Handford, the archivist at Lancing, has identified many of the terms used in this story, some in an article in *TLS*, April 9, 1982, p. 412, and others in personal correspondence with me.

Hyde . . . Jekyll—The split personality of the good Dr. Jekyll and the evil Hyde as portrayed in the novel *The Strange Case of Dr. Jekyll and Mr. Hyde* (1886), by Robert Louis Stevenson.

link his arm in a friend's—A common gesture of friendship among British schoolboys of the time. No impropriety is implied.

lip—Impertinence.

Lovat tweed—Woolen cloth of a greenish color from Scotland.

Medici prints—See Glossary under *BR*.

Milton-on-his-blindness—John Milton's famous sonnet beginning "When I consider how my light is spent. . . ."

Modern Side—Modern languages or sciences with only a small amount of Latin.

Modern Upper—The fifth and sixth forms (classes) were divided into the classical side and the modern side. The classical side emphasized Greek and Latin, while the modern side emphasized science and modern languages. "Modern Upper" means the upper fifth on the modern side.

New Statesman—See Glossary under *VB*.

Old Rugbeian tie—A tie worn by graduates of Rugby School. It is blue-, green-, and white-striped.

Old's House—One of the actual Houses at Lancing. B. W. T. Handford drops the apostrophe.

OTC—Officers Training Corps.

Oxford Movement—An attempt to bring the Anglican Church closer to Roman Catholicism in doctrine and liturgy. The starting point in the movement is usually attributed to a sermon given by John Keble in 1833, but the most famous figure was John Henry Newman, who later converted to Roman Catholicism and became a Cardinal. The Oxford Movement was instrumental in establishing Anglo-Catholicism within the Anglican Church.

Pop. Sci.—In Waugh's time at Lancing, this was a general course in science, largely natural history, for those students who were not placing major emphasis on science.

"Quantum mutatus ab illo Hectore"—A Latin passage from Virgil's *Aeneid*, bk. 2, line 274. Aeneas is describing to Dido the fall of Troy, and he says, "How greatly changed from the Hector who once came back arrayed in the armor of Achilles."

"Qui diligit Deum diligit et fratrem suum"—Latin for "He who loves God also loves his brother." This phrase is inscribed in the Head's Houseroom at

THE GLOSSARY

Lancing, but according to B. W. T. Handford, the Lancing inscription uses the spelling *diligat* after *Deum*.

Ryder — In great part the character is based on Waugh himself.

Salamanca — A reference to the famous university in Salamanca, Spain.

Sandhurst — See Glossary under *OG*.

Second Evening — Prep (homework) time after supper.

Settle — The House Room contained a settle made of oak. If one was promoted to the settle, he not only achieved a mark of distinction but also could possibly in time become house captain.

Shaw's *Alphabets* — A book on letter designing containing alphabets in various styles.

Spierpoint Down — A public school based on Lancing, the school Waugh attended.

subfusc — See Glossary under *BR*.

Tea-cake — The nickname of the master of the Middle-Fifth class. In reality his name was Noel James, and his nickname was "Dough Bun."

"There swimmeth One Who swam e'er rivers were begun, And under that Almighty Fin the littlest fish may enter in" — Lines from the poem "Heaven," by Rupert Brooke (1887–1915).

Third Evening — A prep time when students could read any books they wished but had to do so in the House Room.

Uncle George — The nickname of an actual House Master at Lancing whose full name was George Smythe.

under-school table — The youngest students were assigned certain tables to work at.

"Under the wide and starry sky" — The first line of Robert Louis Stevenson's poem "Requiem."

Upper Dormitory — The dormitory of the Upper boys. The students were divided academically into Upper School and Lower School.

Veniam day — One of the special days honoring particular saints. On such days boys were allowed to socialize with their parents and relatives and visit away from the school.

walked across the Hall — Walked across the dining hall.

"What have I done for you, England, my England . . . ?" — The first line of William E. Henley's poem "England, My England."

"Consequences" (1929)

sidesmen — Men who assist the wardens of an Anglican church by taking up the collection, ushering, and performing similar tasks.

"Cruise: Letters from a Young Lady of Leisure" (1933)

apache — See Glossary under *BR*.

d.v. — *Deo volente*, Latin for "God being willing."

frogs — Derogatory British slang for the French.

gave him the raspberry — Making a rude, contemptuous noise with the lips: here, being sexually unfaithful.

walk out — See Glossary under *HD*.

"Excursion in Reality" (1932)

Boer farms — The Boers were Dutch settlers in South Africa. The Boer War (1899–1902) between the Boers and the British resulted in a British victory and the creation of the Union of South Africa. The word *boer* is Dutch for "farmer."

commissionaire — Doorman.

an extension night — An extension to the license of a restaurant or public house permitting it to serve alcohol after closing time on a given night.

Fuzzie-wuzzies — See Glossary under *DF*.

hosier — One who deals in hosiery.

Mewses — See Glossary under *DF*.

ostlers — See Glossary under *HD*.

sluicing — Washing.

supers — See Glossary under *VB*.

tube stations — Subway stations.

West End — The fashionable section of London, noted especially for theaters and restaurants.

"Incident in Azania" (1933)

See map of Azania, Appendix 4.

Andromeda-like — A figure in Greek myth known for her beauty. On the verge of being seized by a sea

THE SHORT STORIES

monster, she was rescued by Perseus, who married her.
chit — See Glossary under *OG*.
Condominium — A country or territory ruled in common by two or more countries.
Goan — See Glossary under *BM*.
gymkhanas — See Glossary under *VB*.
lawner — See Glossary under *HD*.
O.C. — Officer Commanding.
syce — See Glossary under *BM*.
tarboosh — A red hat, like a fez, worn by Muslim males.
La Vie Parisienne — See Glossary under *VB*.
wallah — See Glossary under *BM*.

"Love in the Slump" (1932)

Bullingdon — See Glossary under *DF*.
Christ Church "grind" — See Glossary under *POMF*.
cobs — Strong, stout horses with short legs.
cow-cake — A pellet rich in protein that is fed to cows.
Crisis years — The depression period in the 1930s.
"43" — A London nightspot notorious for drinking and prostitution. It was founded in 1921 by Mrs. Kate Meyrick at 43 Gerrard Street. See Glossary under *BR*, *Old Hundredth*.
High — See Glossary under *DF*.
Slump — See Glossary under *POMF*.
Third in History — See Glossary under *BR*.

"Mr. Loveday's Little Outing" (1935)

alienist — A psychiatrist.
Home Office — The government department which was in charge of, among other things, state asylums.
monkey-puzzler — A species of evergreen tree with prickly leaves and branches twisting intricately (so that it would puzzle a monkey to make his way through them).

"On Guard" (1934)

Bart. — See Glossary under *VB*.
came out — See Glossary under *EB*.

Mombasa — An island off the southern coast of Kenya, east Africa.
sirens — Beautiful, alluring girls.

"Out of Depth" (1933)

Dominican — See Glossary under *BR*.
du Maurier — George du Maurier (1834-96) French novelist and illustrator. For a time he was a member of the *Punch* staff.
Eros — In Greek myth, the god of love.
Ethelred the Unready — See Glossary under *Sc*.
"Ite, missa est" — Latin for "Go, the Mass is ended," a salutation given by the priest to the congregation near the end of the traditional Roman Catholic Mass. It is spoken before the Last Gospel (John 1:1–14).
Piranesi ruin — A reference to the neoclassical-style architecture created by Giovanni Piranesi; see Glossary under *BR*.
Tiger Tim — The *Tiger Tim Weekly* featured animal stories of characters like Tiger Tim attending an animals' boarding school, which was, of course, a takeoff on boys' boarding schools.

"Period Piece" (1936)

Bessie Cotter — A "slice-of-life" novel by Wallace Smith (1888–1937), published in 1934.
Sanctuary — A raw, brutish novel by William Faulkner (1897–1962), published in 1931.

"Tactical Exercise" (1947)

"Ne pas depasser deux" — French for "Take no more than two."
syndicate — See Glossary under *MA*.
"24 Comprimés narcotiques, hypnotiques" — French for "24 tablets narcotic, hypnotic."

"The Balance" (1926)

Alma Tadema — Sir Lawrence Alma-Tadema (1836–1912), English painter.

THE GLOSSARY

"Ave Imperatrix Immortalis, Moriturus te saluto"—Latin for "Hail, immortal Empress, I who am about to die salute you," an adaptation of "Hail Immortal Emperor, we who are about to die salute you," the greeting of the gladiators to the Roman emperor as they prepared to do battle in the arena.

Bach—Johann Sebastian Bach (1685–1750), German composer best known for his religious music.

blind—Drinking party.

Bronzino Venus—Bronzino was a Florentine painter whose real name was Agnolo di Cosimo di Mariano (1502–72). His portrait *Venus, Folly, Cupid, and Time* is in the National Gallery in London.

Bullingdon tie—See Glossary under *DF*.

Canning—See Glossary under *BR*.

Chatham—See Glossary under *BR*.

Cointreau—A sweet orange-flavored liqueur.

Collections Paper—See Glossary under *BR*.

coo—See Glossary under *VB*.

E.V.—Ernest Vaughan.

Expressionismus—The reference is to expressionism, an artistic movement which originated in Germany at the beginning of the twentieth century. It sought to project thoughts, dreams, and similar mental states in external occurrences. These states were usually presented in a disjointed manner.

fixative—A chemical which holds colors in a fixed position. It is commonly used in art schools.

two Generals Gordon—Two of the guests at the party are dressed like General Charles George Gordon (1833–85). See Glossary under *DF*.

Hydriotaphia—A book by Sir Thomas Browne published in 1658. It is a meditation on funeral customs and other matters relating to death.

"Know you her secret none can utter..."—The first lines of the poem "The Secret of Oxford" by Arthur Quiller-Couch (1863–1944).

Louis Seize—Furniture designed in the neoclassical style common during the reign of the French King Louis XVI (1774–93).

National Gallery—The great London art gallery.

Ozymandias—A poem (1818) by Percy Bysshe Shelley, stressing how a once powerful king had died and been forgotten.

paper games—Games like "consequences" played with paper and pencil; see Glossary under *HD*.

Petronius—First century A.D. Roman author, especially remembered for his *Satyricon*.

Poussin—Nicholas Poussin (1594–1665), French classical painter.

Rape of the Sabines—A myth about the legendary Romulus, who could not find enough wives for his followers. He allegedly invited the Sabine men, who lived in the Apennines, to a banquet. While they were feasting, another group of Romans raided the Sabine area and kidnapped all the women there.

Rhodes trust—A trust fund for scholarships; see Glossary under *Sc*.

Saphist—A follower of Sappho (fl. ca. 600 B.C.), the Greek love poetess of Lesbos. Sappho and her group are associated with lesbianism. Misspelled in the story; "Sapphist" is the correct form.

Larry Semon—A British comic movie actor, a British version of Buster Keaton.

sent down—See Glossary under *BR*.

shingled—Close-cropped.

soft—Silly, follish.

Tatler—See Glossary under *BR*.

the Triple Crown—A book and a triple crown make up the coat of arms of Oxford University. These are the mythical arms which were invented for King Edmund of East Anglia. Edmund was canonized and became an object of veneration at the end of the fourteenth century. The three crowns were associated with King Richard II and were borne as arms by two men who served him in Ireland. One of these men was also chancellor of Oxford.

"Ut exultat in coitu elephas, sic Ricardus"—Latin for "As an elephant enjoys sexual intercourse, so does Richard." A vulgar comment ascribed to Richard Basingstoke to tease him.

Le vin triste—French for "the sad wine." As the story demonstrates, Adam grows sadder as he drinks.

Horace Walpole...Orford one...Strawberry Hill—Horace Walpole (1717–97), English literary figure best known for his mystery romance *The Castle of Otranto* (1764) and his voluminous *Letters*. He was the son of Prime Minister Sir Robert Walpole, first earl of Orford, and he succeeded to the title as the fourth earl of Orford in 1791. For many years he lived at his estate, Strawberry Hill, and he established a printing press there. Donald Greene notes in personal correspondence that Allen T. Hazen's *A Catalogue of Horace Walpole's Library* (3 vols., New Haven, 1969) is the definitive study of Walpole's books and adds: "There was much trouble about 'Orford' bookplates. The late nineteenth-century Earl of Orford designed a bookplate that was almost a duplicate of Horace Walpole's, and no doubt unscrupulous booksellers tried to pass off books containing this as coming from HW's library. Incidentally, Hazen's index lists a number of Sir Thomas Browne's books as having been in HW's library, but not the *Hydriotaphia*. Interesting that Waugh would have known something about this obscure bibliographical puzzle."

Whembley, Mentmore and Thatch—Country houses.

"The Major Intervenes" (1949) (Also published under the title "Compassion")

A.B.C. shop—One of a chain of British tea shops.
Attlee Brigade—Clement Attlee (1883–1967) was an English Labour party leader who succeeded Churchill as Prime Minister in 1945. Attlee was highly supportive of the anti-Franco forces in the Spanish Civil War in the 1930s and went to Spain to review the British unit of the International Brigade. Since Attlee gave the clenched-fist salute to the group during his review and the International Brigade had strong Russian and Communist influence, Attlee was regarded by several critics as supportive of communism. He also gave one of the brigades he reviewed permission to name itself the "Major Attlee Company."
Bari...bones of St. Nicholas—Bari is a city in southeastern Italy on the Adriatic Sea. Saint Nicholas of Myra, a fourth-century bishop, is buried there.
"the City"—See Glossary under *MA*.
Dakotas—See Glossary under *EB*.
fives—A game, somewhat similar to American handball, in which a ball is hit against walls.
Hoppner—John Hoppner (1758–1810), English portrait painter who imitated the style of Sir Joshua Reynolds.
House colours—Many English schools are divided into groups, or Houses, with their own living facilities etc. Sports competition often flourishes among the various Houses.
O.T.C.—Officers' Training Corps.
OZNA—Acronym for Odelenje Zaštite Narodna, the Yugoslavian federal ministry of the interior which with its political police was designed to eliminate opposition to Marshal Tito's dictatorial control.
Palladian—See Glossary under *VB*.
Pont Street—See Glossary under *BR*.
Romneys—Portrait paintings by the English artist George Romney (1734–1802).
Torres Vedras—A town and district in Portugal. A twenty-eight-mile-long series of fortifications was built there and was used as a barrier against the French during the Peninsular War.
Unrra—See Glossary under *EB*.
Ustashi—Members of an extremist group who regarded themselves as Croatian nationalists. They supported the German and Italian fascists.
vet them—Check up on persons to see whether they are socially acceptable, reliable, etc.

"The Manager of The Kremlin" (1930)

Imperial Government—The government of the Russian czars.
Kolchak—Aleksandr Kolchak (1873–1920), Russian officer who after the Bolshevik Revolution of 1917 led armes against the Communist forces. During the period 1918–20 he was probably the most important anti-Bolshevik leader in Russia. He fought a losing cause and was eventually taken prisoner and executed by the Bolsheviks.

"Winner Takes All" (1936)

Badajos—A Spanish city near the Portuguese border. It was seized by the French in the Peninsular War but was recaptured by the Duke of Wellington's forces in 1812.
death duties—See Glossary under *HD*.
dower house—See Glossary under *H*.
Eights Week and Commem.—See Glossary under *BR*.

THE DICTIONARY

DICTIONARY OF EVELYN WAUGH'S FICTION
A Who's Who Among the Characters, and a Listing of the Principal Proper Names, and a Concise Synopsis of the Stories

[Unless otherwise indicated in the particular entry, references to *EB* serve also for *US*.]

A

Aaronson, Baby (*LO*) — The real name of Hollywood starlet Juanita del Pablo.

Abbot, the (*BM*) — The head of the Nestorian monastery of Saint Mark the Evangelist, which is situated deep in the interior of Azania. The autocratic Abbot maintains great independence. Some of his religious views are bizarre. He insists, for example, that the spirits in hell marry and produce hobgoblins. The Abbot and the Earl of Ngumo arrange for the release of Achon, whom they hope to have succeed Seth as emperor. The Abbot receives money for releasing the imprisoned Achon.

Abdul-Akbar, Princess Jenny (*HD*) — A companion and friend of Brenda Last in London. Brenda introduces Jenny to her husband, Tony, hoping that she will distract Tony while Brenda continues her affair with John Beaver. Jenny has been divorced from a Moroccan Moulay who had treated her badly. She is a nonstop talker, scatterbrained, yet exotic. She fascinates the Lasts' young son, John Andrew. Jenny is also mentioned as one of Brenda's friends in "By Special Request" and in the "Alternative Ending" to *HD*.

Abel, Mr. and Mrs. (*DF*) — Devoted parishioners of Mr. Prendergast's church when he was in charge of a parish in Worthing. Mr. Abel was a dentist.

Abel, Mrs. (*BR*) — The cook for Charles Ryder's eccentric and reclusive father.

Abercrombie, Lady (*LO*) — Sir Ambrose Abercrombie's wife.

Abercrombie, Sir Ambrose (*LO*) — The distinguished veteran British actor who serves as the unofficial head of the British film colony in Hollywood. He is in his late fifties and is very concerned about propriety and the British "image" in America and thus reproves Barlow for taking a job at the pet cemetery. It has been suggested that he may have been modeled on film actor Sir C. Aubrey Smith.

Abercrombies (*MA*, *SOH*) — A British family who moved to Jamaica at the beginning of World War II to avoid the conflict.

Achon (*BM*) — The son of the Great Amurath. Although heir to the Azanian throne, he has been incarcerated in a monastery by order of his sister and the Nestorian Patriarch Gorgias. Achon is Seth's uncle. He is eventually released from the monastery when a large sum of money is paid by the Earl of Ngumo. He is very aged and blind. Yet Ngumo, Ballon, and General Connolly intend to use him to overthrow Seth. When he is taken to Debra-Dowa and the heavy imperial crown is placed on his head, the strain proves too great, and he dies immediately.

Ada (*TB*) — A parlormaid in a house in Earls Court. She and her friend Gladys attend a movie and give a running lower-class commentary on the film.

Ada (*HD*) — The Reverend Tendril's respected sister.

Ada (*VB*) — A young housemaid in Colonel Blount's home.

THE DICTIONARY

Addison, Mr. (*OGP*) — One of the passengers aboard the *Caliban*.

Adjutant, the — See *Grace-Groundling-Marchpole*.

(Admin) (*EB, SOH*) — An abbreviation for "administrative officer," a Royal Air Force officer who occasionally visits the emergency ward of the aerodrome where Guy Crouchback is taken after his parachute accident.

Adventist University of Alabama (*Sc*) — The school attended by the unnamed assistant to Dr. Benito. He tries to intimidate William Boot into leaving Jacksonburg, but is butted by a goat at the Pension Dressler.

Agnes (*SP*) — The maid of Mr. and Mrs. James.

Agnes (*VB*) — The kitchen servant of Mrs. Orraway-Smith who may want to invite young suitors into the kitchen as a result of the bad example of Prime Minister James Brown, who is allegedly having wild all-night parties in his home.

Aircastle School (*Sc*) — A correspondence school for anyone who wants to study journalism. Bateson is a graduate of the institution.

Akonanga, Dr. (*EB, SOH*) — A Swahili witch doctor and former abortionist who goes to work for the Ministry of Information using voodoo and similar methods to cast spells on Nazis like Hitler and von Ribbentrop. In his equipment are drums, human bones, and scorpions.

Albert (*HD*) — One of the servants of Brenda and Tony Last at Hetton.

Alberto del Sol (*MA, SOH*) — The later name of the inn, formerly called the Hotel Eden, in Santa Dulcina delle Rocce, Italy.

Albright, Charles (*BSRA*) — The son of Clarence Albright. He desires to marry Basil Seal's daughter Barbara. He is bold, disrespectful, and undisciplined. He has no profession but occasionally plays guitar in a coffeehouse. He hopes to marry Barbara for her money. (Actually he is rather similar in character and behavior to the youthful Basil Seal.) Through a ruse Basil persuades Barbara that Charles is his illegitimate son; Albright's intention to marry Barbara is thus thwarted.

Albright, Clarence (*BSRA*) — An acquaintance of Basil Seal and Peter Pastmaster. He is the father of Charles Albright and is killed in action in 1943.

Albright, Lady Betty (*POMF, BSRA*) — The daughter of the Duke of Stayle. She married Clarence Albright in 1940 and died of cancer in 1956. She had been thrown into a lake by Basil Seal in 1937 at a party at King's Thursday. She was the mother of Charles Albright. She did not succeed in marrying Peter Pastmaster.

Albright, Major Charles (*OG, EB, SOH*) — A planning operations officer at Hazardous Operations Headquarters. He dreams up the "Popgun" campaign, which involves Trimmer and a small uninhabited island, to raise civilian morale.

Aldershot (*POMF, MA, SOH*) — A large British military base in southern England. Guy Crouchback's battalion is stationed there for a time.

Alex (*MA, SOH*) — Molly's husband; he has an important position in the Admiralty. Guy Crouchback writes to Molly hoping that Alex can obtain a position for him in military service.

Alfred (*BR*) — A cousin of the Ryders.

Alfred (*VB*) — The middle-aged husband on vacation who can think only of his job.

Algernon (*POMF*) — A member of the British upper classes who is sent to Syria on a secret mission.

Ali (*BM*) — The Indian secretary to Emperor Seth. During the war with the forces of Prince Seyid, Ali attempts to escape with the crown jewels. He is captured, and although Seth allows him liberty, Major Joab makes certain that Ali is assassinated.

"Ali" (*OG, SOH*) — A nickname Trimmer uses while training on the island of Mugg. It is a short form of Alistair.

Alice (*Sc*) — A friend of Mrs. Stitch.

Alice's (*DF*) — The house — actually a brothel — in Marseilles where Margot Beste-Chetwynde's "entertainers" stay en route to South America. It is also referred to as Chez Alice. Paul Pennyfeather goes there at Margot's request to straighten out details for the trip.

Allan (*BM*) — A friend of Basil Seal's; he was beaten up by some fellows while he and Basil were intoxicated.

Allan (*HD*) — The husband of Brenda Last's sister Lady Marjorie. He is a prospective Conservative candidate for a south London constituency. He tries to effect a reconciliation between Tony and Brenda.

Allgood, Billy (*POMF*) — A member of Cedric Lyne's regiment who broke his collarbone while on leave and was therefore unable to embark for the British military campaign in Norway.

Alopov, Nada (*BR*) — A homosexual prostitute to whom Anthony Blanche takes Sebastian Flyte to lure him away from his alcoholism. Sebastian gives Alopov a bad check.

Aloysius (*BR*) — Sebastian Flyte's teddy bear. Aloysius is frequently in Sebastian's company when the latter attends Oxford.

Alphonse (*Sc*) — A steward aboard a ship William Boot takes on part of his trip to Ishmaelia.

Alphonse (*VB*) — The maitre d'hotel of the expensive Chez Espinosa Restaurant in London.

Amabel (*Sc*) — Priscilla Boot's dog. She is old and dirty and shares a bed with the unwilling Mr. Salter when he stays the night at Boot Magna. In American editions the dog is named Annabel.

Ambrose (*HD, BSR*) — The principal servant of Brenda and Tony Last at Hetton. He also appears in the "Alternative Ending" to *HD*.

Ambrose (*SKME*) — One of Scott-King's recalcitrant classics students at Granchester.

Ambrose (*VB*) — A servant who works for Prime Minister Brown's family.

Amelia, Lady (*PP*) — An aging London matron, the narrator of the story.

American vice-consul (*BM*) — He flees Azania when it appears that Seth will be overthrown by the rebel forces of Prince Seyid.

Amory, Miss (*OGP*) — One of the passengers aboard the *Caliban*.

Amurath (*BM*) — Seth's grandfather. He had immigrated to Azania and eventually commanded the sultan's armies and then his own military force. In time he became Emperor Amurath the Great. He renamed the country and founded a capital at the inland community of Debra-Dowa.

Amurath Café and Universal Stores (*BM*) — A commercial enterprise in Matodi, Azania, under the proprietorship of Mr. Youkoumian.

Anastasia (*H*) — The reference is not perfectly clear but apparently alludes to Constantine's daughter, who is allegedly engaged in a plot against the Emperor. Could refer instead to Constantine's half sister.

Anchorage, Lady (*VB, HD, POMF, BR, PP, WTA*) — A wealthy and prominent British noblewoman. She is mentioned in *VB* and in *HD*. She attends Peter Pastmaster's wedding in *POMF*. She avoids Julia Flyte's and Rex Mottram's wedding in *BR*. In *PP* she is mentioned as a competitor of Viola Chasm for the romantic favors of Ralph Bland. Her husband is never specifically mentioned, but "the Anchorages" are referred to in *BR* and in *WTA*. In *WTA* they are mentioned as staying with the Chasms and are to be invited to the Kent-Cumberlands'.

Anchorage House (*VB, HD, BR*) — The magnificent home of the wealthy, aristocratic Anchorage family. It becomes the last survivor of the large noble townhouses of London. In *BR* we learn that the house is to be demolished, and Celia Ryder promises Lady Anchorage that Charles will paint it before it is destroyed.

Anderson (*CRS*) — The house captain in charge of Charles Ryder's dormitory at Spierpoint.

Anderson (*POMF*) — Lady Seal's butler.

Anderson (*VB*) — A young man working in the radio business and dating Betty Rylands.

Anderson, Dick (*WS*) — An acquaintance of John Plant's father who marries his daughter to a grocer.

Anderson, Professor (*TMWLD*) — The leader of the Anderson expedition to Brazil, who is traveling with Paul Henty. He contracts malaria in the jungle and dies. He is the prototype of Dr. Messinger in *HD*.

Anderson, Sybil (*TB*) — An acquaintance of Adam Doure and Imogen Quest.

Anderson expedition (*TMWLD*) — An exploratory mission to the upper Uraricuera region of Brazil.

Andrew (*BR*) — An acquaintance of Celia and Charles Ryder.

Andrew (*TB*) — A friend of Lady Rosemary Quest.

Andrews (*BM*) — Lady Cynthia Seal's chauffeur.

Andrews, Mrs. (*POMF*) — The doctor's wife in the Grantley Green area, south of Malfrey. She gives the proper amount of money in a subscription collection.

Angel (*OGP*) — The leader of the BBC group that comes to Lychpole to record an interview with Gilbert Pinfold. Pinfold falsely believes that this is the same Angel whose voice torments him on the *Caliban*.

Angel, Mr. and Mrs., and Miss Margaret (*OGP*) — Recorded on the passenger list of the *Caliban*. As sister (Margaret), brother, and sister-in-law (Goneril) they are the voices that Pinfold hears tormenting him. It develops that, as a result of his illness, Pinfold has invented Angel, Margaret, and Goneril.

Angela (*HD*) — An acquaintance of Tony and Brenda Last. She is a gossiping, high-society type. Tony,

THE DICTIONARY

Brenda, and Beaver attend a party at her home during the Christmas holiday season.

Angmering, Billy (*HD*) — One of Brenda Last's acquaintances and a London socialite. Beaver tells Brenda that Billy is having an affair with Sheila Shrub.

Annabel — See *Amabel*.

Anrep, Prince (*VB*) — An acquaintance of Kitty Blackwater and Lady Throbbing.

Anstruther, Betty (*BM*) — The Anstruthers' daughter who is injured when she falls from a pony.

Anstruther, David (*BM*) — The Anstruthers' son who is scheduled to attend Uppingham School, in England.

Anstruther, George (*BR*) — An acquaintance of Rex Mottram's. He is the first to inform Rex that Lady Marchmain is in poor health and does not have long to live.

Anstruther, Jean (*OG, SOH*) — A relative of Angus Anstruther-Kerr mentioned by Mugg.

Anstruther, Mr. and Mrs. Arthur (*BM*) — Members of the British diplomatic legation group in Azania.

Anstruther-Kerr, Angus (*OG, SOH*) — A Scots soldier who has a serious fall on the island of Mugg while practicing commando cliff climbing.

Anthea (*WS*) — A school friend of Julia's. She was fond of the books of Gilbert Warwick. She wrote to him, and he responded with a three-page letter. Later she wrote to him again, and he answered with essentially the same letter, and thus she became disillusioned. She had wanted to carry on a personal correspondence rather than simply receive form letters.

Antoine (*BR*) — Anthony Blanche, occasionally addressed by the French form of his first name.

Antoinette (*HD*) — A girl at a Catholic boarding school in Paris who was expelled for wearing lipstick at Sunday Mass; mentioned by Thérèse de Vitré, who attended the same school.

Antonic, Dr. Bogdan (*SKME*) — The International Secretary of the Committee of the Bellorius Tercentenary Celebration Association. He is cultural adviser to the Ministry of Popular Enlightenment and conceives the idea of honoring Bellorius. He is a sympathetic character, a Croatian who unsuccessfully applies for citizenship in Neutralia. He and his wife are symbolic of the displaced persons of the post–World War II era.

Antonic, Mme. (*SKME*) — The optimistic but nervous Czech wife of Dr. Antonic. She hopes to leave Neutralia with her husband and family.

Antonios, Archimandrite (*POMF*) — A bizarre refugee expelled from Bulgaria who seeks help in the Ministry of Information in London during the "Phoney War" period. The Bulgarians expelled him for "fornications," but he claims that politics was involved. An archimandrite is a high-ranking clergyman in the Eastern Orthodox church.

Apar (*H*) — A Roman praetorian prefect.

Ape, Mrs. Melrose (*VB*) — An American woman evangelist. She is a tough taskmaster to her singing angels and is very concerned with financial profit. Her most famous hymn is "There Ain't No Flies on the Lamb of God." She is modeled on American evangelist Aimée Semple MacPherson.

Apollo (*LO*) — A British magazine for which Francis Hinsley wrote a book review. The February, 1920, issue is found by Dennis Barlow among Hinsley's effects.

Appleby (*WS*) — A friend of Arthur Atwater. Appleby claims to know the location of a cave in Bolivia where the Jesuits stored treasure.

Applejacks (*MA, SOH*) — A sobriquet for the Royal Corps of Halberdiers.

Apthorpe (*CRS*) — Charles Ryder's house captain at Spierpoint.

Apthorpe (*MA, OG, SOH*) — A pompous, stuffy, self-important junior officer in the Halberdiers. He often refers to his experience in Africa. Because he and Guy Crouchback are about the same age they become companions and are called "uncle" by the younger officers. He has a portable latrine which Brigadier Ritchie-Hook discovers and uses. He and Apthorpe engage in a game of hide-and-seek with this commode until Ritchie-Hook booby-traps it and blows it up. Apthorpe is put in command of a company and later promoted to captain. He is extremely officious and is thorny about his rights as a captain. After the expedition to the French African coast, he is given shore leave and develops a tropical illness. Crouchback visits him in the hospital and gives him a bottle of whiskey. Apthorpe makes Guy promise to deliver his gear to Chatty Corner in the event of his death. Apthorpe dies from drinking the whiskey Guy brought him, and at the end of *MA* he is buried in Africa. In *OG*, Guy collects his gear and delivers it to Chatty Corner. Corner informs Guy that Apthorpe worked for a tobacco company in a town in Africa, that he never lived in the "bush," as he had so often claimed.

Aquitania (*OG, SOH*) — A famous Cunard trans-Atlantic liner on which Trimmer served as a hairdresser before the war. He first met Virginia Troy on one of the ship's voyages.

Archie (*Sc*) — The son of the British Minister of Ishmaelia. He cannot obtain a job because he is unable to pass any examinations.

Ardingly (*EB, SOH*) — Batman to both Ludovic and Captain Fremantle at the parachute training base in England. He is especially friendly with Fremantle.

Arkwright (*BR*) — A fictional Oxford lecturer. Charles Ryder's cousin Jasper tells Charles that he should attend Arkwright's lectures on Demosthenes.

Armenian Archbishop in Azania (*BM*) — Deserts the country when it appears that Seth will be overthrown by Prince Seyid. After Seth's victory he returns. Misprinted in some editions as "American Archbishop."

Armstrong (*WS*) — An artist friend of John Plant's father who lets his servants intimidate him.

Arthur (*BM*) — A hall porter at Basil Seal's London club.

Arthur (*Cr*) — A young man whom the young lady fancies briefly, but he turns out to be a homosexual.

Arthur (*LO*) — Mr. and Mrs. Walter Heinkel's pet Sealyham, whose funeral is arranged by the Happier Hunting Ground. He is cremated at the pet cemetery, and the usual anniversary card about the dog wagging his tail in heaven is arranged for.

Arthur (*OGP*) — A friend of the Pinfolds who is an official at the British Broadcasting Corporation. He confirms that Angel of the BBC has been in England and never on the *Caliban*.

Arthur (*Sc*) — An elegant young decorative painter employed by Julia Stitch.

Arthur (*VB*) — A commercial traveler who becomes seasick on the Channel boat to England.

Arundel (*VB*) — At a hotel there Adam Fenwick-Symes and Nina Blount have sexual intercourse for the first time.

Arundell (*EB, SOH*) — A member of a recusant Catholic family who attends the funeral of Guy Crouchback's father.

Athenaeum (*BR*) — A London club (founded 1824) to which Charles Ryder's father belonged.

Athol, Mrs. "Teeny" (née Jackson) (*Sc*) — An important government official of Ishmaelia and aunt of President Rathbone Jackson. Named, like other Jacksons, after real political and intellectual figures of the 1930s whom Waugh thought too "leftist" — in this case, Katherine Stewart-Murray, the "red" Duchess of Atholl (1874–1960). See also *Jackson family*.

Atwater, Arthur (*WS*) — The bold, aggressive stockings salesman whose automobile hits and kills John Plant's father. He has the audacity to keep pestering Plant for money. He uses three aliases — Thurston, Long, and Norton. When brought to trial, he is acquitted of killing Plant's father. He constantly emphasizes the advantages that rich people have over him. In World War II he prospers in the service and is in charge of a large area of conquered Germany.

Atwater, Mr. (*Sc*) — A local troublemaker in the area of Boot Magna.

Audrey (*HD*) — An acquaintance of John Beaver's who invites him to dinner. Beaver usually receives such invitations at the last minute when some other guest "chucks."

Augustus (*MA, EB, SOH*) — One of Virginia Troy's lovers after her divorce from Tommy Blackhouse. He is also known as Gussie.

Aunt at Peterborough — See *Peterborough*.

Aunt at Tunbridge Wells — See *Tunbridge Wells*.

Aunt Greta (*DF*) — Alastair Digby-Vane-Trumpington's aunt (see *Circumference, Countess of*) — who writes to him about Pennyfeather's wedding to Margot. Pennyfeather's arrest, of course, prevents the marriage from occurring.

"Aunt Lydia's Post Bag" (*LO*) — The original name of the newspaper advice column now called "The Wisdom of the Guru Brahmin."

Aunt Margie (*MA, SOH*) — Daisy Leonard's aunt.

Aunt Martha (*LITS*) — Tom Watch's aunt at whose house in Devon Tom and Angela Trench-Troubridge are scheduled to spend their honeymoon.

Aurelian (*H*) — Roman military leader and emperor; Constantine courts his friendship and hopes to rise through this connection. Aurelian is, however, murdered by his own advisers on the shores of the Bosphorus.

Austen (*DF*) — An undergraduate at Scone College who has a grand piano in his room. Some drunken members of the Bollinger Club smash the piano.

Austin (*IA*) — Mr. Kentish's car. He lends the car so

that ransom can be delivered for Prunella Brooks's release.

Austin Seven (*VB*) — A reasonably priced auto driven by "the average reader"; mentioned in ironic contrast with Lady Metroland's Hispano-Suiza, Mrs. Mouse's Rolls Royce, and Lady Circumference's Daimler.

Australian journalist (*IA*) — He works for the *Daily Excess* and reports the Prunella Brooks kidnapping story. He helps deliver the ransom money.

Aylesbury (*VB*) — The county seat of Buckinghamshire. Colonel Blount's estate, Doubting Hall, is near there.

Azania (*BM, IA*) — An island empire off the east coast of Africa. After the death of Emperor Seth the country becomes a joint protectorate of England and France under the League of Nations. It is modeled on Ethiopia, where Waugh served as a newspaper correspondent in 1930 and 1935. In a brief prefatory note to "Incident in Azania," Waugh states that Azania is "in character and history a combination of Zanzibar and Abyssinia."

B

Babbitt (*BM*) — A British Foreign Office official in London who plays chess by cable with Percy Legge in Azania.

Babe (*HD*) — A friend of Jock Grant-Menzies.

Babs (*HD*) — A prostitute friend of Milly's whom Tony and Jock meet at the One Hundredth Club.

Baby (*HD*) — Dan's cheap, low-class, cantankerous girl friend who accompanies him to Brighton, where they met Millie and Tony Last.

Bachelors (*WS*) — A London club mentioned by Arthur Atwater. John Plant has heard of it, and Jimmie Grainger, a friend of Atwater's, belonged.

Bagnold, Clarissa (*OGP*) — A neighbor of the Pinfold family.

Bagnold, Colonel and Mrs. (*OGP*) — Neighbors of the Pinfold family.

Bakic (*C, TMI, EB, SOH*) — A Serbo-Croat interpreter who works for the Yugoslavian partisans. An unpleasant, suspicious, dedicated Communist, he distrusts the British and the Jewish refugees. In the 1930s he had been a political exile in New York, where he had learned some English.

"Balance, The" — A short story by Waugh about a young art student who becomes despondent over a terminated love affair and for a time contemplates suicide. The story appeared in the anthology *Georgian Stories, 1926* (London and New York, 1927).

Balcairn, Countess of — See *Panrast*.

Balcairn, Simon, Earl of (*VB*) — A gossip writer for the London *Daily Excess*. After he is barred from Margot Metroland's party and then caught attending in disguise, he telephones a fictitious story of the scene and commits suicide. Alec Waugh states that Patrick Balfour, later Lord Kinross, who wrote the "Mr. Gossip" column for the *Daily Sketch*, was one of the models for Balcairn.

Baldwin, Mr. (*Sc*) — A powerful, mysterious, and resourceful British financier who parachutes into Jacksonburg and helps prevent the Russians from taking control of Ishmaelia. Baldwin is an alias. His real name is never revealed. Possibly based on the industrialist Sir Antonin Besse (1877–1951), founder of Saint Anthony's College, Oxford, whom Waugh met on his first visit to Ethiopia; *Diaries of Evelyn Waugh*, ed. Michael Davie (Boston, 1976), pp. 340–42.

Ballingar (*BFGP*) — An Irish market town about a five-hour train trip from Dublin. It is near there that Bella Fleace's home is located.

Ballingar House (*BFGP*) — A country home near Fleacetown, in need of repair.

Ballon, Madame (*BM*) — The wife of the French ambassador to Azania, falsely rumored to be carrying on an affair with General Connolly.

Ballon, Monsieur (*BM*) — The French ambassador to Azania. He and his legation seethe with intrigue and spying. He is especially suspicious of the British. He arranges a coup which eventually overthrows Seth.

Bamfshire, Sonia (*BR*) — A woman treated for illness by a doctor in Vienna.

Bane, Sergeant (*OG, SOH*) — A soldier stationed on the isle of Mugg.

Bankes (*CRS*) — One of the wittier students at Spierpoint.

Banks, Archie (*BFPG*) — The heir of Bella Fleace. He is a distant cousin who lives in the South Kensington section of London and works for the British Museum. Bella does not care for him. To prevent him from inheriting all her money, she decides to spend a considerable amount for a lavish party.

THE DICTIONARY

Banks, Olive (*BR*) — A student dismissed from the Catholic school that Cordelia Flyte attended.

Bannister, Jack (*Sc*) — The British Vice-Consul in Ishmaelia. An old school friend of William Boot, he gives William much valuable help and information about the political turmoil occurring there.

Baptist missionary (*IA*) — An American who was killed by the natives. His body was dismembered, and various parts were sent to Matodi.

Barebones-Abraham, Tom (*POMF*) — A nom de plume of Ambrose Silk.

Bari (*C, TMI, EB, SOH*) — A city in Italy, the headquarters of the British Mission to the Anti-Fascist Forces of National Liberation (Adriatic). After a stay there Guy Crouchback is sent to Begoy.

Barker (*BR*) — An Oxford student who is a friend of Collins and Tyngate. He is a candidate for president of the Union.

Barker (*IA*) — An Englishman employed in Azania.

Barlow, Dennis (*LO*) — A twenty-eight-year-old British poet who comes to Hollywood to write a life of Shelley for the movies. Losing his job, he goes to work for the Happier Hunting Ground. For a time he is on the verge of becoming a nonsectarian clergyman. After Aimée Thanatogenos's death he outwits Joyboy and returns to England.

Barnet, Mrs. (*BR, OG, SOH*) — An aged, bedridden woman who never speaks. She is often visited by Guy Crouchback and his mother when Guy is a child. Guy reminisces about her when he is recovering in an Egyptian hospital from his harrowing boat escape from Crete.

Barney, Mrs. (*BR*) — A friend of the Marchmains.

Bartholomew, the Reverend Errol (*LO*) — A nonsectarian clergyman who performs religious funeral services for dead pet animals. The names were chosen from those of movie stars Errol Flynn and Freddie Bartholomew.

Barton, Miss (*Sc*) — An employee of the London store in which William Boot procures his traveler's gear.

Basher (*OGP*) — One of the nicknames of Reginald Graves-Upton. Like his other sobriquets, "Bruiser," "Old Fisticuffs," "Boxer," and "Pug," this name associates him with the Box, supposedly a source of therapeutic power, in which he is greatly interested.

Basilina (*H*) — A Roman allegedly engaged in a plot against Emperor Constantine.

Basil Seal Rides Again or The Rake's Regress — A story by Waugh published in a limited, signed edition in 1963 and reprinted in a British paperback edition in 1967. Basil Seal prevents his daughter from marrying a young scamp by convincing her that her fiance is his illegitimate son. The story takes place in 1961.

Basingstoke, Lord Richard (*TB*) — A well-to-do student at Oxford who cannot dine with Adam Doure becaues he has to complete a Collections Paper.

Bassianus (*H*) — A Roman married to Constantine's half sister, Anastasia; he was allegedly engaged in a plot against Emperor Constantine.

Bat, Bert (*BR*) — One of the older servants at Brideshead Castle. A man named "Bert" is mentioned as a servant. Later Sebastian stops to speak to a man named "Bat" riding a bicycle on the castle grounds. Some readers regard these two men as separate individuals, but possibly the references are to the same character.

Bates, Frank (*CRS*) — The most popular of the housemasters at Spierpoint.

Bateson (*Sc*) — The eager young reporter on the *Beast* assigned to meet William Boot on the latter's return from Ishmaelia. He is a graduate of a correspondence school.

Batts (*DF*) — A London club where Philbrick claims to be staying; he mentions this to Pennyfeather near the end of *DF*. In later novels this club is called Brat's or Bratt's, which see. The reference is to the actual exclusive Pratt's Club in London (founded 1841).

Batulle, Baroness (*BM*) — One of the nobility of Azania.

Baumbein, Otto (*LO*) — A high official at Megalopolitan Pictures. He claims to be too busy to tell Sir Francis Hinsley that the latter has been fired.

Baverstock, Peter (*WS*) — A friend of Lucy Simmonds who had wanted to marry her. He worked in the Malay States, and she corresponded with him regularly.

Bayton (*HD*) — A town near Hetton Abbey. A nearby town called Little Bayton is mentioned in the same novel.

Beamish, Dr. (*LAR*) — Director of the Euthanasia Department in Satellite City. He was a fiery radical in the 1930s and is now disillusioned and embittered.

Bean, Silly, Black Bean, Awful Bean (*MA, SOH*) — Characters in a traditional Halberdier play.

"Beano" (*OG, SOH*) — The nickname of a major-general who is a friend of "Jumbo" Trotter.

Beaseley, Robin (*BSR, HD*) — A former lover of Marjorie, Brenda Last's married sister. In the "Alternative Ending" to *HD* he is mentioned as having carried on an affair with Marjorie. The same information is given in *BSR*, but there the name is spelled Beasley.

Beast — See *Daily Beast*.

"Beastly" (*Sc*) — The private school nickname for William Boot. Jack Bannister recognizes him under this name.

Beaver, John (*BSR, HD*) — The inept, unemployed, and unprincipled man-about-town and lover of Brenda Last. At the beginning of *HD*, Beaver is twenty-five years old. After leaving Oxford, he worked at an advertising agency until the economic depression terminated his job. When Brenda is no longer able to finance their affair, he breaks off the relationship. In "By Special Request" and in the "Alternative Ending" to *HD*, Beaver tires of Brenda, leaves her, and then becomes infatuated with Mrs. Rattery, who takes no interest in him. Beaver's mother finally sends him abroad (to either Berlin or Vienna) as a buyer for her shop.

Beaver, Mrs. (*BSR, HD, Sc*) — The owner of a London interior decorating shop; she also rents and remodels apartments. Oblivious of moral values, she is concerned only with making money. She is the mother of John Beaver in *HD* and is still operating her business in *Sc*. In "By Special Request" and in the "Alternative Ending" to *HD* she arranges for Tony to take over Brenda's flat for, of course, an additional gratuity. Her decor for Brenda's sitting room at Hetton ("white chromium plating and natural sheepskin carpet") is reminiscent of that made fashionable by Syrie Maugham (divorced wife of Somerset Maugham), who specialized in interiors in white. See Donald Greene, "Another Waugh Identification: Mrs. Beaver," *EWN*, Spring, 1987, pp. 1–2.

Beckthorpe (*OGu*) — He runs, for several years, an unsuccessful farm in Kenya.

Beech, Air Marshall (*MA, OG, EB, SOH*) — Ian Kilbannock's pompous and boring military superior whom Guy Crouchback meets at a party. In *MA, SOH*, Beech hopes to become a member of Bellamy's club. In *OG, SOH*, he hides under a billiard table in Bellamy's (he has been elected to membership) during a London air raid (strictly following orders, as he says). In *EB, SOH* it is mentioned that he has published a book of reminiscences. The rank of air marshal in the Royal Air Force is equivalent to that of a full general in the army.

Beefsteak (*POMF*) — A London club (founded 1876) to which Sir Joseph Mainwaring belongs.

Begedbian (*BR*) — An Armenian cook for Sebastian Flyte and Mr. Samgrass during a trip to the Levant. Sebastian is supposed to be with Samgrass but manages to avoid him most of the time.

Begoy (*C, TMI, EB, SOH*) — A fictional town in northern Croatia held by the Yugoslavian partisans. In *EB, SOH*, the British liaison group has its mission there, and an airfield near the town is used to bring in supplies. In *TMI, C*, Major Gordon is stationed there and tries to help the Jewish refugees.

Bell, Monsignor (*BR*) — The chaplain to the Catholic undergraduates at Oxford and a friend of the Marchmain family. It is recommended that Sebastian stay with him to keep the young man's drinking under control.

Bellacita (*SKME*) — The capital city of Neutralia.

"Bella Fleace Gave a Party" — A short story by Waugh (1932) about an elderly grand dame who decides to give a lavish party and then forgets to mail the invitations. The story first appeared in *Harper's Bazaar* (London), December 7, 1932, pp. 12–13, 100–101. It was collected in *Work Suspended and Other Stories Written Before the Second World War* (London, 1949), in *Tactical Exercise* (Boston, 1954), and in *Charles Ryder's Schooldays and Other Stories* (Boston, 1982).

Bellamy's (*MA, OG, OGP, EB, SOH, BSRA*) — A fictional London club on Saint James Street to which Gilbert Pinfold belongs. Guy Crouchback is also a member there. Among other members, mentioned in the trilogy, are Tommy Blackhouse and Ian Kilbannock.

Bellorius (*SKME*) — An imaginary Latin poet alleged to have died in 1646 in a province of the Habsburg Empire (now the fictional Republic of Neutralia). Bellorius's writings are studied by Scott-King, who is invited to a tercentenary celebration in Neutralia honoring the poet. Miss Bombaum confuses him with the hero of Robert Graves's recently published *Count Belisarius*, a biography of the famous Byzantine general.

Ben (*H*) — A ship's bosun with whom Helena becomes friendly while traveling from Britain to Gaul.

THE DICTIONARY

Benakis (*Sc*) — The proprietor of a food store in Jacksonburg, Ishmaelia.

Benfleet, Sam (*VB*) — The junior director of a London publishing firm. Adam Symes's autobiography was supposed to be published by this firm, but the manuscript was confiscated by customs and burned. During the war we hear that Benfleet's "Sword Unsheathed" series, featuring war poets, is very successful.

Benito, Dr. Gabriel (*Sc*) — The director of the press bureau in Ishmaelia. His official title is Minister of Foreign Affairs and Propaganda. He is short, well dressed, self-confident, and energetic. He wishes to overthrow the Jacksons and set up a Soviet state (both the Germans and the Russians are competing primarily to obtain the gold-ore concession there). "Benito" was, of course, the first name of the Italian Fascist dictator, Mussolini.

Benson (*ER*) — Sir James Macrae's chauffeur.

Benson (*POMF*) — One of the Sothill family servants at Malfrey.

Benson, Mr. (*IA*) — A second lieutenant in the native levy.

Benson, Mr. and Mrs. (*OGP*) — Passengers on the *Caliban*. Mrs. Benson becomes chummy with Mrs. Cockson, and both of them enjoy social drinking. Pinfold imagines that she and Mrs. Cockson are involved in some of the last negative hallucinations he experiences.

Bentham, Miss (*ER*) — The night secretary to filmmaker Sir James Macrae.

Bentinck (*Sc*) — A butler in the Boot family.

Bentley (*OD, WS*) — A make of automobile manufactured by Rolls-Royce, almost as expensive but more modest in appearance. Alastair Digby-Vane-Trumpington drives a Bentley in *OD*. Grainger sells his Bentley in *WS*.

Bentley, Geoffrey (*POMF, BSRA*) — The publisher of Ambrose Silk's writing. In *POMF*, during the war he is employed at the Ministry of Information in charge of writers. In *BSRA* he organizes a dinner to honor Ambrose Silk.

Benwell, Mr (*WS*) — John Plant's publisher. He is distressed when John reports that he wants to try some new technique since this might interfere with his best-selling status. He also publishes Roger Simmond's books.

Bergson, Amelia (*LO*) — A writer who makes Before Need arrangements to be buried at Whispering Glades.

Bert — See *Bat, Bert*.

Bertie (*Cr*) — The brother of the young lady letter writer. He spends much of his time drinking, and for a while is engaged to Mabel Phillips.

Bertie (*OG, EB, SOH*) — A grenadier captain stationed on the island of Mugg. In *OG, SOH* he is for a time adjutant to Tommy Blackhouse. He is later taken prisoner by the Germans during the fall of Crete. In *EB, SOH* he is released from a PW camp after the war and returns to England and life revolving around Bellamy's Club.

Bertie (*POMF*) — A member of the upper class looking for a war service position.

Bertie (*VB*) — One of the film workers for Mr. Isaacs.

Bertrand, M. (*BM*) — The owner and editor of the *Courier d'Azanie*. He does not wish to sell the paper because it gives him prestige in Azania. Basil buys the paper and lets Bertrand retain his titles. Basil wishes to use it as a vehicle for the new government ideas of Seth.

Beste-Bingham, Eddie (*POMF*) — A friend of Sir Joseph Mainwaring. He claims that the British have a secret war weapon called RDF (the early form of radar) which will thwart the Germans.

Beste-Chetwynde, Margot (*DF, VB, BM, ER, HD, OD, PP, Sc, POMF, WS, BR, BSRA*) — A wealthy high-society beauty who when we first meet her in *DF* is a widow with a black paramour. She is the sister-in-law of Lord Pastmaster, and it is rumored that she poisoned her first husband. She attends Llannabba Sports Day with Chokey, her lover, since her son, Peter, goes to school there. She achieves a vast financial income by running a string of brothels in South America inherited from her father. She tires of Chokey and decides to marry again to achieve greater respectability. She chooses Paul Pennyfeather for her husband, but before the marriage takes place, Paul is arrested while carrying out arrangements to transport some of Margot's prostitutes. She carries on an affair with Alastair Digby-Vane-Trumpington both before and after her marriage to Maltravers (Lord Metroland). As Lady Metroland she uses her influence with her husband to free Pennyfeather from jail and arrange his "death."

Her first name may come from the most famous real Margot of the time, the second wife of Prime

Minister H. H. Asquith. Her garrulity and love of publicity caused a good deal of disapproval.

In *VB*, Margot maintains her connection with white slavery, offering to get Mrs. Ape's "angel" Chastity a job in South America. She lives in Pastmaster House on Hill Street, one of the finest homes in London. It is rumored that she had an affair with press magnate Lord Monomark before her second marriage. She throws a grand party for Mrs. Ape. In *BM* she gives parties and receives visitors. When Basil Seal returns from Azania, we hear that Margot has closed up her home and is wintering in America. In *HD* and *Sc* Margot continues being a London socialite, giving frequent lunch and dinner parties. In *Sc* she also sponsors charities and is acquainted with Julia Stitch. In *WS* she visits a London art show party given by John Plant's father, and in *BR* she gives a luncheon party in Charles Ryder's honor on the occasion of the exhibit of his Latin-American paintings.

In *POMF* she shuts her London home and moves to the Ritz Hotel. Her home is later destroyed during the German bombing. Peter, her son who in *DF* had inherited from his uncle the title Earl of Pastmaster, announces that he plans to marry Lady Molly Meadowes. Margot and Molly's mother get together to make arrangements for the wedding, and Margot attends the wedding. Also in *POMF*, Sonia and Alastair Digby-Vane-Trumpington invite themselves to luncheon at Margot's. Margot dines with Angela Lyne, and later Basil Seal and Margot converse about Angela's drinking.

In *BSRA* we learn that Margot has lived in the Ritz since the world war (Pastmaster House was never rebuilt) and has become a television addict. In the short stories she is mentioned as giving a party in 1933 in London (*OD*), giving a luncheon (*PP*), and inviting Simon Lent to luncheon (*ER*).

Beste-Chetwynde, Peter (*DF, VB, BM, POMF, BSRA*) — Margot's son. In *DF* he attends Llanabba School and has Paul Pennyfeather as one of his teachers. He becomes friendly with Pennyfeather. He favors the marriage of Paul to Margot although he is aware of his mother's business activities. Upon his uncle's death he succeeds him as the Earl of Pastmaster. After finishing his studies at Llanabba, he goes to Oxford, where he drinks heavily. In *VB*, Peter drinks heavily, and in *BM* he is mentioned as having attended a wild party given by Basil Seal. At some point he serves in the cavalry (mentioned in *POMF*). In *POMF* at the beginning of World War II he is one of the first of his social set in uniform, arousing Alastair Digby-Vane-Trumpington's envy. He decides to marry and courts several eligible girls, finally settling on Molly Meadowes, one of Lady Granchester's daughters. Actually it is really she who proposes when she sees his boyish naïveté after they discover Angela Lyne intoxicated outside a cinema. Peter will be one of the officers in the new commando force and believes one should "hang about" with one's friends in wartime.

In *BSRA*, Peter has become a stout, well-dressed "duffer" very much like Basil Seal although a trifle younger. He and Basil attend the banquet in honor of Ambrose Silk. He is still married happily to the former Lady Molly Meadows (in *POMF* Meadows is spelled Meadowes).

Bettie (*EB, US*) — A homely hospital nurse who in *EB* is the mistress of Brigadier Cape at Bari. In the British edition of *EB* (*US*) the name is spelled Betty.

Betty, Aunt (*BR*) — A relative of the Marchmains. She sends a wedding present to Julia on her marriage to Rex Mottram.

Beverly-Waldorf (*LO*) — A hotel in Los Angeles where Aimée Thanatogenos was employed as a beautician before going to work at Whispering Glades.

Bey, Mme Fifi Fatim (*BM*) — The town courtesan of Debra-Dowa; she is under the protection of Viscount Boaz, Minister of the Interior.

Bianca (*MA, OG, SOH*) — Along with her sister Josefina, the housekeeper at Guy Crouchback's home in Santa Dulcina delle Rocce, Italy.

Bicesters (*VB*) — A family who sponsors a dance. Jane Brown, the prime minister's daughter, tells her mother the dance was lovely.

Bickerton-Gibbs, Mr. (*TB*) — A student at Oxford and friend of Henry Quest.

Bigod (*EB, SOH*) — A member of an old recusant Catholic family who attends the funeral of Guy Crouchback's father.

Bill (*Cr*) — A passenger aboard ship described by the young lady letter writer; he is disillusioned by his wife's behavior with a foreigner.

Bill (*DF*) — A detective seeking to arrest Philbrick on charges of false pretences and impersonation.

Bill (*DF*) — A friend of Grimes in charge of a group of Margot Beste-Chetwynde's places of prostitution.

Bill (*POMF*) — The husband of the unnamed lovely girl

living at Malt House, Grantley Green, with whom Basil has an affair. Bill is serving in the army, and Basil meets his wife while attempting to billet the Connollies in the Prettyman-Partridge house. He carries on an affair with the young woman until her husband's yeomanry unit returns home. The last name of Bill and his wife is never given.

Bill (*VB*) — A commercial traveler who becomes seasick on the English Channel boat to England.

Billy (*OGP*) — A character Pinfold hears speaking on the *Caliban*. Billy is speaking about his impurity and confessing it to a clergyman.

Bishop (*BR*) — A Episcopal clergyman who is one of the passengers on the liner taking Charles, Celia, and Julia to England. He sits at the captain's table.

Bishop of Chertsey, the younger sister of (*VB*) — Her engagement is mentioned in the Mr. Chatterbox column. Chertsey is an undistinguished suburb in south London, and presumably the doings of younger relatives of its bishop would be of no great interest to the readers of society columns.

Blackadder, Mr. (*OGP*) — A passenger on the *Caliban*.

Blackall (*DF*) — An Oxford gate porter who predicts that Pennyfeather will probably become a schoolmaster after having been sent down for indecent behavior since most students expelled for that reason enter the teaching profession.

Blackberry (*HD*) — The cat at the Sixty-four Club at 64 Sink Street, London.

Black Bitch (*BM*) — General Connolly's native African wife. She becomes a duchess when her husband is created Duke of Ukaka for his victory over Seyid. She is devoted to the general, and he in turn is very fond of her; he uses the term affectionately.

Blackhouse, Tommy (*MA, OG, EB, SOH*) — In *MA, SOH* the man with whom Guy Crouchback's first wife falls in love; as a consequence, she obtains a divorce from Guy. Blackhouse marries Virginia but is later divorced from her, although they remain friends. In *OG, SOH* he gets friendly with Guy and becomes Guy's commanding officer on the Isle of Mugg. He goes to Egypt with Hookforce. Although he is scheduled to land on Crete with Hookforce, he accidentally breaks his leg aboard ship and does not participate in the debacle on that island. He recuperates in a hospital in Egypt. In *EB, SOH* he returns to England from convalescence to raise another Special Service Force. He offers Crouchback a post on his staff, but Guy decides to stay with the Halberdiers. At the end of the war Blackhouse has risen to the rank of major general. In 1951 he retires from military service with many decorations and has also acquired a new, attractive wife.

Black Mischief — A novel (1932) starring the modernistically obsessed Emperor Seth of Azania and Basil Seal. Through a series of impractical theories conceived by Seth and carried out by Seal, chaos ensues, and Seth is overthrown and slain.

Blackstone Gaol (*DF*) — The prison where Pennyfeather is confined and Sir Wilfrid Lucas-Dockery carries out his bizarre experiments. It is named no doubt for Sir William Blackstone, the famous eighteenth-century jurist and author of *Commentaries on the Law of England*, a widely used textbook. It describes the harsh terms of the punishment of crime during the century.

Blackwater, Mrs. Kitty (*VB*) — The twin sister of Lady Throbbing. She is an old gossip and like her sister is obsessed with sexual topics.

Blackwell (*Sc*) — The country estate where Julia Stitch and others read John Courteney Boot's book *Waste of Time* aloud.

Blade, Millicent (Milly) (*OGu*) — The attractive young protagonist. Her nose allures men until Hector, the dog, bites it off.

Blades (*WS*) — One of the fellows in the old John Plant–Roger Simmonds social set. Blades is now a member of Parliament. He is referred to only in the 1942 edition of *WS*.

Blake (*BSR, HD*) — The chauffeur of Tony and Brenda Last (also in the "Alternative Ending" to *HD*). He is called Dawson in *HD*.

Blake, Corporal (*OG, SOH*) — A soldier hurt in a fall while climbing a cliff during commando training on the island of Mugg.

Blake, Tubby (*MA, SOH*) — One of the older Halberdiers. Stout and genial, he was a schoolmaster in civilian life.

Blake-Blakiston, Lt. Cmdr. (*OG, SOH*) — The captain of the boat that lands HQ Hookforce and some of B Commando at Crete.

Blanche, Anthony (*BR*) — The "aesthete" par excellence of Oxford. He is intellectual and cultured to the highest degree. He is a homosexual and a fascinating conversationalist. He leaves Oxford and takes a flat in Munich, having formed an attachment to a policeman there. Eventually he meets Samgrass and Sebastian by chance in Constantinople and spends some time with them. He later visits Charles Ryder's art exhibit in London and comments on the paintings. He is modeled on Brian Howard and Harold Acton.

Bland, Ralph (*PP*) — Billy Cornphillip's closest relative and heir until Cornphillip's marriage. They quarrel, and Bland runs off to Venice for a time with Billy's wife. She becomes pregnant by him, but he leaves her for an American woman. She returns to her husband.

Bland, William (*BM*) — The young honorary attaché at the British legation in Azania. For a time he is Prudence Courteney's lover; then she becomes involved with Basil Seal. He is very casual about his legation duties. In some editions of *BM* — for example, in the first English and first American — he is on occasion mistakenly called William Trench. This error persists in the latest (1977) Little, Brown reprinting of *BM*.

Blank, Prudence (*Sc*) — Known also as "the Mary Selena Wilmark of Britain"; she dines with journalist Wenlock Jakes.

Blenheim, Lady Belinda (*WS*) — Her spaniel is killed "in atrocious circumstances" in John Plant's *The Frightened Footman*. Lady Belinda is mentioned only in the 1942 edition of *WS*.

Blenkinsop (*HD*) — A private detective working on the Tony–Brenda Last divorce case who is concerned about Milly's daughter being along on the trip to Brighton.

Blenkinsop (*POMF*) — A pseudonym given to Basil Seal in a fantasy.

Blenkinsop, Major (*EB, SOH*) — A military doctor who treats Guy Crouchback's knee after his parachute accident.

Blenkinsop, Mr. (*VB*) — Margot Metroland's butler.

Blight Street, 14 (*EB, SOH*) — The rather appropriate address of Dr. Akonanga's office in London before he moves on to the Ministry of Information.

Block, Sergeant (*BR*) — One of the soldiers in Charles Ryder's military unit. He is sent with a group of men to collect bedstraw when the army prepares to camp at Brideshead.

Bloggs, Nannie (*Sc*) — The elderly and bedridden nannie to the Boot family. She reputedly has a considerable amount of money and frequently won bets on the horse races. She enjoys telling the various members of the family that each is her heir. She plays dominoes and cards for money and usually wins. Near the end of some British editions she is mistakenly called Nannie Price.

Blount, Colonel (*VB*) — Nina's absentminded and eccentric father. He lives on a large country estate called Doubting Hall and allows the estate to be used for filming a saga about John Wesley. He enjoys appearing in the film as an extra. Eventually he buys the movie and takes considerable delight in showing it. At one point he writes out a check for a thousand pounds for Adam Symes and signs it "Charlie Chaplin."

Blount, Nina (*VB*) — The fiancée of Adam Fenwick-Symes. She has an off-and-on engagement with Adam throughout the novel but ultimately marries Eddy Littlejohn (Ginger). Ginger goes to military duty. Nina and Adam renew their affair, and Nina becomes pregnant.

Blouse, Mrs. (*VB*) — One of Margot Metroland's servants.

Blue Grotto Club (*BR*) — A bar in London catering to homosexuals. Anthony Blanche goes there with Charles Ryder.

Boaz, Viscount (*BM*) — The Minister of the Interior in Azania. Near the end of the novel he captures Seth and murders him. He himself is eventually killed by Major Joab. Boaz was Waugh's nickname among the Lygon girls and their group during the early 1930s (Boaz was the kindly kinsman and later husband of Ruth in the biblical book of Ruth).

Bob (*VB*) — A young man, dissatisfied with his present job, who desires to go into the automobile business.

Boggett (*EH*) — The gardener on Beverly Metcalfe's country estate.

Bogolov, Mr. and Mrs. (*LO*) — Customers of Whispering Glades. Mrs. Bogolov makes arrangements for her husband's burial; she is distressed when she learns that Whispering Glades does not allow floral arrangements in the form of wreaths and crosses.

Bollinger Club (*DF*) — A group of Oxford undergraduates and former Oxford students who usually hold an annual dinner. The heavy drinking of this group leads to much destruction of property and to Paul Pennyfeather's expulsion from Oxford. Near the end of *DF* we learn that Peter Pastmaster has become a member of this group.

Bombaum, Miss Martha (*SKME*) — The cynical, aggressive newspaper columnist and political activist who attends the Bellorius celebration in Neutralia.

She is perhaps based on the American journalist Dorothy Thompson.

Boot, Bernard (*Sc*) — An uncle of William Boot. He is a researcher in his family's genealogy.

Boot, John Courteney (*Sc*) — A popular British novelist who also writes travel and history books. He hopes to be sent to Ishmaelia as a foreign correspondent through the influence of Julia Stitch. Mrs. Stitch makes the contact with newspaper magnate Lord Copper, but by mistake William Boot is sent instead. Later John Courteney is given a knighthood that was really intended for William. Near the end of *Sc* he is hired by the *Beast* and sent to the Antarctic on an assignment.

Boot, Mrs. (*Sc*) — William's bedridden widowed grandmother who possesses the money in the family.

Boot, Mrs. (*Sc*) — William's widowed mother, who owns the contents of Boot Magna and has some ownership rights to the flower garden.

Boot, Priscilla (*Sc*) — William Boot's younger sister. She causes her brother considerable difficulty when as a joke she changes the "great crested grebe" to "badger" in one of his nature newspaper columns.

Boot, Roderick (*Sc*) — An uncle of William Boot. He manages the Boot estate and household.

Boot, Theodore (*Sc*) — An uncle of William Boot who likes to sneak off to London and engage in bawdy activity. When John Courteney Boot and William Boot do not attend Lord Copper's banquet honoring Boot of the *Beast*, old Uncle Theodore is hired by the newspaper and enjoys the banquet immensely. His salary will give him the opportunity to return to his old roué, man-about-town way of living.

Boot, William (*Sc*) — The writer of a nature column for Lord Copper's *Beast*, sent by error to Ishmaelia. He achieves the major scoop of the attempted Russian power grab and returns to England in triumph. He decides to retain his old job of writing a column about rural life.

Boot Magna (*Sc*) — The large, ramshackle country home of the Boot family. Also called Boot Magna Hall.

Boot Magna Halt (*Sc*) — The station for Boot Magna on the railway branch line.

Booth-Bryce, Bertie (*Sc*) — A man about whom Uncle Theodore and another guest at the banquet given by Lord Copper reminisce, both having known him many years ago. In the first edition and in some other editions of *Sc* this character's name is Bertie Wodehouse-Bonner, indicating Waugh's admiration for the writings of P. G. Wodehouse, one of whose most famous fictional creations was Bertie Wooster.

Borethus, Dr. (*BR*) — He runs a sanatorium in Zurich for alcoholics and people with psychiatric problems; Rex Mottram is taking Sebastian Flyte there for treatment, but Sebastian flees from Rex's guardianship.

Boris (*MK*) — The manager of the Kremlin restaurant and nightclub in Paris. Boris, a young military cadet, escapes from Russia after the Bolshevik revolution and through the help of a wealthy French friend, opens a successful restaurant with a Russian motif. He realizes that the restaurant is not genuinely Russian and is an inadequate exchange for the loss of homeland.

Bosanquet, Captain (*MA, SOH*) — A Halberdier adjutant.

Bosworth, Mike (*OGu*) — One of Millicent Blade's unsuccessful suitors.

Boucher's (*CRS*) — One of the houses at Spierpoint.

Boughton (*BR, CRS*) — The ancestral home village of the Ryder family.

Bourne Mansions (*EB, SOH*) — In Carlisle Place, London, adjacent to Westminster Cathedral. Uncle Peregrine Crouchback has an apartment there. He, Virginia, and Mrs. Corner are killed there by a German bomb. Named no doubt for Francis Bourne, Cardinal Archbishop of Westminster, 1903–35, whom Waugh detested.

Box — See *Box-Bender, Arthur*.

Box, the (*OGP*) — A mechanical device supposed to possess diagnostic and therapeutic powers. It looks somewhat like a wireless unit. If a part, e.g., some blood, of a sick person or animal is placed in the Box and the Box is tuned to the patient's Life-Waves, the nature of the sickness could allegedly be perceived and then a remedy would be proposed. When he is tormented by the voices aboard the *Caliban*, Pinfold theorizes that Angel has an advanced kind of "Box" which speaks and hears. His wife, after consulting Father Westmacott, assures him that such a gadget is a figment of his imagination. Christopher Sykes, in *Evelyn Waugh: A Biography* (Boston, 1975), p. 359, gives more detail about the Box.

Box-Bender, Angela (*MA, OG, EB, SOH*) — A kindly,

sympathetic older sister of Guy Crouchback, wife of Arthur, and mother of Tony. In *EB, SOH* she takes care of Trimmer's son for a time while Guy is overseas, but then Eloise and Domenica Plessington rear the child until Domenica's marriage to Guy.

Box-Bender, Arthur (*MA, OG, EB, SOH*) — The husband of Guy Crouchback's sister Angela. His family name was Box, but his father added the Bender in 1897. A practical, rather insensitive man, he is a member of Parliament. He is fifty-six years old at the beginning of *MA, SOH*. In *OG, SOH* he is very concerned over his son's request for religious books. In *EB, SOH* it is mentioned that he retains his seat in Parliament throughout the war but loses in the election of 1945, when Winston Churchill's Conservatives are defeated. He seems to spend much of his time in Bellamy's Club.

Box-Bender, Tony (*MA, OG, EB, SOH*) — The son of Angela and Arthur Box-Bender and Guy Crouchback's nephew. In *MA, SOH* he is a young, pleasant British soldier who sees service in France, where he is taken prisoner by the Germans at Calais. Throughout *OG, SOH* he is a German prisoner of war. In one of his letters he requests several religious books. In *EB, SOH* he is still a prisoner of war and thinking about becoming a monk. At the end of the war he enters a monastery, much to the annoyance of his father. There was a revival of monasticism in the 1940s and 1950s, the most famous figure of the movement being Thomas Merton.

Boxer (*OGP*) — A nickname for Reginald Graves-Upton.

Boycott, Castle — see *Castle Boycott*.

Brace, Mrs. (*VB*) — The social editor of the *Daily Excess*. Simon Balcairn writes his gossip column for this paper and works under her. Later Adam Symes and then Miles Malpractice succeed to the gossip column and report to her.

Brace, Mrs. Sam (*HD*) — A farmer's wife who goes up to London for a visit and does not want to return to her home near Hetton. Her husband has to go up to London to bring her back, and after their return to the country, she beats him up.

Bradshawe (*BM*) — Lady Seal's devoted maid.

Bradshawes (*MA, SOH*) — Acquaintances of Guy Crouchback.

Braganza Hotel (*Sc*) — The scene of Lord Copper's banquet honoring Boot of the *Beast*. Uncle Theodore Boot attends in William's stead, much to Lord Copper's bafflement.

Brakehurst, Lord and Lady (*EH*) — The owners of a large country estate near the home of Beverly Metcalfe. The local hotel was named the Brakehurst Arms but later was changed to the Metcalfe Arms.

Brakeleigh (*HD*) — The family estate of Reggie St. Cloud's parents. Reggie has no sentimental involvement and sells it after his parents' deaths.

Brand from the Burning, A (*VB*) — The title of the film about the life of John Wesley made at Colonel Blount's estate. Colonel Blount eventually buys the film. See *Epworth Rectory*, and also see Glossary under *Vile Bodies*.

Bratt's (*HD, POMF, BR, BSRA*) — A men's club in London. In *HD*, Tony Last, Jock Grant-Menzies, and John Beaver are members there. In *POMF*, Peter Pastmaster and Alastair Digby-Vane-Trumpington are mentioned as members, and in *BR*, Rex Mottram is a member. The club is also referred to in *BSRA*. In *HD* the club's name is spelled Brat's, having only one *t*. It is based on the real Pratt's Club (founded 1841).

Breen, Halberdier Sergeant-Major (*MA, SOH*) — A participant in the ancient Battle of Malplaquet. He was in charge of a group of Halberdiers who drove off French attackers by pelting them with apples from an orchard.

Brenda (*OG, EB, SOH*) — A friend of Kerstie Kilbannock who works with her in a London canteen. Brenda also lives with the Kilbannocks for a time. Possibly the same as Brenda Last in *HD*.

Brendan (*OG, SOH*) — An individual referred to by Ivor Claire. While the Trimmer "Popgun" publicity account is newsworthy, Claire remarks that it was a stunt dreamed up by Brendan. In the American edition of *OG* the name is spelled Brendon. The name is omitted completely from *SOH*. Very probably a reference to the real-life Brendan Bracken (1901–58), a political ally of Winston Churchill who became Minister of Information in 1941.

Brendon, Baron (*VB*) — One of the titles of gossip columnist Lord Vanburgh.

Brent, Bill (*MA, OG, SOH*) — In *MA, OG*, a young Halberdier who for a time is Guy Crouchback's second-in-command. In *OG, SOH* he is one of the soldiers fighting on Crete.

Brent's (*CRS*) — One of the houses at Spierpoint.

Bretherton (*BM, IA*) — A sanitary inspector in Azania

after it becomes a protectorate of the League of Nations. He and his wife are friends of the Reppingtons.

Bride (*BR*) — A stream which begins at a farm named Bridesprings, about two miles from Brideshead Castle. The stream eventually becomes a large river and flows into the Avon.

Bride of Grantley Green (*POMF*) — Basil Seal visits Malt House, Grantley Green, to billet the Connollies with elderly Mr. and Mrs. Prettyman-Partridge, only to learn that one of them has died and the house has been sold to a young married couple. The husband, Bill, is serving in the army. Basil carries on an affair with this bride of Grantley Green until her husband returns to the area for further military training.

Brideshead, Earl of (*BR*) — The courtesy title of the oldest son in the Flyte family, the older brother of Julia, Sebastian, and Cordelia. He is usually referred to as Bridey; his baptismal name is never given. A strict and rigorous Catholic, he had wanted to become a priest, but his family was opposed. He eventually marries a middle-aged Catholic widow who has three children. At the end of *BR* he is serving in the British army during World War II (he is only three years older than Sebastian, although the age difference between the two appears much greater). Auberon Waugh and others believe that Bridey was based on the eighth Earl Beauchamp (whom Waugh had known at Oxford as Lord Elmley). For Elmley's younger brother, the Hon. Hugh Lygon, see *Flyte, Lord Sebastian*. After his father's death, Brideshead succeeds as marquess of Marchmain.

Brideshead (*BR*) — This name is sometimes used to refer to Brideshead Castle.

Brideshead Castle (*BR*) — The impressive baroque country estate of the Marchmain family in Wiltshire.

Brideshead Revisited — A novel (1945) in which the hero, Charles Ryder, reminisces about his Oxford years and his subsequent experiences with the aristocratic Marchmain family. Ryder recalls these events when his World War II unit is stationed at requisitioned Brideshead Castle. Waugh later published a revised edition of *BR* in which he made many deletions and changes (London, 1960).

Brides-in-the-Bath (*EB, SOH*) — A sobriquet for General Whale, so called because most of the military operations he proposes or supports seem to require a bloodbath — the death of everyone involved. The reference is to one of the most famous of British murder cases in which George Joseph Smith married three older women in quick succession and promptly drowned each of them in his bathtub to obtain their insurance benefits. He was convicted and hanged in 1915.

Bridey (*BR*) — A sobriquet of the Earl of Brideshead.

Brigadier (*EB, SOH*) — The unnamed military official who with Ralph Brompton decides that Guy Crouchback should be sent on the military mission to Yugoslavia.

Briggs (*DF*) — A student at Llanabba, nicknamed Brolly.

Briggs, Mr. (*ER*) — An employee of Sir James Macrae's film studio.

Briggs, Sister (*VB*) — An overindulgent nurse at the nursing home where Agatha Runcible is a patient.

Brighton (*HD*) — The seaside resort where Tony Last spends a weekend with Milly to furnish legal grounds for divorce proceedings.

Brink, Colonel and Mrs. (*HD*) — Acquaintances of Tony Last.

Brink, Mr. (*HD*) — A genial fellow passenger of Tony Last and Dr. Messenger on the cruise from England to South America.

Brinkman (*MA, SOH*) — A young football goalie at Staplehurst School. Apthorpe is his substitute.

Brinkwell (*HD*) — A man who hires out horses near Hetton.

Bristow, Mrs. (*EB, SOH*) — A charwoman who works for the Kilbannocks. She supplies the names of some abortionists whom Virginia Troy tries to find.

Brittling (*Sc*) — Julia Stitch's maid.

Brixton Gaol (*POMF*) — The prison where Mr. Rampole is incarcerated because of his publication of Ambrose Silk's subversive *Ivory Tower* even though he is unaware of the review's publication or contents. He eventually settles into his cell, comfortably spending delightful hours reading the charming novels of Ruth Mountdragon.

Brodie (*POMF*) — A former lawyer, now a soldier sent to officer training school.

Brolly — See *Briggs*.

Brompton, Sir Ralph (*EB, SOH*) — The diplomatic adviser to H.O.O.H.Q. He is a "tall, grey civilian dandy." A retired ambassador and interested in Communist indoctrination, he is very much involved in supporting Tito and in recommending personnel who will work for Communist goals. He is also a homosexual who had at one time an affair with Ludovic. Donald Greene believes that Brompton is based on Sir Harold Nicolson; *EWN*, Winter, 1974, pp. 1–2.

Brook Park (*MA, OG, EB, SOH*) — A park surrounding a large house in Cornwall, one of the locations where the Halberdiers are assembled and stationed for a time near the end of *MA, SOH*. Also mentioned in *OG, SOH, EB*. In *OG* it is also called Brookwood.

Brooks, Mr. (*IA*) — An oil-company agent in Azania and the father of the "kidnapped" Prunella Brooks.

Brooks, Prunella (*IA*) — The pretty, lively, and appealing daughter of an oil-company agent in Azania. She is courted by all the eligible men in Azania but falls in love with an impoverished remittance man who has fled his creditors in Kenya. She and her lover stage a fake kidnapping, obtain ransom money, return to England, and marry.

Brookwood (*POMF*) — Alastair Trumpington is stationed near this park when he joins the army in World War II. See *Brook Park*.

Broome (*MA, OG, EB, SOH*) — A small English village associated with the Crouchbacks.

Broome Hall (*MA, OG, EB, SOH*) — The ancestral English estate of the Crouchback family, eventually rented for a convent. In some references "Hall" is omitted, and just "Broome" is used to refer to the family home and grounds.

Brother Grandee (*BR*) — A term used for Bridey at his club.

Brough, Mr. (*TMWLD*) — A surveyor, wireless operator, and mechanic scheduled to take part in the Anderson expedition. He becomes engaged on board ship. When the boat arrives in Brazil, he boards a return ship, goes back to England, and marries, but not the girl he got engaged to on the boat. Thus he does not join the expedition into Brazil.

Brown, Bessy (*DF*) — A prostitute interviewed for a job by Margot Beste-Chetwynde. See also *de la Conradine, Pompilia*.

Brown, Captain (*POMF*) — An officer in Alastair Digby-Vane-Trumpington's unit. Another Captain Brown appears in Charles Ryder's regiment in *BR*, probably the same figure.

Brown, Miss Jane (*VB*) — The daughter of British Prime Minister Sir James Brown. She hosts the remnants of a party which causes such a scandal that her father is forced to resign.

Brown, Mrs. Martha (*VB*) — The wife of British Prime Minister Sir James Brown.

Brown, Sir James (*VB*) — For a time he is Conservative Prime Minister of England. He is forced to resign his post because of his daughter's party-giving for some of the Bright Young People. Possibly based on Stanley Baldwin. See *Outrage, the Right Honourable Walter*.

Brown's (*BSR, HD*) — A fashionable London men's club in *HD*. Jock Grant-Menzies and Tony Last are members. In *BSR* and in the "Alternative Ending" to *HD*, John Beaver unsuccessfully attempts to gain admission. The reference is probably to White's, the oldest (founded 1693) and most exclusive of London clubs. Waugh was elected to membership in 1941.

Bruce, Inspector (*DF*) — The policeman who arrests Paul Pennyfeather for white slavery just before Paul's intended wedding to Margot Beste-Chetwynde.

"Bruiser" (*OGP*) — The most common nickname of Reginald Graves-Upton.

Brunner, Mrs. Hacking (*BR*) — She and her charming heiress-daughter are invited to luncheon by Cara.

Brute — See *Daily Brute*.

Bruton Wood (*HD*) — An area near Hetton drawn by the fox hunt on the day John Andrew Last is killed.

Bundle, Mr. and Mrs., and son (*DF*) — Friends of Mr. Prendergast's mother when Prendergast is parish priest. They invite the Prendergasts to supper every Sunday after Evensong.

Bunny (*HD*) — A Shetland pony belonging to John Andrew Last. He rides it before the arrival of Thunderclap.

Bunny (*VB*) — The name used by the British soldiers for Chastity who became a prostitute and for a time served the men training at Salisbury Plain.

Bunty (*BR*) — An acquaintance of Effie at the Old Hundredth Club. They once hid in the dust closet there during a police raid.

Bunyan, Lady (*DF*) — A visitor to Llanabba School who is taken ill because of the liver sausage served on one of the sports days.

Burns, Halberdier (*OG, SOH*) — Colonel Jumbo Trotter's aged and devoted servant.

Bush, Major (*POMF*) — An officer in Alastair Digby-Vane-Trumpington's unit.

Bush Thunder-box (*MA, SOH*) — A portable toilet

owned by Apthorpe. It is eventually blown up during Apthorpe's struggle with Ritchie-Hook for its use.

Butcher (*LITS*) — A housemaster at Eton who teaches Tom Watch's friend. This friend seduces Tom's wife.

Butterworth, Mr. (*HG*) — An acquaintance of Ernest Vaughan's.

Byng (*HG*) — A servant of the Duke and Duchess of Vanburgh.

"By Special Request" — The alternative ending to *HD*. It was subtitled "The Next Winter" and took the place of chapters 5–7. Tony and Brenda are reconciled and return to Hetton, but Tony keeps Brenda's flat in London for himself. It was published in *Mr. Loveday's Little Outing and Other Sad Stories* and is the same text as the "Alternative Ending" to *HD* (London: Chapman and Hall, 1964). It was part of the serial version of *A Handful of Dust* which was entitled "A Flat in London." Under this title the novel appeared in five installments in *Harper's Bazaar* (New York) in the June–October, 1934, issues. "By Special Request" had to be used in the serial publication in *Harper's* because the original ending was essentially that of "The Man Who Liked Dickens." The serial rights to this story had already been sold.

C

Café de la Paix (*VB, HD*) — A London restaurant, probably based on the Café Royal, which also has a "gallery".

Café Lenin (*Sc*) — During the brief Communist revolution in Ishmaelia, this name was given to the Café Wilberforce.

Café Royal (*POMF, BR, MA, SOH*) — In *POMF* a favorite meeting spot of Poppet Green and her friends on Regent Street in London. It is also mentioned in *BR*. Frank de Souza and his girl friend Pat dine there in *MA, SOH*. It was famous in the nineteenth century as a meeting place of Oscar Wilde and his circle.

Café Royal (*VB*) — An eating establishment in the town where the car race was held.

Café Wilberforce (*Sc*) — An eating establishment in Jacksonburg, Ishmaelia. William Wilberforce (1759–1833) was the famous leader of the British movement for the abolition of black slavery.

Caldicote, Miss (*Sc*) — A girl whom William Boot's relatives thought he was romantically interested in. There was no truth in their theory.

Caliban (*OGP*) — The ship on which Gilbert Pinfold takes passage from England and suffers his strange hallucinations. The S.S. *Caliban* was clean and serviceable, but far from luxurious. The name, from the monster in Shakespeare's *The Tempest*, is significant.

Calpurnia (*H*) — A friend and confidante of Helena in Dalmatia.

Campbell (*OG, SOH*) — Colonel Hector Campbell's butler.

Campbell, Colonel Hector (*OG, SOH*) — The hard-of-hearing laird on the island of Mugg, in the Hebrides. In *OG* he is obsessed with explosives and wants part of the cliffs of Mugg blown up. He steals some explosives from the commando stores, and an explosion occurs. In *SOH* we learn that the laird and his great-niece were killed in the explosion.

Campbell, Mrs. Hector (*OG, SOH*) — The wife of the eccentric laird on the island of Mugg.

Campbells (*MA*) — One of the clans that joins Prince Charles in a movie version of the Rising of 1745.

Canadian priest (*BM*) — A Roman Catholic missionary of huge physical proportions who uses force to keep unruly soldiers away from his mission in Azania.

Canary Castle (*OG, SOH*) — The dilapidated ship on which Guy Crouchback is sent back to England from Egypt after he recovers from the ordeal of escaping from Crete.

Canterbury, Archbishop of (*VB*) — A guest at Margot Metroland's lavish party for Mrs. Ape. Simon Balcairn phones in for his final newspaper gossip column that, as a result of Mrs. Ape's revivalism, the Archbishop confessed doing something improper at Eton with former Prime Minister Sir James Brown — no doubt engaging in homosexuality. The Archbishop of Canterbury is the unofficial head of the Anglican communion. At the time of the novel, he was the stern moralist Cosmo Gordon Lang (1864–1945), whose objections to King Edward VIII's marriage to an American divorcée led to the king's abdication.

Cape, Brigadier (*EB, SOH*) — The commander of the British mission to the Anti-Fascist Forces of National Liberation (Adriatic) with headquarters at Bari, Italy. A friendly, direct figure, he had been wounded at Salerno.

THE DICTIONARY

Captain, the (*LITS*) — The old school friend of Tom Watch who becomes Angela's lover.

Captain, the (*VB*) — The skipper of the Channel boat on the storm-tossed voyage to England at the beginning of the novel.

Cara (*BR*) — The pleasant, well-mannered, middle-aged mistress of Lord Marchmain. She was originally a dancer. Legally, Cara is Mrs. Hicks, a British subject by marriage. The word in Italian means "dear."

Carausius (*H*) — The commander of a Roman fleet in the English Channel.

Cardenas, General (*SKME*) — A military officer shot by anarchists in Neutralia during the civil war there. General Lázaro Cárdenas was the president of Mexico who nationalized foreign oil holdings, an action against which Waugh's *Robbery Under Law* (Boston, 1939) was a bitter protest.

Carinus (*H*) — The son of Carus who for a time was put in charge of Rome and administered it badly. He was eventually murdered.

Carlisle Place — See *Bourne Mansions*.

Carlton Club (*VB*) — A London men's club (founded 1832) to which Lord Chasm belongs. It is the official club of members of the British Conservative party.

Carlton House Terrace (*DF*) — Philbrick claimed to have a large home in this luxurious street in London.

Carmichael, A. A. (*CRS*) — The most illustrious scholar among the schoolmasters at Spierpoint.

Carmichael, Kate (*OG, SOH*) — The great-niece of Colonel Hector Campbell. She comes from Edinburgh, is in her mid-twenties, and is a crazed Scottish nationalist. Mrs. Campbell explains that Katie had overworked while studying for college exams. In *SOH* we learn that she has been killed in the explosion initiated by Campbell at Mugg.

Caroline (*BR*) — Charles Ryder's very young daughter by his wife, Celia. In personal correspondence Donald Greene has commented that Caroline is very likely the product of Celia's adultery.

Carpenter, the (*DF*) — A deranged "religious nut" sent to Blackstone Gaol for murder. He claims that the Angel of the Lord orders him to kill. As a result of Sir Wilfred Lucas-Dockery's creative-instinct theories, the carpenter is allowed tools, which he uses to saw off Mr. Prendergast's head.

Carter (*HD*) — An acquaintance of Tony Last, probably an estate or farm agent.

Carus (*H*) — A rival of Constantius for power, he is one of Probus's chiefs of staff. He follows Probus as the new Emperor of Rome. He is eventually killed while his army is invading Persia.

Carver, Mrs. (*POMF*) — She does domestic work for Ambrose Silk in *POMF*. When Silk flees to Ireland, Basil Seal takes over Ambrose's apartment, and Mrs. Carver then cleans the flat for Basil.

Casa Gluck (*MA, SOH*) — The estate of the Gräfin von Gluck at Santa Dulcina delle Rocce, Italy.

Casanova Hotel (*LO*) — A staid but fashionable hotel in London's Bloomsbury section where liquor is not served. It is mentioned by Adam when he writes the Mr. Chatterbox column. As a result of the publicity Eddy ("Ginger") Littlejohn goes there, but is very disappointed.

Casket, The (*LO*) — A magazine devoted to the doings of morticians. Joyboy regularly contributes articles to this publication.

Castelletto Musgrave (*MA, SOH*) — The estate of the Wilmots at Santa Dulcina delle Rocce, Italy.

Castello Crouchback (*MA, OG, EB, SOH*) — In *MA* the name of the home of Gervase and Hermione Crouchback in Santa Dulcina delle Rocce, Italy. In *SOH* it is called Castello Crauccibac (in Italian pronounced "Crouchback") as well as Castello Crouchback. After World War II it is sold by Guy Crouchback to Ludovic.

Castle — See *New Castle*.

Castle Boycott (*BFGP*) — A country home near Fleacetown, Ireland, in need of repair. Captain Charles Boycott (1832–97) was the land agent for the Irish estate of an English absentee nobleman. His oppressive treatment of the Irish tenants led to retaliation which gave rise to the verb *to boycott*. The name here is symbolic of the decay of the "ascendancy" in Ireland.

Castle Hill (*BR*) — The field where the former Marchmain home stood before Brideshead Castle was built.

Castle Mockstock (*BFGP*) — An impressive country home near Fleacetown, Ireland. Lord Mockstock lives there with his wife, a draper's daughter.

Castle Tangent (*DF*) — The country home of Lord and Lady Circumference.

Castleton (*DF*) — A student at Scone College, Oxford. He is a friend of Alastair Digby-Vane-Trumpington.

132

THE DICTIONARY

Cathcart, Major Jack (*POMF*) — An officer in Freddy Sothill's army unit.

Cattermole, Major Joe (*EB, SOH*) — An officer at the British mission in Italy. He had been a professor at All Souls College, Oxford, and during the war he had been wounded in Yugoslavia. An ascetic, hardworking Communist, he is thoroughly supportive of Tito and the partisans. He is noted for his very pleasant disposition. He succeeds Brigadier Cape as commander of the mission to the Yugoslavian partisans. He is based in part on William (later Sir William) Deakin, fellow of Wadham College, Oxford, who served with Waugh in Yugoslavia.

Cavanagh, Binkie (*OG, SOH*) — A member of Bellamy's club who is insane. At times he sits under the billiard-room table.

Cecil Hotel (*OG, SOH*) — A hotel in Alexandria, Egypt. Its bar and restaurant are frequented by Guy Crouchback and other members of the British military.

Celia (*BR*) — The sister of Boy Mulcaster; she becomes the wife of Charles Ryder. She is pretty, pert, and efficient. She carries on a brief affair while married to Ryder but is particularly helpful in publicizing his career. After Ryder takes up with Julia, Celia agrees to divorce him and soon remarries.

Cernic, Major (*EB, SOH*) — One of Tito's partisans in the Yugoslavian campaign in World War II.

Chadwick, Mrs. (*HD, MA*) — An acquaintance of Guy Crouchback's father. When the auction sale of the contents of Broome is held, she buys a stuffed bear.

Chambers (*HD*) — Mrs. Beaver's cook.

Champion, Mrs. Brenda (*BR*) — A fashionable and important socialite who is Rex Mottram's mistress for a time; after his marriage to Julia Flyte he still keeps a romantic connection with her.

Chandler, Mrs. (*BR*) — One of the servants at Brideshead Castle.

Chaplain (*C*) — He is in Major Gordon's regiment. he feels that Major Gordon's attempt to help the Kanyis was an important spiritual action even if it did not succeed.

Chaplain at Egdon Heath Penal Settlement (*DF*) — He is involved in Margot's plan to give Pennyfeather special favors in prison.

Charity (*VB*) — One of Mrs. Ape's "angels."

Charles — See *Albright, Major Charles*.

Charles, Prince (*MA*) — Mentioned in connection with a film Guy Crouchback once saw concerning Bonnie Prince Charlie and the Rising of 1745.

Charles Ryder's Schooldays and Other Stories — Published in Boston in 1982, this collection contains the same stories found in *Mr. Loveday's Little Outing and Other Sad Stories* (which see) with the addition of "Charles Ryder's Schooldays." The latter narrative consists of one chapter of an unfinished novel first published in *TLS*, March 5, 1982. This chapter was entitled "Ryder by Gaslight." The story is an autobiographical account of some happenings at Spierpoint (for which read Lancing, Waugh's own public school). Ryder and other youths resent an unworthy student named Desmond O'Malley being given authority over them.

Charlie (*OG, SOH*) — A wounded New Zealand brigade major at Crete who is being transported in a commandeered car. Fido Hound travels in this car for a while.

Chasm, Lady Viola (*VB, HD, PP, Sc, BR*) — A wealthy London society woman. In *PP* she is described as "chic and plump." She is the mother of Agatha Runcible. Mrs. Beaver goes to one of her luncheon parties in *HD*. She is mentioned in *Sc*. In *PP* it is stated that she is very much in love with Ralph Bland. While they were courting, Julia Flyte and Rex Mottram spent a weekend at the Chasms' country house. In *BR* the Chasms refused to attend Julia and Rex's wedding.

Chasm, Lord Archie (*VB, WTA*) — Agatha Runcible's father. He had at one time been governor-general of Australia.

Chasm's cousin (*BSR*) — Viola Chasm's young cousin who is interested in taking over Brenda Last's flat in London. This young cousin also appears in the "Alternative Ending" to *HD*.

Chastity (*VB*) — One of Mrs. Ape's "angels." She eventually goes to South America to work in Margot Metroland's brothel. Later she returns to England and becomes a prostitute among soldiers both in England and on the Continent. She becomes the companion of the drunken major — now a general — during the war at the end of the novel.

Château de Madrid (*OG, SOH*) — A restaurant in Glasgow where Trimmer renews his acquaintance with Virginia Troy, and then, while in Glasgow, he carries on an affair with her.

Chatterbox, Canon (*VB*) — An old Oxford college friend of Colonel Blount who was a chaplain abroad and then was assigned to a parish in Worcester. Blount confused him with Mr. Chatterbox. *Chatterbox* was the title of a popular children's annual in the early twentieth century.

Chatterbox, Mr. (*VB*) — The title used by Simon Balcairn for his newspaper gossip column in the *Daily Excess*. After Simon commits suicide, Adam Symes writes the column, and later Miles Malpractice takes the job.

Chesham Bois (*VB*) — A town in Buckinghamshire near Aylesbury — see *Cruttwell, Captain*.

Chester-Martins (*MCLO, MCO, MLLO*) — Guests at a party given by Lord and Lady Moping during which Lord Moping attempts to hang himself in the orangery.

Cheyne Row (*EB, SOH*) — The site of Everard Spruce's home in London. His home housed the editorial offices of *Survival*. Both it and Cheyne Walk are in fashionable and "intellectual and artistic" Chelsea in southwest central London.

Cheyne Walk (*DF, EB, SOH*) — In *DF*, Philbrick claims to have a large home in that section of London. In *EB, SOH*, Everard Spruce lives there.

Chez Espinosa — See *Espinosa's*.

Chief Guide (*LAR*) — A penology official.

Chief Officer (*VB*) — The chief officer of the Channel boat on the storm-tossed voyage to England.

Chivers (*HD*) — A local farmer who sells rabbits to the Richard Lasts. The rabbits are fed to the silver foxes being raised at Hetton.

Chlorus (*H*) — A designation added to Constantius's name. Constantius came to be called Constantius Chlorus ("Green").

"Chokey" (*DF*) — The nickname of Sebastian Cholmondley, a black with intellectual pretensions; for a time he was the paramour of Margot Beste-Chetwynde. He visits Llanabba School with Margot on sports day. This character is sometimes thought to be based on the singer and actor Paul Robeson. Another possibility is Leslie Hutchinson, the singer-pianist known as "Hutch."

Cholmondley, Sebastian — See *"Chokey."*

Christabelle (*HD*) — The original name of Thunderclap, John Andrew Last's horse.

Chrystabel, Mrs. (*Co*) — Out of kindness she gives heavy-drinking Bill Scroggs money, which leads to a series of events culminating in a war in which she is killed.

Church and Gargoyle (*DF*) — An employment agency for teachers. Pennyfeather obtains his teaching position at Llanabba School through this firm.

Churchill, Winston (*MA, OG, EB, SOH*) — Conservative political leader (1874–1965), England's Prime Minister during World War II., He has a brief quotation part in *OG, SOH*. He directs in written form that Ritchie-Hook be returned to duty. Churchill is also mentioned in *MA, SOH*. In *EB, SOH* there is a comment that Churchill will be no match in a meeting with Tito since Tito is a well-trained politician while Churchill's ability is as an orator and a parliamentarian.

Cincinnati, Count (*VB*) — A mythical government official stationed at the Italian embassy in London; invented by Adam Symes for his Chatterbox gossip column.

Circumference, Countess of (*DF, VB*) — The stout, elderly mother of Lord Tangent. Her first name is Greta. In *DF* she is domineering, talkative, and quarrelsome and regards herself as high society of the most proper and authoritative type. In *VB* she attends a party at Lady Metroland's London home. She loudly denigrates Mrs. Ape when the latter gives one of her orations urging the listeners to confess their sins. Later in *VB* she attends a party at Anchorage House. She is reputed to be based on Alastair Graham's mother (see Waugh's autobiography *A Little Learning* [Boston, 1964], p. 192). Sir Maurice Bowra's description (in his *Memoirs* [London, 1966], pp. 164–65) of Mrs. Vincent Yorke, the aristocratic mother of Waugh's friend the novelist "Henry Green," makes her way of speaking sound very much like Lady Circumference's.

Circumference, Earl of (*DF*) — The gentle, rather timid father of Tangent and husband of Lady Circumference. He is not mentioned in *VB*, but his butler furnishes the Mr. Chatterbox column some material in that novel.

Citroen (*BM*) — Seth drives this make of car.

Claire, Ivor (*OG, EB, SOH*) — A captain of the Blues (Royal Horse Guards) who comes from a very wealthy family. He is a horseman of repute and is possessed of aesthetic tastes, although his personality is aloof and his sense of humor melancholy. He represents at least one type of English aristocrat. In *OG, SOH* on the island of Crete he deserts his unit and takes a boat back to Egypt. Because of his aristocratic connections, Ivor is safely transferred to India through the influence of Julia Stitch. In *EB*,

SOH it is learned that Claire has joined the Chindits fighting in Burma. He fights well there, receiving a DSO and an incapacitating wound. After the war he frequently visits Bellamy's Club, and his disgraceful action at Crete is almost forgotten.

Clara (*LAR*) — The bearded ballet dancer with whom Miles Plastic falls in love; after her thick, blond beard is removed and plastic surgery is performed, Miles loses interest in her.

Clarence, Duke and Duchess of (*BR*) — They visit Charles Ryder's London exhibit of his Latin American paintings. The Clarences are members of the royal family, as Lady Celia's curtseying to them indicates. "Clarence" is traditionally the title of one of the royal dukedoms. In the early autumn of 1936, the date of the scene in *BR*, the duke could be one of King Edward VIII's brothers — the duke of York (soon to become King George VI), of Gloucester, or of Kent, and his wife (see under *Kent*). In the 1920s they were the "young princes" of chap. 7 of *BR* whom Julia, as a Roman Catholic, was ineligible to marry.

Claridge's (*MA, OG, EB, SOH, BSRA*) — A luxurious London hotel. In *MA, SOH* it is there that Guy Crouchback attempts unsuccessfully to have sexual relations with Virginia Troy, his divorced wife.

Clark, Mrs. (*BR*) — An attendant stewardess to Celia Ryder on the passenger liner to England.

Claudius (*H*) — Constantius's uncle, a Roman general and later emperor.

Cleopatra (*OG, SOH*) — Julia Stitch's yacht, commandeered for military use in World War II. It helps transport X Commando unit off the island of Mugg.

Cliff Place (*DF*) — A private sanatorium in Worthing. It is there that Paul Pennyfeather is taken from prison ostensibly to have his appendix removed. The home is run by Dr. Fagan.

Clutterbuck, John (*DF*) — Father of Sam and Percy and the head of a successful brewery and wine business. He offers Grimes a job checking the quality of his product after the last employee developed DT's. The official name of the company is John Clutterbuck and Sons.

Clutterbuck, Martha (*DF*) — Wife of John Clutterbuck and mother of Sam and Percy. She attends the Sports Day at Llanabba.

Clutterbuck, Percy (*DF*) — A clever, dishonest, troublesome student at Llanabba School. He smokes cigars in the boiler room and cheats during a race on sports day.

Clutterbuck, Sam (*DF*) — The Clutterbucks' older son. He joins his father in the brewery business.

Clutton-Cornforth, Algernon (*OGP*) — The editor of a literary weekly who speaks on the BBC Third Programme. During his illness on shipboard Pinfold hears himself and his writing ridiculed by Clutton-Cornforth. This character was probably based on critic Cyril Connolly.

Cockatrice Club (*TB*) — A London night club.

Cockpurse, Lord (*HD*) — A well-liked and pleasant earl, the husband of Polly Cockpurse.

Cockpurse, Polly, Lady (Countess of) (*BSR, HD, Sc*) — A gossipy, amoral socialite friend of Brenda Last. Her origins are obscure and questionable, but in time she marries a respectable earl and becomes an important member of London society. In *BSR* and in the "Alternative Ending" to *HD*, after Beaver deserts Brenda, she travels to America for a while but then returns to the London scene. In *Sc* she attends one of Margot Metroland's parties and is acquainted with Mrs. Stitch.

Cockson, Major and Mrs. (*OGP*) — Passengers on the *Caliban*. Mrs. Cockson becomes very friendly with Mrs. Benson.

Coel, King (*H*) — The Paramount Chief of the Trinovantes and father of Helena. He resides in Colchester, England. He is supposed to have been the "Old King Cole — the merry old soul" of the nursery rhyme.

Cohen, Dr. and Mrs. (*Sc*) — William Boot mistakenly rings the bell of their London home while looking for the Ishmaelite legation to get a visa. The legation is in the basement downstairs.

Colchester (*H*) — The English city in Essex where, according to Waugh's novel, Helena was born and reared. It is named for King Coel.

Colenso (*MA*) — One of the Training Depot group of Halberdiers. He is described as a malcontent like Sarum-Smith.

Collins (*BR*) — An Oxford student who is a friend of Charles Ryder. Collins is a Wykehamist and an embryo don. He eventually becomes a well-known scholar.

Commander-in-Chief (*OG*) — He attends a party given by the Stitches in Egypt. He quotes poetry at the gathering and has his chauffeur drive Guy Crouchback back to Guy's camp. The Commander is Field Marshal Lord Wavell. See Glossary under *OG.*

Commanding officer *(BR)* — The leader of the battalion in which Charles Ryder is a captain. He is very blustery and very petty.

Commissar *(C, TMI, EB, SOH)* — A member of the partisan "general staff" in Yugoslavia. He is a veteran of the International Brigade in Spain.

"Compassion" — A short story by Waugh about a British major stationed in Yugoslavia during World War II. He tries to help a band of Jewish refugees escape the clutches of Tito's partisans. The story appeared in the *Month*, vol. 2, n.s. (August, 1949): 79–98. It was also published with some additional material as "The Major Intervenes" in *Atlantic*, July, 1949, pp. 34–41. Much of the material was reworked into *EB* and hence *SOH.*

Compton Last *(HD)* — A village near Hetton.

Coney *(EB, SOH)* — One of Everard Spruce's secretaries. She does cooking and other domestic tasks as well as serving on the staff of *Survival*. She and Frankie, another secretary, are based on Cyril Connolly's two "acolytes"; see Peter Quennell, *The Wanton Chase* (New York, 1980), p. 22.

Congreve, Captain *(MA)* — A figure in Guy Crouchback's boyhood reading who refuses to sail with his regiment when they are posted for foreign action but who later saves the hero, Captain Truslove.

Connollies *(POMF)* — Three children, the oldest, Doris, being about sixteen. They are wild, incredibly mischievous war evacuees from the city whom Basil Seal billets on various country families. Doris is voluptuous and amorous; Mickey is a foul-mouthed and scowling boy; and Marlene is simple-minded. Despite the slight spelling difference, it is evident that Waugh is comically alluding to and satirizing literary critic Cyril Connolly.

Connolly, General *(BM)* — A middle-aged British soldier of fortune, the commander of Seth's army who puts down the rebellion by Prince Seyid. He is given a noble title by Seth but disagrees with Basil Seal's plan for army boots and falls into disfavor. With the aid of the French and the Earl of Ngumo, he and his men overthrow Seth and crown Achon Emperor. When Achon dies, Azania becomes a League of Nations protectorate, and Connolly and his wife are slated for deportation. Connolly has lost all his money in the revolution. It is pointed out that he served with the Black and Tans in Ireland, was a policeman in South Africa, and also worked at the Kenya Game Reserves before going into Seth's service.

Connolly's Chemical Closet *(MA, SOH)* — The trade name for Apthorpe's portable toilet. Waugh is poking fun at Cyril Connolly.

"Consequences" — A short story by Waugh in which a heavy drinker popular with almost everybody casts the deciding parliamentary vote to start a war. The war kills his initial benefactress who started him on the road to financial and career success. The story appeared in the *Manchester Guardian*, April 4, 1929, p. 18.

Constant *(MA)* — An acquaintance of Frank de Souza and his mistress, Pat.

Constantia *(H)* — The widow of Licinius, mother of Licinianus, and half sister of Constantine. She is accused of plotting against Constantine but is spared by him.

Constantine *(H)* — The son of Constantius and Helena. He eventually became Constantine the Great, emperor of Rome. He supported Christianity, although he was not baptized until near the end of his life.

Constantine *(H)* — A Roman accused by Fausta of treason.

Constantius Chlorus *(H)* — A great-nephew of emperors Claudius and Quintilius, he is a staff officer who arrives in Britain from Gaul. He marries Helena, rises in military prestige and power, and becomes a Caesar. He is appointed governor of Dalmatia and takes a mistress (who several years later is strangled to death). In order to become a Caesar under Diocletian, he divorces Helena and marries Maximian's daughter Theodora. He becomes ruler of Gaul but never realizes his abiding ambition to become Emperor. His son does achieve this goal, becoming Constantine the Great.

Constantius Flavius *(H)* — A Roman allegedly engaged in a plot against Emperor Constantine.

Consul-General of Ishmaelia *(Sc)* — A black communistic zealot who is a graduate of the Baptist college in Antigua. He issues William Boot's visa from his London office. There is a rival pseudo-consul in London who is a Fascist.

Continental Daily Mail *(BR)* — A newspaper published in Paris until recently. While living abroad,

Charles Ryder reads in this newspaper of Julia Flyte's engagement to Rex Mottram.

Cook, Colour Sergeant (*MA, SOH*) — A military instructor in the Halberdiers.

Copper, Lord (*Sc, POMF, BR, OG, SOH*) — The head of the Megalopolitan Newspaper Corporation, owner of the *Daily Beast*. In *Sc* he is remote and pompous and becomes especially confused when Uncle Theodore Boot attends his banquet as the featured guest. He is also mentioned in *POMF* (where he is described as "hard-boiled and rich" and a friend of Angela Lyne's father) and in *BR*. In *OG, SOH* he uses the *Daily Beast* to praise Trimmer and denigrate the upper-class establishment aspects of the military since he dislikes the old school tie of the British officers. Copper was modeled on press magnate Lord Beaverbrook.

Copper Heels (*MA, SOH*) — A sobriquet for the Royal Corps of Halberdiers. In American editions the word Copperhead is used.

Copper House — See *Megalopolitan Building*.

Cordelia — See *Flyte, Lady Cordelia*.

Corfu (*DF*) — An island off the coast of Greece where Margot Beste-Chetwynde has a villa. Paul Pennyfeather stays there after he "escapes" from prison. Otto Silenus also spends time at Margot's villa.

Corker (*Sc*) — A journalist working for Universal News, a British news agency. He is sent to Ishmaelia to cover the war there. He collects Oriental curios and becomes friendly with William Boot, especially after the *Beast* patches up its quarrel with Universal News, so that the two reporters are no longer in real competition. Corker and another journalist leave the capital to pursue a story, but they are marooned when their lorry becomes stuck in mud in a remote area of the countryside. Eventually they travel on to the border of the Soudan. From there they will return to England.

Corner, James Pendennis (*MA, OG, SOH*) — Nicknamed "Chatty." In *MA, SOH* he is an African acquaintance of Apthorpe's and is supposedly an expert on gorillas. He himself is gorilla-like in appearance. In *OG, SOH* he comes to the island of Mugg to train the soldiers in mountain climbing and receives the name "King Kong." He accepts Apthorpe's gear delivered to him by Guy Crouchback.

Corner, Mrs. (*EB, SOH*) — Uncle Peregrine Crouchback's very proper and efficient housekeeper. She is killed when a German buzz bomb lands on Peregrine Crouchback's apartment. In his *Letters*, Waugh admitted that he made an error when he gave her the same last name as Chatty Corner.

Cornphillip, Lady Etty (*PP*) — The lively wife of Billy Cornphillip. She is a cousin of Lady Amelia's mother. She runs off to Venice with Ralph Bland but is deserted and then returns to her husband after becoming pregnant. Billy accepts the child as his own.

Cornphillip, Lord (*PP*) — The heir of Lord Billy Cornphillip's estate, the probable son of Ralph Bland by Etty Cornphillip.

Cornphillip, Lord Billy (*PP*) — A wealthy aristocrat noted for his dullness. Even among a very dull group, his dullness is notorious. He feuds with his cousin Ralph Bland, who runs away with Billy's wife, Etty, to Venice. After a short time Ralph deserts her, and she returns to her husband. She has a child which is obviously Bland's.

Corombona, Vittoria (*BR*) — An Italian noblewoman who gives a ball at her palazzo and invites Lord Marchmain and Cara. Historically, Vittoria Corombona was the wife of the Duke of Bracciano. She was murdered after his death in sixteenth-century Italy. Her story was dramatized in John Webster's play *The White Devil* (1612). The Palazzo Corombona is mentioned in *EB, SOH*. Virginia Troy mentions having fallen downstairs there.

Corporal-major (*OG, EB*) — Ludovic's rank as a warrant officer.

Corporal-major (*H*) — Constantius's military assistant in Britain.

Country Home for Mental Defectives (*MCLO, MCO, MLLO*) — The institution where Lord Moping is an inmate.

Courier (*HG*) — An acquaintance of Ernest Vaughan's.

Courier (*POMF*) — The local newspaper in the Malfrey area. Basil Seal consults it to find billets for the Connollies.

Courier d'Azanie (*BM*) — The principal newspaper of Azania.

Courteney, Lady (*BM*) — The wife of the British minister to Azania. Her main interest is gardening.

Courteney, Prudence (*BM*) — The daughter of the British minister to Azania. Restless and undisciplined, she carries on an affair with William Bland and later with Basil Seal. When the British evacuate Azania, the plane which carries her makes a forced landing in the jungle, and she is ultimately eaten by cannibals.

Courteney, Sir Samson (*BM, SKME*) — The British minister to Azania. He had a brilliant university career and great things were predicted for him, but he always became diverted by hobbies and recreations and never attained significance in several embassy posts. Because of family influence he was kept in the foreign service and relegated to Azania. He is totally casual, a symbol of British imperturbability. For a time he was *chargé d'affaires* at the British embassy in Stockholm. Scott-King met him there and was pleased by his "nonchalant benevolence." It is generally agreed that Courteney was based on Sir Sidney Barton (1876–1946), Envoy Extraordinary and Minister Plenipotentiary in Addis Ababa.

Crambo (*OGP*) — A member of Bellamy's Club who, according to an eccentric earl there, was becoming excessively fat.

Cramp (*OG, SOH*) — A soldier hurt in a fall during the cliff-climbing commando training on the island of Mugg.

Creative Endeavour (*VB*) — One of Mrs. Ape's "angels." She tends to be somewhat undisciplined.

Creforce (*OG, SOH*) — A British military force overwhelmed by the German attack on Crete.

Cricket Club (*LO*) — The social and sporting club of the British movie colony in Hollywood.

Crispus (*H*) — The son of Constantine and Minervina, thus Helena's grandson. He is executed for allegedly plotting against his father. He is sometimes called Tarquin.

Crock (*MA, OG, SOH*) — One of the Halberdiers' duty servants. Apthorpe incorrectly thinks that Crock's name is Smethers.

Crouchback, Angela — See *Box-Bender, Angela*.

Crouchback, Blessed Gervase (*MA, OG, EB, SOH*) — A Roman Catholic priest in Elizabethan times who was caught by the authorities and executed because of his religion. He is one of the Crouchback family ancestors and a candidate for canonization. He is not mentioned in the *MA* segment of the *SOH* trilogy.

Crouchback, Gervase (*MA, EB, SOH*) — An older brother of Guy Crouchback. He was killed in France by a sniper in World War I. He is mentioned in *EB* but not in the equivalent *SOH* paragraph.

Crouchback, Gervase (*EB, SOH*) — The son of Virginia and Trimmer whom Guy Crouchback takes as his own legal son. At Virginia's insistence Angela Box-Bender takes Gervase to her country home, and he thus avoids the fate of his mother. He is cared for by Dominica Plessington and her mother and then reared by Guy and Dominica when they marry.

Crouchback, Gervase (*MA, OG, EB, SOH*) — Guy Crouchback's father. In *MA, SOH*, Mr. Crouchback leaves the ancestral estate, Broome, and rents it to a convent. Innocent, benevolent, good-humored, humble, and tolerant, he lives at the Marine Hotel in Matchet. A boys' prep school moves there from the east coast, and since there is a shortage of schoolmasters, Mr. Crouchback is given a form to teach. Throughout *OG, SOH* he continues teaching at Our Lady of Victory's Preparatory School. In *EB, SOH* his health declines, and he has to give up his teaching position. He dies early in *EB, SOH*.

Crouchback, Gervase and Hermione (*MA, EB, SOH*) — The grandparents of Guy Crouchback. They spent their honeymoon in Italy and established a villa there at Santa Dulcina delle Rocce.

Crouchback, Guy (*MA, OG, EB, SOH*) — The protagonist of these works. In *MA, SOH*, at age thirty-five he leaves his Italian villa to return to England and enlist in the army. He had been married to Virginia Troy, and they had settled in Kenya to farm. His wife returned to England for a time and wrote that she had fallen in love with Tommy Blackhouse and wanted a divorce. Guy proceeds through the vicissitudes of military life and is eventually made a platoon commander of D Company when the regular Halberdier group is assigned to France. His group never reaches France, but he participates in a patrol raid on the French West African coast with the disguised Ritchie-Hook. Since this raid is not authorized and Ritchie-Hook is wounded, Guy and Ritchie-Hook are relieved of their duties and sent back to England with shadows over their careers.

At the beginning of *OG, SOH*, Guy arrives in London and is given leave to collect the dead Apthorpe's gear and deliver it to his designated heir, Chatty Corner. Guy trains with X Commando on the island of Mugg and then sails to Egypt with Hookforce. He participates in the debacle at Crete, escaping from the Germans in a boat with several other soldiers. While recuperating in Egypt, he meets Julia Stitch, who has him transferred back to

England because she learns that Ritchie-Hook is coming to Egypt, and she is afraid that Guy will tell the Brigadier of Ivor Claire's cowardice and Claire would then be court-martialed.

In *EB, SOH*, Guy is sent back to England in a very slow vessel. He stays with the Halberdiers and is useful in training. When the unit is assigned to go overseas, he is refused permission to go because of his relatively advanced age. He then takes an assignment to Special Services Forces Liaison Office. He injures a leg in parachute training and recuperates in Peregrine Crouchback's apartment. He eventually remarries Virginia when he learns that she is pregnant and impoverished. He is then sent to Yugoslavia as a military liaison officer. He learns of Virginia's death, carries out his function with the partisans, and befriends several Jewish refugees. He returns to England and after the war marries Domenica Plessington.

Crouchback, Ivo (*MA, OG, EB, SOH*) — An older brother of Guy Crouchback who was melancholic and a loner. He eventually became insane and starved himself to death in the London slums. He died in 1931.

Crouchback, Peregrine (*MA, EB, SOH*) — Guy Crouchback's uncle. He is well read, well dressed, a collector of bibelots, and a student of history and genealogy. He served in World War I and was for a time in the diplomatic service. He is impervious to ridicule because of his considerable self-esteem and is a bore. He makes the arrangements for Guy's father's funeral. He is killed when a German buzz bomb lands on his London apartment.

"Crouchers" (*OG, SOH*) — A nickname for Guy Crouchback's father, given to him by his students at Matchet.

Crown, The (*TB*) — A restaurant in Oxford where Adam Doure and Ernest Vaughan dine.

"Cruise" — A short story by Waugh consisting of letters and postcards written by a young lady of well-to-do parents who takes a cruise in the Mediterranean with her family. She describes the adventures — mostly sexual misadventures — that occur on the trip. It was published in *Harper's Bazaar* (London), February, 1933, pp. 12–13, 80; and appeared in the *Mr. Loveday's Little Outing*, *Work Suspended*, *Tactical Exercise*, and *Charles Ryder's Schooldays* collections.

Crump, Lottie (*VB, BM*) — The eccentric proprietor of Shepheard's Hotel in London. She also places bets on the horse races. It is mentioned in *BM* that Basil Seal, Peter Pastmaster, and Alastair Trumpington begin a five-day drunk at her hotel. She is based on the real-life Rosa Lewis, who ran the Cavendish Hotel in London. Waugh helped his friend Daphne Vivian write a biography of her, *The Duchess of Jermyn Street* (1964). A successful television series was based on it.

Crump, Mrs. (*DF*) — The mother of Mrs. Bundle and a friend of Prendergast's mother when Prendergast was an Anglican clergyman.

Cruttwell, Captain (*VB*) — A Conservative member of Parliament from Chesham Bois. The Ladies' Conservative Association at Chesham Bois asks him to protest the misdoings at Prime Minister Brown's home when Jane Brown invites some of the Bright Young Things to gather there after a night of partygoing.

Cruttwell, General (*Sc*) — An explorer and world traveler who works for a store dealing in traveler's gear. Many objects were named for him, such as the Cruttwell Glacier, in Norway, and Cruttwell Falls, in Venezuela. He is disgusted when William Boot asks for some cleft sticks and summons Miss Barton to wait on him.

Cruttwell, Gladys (*WTA*) — Tom Kent-Cumberland falls in love with her, and before he leaves for Australia they become engaged. Later, when he returns to England and his new girl friend is taken over by his mother and brother, he and Gladys marry, and they go to live in Australia.

Cruttwell, Mr. (*EH*) — Mentioned as having trouble keeping the Wolf Cub account. See Glossary under *EH*.

Cruttwell, Mr. (*HD*) — Brenda Last's and her sister Marjorie's osteopath. His office is in London. He refuses to work on Marjorie's dog Djinn.

Cruttwell, Toby (*DF, VB, BM*) — A friend of Philbrick's and former burglar who went to war, won the Victoria Cross, and turned respectable. He is now a member of Parliament. He is obviously the Captain Cruttwell in *VB* who is described as a Conservative M.P. from the Chesham Bois district. In *BM* he is a last-minute dinner guest at Lady Seal's party. She regards him as "silly."

Crutwell, Mr. (*MCLO, MCO, MLLO*) — The seemingly innocent, elderly attendant to Lord Moping at the County Home for Mental Defectives. He is renamed Loveday in "Mr. Loveday's Little Outing."

THE DICTIONARY

Waugh disliked his Oxford history tutor, C. R. M. F. Cruttwell, and used his name for several characters in his novels. In the "Little Outing" stories only one *t* is used in the name.

Cumberland, Colonel Jasper (*WTA*) — An ancestor of the Kent-Cumberland family who kept a journal during the Peninsular War; this journal is discovered by younger brother Tom Kent-Cumberland, and Tom writes an introduction and notes. This material is appropriated by his mother and later published. His brother, Gervase Kent-Cumberland, receives all the credit for the book.

Cumberland Arms (*WTA*) — A small inn near Tomb where Tom Kent-Cumberland spends the night on the occasion of his brother's twenty-first birthday. His own room at Tomb has been assigned to a guest.

Cumberleigh, June (*OGP*) — A commentator on a BBC program that Pinfold hears during his illness aboard the *Caliban*. She is a respectable, proper young woman, but in speaking about Pinfold, she is rude and vicious. She appears on the program with James Lance.

Curly — See *Susie*.

"Curse of the Horse Race, The" — A short story written by Waugh when he was seven years old. The grotesquely turned point of the story is to avoid betting. Rupert bets on a horse who loses, eventually kills a policeman, is convicted, and is executed. It was published as part of an anthology, *Little Innocents: Childhood Reminiscences* (London, 1932). It appeared as the first story in the *Tactical Exercise* collection (Boston, 1954). A facsimile of this manuscript is in Waugh's autobiography, *A Little Learning* (Boston, 1964).

Curtis-Dunne (*CRS*) — A student at Spierpoint who wants to start a political club.

Curtis-Dunne, Sir Samson (*CRS*) — The wealthy and prominent father of Curtis-Dunne.

Cuthbert (*Sc*) — The soldierly valet to Mr. Baldwin. He served with Baldwin in World War I, won the Victoria Cross, is very loyal, and is always armed.

Cuthberts (*MA, OG, EB, SOH*) — The husband and wife who are the proprietors of the Marine Hotel, Matchet. They would like to have Guy Crouchback's father evicted so that they can rent his rooms for a higher price. This is prevented by Jumbo Trotter, who intervenes with Grigshawe, the quartering officer in that part of the country. The Cuthberts totally fail to understand Mr. Crouchback's goodness.

Cutler, Sarah Evangeline (*BR*) — Rex Mottram's first wife. A Canadian, she was divorced from Rex in 1919.

Cutter, General (*MA, SOH*) — Guy Crouchback writes to him seeking a war service position.

Cynthia (*BR*) — An acquaintance of Celia and Charles Ryder.

Cyril (*BR*) — A bartender at the Blue Grotto Club.

Cyril (*Sc*) — A page boy working for the *Beast*.

D

Dacre (*EB, SOH*) — An old recusant Catholic family, a member of which attends the funeral of Guy Crouchback's father.

Daily Beast (*Sc, POMF, BR, OG, SOH*) — The newspaper for which William Boot writes the nature column. It is controlled by Lord Copper and housed in the Megalopolitan Building, on London's Fleet Street. In *Sc*, Boot is sent to cover the war in Ishmaelia for the *Beast* and secures the scoop for the paper. In *POMF* it is mentioned that Basil Seal worked briefly for the paper. It is also mentioned in *BR*, where we learn that Mr. Samgrass is now working for this newspaper. In *OG, SOH* its news policy cricitizes the army for being too aristocracy-oriented and lauds the exploits of Trimmer.

Daily Brute (*Sc*) — A rival London newspaper of Lord Copper's *Beast*. Lord Zinc controls the *Brute*.

Daily Excess (*IA, VB*) — A London newspaper owned by Lord Monomark. In *VB*, Simon Balcairn writes the Chatterbox gossip column for this paper. The paper is mentioned in *IA*. In both works it is sometimes referred to as just *Excess*.

Daily Express (*WS, OG, EB, SOH*) — An actual London newspaper whose gossip columnist suggests that the Sword of Stalingrad be displayed throughout England. The paper was also mentioned in *OG, SOH*, and in the 1942 edition of *WS*. Owned by Lord Beaverbrook. See *Copper*.

Daily Mirror (*POMF, EB, SOH*) — An actual London newspaper, one of the cheaper, more sensational ones, with a leftist bias. It is read by one of the air force officers while Guy Crouchback is recovering from his parachute accident.

Daily Twopence (*Sc*) — The London newspaper for which Pappenhacker reported on the Ishmaelian

THE DICTIONARY

conflict. It is modeled on the London *Times*, which then charged twice the penny a copy for which the less erudite London dailies sold.

Daimler (*DF, VB, Sc*) — This expensive auto appears in several of the novels. In *DF*, Sir Humphrey Maltravers owns one. Three Daimlers appear in *VB*: Lady Circumference owns a 1912 model; Adam Symes hires one to go riding with Nina Blount; and a Daimler is sunk in mud on a European battlefield. In it the drunken Major (now a General), Adam Symes, and Chastity take shelter and have a drink. In *Sc*, Mr. Stitch is mentioned as owning a Daimler.

Daisy (*BSR, HD*) — The proprietor of unsuccessful London restaurants frequented by the wealthy, amoral London social set. In *HD*, Daisy, a friend of Brenda's, is herself a member of this group. In *BSR* and in the "Alternative Ending" to *HD*, Brenda works for Daisy trying to encourage people to patronize her latest restaurant.

Dakar (*MA, SOH*) — A city on the Atlantic coast of west Africa. The reconnaissance party with Ritchie-Hook and Guy Crouchback land near there, and Ritchie-Hook is injured in this operation. For data on the actual Dakar operation, which took place in September, 1940, see Waugh's *Diaries*, pp. 481–83.

Dalmatius Annibabianus (*H*) — A half brother of Constantine. He was allegedly engaged in a plot against the Emperor.

Dalmatius Caesar (*H*) — A nephew of Constantine allegedly engaged in a plot against the Emperor.

Dalmatius Rex (*H*) — A half brother of Constantine allegedly engaged in a plot against the Emperor.

Dalmatius's wife (*H*) — One of the women about the Emperor's court in Rome. Dalmatius was one of Constantine's brothers.

Dan (*HD*) — A friend of Milly's who appears at Brighton during Milly's and Tony's visit there for divorce purposes. Dan and his girl friend go to a party there with Milly and Tony.

David (*POMF*) — A friend of Ambrose Silk's who in 1929 committed suicide by jumping under a train.

Davidson (*MA*) — The Halberdier commander of X Battalion.

Davies, Mr. (*DF*) — The Llanabba stationmaster and leader of the Llanabba Silver Band. On any convenient occasion he offers his sister-in-law for prostitution. In the original version (published by Chapman and Hall in 1962), Davies kept offering his sister, rather than his sister-in-law.

Dawkins (*EB, SOH*) — The devoted Halberdier servant of Ritchie-Hook. He is severely burned while rescuing Ritchie-Hook's gear from the crashed plane in Yugoslavia.

Dawkins, Miss (*ER*) — A stenographer attached to Sir James Macrae's film studio.

Dawson (*HD*) — The chauffeur for Brenda and Tony Last. See also *Blake*.

Deacon, Corporal (*POMF*) — A soldier in Alastair Digby-Vane-Trumpington's unit.

Deane, Mrs. Jimmy (*HD*) — A London party giver.

Death in the Dukeries (*WS*) — The title of one of John Plant's detective stories. The Dukeries consist of the district in north-central England where many high-ranking noblemen have country estates. The title is mentioned only in the 1942 edition.

Death's Head (*BR*) — The nickname of one of the party girls at the Old Hundredth Club. She joins Charles, Sebastian, and Mulcaster at their table.

Death Wish, The (*EB, SOH*) — The title of Ludovic's best-selling romantic novel with a diplomatic society setting.

Debra-Dowa (*BM, IA*) — The chief inland city of Azania. Under Amurath it became the capital of the country. It is based on Addis Ababa, capital of Ethiopia.

de Brissac la Motte, Jean (*BR*) — A Belgian Futurist who lived under an assumed name.

Decline and Fall — A novel by Waugh (1928) in which Paul Pennyfeather, a mild-mannered Oxford student, is expelled and then experiences a wild series of adventures before he is able to return to college a year later. The original manuscript was censored by the publisher on the grounds of impropriety. Waugh published *DF* in its original version in England in 1962.

de Foucauld-Esterhazy, Souki (*HD*) — A member of the fashionable, amoral, gossipy social set. She is American by origin. The Princes Esterhazy were among the oldest and most distinguished members of Hungarian aristocracy.

de Grenet, Alphonse and Madame (*BR*) — Acquaintances of Cara.

de la Conradine, Pompilia (*DF*) — The working name of a prostitute whose real name is Bessy Brown. She unsuccessfully applies for a job as a prostitute working for Margot Beste-Chetwynde's

THE DICTIONARY

syndicate. She is rejected because she has some form of venereal disease.

del Pablo, Juanita (*LO*) — A temperamental Hollywood starlet. Her real name is Baby Aaronson, and although she is publicized as sexy, her personality is very unpleasant, and her legs are repulsive. She turns against Sir Francis Hinsley, who has done much to further her career. At his funeral she sings "The Wearing of the Green," which is to be used in her next film. The fact that this is a famous anti-British Irish rebel song further heightens the irony.

Demerara (*HD*) — A district and the chief river in Guyana (formerly British Guiana). Tony Last and Dr. Messinger are bound there when they leave England on the liner for South America.

de Pañoses (*BR*) — Friends of the Maltons in Venice.

de Portallon, Prince (*BR*) — A French nobleman whom Anthony Blanche professes to know.

Deputy-Chief-Guide (*LAR*) — A prison official at Mountjoy.

Desert, Andrew (*WS*) — He and his wife are friends of John Plant. They attend a luncheon at the Ritz which John gives for Lucy and Roger Simmonds.

de Souza, Frank (*MA, OG, EB, SOH*) — In *MA, SOH* a Cambridge University graduate who joins the Halberdiers. In *OG, SOH* he and his platoon fight on Crete, and there he is wounded in the ear, but not severely. In *EB, SOH* he meets Guy Crouchback at the parachute training base. He had commanded D Company of the Halberdiers until he decided to ask for the Serbo-Croat mission assignment in Yugoslavia. A friend of Ralph Brompton and a convinced Communist, de Souza eventually becomes a major, and he is Crouchback's commanding officer in Yugoslavia. He is very much involved with Tito's partisans and their cause.

Despatch (*VB*) — The newspaper for which young Lord Vanburgh writes his gossip column. The paper is also referred to as the *London Despatch* and the *Morning Despatch*. It organizes and sponsors the car race.

de Supplice, Madame (*HD*) — The principal of the Catholic school that Thérèse de Vitré attended in Paris.

de Trommet, Mrs. (*HD*) — An American woman living in London who is acquainted with the Beavers. She owes Mrs. Beaver money for chair covers.

de Vincennes, Armand (*BR*) — The Duc de Vincennes. He allegedly quarreled with Anthony Blanche as a result of the latter's attention to the Duchess Stefanie.

de Vincennes, Philippe (*BR*) — A Duc de Vincennes.

de Vincennes, Poppy (*BR*) — One of the Duchesses de Vincennes.

de Vincennes, Stefanie (*BR*) — Anthony Blanche claims to have fallen deeply in love with her when he was seventeen.

de Vitré, Thérèse (*HD*) — An eighteen-year-old girl who attracts Tony Last aboard ship on his trip to Brazil. She is returning to Trinidad after attending school in Paris. Her family is of the aristocratic upper class in Trinidad. A romance begins to blossom between the two until Thérèse, a devout Catholic, discovers that he is married. To a slight degree she may be based on Teresa Jungman, a Catholic whom Waugh wished to marry in the 1930s.

Devonshire, Duchess of (*VB*) — A member of the English aristocracy. At the time of the novel the duchess was Lady Evelyn FitzMaurice, wife of the ninth Duke, a formidably correct lady. She was Mistress of the Robes to Queen Mary. Waugh was later on friendly terms with Deborah Mitford, Nancy's youngest sister, wife of the present eleventh duke.

Digby-Smith (*POMF*) — An official in the Ministry of Information who handles propaganda and subversive activities in enemy territory. He is later transferred to matters dealing with the Arctic Circle.

Digby-Vane-Trumpington, Lady Sonia (*BM, POMF, BSRA*) — Alastair's pleasant, outgoing wife. In *BM*, when she first meets Alastair, he is Margot Metroland's lover, but Margot has tired of him. Basil Seal visits Sonia and her husband both before and after his trip to Azania. In *POMF*, Basil also visits them and Alastair joins the army and Sonia travels about to be close to him. In *BSRA* we learn that she never remarries after Alastair's death. She shares a flat in London with her son, Robin, and occupies herself with sewing and charity work.

Digby-Vane-Trumpington, Sir Alastair (*DF, VB, BM, OD, POMF, BSRA*) — In *DF* he is the wealthy but undisciplined Oxford undergraduate who after a drunken outing is one of the members of the Bollinger Club who remove Paul Pennyfeather's trousers and is therefore responsible for Pennyfeather's expulsion from the college. He later sends his apologies and £20 through Potts. Pen-

THE DICTIONARY

nyfeather eventually chooses him to be the best man at his proposed marriage to Margot. After Pennyfeather is sent to prison, Alastair becomes Margot's lover and continues in that role even after she marries Maltravers (Lord Metroland). Maltravers is aware of his wife's infidelity and does nothing to thwart it. Alastair is twenty-one years old when the affairs starts, and it lasts a year. In *VB* the affair continues. In *BM*, Alastair is married to Sonia. He attends a wild party given by Basil Seal, and he and Sonia entertain Basil on several occasions.

In *POMF*, Alastair joins the army. He refuses to accept training for officer's school since he does not wish to receive special favors because of his aristocratic background. His army unit is assigned to coastal defense. He becomes bored with such unexciting routine and volunteers for a special forces commando unit so that he can see immediate action. In *BSRA* we learn that he is killed in the war. In some editions of *DF* the middle element is spelled Vaine rather than Vane.

In the short story "Out of Depth," Alastair attends a party at Margot's home in 1933. As a result of the magic of Dr. Kakophilos and the effects of a car accident, Alastair dreams that he is back in the Middle Ages. He returns to consciousness asking for a priest. In "Out of Depth" his last name is misprinted with three t's — Trumptington.

Sir Alastair is a baronet; that is, his title "Sir" has been inherited from his father, not awarded (like a knighthood) for services of his own. Digby and Vane are among the oldest of distinguished historical British aristocratic family names; "Trumpington," however, is merely a small village near Cambridge. Inheritances from wealthy ancestral families often gave rise to such hyphenated family names.

Dime, Air Marshal (*OG, SOH*) — A British officer.

Dina — See *Dingy*.

Dingy (*DF*) — A nickname of Dr. Fagan's daughter Diana, who does most of the housekeeping for her father. Philbrick claims to be in love with her and he calls her Dina. She later appears helping her father run his sanatorium.

Director of International Relations (*LO*) — One of the numerous officials at Megalopolitan Pictures, where bureaucracy is incredibly excessive.

Director of Personality (*LO*) — One of the numerous officials at Megalopolitan Pictures.

District Commander (*H*) — A military general in the Roman Empire whose assigned territory is England.

Divine Discontent (*VB*) — One of Mrs. Ape's "angels." She eventually goes to South America to work in one of Margot Metroland's brothels.

Djinñ (*HD*) — Brenda Last's sister Marjorie's unpleasant Pekingese.

Doge (*VB*) — The headwaiter of Lottie Crump's hotel. He is elderly and in poor health. He was once one of the Rothschilds' butlers.

Dome of Security (*LAR*) — The principal government office in Satellite City. During an international crisis its windows were blackened so that the bureaucrats worked in darkened light. The symbolism is evident.

Dorchester (*EB, SOH*) — An expensive hotel on Park Lane, in London.

Doubting (*VB*) — A village near Colonel Blount's estate.

Doubting Hall (*VB*) — The house near Aylesbury where Colonel Blount lives.

Doure, Adam (*TB*) — The twenty-two-year-old London art student in love with Imogen Quest. When her mother sends her away from London, Adam almost commits suicide but he comes to his senses.

Doure, Mrs. (*TB*) — Adam Doure's mother.

Doure, Professor (*TB*) — Adam Doure's father.

Dracilianus (*H*) — The architect who undertakes the work of building a basilica on the site of the Holy Sepulchre in Jerusalem.

Dracula, Major (*EB, SOH*) — A nickname applied to Ludovic by de Souza because of Ludovic's strange behavior at the parachute training center when he learns that Guy Crouchback has been sent there.

Drage, Jimmy (*DF*) — An underworld figure who knows Philbrick and Toby Cruttwell. He kidnaps Lord Utteridge's son but has to return the lad when the father is delighted to be relieved of him and refuses to pay ransom.

Drake, Dr. (*OGP*) — Gilbert Pinfold's down-to-earth, sensible physician at Lychpole.

Dreadnought, Major Sir Alexander (*OGu*) — A patient, formidable, and appropriately named suitor for the hand of Millicent Blade. The dog Hector finally discourages Dreadnought's romantic pursuit by biting off Millicent's delightfully enticing nose.

Dreamer (*LO*) — A sobriquet for Wilbur Kenworthy, the founder of Whispering Glades Cemetery.

THE DICTIONARY

Dressler, Frau (*Sc*) — The large, energetic proprietress of a boardinghouse in Jacksonburg, Ishmaelia, where William Boot stays for a time. She has in some way separated from her husband. She welcomes Europeans at the Pension Dressler, and Germans feel especially at home there.

Drunken Major — See *Major*.

Ducane, Florence — See *Flossie*.

Duc de Vincennes — See *de Vincennes*.

Duchess of Clarence (*POMF*) — A troopship. The Highlanders were assigned to embark for Norway on this ship, but since it was not in port, they boarded the *Cumberland* through error.

Duchess of Cumberland (*POMF*) — A troopship. Cedric Lyne's unit is to embark for Norway on this ship, but a frightful mixup occurs when his unit and a Highlander regiment attempt to embark on the overcrowded vessel.

Duchess of Stayle's eldest daughter (*VB*) — Lady Ursula, who rather indifferently becomes engaged to Edward Throbbing. She is really forced by her mother to accept his wedding proposal.

Duke of Clarence — See *Clarence, Duke and Duchess of*.

Duke of Omnium (*MA*, *SOH*) — An English nobleman whose wealth originally came from monastic spoils. The name is taken from a central character in Anthony Trollope's series of "Palliser," or "Parliamentary," novels.

Dumbleton, Simon (*OGP*) — A nobleman friend of Gilbert Pinfold.

Duncan (*OG*, *SOH*) — One of the officers serving on the island of Mugg.

Dundee (*MA*) — One of the clans that joins Prince Charles in a movie version of the Rising of 1745.

Dunn, Lt. (*MA*, *SOH*) — A signals officer in the Royal Corps of Signals. He and Apthorpe have several disputes over who is in charge of the Signallers, and over Apthorpe's cutting up the boots of one of Dunn's soldiers.

Dunz, Scab (*OG*, *SOH*) — An American newsman in England during World War II; he interviews Trimmer.

E

Easton (*CRS*) — A student at Spierpoint.

Ebury Street (*WS*, *EB*, *SOH*) — In *WS* a street in London where John Plant takes rooms aftter his father's house is sold. In *EB*, *SOH*, Sir Ralph Brompton has rooms there.

Eddie (*OG*, *SOH*) — A Halberdier officer training on the Isle of Mugg. He is later taken prisoner in the campaign on Crete.

Edith (*POMF*) — A housemaid of the Sothills who leaves Malfrey to work in a wartime airplane factory.

Edwards (*TB*) — A servant in the Hay family.

Edwards (*VB*) — The chief mechanic of Miles's friend the racing-car driver, the owner of car 13.

Edwards, Mr. (*VB*) — A newspaper worker at the *Excess* office.

Effie (*BR*) — A cheap nightclub girl whom Boy Mulcaster knows. She works at a seedy spot in London called the Old Hundredth and goes with Sebastian, Mulcaster, and Ryder when they leave the club. She is in the car when the police appear to question the intoxicated Sebastian. She flees before the police can detain her.

Effie (*BR*) — A servant at Brideshead who tends Nanny Hawkins during World War II.

Effie (*Sc*) — A servant of the Cohens.

Egbertson (*MCLO*, *MCO*, *MLLO*) — In *MLLO* the uncouth young man with whom Lady Moping thinks her daughter may have fallen in love. In reality, the daughter is distracted by attempting to free Loveday. Egbertson is mentioned in an earlier publication of the story, "Mr. Crutwell's Outing" and "Mr. Crutwell's Little Outing."

Egdon Heath Penal Settlement (*DF*) — The prison to which Paul Pennyfeather is transferred after a period of time in Blackstone Gaol. It is there that Grimes makes his escape attempt and presumably drowns in the swampy land surrounding the prison. Probably based on Dartmoor, in western England.

Egerton-Verschoyle, Mr. (*TB*) — A student at Oxford who happens to be drunk when he is visited by Adam Doure.

Eigg (*OG*, *SOH*) — An island off the west coast of Scotland, quite a distance from Mugg. Spelled Egg in American editions.

Elderbury (*OG*, *EB*, *SOH*) — A member of Parliament and friend of Arthur Box-Bender. Although he served in Parliament during the war, he was defeated in the post-war elections. He sits around Bellamy's most of the time with nothing to do. In *OG* the name is spelled Elderbury, but in *EB, SOH* it is spelled Elderberry.

Eldoret (*MA, SOH*) — The location of the farm Guy Crouchback owned in Kenya. Guy sold it after his wife Virginia deserted him.

Electra Palace (*VB*) — A movie theater in Aylesbury where Colonel Blount often goes to watch films. When Adam Fenwick-Symes first visits the colonel, the film *Venetian Kisses*, starring Greta Garbo, is showing there.

Elena of Russia (*MA, SOH*) — The Grand Duchess, regarded as a patron of the Halberdiers. She is toasted at the guest-night celebration. She accepted the honor as a beautiful young woman in 1902; she is now elderly and living in Nice.

Ellis, Peter (*OG, SOH*) — A friend of Guy Crouchback who teaches at the University of Edinburgh.

Elphinstone, Mrs. (*POMF*) — A kitchen servant of the Sothills at Malfrey.

Elsengratz (*Sc*) — Managing Director, Megalopolitan newspapers.

Embassy (*HD*) — A fashionable London restaurant.

Embury, Mrs. (*EB, US, SOH*) — Sir Ralph Brompton's devoted housekeeper.

Emden, Sir Joseph (*BR*) — An architect. Charles Ryder's wife hires him to change an old barn on their country estate into a modern studio.

Emily (*DF*) — A servant employed by the Fagans at Llanabba School.

Emily (*VB*) — The name given to the prostitute Chastity by an American doctor who "picked her up" in France.

Emolphus, "Professor" (*H*) — The designer of Emperor Constantine's arch in Rome.

Emperor of Azania — See *Seth*.

End of the Battle, The — A novel (1961) by Waugh concluding the *Sword of Honour* trilogy. It was published as *Unconditional Surrender* except in the United States where a book with a similar title had recently been issued. To avoid confusion the title was changed to *EB*. In this volume Guy Crouchback undergoes parachute training and is eventually sent to a British mission among Tito's partisans in Yugoslavia. Before leaving he remarries Virginia when he discovers that she is pregnant and requires a father for her child. After giving birth to Trimmer's child, Virginia is eventually killed during a rocket attack on London. In Yugoslavia the Communist partisans cause many difficulties and do everything possible to thwart Guy's attempts to aid a group of hapless Jewish refugees. Guy eventually returns to England and after the war marries and settles in the rural countryside.

Ending, Major (*DF*) — The people's warden of the parish where Mr. Prendergast had been an Anglican clergyman.

Englefield (*EB, SOH*) — A member of a recusant Catholic family, who attends the funeral of Guy Crouchback's father.

"Englishman's Home, An" — A short story in which two brothers run a profitable racket. They pretend to build an industrial laboratory in a beautiful rural area and then sell the land at a profit to the neighbors who do not want the tranquillity and arcadian atmosphere to be polluted. The story was published in *Good Housekeeping*, August 1939, pp. 12–25, 100–104. The story appeared in both the *Work Suspended and Other Stories Written before the Second World War* and *Tactical Exercise* collections.

"Entirely New Angle, An" — See *"Excursion in Reality."*

Eric (*VB*) — Colonel Blount's brother.

Erikson, Mr. (*LO*) — A heartless movie official at Megalopolitan Pictures. He gives Sir Francis Hinsley his termination notice.

Ernie (*HD*) — A passenger aboard the ship Tony Last takes to South America.

Erskine, Major (*MA, OG, EB, SOH*) — A Halberdier officer commanding D Company. A quiet, sensible, mature man, in *MA, SOH* he becomes friendly with Guy Crouchback. In *OG, SOH* he is one of the Halberdiers fighting on Crete. In *EB, SOH* he commands the Second Battalion of Halberdiers.

Espinosa's (*VB, HD, ER*) — A fashionable, elegant London restaurant. Also called Chez Espinosa. In *ER* it is spelled Espinoza.

Etheridge (*WS*) — A friend of John Plant's father. He reads John Plant's novels and enjoys them. Etheridge is still supporting his own thirty-seven-year-old son.

Etheridge, Major (*PP*) — A friend of Lady Amelia's whom the Vicar accuses of persecuting him.

Eusebius of Caesarea (*H*) — An early Church historian. He is a friend of Fausta and a bishop who took part in the Council of Nicaea. He is presented as an unscrupulous individual and a supporter of Arianism. Fausta sometimes calls him Caesarea for short.

Eusebius of Nicomedia (*H*) — The bishop of Nicomedia and a friend of Arius and Fausta. He and Eusebius of Caesarea are cousins.

Eustace (*BR*) — An imaginary suitor that Julia Flyte thought would be ideal for her to marry eventually. He would be a widower and a diplomat. Rex too was in search of a kind of female Eustace who would make the perfect married partner for his career.

Euthanasia Department (*LAR*) — One of the key government offices of the New Britain. It is used extensively there and is an expanding unit, soon ready to eliminate the Department of Pensions. The Teachers' Union wants to send difficult children to this bureau. Miles Plastic is assigned there after being released from Mountjoy. The word means "happy death."

Eutropia (*H*) — A half sister of Constantine, allegedly engaged in a plot against the emperor.

Evening Mail (*VB*) — The newspaper that carries an article censuring the activities at Prime Minister Brown's home when Jane Brown invites Agatha Runcible and some of the other Bright Young Things there. In American editions of the novel *Evening Standard* is used in place of *Evening Mail*.

Everyman, Lady (Countess of Everyman) (*VB, BM*) — A fashionable London socialite, in *VB* one of the guests at Margot Metroland's party. In *BM* she is mentioned as a friend of Lord Monomark.

Excess — See *Daily Excess*.

"Excursion in Reality" — A short story by Waugh (1932) in which a writer is hired to write a scenario for a film version of *Hamlet*, changing the dialogue and many episodes. The chaos of movie producing is heavily emphasized as the writer suffers through the vagaries of script writing and is finally dismissed from the project. The story was originally entitled "An Entirely New Angle" and appeared in *Harpers Bazaar* (New York) 66 (July, 1932): 22, 23, 78, 80, 82 and appeared under its later title in *Mr. Loveday's Little Outing and Other Sad Stories* (1936), *Tactical Exercise* (1954), and *Charles Ryder's Schooldays and Other Stories* (1982).

Express — See *Daily Express*.

Eyre, Trooper (*OG, SOH*) — A soldier hurt in a fall during cliff-climbing training on the island of Mugg.

F

Fagan, Augustus (*DF*) — The pompous but amusing proprietor of Llanabba School and later the owner of a nursing home–private sanatorium. While directing the school he is a Ph.D.; while running the sanatorium he is an M.D. Eventually he writes a best-selling book about Wales, leaves his daughters, and remarries.

Fagan, Diana (*DF*) — Nicknamed "Dina" and "Dingy," the younger daughter of Augustus Fagan. According to a story Philbrick tells Pennyfeather, he and Diana are engaged to marry, but no more is heard of this, and apparently it is a concoction of Philbrick's imagination. In the original manuscript (published by Chapman and Hall in 1962) Diana and Philbrick were seemingly engaged in a romantic affair. Diana does housekeeping work for her father at Llanabba School, and when Dr. Fagan gives up the school, she works at the nursing home that her father has purchased.

Fagan, Florence Selina (*DF*) — Commonly called Flossie, the older of Dr. Fagan's daughters who eventually marries Grimes not knowing that he is already married.

Faith (*VB*) — One of Mrs. Ape's "angels."

Farm Street (*BR*) — Farm Street Church in London, directed by the Jesuits.

Fatima (*WS*) — A prostitute in the Moulay Abdullah quarter of Fez whom John Plant visits regularly when he stays in Morocco. Fatima possesses a friendly, relaxed personality.

Fausta (*H*) — A daughter of Emperor Maximian and the second wife of Constantine. She becomes Empress when her husband ascends the throne. She is an insidious schemer and troublemaker and accuses many prominent Romans of treason. She is eventually killed by her husband's order after she goes too far and suggests that Helena is a traitor.

Fawdle, Mrs. and Miss (*OGP*) — Neighbors of the Pinfold family.

Fawdle-Upton, Lady (*OGP*) — A neighbor of the Pinfold family. The Box had presumably cured her nettle rash.

Fe, Dr. Arturo (*SKME*) — Scholar, lawyer, judge, the editor of the *Historical Review*, government official, and guide of the visitors to the Bellorius celebration in Neutralia. In the uncertain political climate he falls into disfavor and loses his positions.

Felix (*MA, OG, EB, SOH*) — Guy Crouchback's father's golden retriever. After Mr. Crouchback's death Angela Box-Bender takes Felix to her home in the Cotswolds.

THE DICTIONARY

Fender, Colonel (*BR*) — The estate agent who meets Brideshead and lunches with him during the agricultural show.

Fenwick-Symes, Adam (*VB*) — The protagonist of the novel, who hopes to marry Nina Blount but encounters financial difficulties which prevent marriage. He writes an autobiography which is confiscated and burned as pornography by English customs agents. For a time he writes a gossip column (as Mr. Chatterbox), and although Nina eventually marries Ginger Littlejohn, she is pregnant by Adam. At the novel's end he is a soldier on a European battlefield during another world war.

Fenwick-Symes, Professor Oliver (*VB*) — The father of Adam Fenwick-Symes.

Fez (*WS, BR*) — In *WS* the town in Morocco where John Plant liked to write his novels without the distractions of England. In *BR*, Sebastian Flyte lives there for a time after he leaves England.

Fido (*EB, SOH*) — Major Ludovic's Pekinese puppy. The dog was named for Major Fido Hound.

Fifi — See *Bey, Mme.*

Fifi (*WS*) — A prostitute in Morocco.

Fiji (*MA, SOH*) — A British cruiser torpedoed while on duty in the convoy to Dakar.

Fischbaum, Mrs. Arnold (*HD*) — She lives in California and is visited by John Beaver and his mother.

FitzBourke, Kathleen (*LO*) — The heroine of a film story on which Francis Hinsley works for Juanita del Pablo. The scenario never fully materializes, for Hinsley is fired in the midst of preparing the version.

Fitz Clarence (*HD*) — Alias of Ponsonby. He has robbed Dr. Messinger of two machine guns and £200.

Flanagan, Father (*POMF*) — A Jesuit and professor in Dublin University. He comes to the Ministry of Information hoping to get permission to visit the Maginot Line during his vacation. Basil Seal steals his passport and later gives it to Ambrose Silk so that the latter can escape to Ireland. In Dublin University Waugh is probably satirizing Trinity College, Dublin. Trinity was Protestant and would not then have allowed a Jesuit on its faculty. Father Flanagan would be at the (Catholic) National University of Ireland (which James Joyce attended and describes in *Portrait of the Artist as a Young Man*).

"Flat in London, A" — The serial version of Waugh's *A Handful of Dust*, which appeared in both the London and the New York *Harper's Bazaar* in five installments from June to October, 1934.

Flavius, Madame (*H*) — A name used for Helena since by marrying Constantius she became a member of the Flavius family.

Flavius Popilius Nepotianus (*H*) — A Roman allegedly engaged in a plot against Emperor Constantine.

Fleace (*BFGP*) — Bella Fleace's brother. He was obsessed with painting pictures of assassinations.

Fleace, Bella (*BFGP*) — The aged protagonist of the story who decides to give a lavish Christmas party but forgets to mail the invitations.

Fleacetown (*BFGP*) — The abode of Bella Fleace, about fifteen miles from Ballingar, Ireland.

Fletcher (*CRS*) — A student at Spierpoint.

Fleysers (*BFGP*) — Many generations of the Fleyser family had lived for centuries in the area of Fleacetown, Ireland.

Flintshire, Etty, Countess or Marchioness of (*POMF*) — A London socialite who hopes her daughter will marry Peter Pastmaster. We do not know the family name of the Flintshire figures. Flintshire is a title, not a surname.

Flintshire, John, Lord (Earl or Marquess of) (*BSRA*) — A brother of Lady Sarah (or Sally), one of the fashionable London girls of the 1930s.

Flintshire's daughter (*POMF, BSRA*) — Lord and Lady Flintshire's daughter Sarah (or Sally), one of the three girls Peter Pastmaster considered for marriage. She was a friend of Emma Granchester's daughter Molly, who relates the story of Angela Lyne's drunkenness to her in *POMF*.

Floreau, Monsieur (*BM*) — A member of the French legation staff at Debra-Dowa. He is sent by Ballon to escort the legation ladies to the coast and to blow up the Lumo bridge. These preparations are made for the coup that is to overthrow Seth and put Achon on the throne of Azania.

Florian's (*BR*) — A restaurant in Venice where Lord Marchmain, Sebastian and Charles Ryder stop for coffee.

Florin, Mr. and Mrs. (*VB*) — Colonel Blount's servants.

Flossie (*VB*) — A call girl who accidentally kills herself while swinging on a chandelier at Lottie Crump's hotel. In the newspaper account of her death her name is given as Florence Ducane.

Flower, Miss (*LAR*) — A government assistant who is

THE DICTIONARY

assigned to accompany Miles Plastic as he tours the country lecturing about his rehabilitation from arson and the new Mountjoy prison. She and Miles marry at the insistence of governmental officials.

Flyte, Lady Cordelia (*BR*) — The youngest member of the Flyte family. She is very friendly and outgoing and grows up to be plain and pious. She drives an ambulance in Spain and after the war does humanitarian work there. She returns to Brideshead Castle to take care of her father during his last illness. She does woman's service for England in World War II. Some critics have claimed that Penelope, Lady Betjeman (née Chetwode), was at least in part the model for Cordelia.

Flyte, Lady Julia (*BR*) — The Marchmains' older daughter. A popular debutante, she falls in love with Rex Mottram, and despite her strong Roman Catholic background, she marries him in a civil ceremony when it is discovered that he has previously been divorced. The marriage is not successful, and eventually she has an affair with Charles Ryder. She decides to marry Ryder, but her father's deathbed return to Catholicism and the promptings of God's grace convince her that marrying the divorced Charles would be a sinful act. She is bequeathed Brideshead Castle by her father, and during World War II she performs in woman's service for England somewhere abroad, apparently in Palestine.

Flyte, Lord Sebastian (*BR*) — The second son of the Marquis of Marchmain. His beauty and charm appeal to everyone and especially to Charles Ryder, who meets him at Oxford. The family's demands on Sebastian to be upright and religious put a heavy burden on him, and he takes to drinking. He leaves England and goes to northern Africa, where he takes up with a young German named Kurt. Kurt has deliberately shot himself to be released from service in the Foreign Legion. After a stay in Africa, Sebastian and Kurt go to Greece, where Kurt is seized by the Germans and conscripted into military service. He escapes, is put in prison, and there hangs himself. After Sebastian learns of Kurt's fate, he returns to Tunis and is taken to an infirmary run by monks. There at the monastery he is ultimately made into a kind of underporter, still on occasion drinking excessively. Waugh is reputed to have used Hugh Lygon and Alastair Graham as models for Sebastian.

Flyte St. Mary (*BR*) — A small village near Brideshead Castle. It had a post office and one pub.

Fogliere, the Principessa (Princess) (*BR*) — The chief female figure in the Fogliere family. She gives a lavish ball in Venice.

Foglieres (*BR*) — Relatives of Lady Marchmain living in Venice.

Forbes, Mr. (*HD*) — The former lover of Rosa, the Macushi woman who speaks broken English to Tony and Dr. Messinger.

Ford (*VB*) — Adam Fenwick-Symes first arrives at Colonel Blount's home in a Ford taxi.

Fortitude (*VB*) — One of Mrs. Ape's "angels."

Forty-three (*LITS*) — A shady London nightclub about which Tom Watch and his old bachelor friend reminisce.

Fosker (*OGP*) — An antagonist of Pinfold whose voice Pinfold imagines he hears on the *Caliban*. Pinfold theorizes that Fosker has been in a jazz band. Fosker and his unidentified companion torture the protagonist with insulting musical lyrics and threats of bodily harm.

Foulenough (*BR*) — An eccentric red-haired traveler met by Charles and Celia Ryder on the passenger liner to England. Foulenough was not his real name, but since no one seemed to know his true identity, he was given that surname after the despicable Captain Foulenough in "Beachcomber's" (J. B. Morton's) humorous columns in the London *Daily Express* in the 1920s and 1930s.

Four Square Gospel Temple — The headquarters of Aimée Semple Macpherson's evangelical mission in Hollywood, satirized as Mrs. Ape in *VB*. See Appendix 3, "Evelyn Waugh's Hollywood," by Donald Greene.

Frances (*HD*) — Tony Last's caustic aunt.

Francesca (*BR*) — The Italian cousin of the Marchmains. She is mentioned as having received an annulment and having married again.

Francis Xavier (*BR*) — Cordelia's pig. He wins special mention in the agricultural show. He is named, of course, for the famous Jesuit missionary Saint Francix Xavier (1506–52).

Francmaçon (*Sc*) — An old passenger ship, originally built for North Atlantic service, on which William Boot sails from France to Aden on his way to Ishmaelia.

Frank (*BM*) — One of the servants at Lady Cynthia Seal's home.

THE DICTIONARY

Frankie (*EB, SOH*) — A barefoot secretary to Everard Spruce. Like Coney she does domestic duties for Spruce as well as work for *Survival*.

Franks, Professor (*DF*) — An architectural expert who praises the original King's Thursday as a splendid example of domestic Tudor. This is before it is rebuilt by Margot Beste-Chetwynde and Professor Silenus.

Fred (*TB*) — Gladys's husband.

Freda (*OG, EB, SOH*) — Ivor Claire's white pekinese.

Free Man Greets the Dawn, A (*LO*) — The most famous book written by Sir Francis Hinsley.

Fremantle (*EB, SOH*) — Ludovic's Staff Captain at the parachute training base. He is puzzled by Ludovic's attempts to avoid seeing Guy Crouchback and by Ludovic's other eccentric actions.

Fremlin, Mrs. (*POMF*) — A leader of the Girl Guides; she delivers the Connollies back to Barbara Sothill.

French military attaché (*MK*) — A French cavalry officer who meets and becomes friendly with Boris at the time of the Bolshevik Revolution. They help each other and manage to escape from Russia. Later they meet in Paris, where the attaché has developed a succcessful business. He finances Boris in his venture with the Kremlin restaurant.

French-Wise, Freddy (*DF*) — A student at Scone College, Oxford. He is a friend of Alastair Digby-Vane-Trumpington.

Frickheimer, Mrs. Arnold (*BR*) — She is hit in the head with a bottle of milk by one of the members of the Black Birds.

Frightened Footman, The (*WS*) — The title of one of John Plant's detective stories.

Fu, Mr. (*SKME*) — A Cantonese scholar who attends the Bellorius celebration in Neutralia. He is captured by rebel partisans.

Furness, Mr. (*TB*) — A former student at Oxford; he had been expelled.

G

G, Lady (*Sc*) — The wife of the British Consul in Ishmaelia.

Gabriel (*TB*) — A wealthy student at Oxford.

Galerus (*H*) — A Roman leader and military figure, a rival of Constantius in the power struggle for leadership in Rome. He is one of Probus's chiefs-of-staff and is eventually appointed a Caesar by Diocletian.

Galla (*BM*) — Arabic immigrants who had come to Azania.

Gamage, Sister (*BSRA*) — An employee of the health spa visited by Angela and Basil Seal.

Garbett, Colonel and Miss (*OGP*) — Neighbors of the Pinfold family.

Garcia, Engineer (*SKME*) — A Neutralian who chats with Scott-King at the celebration for Bellorius. He is alleged to be an enemy of Dr. Fe who intends to succeed Fe in some of his government positions.

Garesby (*MA*) — The ancestral estate of the Wrothman family.

Garibaldi (*MA, OG, SOH*) — A restaurant Guy Crouchback frequents while in the Halberdiers. The restaurant was closed, and Mr. Pelici, its owner, was arrested as a spy.

Garrick Club (*ER*) — A London club (founded 1841), primarily for those connected with the theater. Sir James Macrae, the film producer, is a member there.

Garry, Mrs. (*MA, SOH*) — A neighbor of Guy Crouchback at Santa Dulcina delle Rocce, Italy. She collects stray cats, distributes Protestant tracts, and disturbs the octopus fishermen.

Gassoway, John (*Sc*) — A friend of the Stitches who has been seeking a knighthood. Brian Howard's father was supposed to have been named "Gassaway" (see Waugh's *A Little Learning*, pp. 204-205).

Gaston (*BR*) — A Swiss valet who serves Lord Marchmain.

Gaythorne-Brodie, Martin (*DF*) — A homosexual partygoer and friend of David Lennox in the first English edition. Because this name is so similar to that of the real-life Edward Gathorne-Hardy, it was changed to Miles Malpractice in the first American edition and all later editions.

Gazette (*EH*) — A local Cotswold newspaper.

General (*C, TMI, EB, SOH*) — A member of the partisan "general staff" in Yugoslavia. He was a veteran of the International Brigade in Spain.

General (*OGP*) — One of the voices Pinfold hears on the *Caliban*. He is the father of Margaret and encourages his daughter to have sexual relations with Pinfold. Pinfold also hears a second General's voice aboard the ship.

Gentakian, Mr. (*Sc*) — The proprietor of a shop in Jacksonburg, Ishmaelia. He is a friend of Kätchen's.

THE DICTIONARY

Geoghan, Canon (*MA, SOH*) — The Catholic priest at Saint Augustine's Church, in Southsand, where the Halberdiers are stationed for a time.

Geoghegan (*CRS*) — The head of the house who whips Charles Ryder and some of the other Spierpoint students for disobeying O'Malley's order.

Geoghegan, Father (*EB, SOH*) — A Catholic priest active in the funeral ceremony for Guy Crouchback's father.

Gibbs (*BR*) — One of the Marchmain servants at Brideshead.

Giles (*OG, SOH*) — A New Zealand soldier who participates in the evacuation from Crete. He surrenders his place in a military vehicle to the fleeing Major Hound.

G.I. Liberation Italy (*EB, SOH*) — A British lieutenant colonel who in *EB* used this designation in correspondence. In some editions and in *SOH* the title G.I. Liberation of Italy is used. The *I* may be a misprint for *S*, meaning General Staff [officer], or the *I* may be "one," i.e., General Staff Officer, Grade One.

Gilmour, Bill (*VB*) — A cantankerous drunkard. He is an old friend of Eddy Littlejohn's.

Gilpin (*EB, SOH*) — A stern, suspicious, and officious officer who trains for special foreign missions. He had been a schoolteacher in civilian life and was in the Education Corps. He is of Ralph Brompton's set and therefore has strong Communist sympathies. He is later attached to the Headquarters of the British Mission to the Anti-Fascist Forces of National Liberation at Bari, Italy. At the end of the war he had defeated Elderberry for a seat in parliament and was becoming prominent. He recently had become Under-Secretary.

Ginger (*VB*) — A nickname for Eddy Littlejohn, because of his red hair.

Giraud, M. (*Sc*) — A railroad employee in Ishmaelia but really doing secret agent work for Mr. Baldwin.

Gladys (*TB*) — The cook from a house in Earl's Court; she attends a movie with her friend Ada and provides a running commentary on the film.

Glass (*MA, SOH*) — A Halberdier who is Guy Crouchback's batman. He tends to be surly and negative.

Glendening-Rees, Dr. (*OG, EB, SOH*) — An expert on dietetics, he is sent to the isle of Mugg with ideas about emergency food supplies. In *OG* he leads a group of soldiers on Mugg to live just on seaweed and heather and returns on a stretcher. In *EB, SOH* he continues to conduct his dietary experiments.

Glenobans (*EB, SOH*) — A noble Scottish family.

***Glory of Greece*, S.S.** (*Cr*) — The passenger liner on which the young lady of leisure takes a sea voyage.

Gloucestershire (*MA, SOH*) — The county in western England where Angela and Arthur Box-Bender's country home is situated. For many years Waugh lived at Piers Court, in Gloucestershire.

Glover (*OGP*) — A young manager of a tea plantation in Ceylon and a passenger on the *Caliban*. He is especially fond of golf. His cabin is next to Pinfold's, and Pinfold assumes that Glover must hear the same voices. Glover is always polite but obviously believes that Pinfold is an alcoholic.

Glover, Colonel (*MA, SOH*) — Guy Crouchback writes to him seeking a war service position.

Godley, Mr. — See *Goodchild and Godley*.

Gold, Halberdier (*MA, OG, SOH*) — A military aide assigned to Major Tickeridge; mentioned in *MA*. In *OG, SOH* he is one of the soldiers on Crete.

Goneril (*OGP*) — A nickname given to a mysterious, cruel, and vicious woman whose voice Pinfold hears on the *Caliban*.

Goodall, Ambrose (*MA, OG, SOH*) — In *MA, SOH* a parishioner of Saint Augustine's Church, in Southsand, whom Guy Crouchback meets when he is stationed with the Halberdiers in that section of England. Goodall is a bachelor and lives with his unmarried sister. A convert to Roman Catholicism, he is an expert on heraldry. He tutors, lectures, and writes book reviews. He had taught Apthorpe at Staplehurst. In *OG, SOH* Guy visits Mr. Goodall and finds that he expects a religious revival restoring peace and goodness to the earth. Guy also encounters him at church on All Souls' Day.

Goodchild, Bishop (*BM*) — The Anglican Bishop of Debra-Dowa who is a frequent visitor to the British legation. Although not in the best of health, he is very knowledgeable on most aspects of Azanian life.

Goodchild and Godley (*WS*) — Art dealers who employ John Plant's father to do "restorations," imitating the famous English portrait painters. He does not object that these pictures may be sold as originals.

Good Hope Fort (*TE*) — The stone house on the Cornish coast cliff where John and Elizabeth Verney spend their vacation and from which she presumably pushes him to his death after drugging him.

THE DICTIONARY

Gordon, Major (*C*, *TMI*, *EB*, *SOH*) — A British military liaison officer to the Tito partisans in Yugoslavia. In *C*, *TMI* he attempts to help the Jewish refugees. In *EB*, *SOH* this role is given to Guy Crouchback.

Gordon, Sir Samuel and Lady (*BFGP*) — Wealthy landowners living near Bella Fleace who come uninvited to Bella's party. Bella, who looks down upon the Gordons because Lady Gordon is an American, refuses to entertain them.

Gordontown (*BFGP*) — An Irish country estate with several modern conveniences such as an elevator and electric lights. Lady Gordon, an American, had insisted on these improvements.

Gore, Sir Lionel (*MA*, *SOH*) — The Commodore of the Southsand and Mudshire Yacht Squadron. He is a retired physician.

Gorgias (*BM*) — The predecessor of the present Nestorian patriarch of Azania.

Governor's wife (*H*) — Residing in Ratisbon, she looks after Helena while Constantius is traveling.

Gracchus (*H*) — Another name used for Constantine.

Grace, Mr. and Mrs. (*POMF*) — They billet the Connollies for a brief time. He is a portrait painter, and she is in delicate health.

Grace-Groundling-Marchpole (*MA*, *OG*, *EB*, *SOH*) — A Halberdier major whose brother is the colonel in London in charge of secret intelligence reports. He and Guy Crouchback occasionally meet at various times during the war, and Guy never learns his name until the last book of the trilogy. At various times in the trilogy he is referred to as the Adjutant, the unknown adjutant, the nameless major, and the unknown major. Among the places where Guy encounters him are Penkirk, Brook Park, and Bari. His first name is never indicated.

Grace-Groundling-Marchpole, Colonel (*MA*, *OG*, *EB*, *SOH*) — In *MA*, *SOH*, an officer in the British intelligence unit dealing with spying and treasonable activities by Englishmen. In *OG*, *SOH* he has become the head of his secret department and is filing material suggesting treasonable activities by Guy Crouchback. In *EB*, *SOH* because of false information indicating that Guy has been engaged in treasonable behavior, he rejects Guy's assignment to secret service work in Italy.

Graceful, Mr. (*HD*) — The very proper and dignified lawyer for Tony Last.

Gracie (*DF*) — The sister of Philbrick in one of the stories he makes up about himself. She commits suicide because Philbrick won all the father's attention and inherited his money. Gracie haunts Philbrick with cooking smells until by way of reparation he agrees to live among servants for a year and write a book that will improve their conditions.

Gräfin von Gluck — See *von Gluck*.

Grainger (*POMF*) — Angela Lyne's devoted maid.

Grainger (*Sc*) — A nurse employed by the Boot family. In American editions the name is spelled Granger. Grainger was the name of Lady Mary Lygon's Pekinese dog; see *Letters of Evelyn Waugh*, ed. Mark Amory (New Haven, Conn., and New York, 1980), p. 58.

Grainger, Jimmie (*WS*) — A friend of Archie Atwater's.

Grainger, Mr. (*BM*, *IA*) — He is appointed immigration officer in Azania after it becomes a joint British-French protectorate of the League of Nations. He and his wife are friends of the Lepperidges and the Reppingtons.

Granchester (*SKME*) — The boy's prep school at which Scott-King's teaches classics. The town of Granchester, near Cambridge, provides the title for one of Rupert Brooke's best-known poems.

Granchester, Emma, Countess or Marchioness of (*POMF*) — A London society woman who had been friendly with the German diplomat Joachim von Ribbentrop. Her daughter marries Peter Pastmaster. Granchester was also the name of the family country estate. In some English editions the estate is spelled Grandchester.

Grand, the (*MA*, *SOH*) — A pub near Kut-al-Imara Preparatory School.

Grand Azanian Hotel (*BM*) — The principal hostel in Matodi, Azania. The official title was Grand Hotel de l'Empereur Amurath.

Grand Café et Hotel Restaurant de l'Empereur Seth (*BM*) — A seedy establishment run by Mr. Youkoumian at Debra-Dowa. Mildred Porch and Sarah Tin stay there and observe the revolution against Seth from the building's roof.

Grand Chemin de Fer d'Azania (*BM*) — The very bizarre and unreliable railroad running between the Azania cities of Matodi and Debra-Dowa.

Grand Hotel (*MA*, *OG*, *SOH*) — A hotel in Southsand. In *MA* while the Halberdiers train nearby, Guy Crouchback lives there for a time. In *OG*, *SOH*, Guy stays there while waiting for Chatty Corner to make contact with him.

Grandee, Brother (*BR*) — The sobriquet of Lord Brideshead at his dining club.

Granger, Nurse — See *Grainger*.

Grant-Menzies, Jocelyn (Jock) (*BSR, HD*) — In *HD* a close friend of Tony Last. He is a member of Parliament and man-about-town. He carries on an affair with Mrs. Rattery. After Tony is declared legally dead, he marries Brenda Last. He is mentioned in *BSR* and in the "Alternative Ending" to *HD*, in which he informs Brenda of the exact time that Tony is returning from his trip abroad.

Grass, Bartholomew (*POMF*) — A nom de plume of Ambrose Silk. The name is used as the author of one of the *Ivory Tower* articles written by Silk.

Graves, Father (*BR*) — A Catholic priest who was a friend of Father Phipps and takes him to a cricket match.

Graves, Mr. (*CRS*) — One of the schoolmasters at Spierpoint.

Graves, Mr. and Mrs. (*OGP*) — Neighbors of the Pinfold family at Lychpole. Fanny Graves used the Box to treat her dog for worms.

Graves, Major (*OG, SOH*) — An officer on the island of Mugg; he is experienced in mountain warfare. He goes to the Middle East with Hookforce.

Graves-Upton, Reginald (*OGP*) — A friend of the Pinfold family. He is a gentle, refined, bee-keeping old bachelor who is the Pinfolds' closest neighbor. Every Sunday he leaves his terrier at the Pinfolds' while he goes to Matins. Afterward he always has a short visit with the Pinfolds. He has various nicknames: "the Bruiser," "Pug," "Basher," and "Old Fisticuffs." All of these aliases derived from the term "Boxer," because Graves-Upton has recently been involved with an object called the Box, which supposedly relieves people of various maladies. His nephew and niece live at Upper Mewling. Margaret claims that her father, Angel, is a cousin of Reginald.

Graybridge, Lady (*VB*) — Her servant has been letting rooms in her mansion without her knowledge.

Great Missenden — See *Princes Risborough*.

Green, Captain-Commandant Geoffrey (*MA, OG, SOH*) — A full colonel with the honorary appointment of "Captain-Commandant" of the Halberdiers regiment.

Green, Goridge and Wright, Ltd. (*SKME*) — An English engineering firm.

Green, Miss (*MA, SOH*) — The daughter of the Halberdiers' "Captain-Commandant."

Green, Mrs. (*MA, SOH*) — The agreeable, sensible wife of the "Captain-Commandant" of the Halberdiers.

Green, Poppet (*POMF*) — A silly modernistic London artist, one of Basil Seal's girl friends.

Greenidge, Lady (*Sc*) — London socialite, a friend of John Courteney Boot. Waugh took the name from his Oxford friend Terence Greenidge.

Green Park (*BR*) — A lovely park in central London, just north of Buckingham Palace and northwest of Saint James's Park. One side of the Marchmains' London house overlooks it.

Gregson (*BR*) — Lord Marchmain's lawyer. He is summoned so that Marchmain's will can be changed to leave Brideshead Castle to Julia.

Greswold (*OG, SOH*) — A student of Mr. Crouchback's at Our Lady of Victory's Preparatory School who is adept at sports and at having Crouchback reminisce during classes about his family history.

Greville (*HD*) — A London men's club; Tony Last is a member. It is there that Tony first meets Dr. Messinger. "A club of intellectual flavour" — possibly the Athenaeum or the Travellers.

Griffenbach (*BM*) — A scientist, mentioned by Basil Seal, who supposedly demonstrated that an onion-and-porridge diet is not helpful. Basil supplies that information to press magnate Lord Monomark, who believes in this health regimen.

Griffiths, Sir Almeric (*EB, SOH*) — British orchestral conductor, one of the official visitors to the Yugoslav partisans. He is killed in a plane crash in Yugoslavia.

Grigg (*BR*) — The strict judge before whom Sebastian, Mulcaster, and Ryder appear on the charge of public drunkenness.

Griggs, Mr. (*SKME*) — A teacher of civics at Granchester. He is critical of classical studies.

Grigshawe (*OG, SOH*) — A major who serves as a Quartering Commandant and tries to evict the senior Crouchback from his rooms at the Marine Hotel. Grigshawe's effort is forestalled by "Jumbo" Trotter.

Grimes, Captain Edgar (*DF*) — A roguish homosexual schoolmaster at Llanabba. He is about thirty years old and has an artificial leg (he lost his leg after being hit by a trolley during one of his drinking bouts). He has a red moustache, and is slightly bald.

His World War II service was dishonorable, but he was saved from a court martial through an old Public School connection. Grimes marries Flossie Fagan, although he is already married to an Irish woman. After faking suicide, he works for the Latin-American Entertainment Co., Ltd. He is sent to Egdon Heath Penal Settlement (where Pennyfeather again meets him) and is perhaps killed in the swamps near the prison while trying to escape. The original edition, censored by the publishers in 1928, was made available in the Chapman and Hall 1962 issue. The original text contains more direct reference to Grimes's homosexuality.

Grimes was based on a Richard Young (d. 1972), a fellow teacher of Waugh's at Arnold House who later gave Waugh permission to make the identification; see *Letters*, p. 616.

Grimes, Jane (*DF*) — First wife of Grimes; she goes to work for Margot Beste-Chetwynde as a prostitute in South America.

Grimshawe (*HD*) — A woman servant of the Last family, serving Brenda.

Grits, Miss Elfreda (*ER*) — She works on scenarios of various films and is presently employed by Sir James Macrae; she works with Simon Lent on the scenario for a modern dialogue version of *Hamlet*, and during that period they have an affair.

Grizel (*BR*) — A woman guest of Rex Mottram's at a gathering at Brideshead Castle.

Groat, Mrs. (*MA, SOH*) — A house servant employed by Angela and Arthur Box-Bender.

Grocer from Mostar (*C, TMI, EB, SOH*) — One of the Jewish refugees in Yugoslavia whom Guy Crouchback tries to help.

Groggin, Sergeant Major (*MA, SOH*) — A Halberdier who is in charge of kitchen supplies. He trains the Halberdiers in judging meat so that they will not be cheated by civilian contractors.

Grumps (*EH*) — The previous name of Much Malcock Hall.

Gryll, Blessed John (*MA*) — An English Roman Catholic candidate for canonization.

Grylls (*MA*) — An ancient English Roman Catholic family from whom the Crouchbacks may be descended; mentioned by Ambose Goodall.

Guernica Revisited (*POMF*) — A book of poems by Parsnip. Picasso's famous painting *Guernica* of the bombing of a town during the Spanish Civil War doubtless furnished the first part of the title.

Gunter's (*BR*) — A London restaurant where Julia Flyte meets her brother Sebastian and Charles Ryder after they have been freed from jail. They were incarcerated because of Sebastian's drunken driving after leaving Ma Mayfield's.

Guru Brahmin (*LO*) — The "writer" of "The Wisdom of the Guru Brahmin," the advice-to-the-lovelorn newspaper column which Aimée Thanatogenos consults. It is actually compiled by two newsmen and a secretary, Mr. Slump being the most prominent of the three in the story.

Gussie — See *Augustus*.

Gustave (*OG, SOH*) — The fictitious name Trimmer used when he worked as a hairdresser on the *Aquitania*.

H

Hacket, Ben (*HD*) — The vulgar horse groom at the Hetton estate of Tony and Brenda Last who encourages John Andrew Last to ride and teaches him basic horsemanship.

Hall, Halberdier (*MA*) — A name mentioned once. It is an error for Halberdier Glass and is corrected in *SOH*.

Hamilton-Grand, General (*OG*) — Jumbo Trotter serves on his staff at Gibraltar. In English editions the general's name appears as Hamilton-Brand.

Handful of Dust, A — A novel by Waugh (1934) in which Tony Last, the protagonist, is cuckolded by his wife and then sued for divorce. Last goes to the primitive jungles of South America, where he is trapped by a maniac and forced to read Dickens's novels interminably.

Hans (*POMF*) — A former lover of Ambrose Silk, now imprisoned in Germany.

Happier Hunting Ground (*LO*) — The pet mortuary in Hollywood where Dennis Barlow is employed. According to popular legend, Indians called their version of heaven "the happy hunting ground."

Hardcastle (*BR*) — Described as a gloomy student at Oxford with whom Sebastian Flyte is acquainted. Sebastian likes to borrow his car.

Hardcastle, Alfred (*WS*) — A real estate director who purchases John Plant's father's house to tear it down and build apartments.

Hargood-Hood, Jock (*EH*) — He purchases land in

the countryside and, after threatening to build a factorylike laboratory there, sells the land at a considerable profit. He uses the money to keep his family estate solvent.

Hargood-Hood's brother (*EH*) — A lawyer who assists in the profit-making land scheme.

Harkness, Mr. and Mrs. (*POMF*) — A quiet middle-aged couple with whom the Connollies are billeted for a time. They live in a pleasant, idyllic area of rural England. They are the first to pay Basil for taking the Connollies off their hands.

Harper, Miss (*ER*) — A day secretary to the extremely busy film maker Sir James Macrae.

Harriet (*BM*) — Prudence Courteney's aunt who lives in Belgrave Place, London.

Harris, Sergeant (*POMF*) — An excellent soldier and football player. He cannot be sent to officer school because he is too valuable to his military unit as a football player.

Hat (*POMF*) — A friend of Ambrose Silk who with Silk and Malpractice once issued an invitation to a social gathering in manifesto form.

Havas (*Sc*) — A correspondent from this publication is in Ishmaelia to cover the crisis there.

Hawkins, Nanny (*BR*) — The nanny (children's nurse) of the Flytes — Brideshead, Julia, Sebastian, and Cordelia — she lives in retirement at Brideshead Castle. She is kindly, religious, and totally devoted to the Marchmain family.

Hay, Basil (*TB*) — A young Oxford student who is friendly with Imogen and Henry Quest.

Hay, Mrs. (*TB*) — The well-to-do mother of Basil Hay.

Hayter (*BR*) — The servant of Charles Ryder's father.

Hayter (*MA, SOH*) — A Halberdier who is appointed second-in-command of D Company. He is unduly forward and cocky. Major Erskine recommends him for special training in Air Liaison so that the Halberdiers can get rid of him. Hayter is thus transferred.

Hazardous Offensive Operations Headquarters (*OG, EB, SOH*) — Fictional title for a group of offices on Saint James's Street, London, which provided the military with experts or alleged experts in all areas of warfare. General Whale headed its Land Forces operations, while Sir Ralph Brompton was its diplomatic adviser. Waugh sometimes uses the term Hazardous Offensive Operations instead of Hostile Offensive Operations. Donald Greene discusses the actual site of H.O.O.H.Q. in "Reality into Art: Some Detective Notes on Waugh," *EWN*, Spring, 1986, p. 3.

Headlong Corner (*VB*) — The most dangerous part of the car race course where accidents and deaths often occur. It is considered the fun spot from which to watch the race.

Headmaster of Granchester (*SKME*) — He chats briefly with Scott-King.

Headmaster of Our Lady of Victories (*MA, EB, SOH*) — The headmaster of the school at which Guy Crouchback's father taught for a while during his retirement. He attends Mr. Crouchback's funeral.

Hector (*OGu*) — A suitor of Millicent Blade's who hopes to marry her after his farming in Kenya becomes successful. He gives her a dog as a present, names it after himself, and admonishes the animal to ward off rivals.

Hector (*OGu*) — The dog assigned to keep Millicent Blade's suitors — other than his purchaser (who runs a farm in Kenya) — away from her. To fulfill his assignment, he ultimately bites off her attractively enticing nose.

Heinkel, Theodora (*LO*) — With her husband, Walter, a client of the Happier Hunting Ground when their pet dog Arthur dies.

Helena (*H*) — The heroine of the novel. She is portrayed as the youngest daughter of King Coel of Britain. She marries Constantius, leaves England, and travels about on the Continent. She becomes the mother of the future Emperor Constantine. For political advantage Constantius divorces her. She eventually becomes the Empress Dowager and is converted to Christianity. Later she leads the search to find the Cross on which Christ was crucified. After its discovery she returns to Europe and dies at a venerable age. She is buried at Rome and canonized as Saint Helena. Her early interest in horses seems to be a trait taken from Penelope (Mrs. John, later Lady) Betjeman (née Chetwode), to whom the book is dedicated. The novel mixes fact, legend, and fiction.

Helena — A novel by Waugh published in 1950 which traces the life of Saint Helena: her birth in Britain, her marriage to Constantius, her motherhood of the future emperor Constantine, her conversion to Christianity, her role as empress dowager, and her ultimate discovery of the True Cross. Waugh wrote an earlier short story entitled "St. Helena Meets Constantius" (*Tablet*, December 22, 1945, pp. 299–

THE DICTIONARY

302), which comprises, with some slight changes, most of the first chapter and parts of two other chapters of the novel.

"**Hell Ship, the**" (*MA, SOH*) — A title for the *Altmark*; see Glossary under *SOH*.

Helm (*MA*) — One of the Halberdiers in training. He is severed from the outfit by Ritchie-Hook.

Helm-Hubbards (*HD*) — A London society couple whose marriage is in difficulty; this information is mentioned in gossip between Beaver and Brenda Last.

Hemingway, Mrs. (*VB*) — She and her son are mentioned: the son cannot find a job and is taking a correspondence course in civil engineering.

Hemp (*MA*) — An officer with the Training Depot group of Halberdiers. He is described as a black sheep like Trimmer. He is nominally a Catholic but does not take his religious obligations seriously.

Henderson, Mr. (*VB*) — A commercial traveler who becomes seasick on the Channel boat to England.

Henty, Paul (*TMWLD*) — A well-to-do Englishman whose wife's adultery causes him to travel to Brazil, where he is trapped into reading Dickens. He is the prototype of Tony Last in *HD*.

Henty, Mrs. Paul (*TMWLD*) — Her adultery with a captain in the Coldstream Guards causes Henty to leave London and travel on the Anderson expedition to Brazil. She is a variant of Brenda Last in *HD*.

Hercules (*OG, SOH*) — One of the dogs belonging to Colonel Hector Campbell at Mugg.

Hermogenes (*H*) — A soothsayer in Rome.

Hesketh-Smithers, Sir Philip (*POMF*) — An officious departmental Assistant Director in the Ministry of Information. He is eventually transferred to the Folk-Dancing Department.

Hetton (*BSR, HD*) — In *HD* the name of Brenda and Tony Last's large Gothic country home, also called Hetton Abbey. There is also a small nearby village called Hetton. Hetton is mentioned in *BSR* and in the "Alternative Ending" to *HD*.

Hicks, Mrs. — See *Cara*.

Hill (*OGP*) — A grazier who rented the fields of the Pinfold estate during World War II and fights a legal battle for years to retain use of the land, thus causing Mrs. Pinfold much anguish.

Hill, Corporal (*MA, SOH*) — A Halberdier who commits suicide during training.

Hinsley, Sir Francis (*LO*) — A former chief script writer for Megalopolitan Pictures, he later works in the Publicity Department of that studio. He commits suicide by hanging after being fired from his job. He is succeeded by Lorenzo Medici.

Hispano-Suiza (*DF, VB*) — Margot Beste-Chetwynde's (Lady Metroland's) car. In *DF* we are told that she actually owned two of these expensive autos. Rex Mottram also has a Hispano in *BR*.

Historical Review (*SKME*) — A magazine edited by Dr. Arturo Fe in Neutralia.

Hitchcock, Sir Jocelyn (*Sc*) — A world-famous British newspaper correspondent who is covering the events in Ishmaelia. He moves about secretly and is a loner in gathering news. He is the British equivalent of Wenlock Jakes. He sends the journalists off to Laku, a town in the interior which actually does not exist. He then gets permission from his paper to leave for Lucerne to cover an economic conference. Hitchcock's real-life model was Sir Percival Phillips (1877–1937), one of England's most famous correspondents. He worked for various British newspapers and was special correspondent for the *Daily Mail* from 1922 to 1934. He covered wars, revolutions, coronations, and similar events all over the world from the World War I trenches to the Balkans and India.

Hobson (*BR*) — Sebastian Flyte's servant at Oxford.

Hodge, Colonel (*EH*) — A neighbor of the Metcalfes. He devises the plan to buy the land threatened by a factory site for a scout clubroom. Everyone can then donate money for the public benefit rather than feel cheated by spending an unequal share for the purchase of the land.

Hodges (*TB*) — A female servant of the Quest family. She sees that Imogen leaves London and travels to Thatch.

Hogbaum, Mrs. (*Sc*) — A publisher's wife.

Holloway, Miss (*Sc*) — The secretary of Julia Stitch.

Honest Injun (*VB*) — A tea shop–restaurant in the town where the auto race takes place.

Honoré (*HD*) — One of Thérèse de Vitré's potential suitors in Trinidad.

Hookforce (*OG, SOH*) — The British force, including Guy Crouchback and commanded by Ben Ritchie-Hook, which lands on Crete to relieve the troops there. They are eventually forced to surrender to the Germans, although they cover the evacuation of other British units taken off the island by ship.

Hoop, Johnnie (*VB*) — A man-about-town. He likes to send clever invitations to fashionable parties and get-togethers; for example, he invites people to a party that is to be held in a captive dirigible. His autobiography is published by the Rampole-Benfleet firm. Near the end of the novel he goes to France to study painting.

Hoop, Mrs. (*VB*) — One of the fashionable older women-about-town, the mother of Johnnie Hoop. She decides to give up theosophy after the storm-tossed English Channel crossing. She attends various stylish parties. She announces that the fictitious sculptor Provna (invented by Adam Fenwick-Symes) was working on a bust of her son.

Hooper (*BR*) — A platoon commander in Charles Ryder's World War II unit. Hooper is a young commoner who is poorly educated; he is also careless and unreliable in his military assignments.

Hope-Browne, Mr. and Mrs. (*DF*) — Guests at the sports day at Llanabba School.

Horlick's field (*BR*) — The field where the former Marchmain home was situated before Brideshead Castle was built.

Hornbeam, Mr. and Mrs. (*EH*) — Neighbors of the Metcalfes. They live in quiet retirement at a house called Old Mill, devoting their days to arts and crafts. They are especially distressed to hear that the Westmacott property may be sold for a factory site.

Hornyold (*EB, SOH*) — A recusant Catholic family, a member of which attends the funeral of Guy Crouchback's father.

Hostile Offensive Operations — See *Hazardous Offensive Operations Headquarters*.

Hotel Eden (*MA, SOH*) — An inn in Santa Dulcina delle Rocce, Italy.

Hotel Liberty (*Sc*) — The principal place of accommodation for foreigners in Ishmaelia. The foreign correspondents stay there, much to the annoyance of the proprietor, Mrs. Earl Russell Jackson, whose pleasures are smoking a pipe and reading the Bible.

Hotel Metropole (*DF*) — The finest hotel in northern Wales. It is situated at Cwmpryddyg and is the scene of a lavish pre-wedding meal for Grimes attended by Pennyfeather and Prendergast.

Hôtel 22nd March (*SKME*) — The principal hotel in Neutralia, known also at various times as the Royal, the October Revolution, the Empire, the President Coolidge, and the Duchess of Windsor; popularly called the Ritz.

Hound, Major "Fido" (*OG, SOH*) — A stiff, officious officer who joins Operation B Commando unit in Egypt as Brigade Major. During the campaign in Crete he shows poor judgment and cowardice. He is particularly negatively affected by hunger. He leaves his post and makes his way to the harbor hoping to find a boat and leave his men behind. Only Ludovic knows his fate — he is presumably killed by Ludovic during the confusion of the evacuation and surrender at Crete. Hound had originally chosen a military career because he was an able civil servant. His talent was for administration, not for field commanding. "Fido" ("Faithful") is, of course, a popular name for a dog.

"House of Gentlefolks, A" — A short story by Waugh which appeared in *The New Decameron: The Fifth Day* (Oxford and New York, 1927). Members of a noble English family prefer to keep the heir over-sheltered because they regard him as insane when in reality he is the only sane member of the household. The title derives from Turgenev's *A Nest of Gentlefolk*.

Humber Snipe (*POMF, BR*) — A small British-made passenger car. Many Humber Snipes were modified for military use in World War II. In personal correspondence John St. John, who served with Waugh and wrote the memoir *To the War With Waugh* (London, 1973), noted that a Humber Snipe was attached to battalion headquarters; it was fitted to carry both passengers and equipment. In *POMF* the Commanding Officer travels with the Adjutant in a Humber Snipe. In *BR* it is noted that Charles Ryder's uncle owned a Humber.

Humility (*VB*) — One of Mrs. Ape's "angels."

Huntingdon, Countess of (*VB*) — Effie La Touche plays this role in the film about John Wesley. The Countess was Selina Hastings (1707–91), an important supporter of the Wesleys at the beginning of the Methodist movement.

I

Iago, Dr. (*EB, SOH*) — A professor of literature from Coimbra who attends Everard Spruce's party.

Ian (*OG, SOH*) — The first name of a Halberdier officer who is apparently injured in a fall on the cliffs on the island of Mugg while engaged in Commando training.

THE DICTIONARY

Île St. Louis (*BR*) — The district of Paris where Charles Ryder lived when he attended art school.

"Il Santo Inglese" (*MA, EB, SOH*) — "The Holy Englishman" or "the English saint," the local Italian name for Sir Roger of Waybroke, buried in Santa Dulcina delle Rocce, Italy. The Italian phrase is mentioned in *EB* but not in the equivalent *SOH* passage.

Imperial Hotel (*VB*) — The most prestigious hotel in the English town where the car race is held.

Inch, Colonel (*HD*) — The master of a fox-hunting group in the Hetton area.

"Incident in Azania" — A short story by Waugh (1933) involving the alleged kidnapping of Prunella Brooks. This story occurs after the events in *BM* have concluded. At the time of the story Azania has become a joint protectorate under British and French rule. The story first appeared in the *Windsor Magazine*, December, 1933, pp. 91–100; and later was published in *Mr. Loveday's Little Outing and Other Sad Stories* (London and Boston, 1936), and in *Charles Ryder's Schooldays and Other Stories* (Boston, 1982).

Indian Runner (*VB*) — The horse that easily wins the November Handicap. The drunk major claims to have bet Adam Symes's money on this horse and to have won thirty-five thousand pounds. The horse is owned by Mary Mouse's mother.

Inspector (*VB*) — The police official who investigates Flossie Ducane's death after she falls while swinging from a chandelier in Lottie Crump's hotel.

Instow, Lady (*PP*) — The mistress of Billy Cornphillip until his marriage to Etty.

Internal Combustion (*WS*) — The title of a Socialist expressionist play by Roger Simmonds.

Interpreter (*C, TMI, EB, SOH*) — An alleged lecturer in English from Zagreb University who serves as an interpreter for the partisan "general staff."

Invercauld (*MA*) — One of the clans which joins Prince Charles in a movie version of the Rising of 1745.

Ironside, General — See Glossary under *MA*.

Irwin — See Glossary under *BR*.

Isaacs, Mr. (*VB*) — The head of the Wonderfilm Company of Great Britain who makes a film about John Wesley using Colonel Blount's estate as the setting. He is an amateur working with very little money. He tries to sell the film or a share in the film to Adam Symes. Later he manages to sell the film to Colonel Blount.

Ishmaelia (*Sc*) — A country in northeast Africa where William Boot is sent as a correspondent. In several ways it parallels Ethiopia, where Waugh served as a newspaper correspondent.

Ithewaite, Mrs. (*VB*) — A member of a Conservative association at Chesham Bois. She is one of the protestors of the alleged wild party held at Prime Minister Brown's home at 10 Downing Street.

Ivory Tower (*POMF*) — The literary review started by Ambrose Silk.

J

Jack (*BM*) — A member of the British legation staff in Azania. He receives a letter from Sybil which is presumably read by almost everyone at the legation.

Jack (*EB*) — A name incorrectly used in one passage to designate Everard Spruce. In *US, SOH* this name is deleted, and Everard is substituted.

Jackson (*MA, SOH*) — One of the Halberdiers.

Jackson, Garnett (*Sc*) — An important government official of Ishmaelia.

Jackson, General Gollancz (*Sc*) — The official in charge of national defense and inland revenue in Ishmaelia. His soldiers collect taxes and equivalent commodities by force.

Jackson, Huxley (*Sc*) — An important government official of Ishmaelia.

Jackson, Mander (*Sc*) — An important government official of Ishmaelia.

Jackson, Mrs Earl Russell (*Sc*) — The pipe-smoking, Bible-reading proprietor of the Hotel Liberty, in Jacksonburg, Ishmaelia.

Jackson, Pankhurst (*Sc*) — The second president of Ishmaelia.

Jackson, Rathbone (*Sc*) — The third president of Ishmaelia, the grandson of the first president. When Dr. Benito and the Russian agent attempt to seize control of the country, they lock up Rathbone and the other Jacksons until Mr. Baldwin and Olafsen manage to restore the Jacksons to power.

Jackson, Samuel Smiles (*Sc*) — A proper, elderly black from Alabama who was chosen to be the first president of the Republic of Ishmaelia. As the years passed, the Jackson family became ascendant and held the chief positions in the government.

Jacksonburg (*Sc*) — The capital city of the Republic of Ishmaelia.

Jackson family (*Sc*) — The family in control of Ishmaelia. Although *Scoop* is clearly set in the Ethiopia of 1938, the Jackson family is evidently based on the ruling clique of the Republic of Liberia. Liberia was colonized in the early nineteenth century as a home for freed American slaves, and until very recently intermarried groups of (originally) American blacks ruled it. Waugh has given the members of the Jackson family first names taken from various real-life individuals whose views he distrusted or whose names could furnish comic allusions:

Samuel Smiles (1812–1904), author of many self-help books (his most popular book, entitled *Self-Help*, was published in 1859).

Gollancz, Sir Victor (1893–1967), publisher and founder of the influential Left Book Club.

Huxley, Sir Julian (1887–1975), scientist and first secretary of UNESCO. There may also be an allusion to his brother Aldous, the novelist, and their grandfather, the great agnostic scientist Thomas Henry Huxley (see also Glossary under *VB*, *Huxdane-Halley bomb*).

Garnett, J. C. M. (1880–1958), who resigned as secretary of the League of Nations Union in 1938 over the suggestion that the league might employ sanctions against Italy for its invasion of Ethiopia.

Mander, L. H. M. (1888–1946), author, film producer, political radio commentator, member of the Fabian Society, and Labour candidate for election to Parliament.

Russell, Bertrand, third Earl Russell (1872–1970), philosopher, radical, pacifist. Russell on inheriting his earldom at first "democratically" disclaimed use of his title; hence Waugh makes a point of including "Earl" in Mrs. Jackson's name.

Athol, Mrs. (née Jackson). See *Athol*.

Pankhurst, Emmeline (1858–1928) and her daughter Christabel (1880–1958), famous agitators for woman suffrage; possibly also Christabel's younger sister, Sylvia, a supporter of the Russian revolution and of Abyssinian independence.

Rathbone, Eleanor (1872–1946), Independent Member of Parliament and worker for woman suffrage and other reform movements.

Jagger, Mr. (*BM*) — A contractor engaged at Seth's order to demolish the Anglican cathedral in Debra-Dowa as a step toward remodeling and modernizing the town. Jagger protests Seth issuing his own currency to pay for the job. The name came from a Miss Jagger who lived with Waugh's friends the Lygons. The name referred to someone who was pleased to perform menial or tiresome tasks, not necessarily in a sycophantic manner. See *Letters*, p. 58 n. 3.

Jagger, Mr. (*IA*) — A repulsive Englishman who worked for the bank at Matodi.

Jakes, Wenlock (*Sc*) — The famous, highest-paid American journalist whose column is syndicated all over the United States. Jakes had won the Nobel Peace Prize for reporting about the carnage during a revolution in a Balkan country. He invented the revolution for his newspaper article, and soon a real revolution occurred. He is now writing a book of his experiences to be entitled *Under the Ermine*.

James (*POMF*) — A Sothill family servant who leaves for World War II army service.

James (*Sc*) — The first footman in the Boot family. He is not in good health and is able to serve the family only occasionally.

James, Mr. (*HD*) — One of the detectives hired to follow Tony Last and Milly to Brighton so that evidence can be collected for the divorce from Brenda.

James, Mr. (*IA*) — He worked for the Eastern Exchange Telegraph Company at Matodi.

James, Mr. (*SP*) — A middle-aged resident of the suburbs who hates radio programs.

James, Mrs. (*SP*) — Mr. James's wife, who enjoys radio programs.

Jane (*DF*) — A servant employed at Llanabba School by the Fagans.

Jane (*MA*, *SOH*) — An acquaintance of Frank de Souza's and of his mistress, Pat.

Jane (*VB*) — An elderly London woman who listens to her friend's tirade against the customs officials who searched Agatha Runcible at Dover. The woman reads an account of the incident in the newspaper.

Jane, Miss (*TB*) — Adam Doure's pimply sister.

Janet (*BR*) — An acquaintance of the Ryders who is on the passenger liner from the United States to England.

Japheth, Duke (*BM*) — The leader of a rebellion in Azania before the time of Seth.

THE DICTIONARY

Jason (*OG, SOH*) — One of the dogs belonging to Colonel Hector Campbell on Mugg.

Jasper (*BR*) — Charles Ryder's cousin who as an experienced, older student gives Charles advice about the most beneficial ways of studying and behaving at Oxford.

Jazz Girl (*HD*) — The name of a speed boat, in constant use, observed by Tony and Brenda Last on their honeymoon in Italy.

Jean, Lady (*Sc*) — She receives a wedding present from the Stitches. They paid Mrs. Beaver twenty pounds for the gift.

Jean, Monsieur (*BM*) — The first secretary of the French legation in Azania. He is disturbed about Madame Ballon's alleged love affair with General Connolly.

Jeannette (*LO*) — The cosmetic firm that produces "Jungle Venom."

Jebb, Mr. (*LO*) — The manager of the beauty parlor in the Beverly-Waldorf. Aimée Thanatogenos was employed there before going to work at Whispering Glades.

Jellaby, Mr. and Mrs. T. (*WS*) — The devoted servants of John Plant's father. After his death they settle in Portsmouth and sell radio materials and supplies.

Jellaby, Professor (*Sc*) — A scholar who writes a feature article for the *Beast* that no one can understand.

Jenkins, Sister — See *Jenny*.

Jenny (*EB, SOH*) — A short form for Sister Jenkins, the midwife of Virginia Troy's baby. In a letter to Guy, Virginia calls the midwife Sister Jennings. In *SOH* the same Sister Jenkins is not used; she is referred to as Jenny or as Sister Jennings.

Jepson (*Sc*) — One of the *Beast*'s foreign correspondents.

Jerningham (*EB, SOH*) — A recusant Roman Catholic who attends the funeral of Guy Crouchback's father.

Jervis (*MA, SOH*) — One of the Halberdier platoon commanders of D Company.

Jim (*MA*) — A Loamshire officer who for a time is suspected by Guy Crouchback of being a fifth columnist.

Jim (*WS*) — The barman at the Wimpole Club. He drinks with Atwater and John Plant.

Joab (*IA*) — A member of the Sakuyu tribe who commands a band of brigands in Azania. He is falsely accused of kidnapping Prunella Brooke. He is probably the Major Joab in *BM*.

Joab, Major (*BM*) — The captain of the Azanian infantry in Seth's army. He remains loyal to Seth and ultimately avenges the Emperor's death by killing Boaz. In the Bible (2 Samuel) Joab is David's strong-minded and ruthless army commander. There are interesting parallels between Joab's relationship to David and Major Joab's to Seth.

Job (*OG, EB, SOH*) — The night porter at Bellamy's Club, in London.

John (*LITS*) — A friend of Tom Watch and Angela Trench-Troubridge who attends their wedding.

John (*POMF*) — A member of the upper class looking for a war service position.

Johnjohn (*BR*) — Charles Ryder's young son by his wife, Celia.

Jorkins (*BR*) — An old school acquaintance of Charles Ryder's; Charles brings him to dinner at his father's. The father plays an elaborate charade throughout the meal, pretending to think that Jorkins is American. He is presumably the same Jorkins who appears in *CRS*.

Josefina (*MA, OG, SOH*) — With her sister Bianca she does the housework in Guy Crouchback's home in Santa Dulcina delle Rocce, Italy.

Journal of an English Cavalry Officer During the Peninsular War, The (*WTA*) — A journal kept by Colonel Jasper Cumberland, published with notes and introduction by Gervase Kent-Cumberland. Actually it was Gervase's younger brother, Tom, who found the manuscript of the journal and compiled the notes and introduction.

Joyboy, Mr. (*LO*) — The senior mortician of Whispering Glades. He is a mama's boy and is also Aimée's fiance. When he is happy, he sends the embalmed corpses with smiles on their faces for Aimée's cosmetic treatments.

Joyboy, Mrs. (*LO*) — The selfish and cranky mother of Joyboy. She appears mainly interested in political commentary on the radio and in her parrots.

Joyce (*HD*) — An employee at Mrs. Beaver's interior-decorating shop; she has paid to be an apprentice there and learn the trade but is relegated to the cellar packing area.

Julia (*HG*) — A friend of Ernest Vaughan.

Julia (*POMF*) — A dogmatic Communist from the London School of Economics; she frequently associates with Poppet Green's set.

Julia (*WS*) — Lucy Simmond's pretty eighteen-year-old cousin who becomes infatuated with author John Plant. Julia is cheerful and outgoing and dotes on

John but astutely perceives that he is in love with Lucy. Julia's father was an army major at Aldershot.

Julia, Aunt (*BR*) — An older member of the Marchmain family.

Julius Constantius's wife (*H*) — One of the women in the emperor's court in Rome. Julius Constantius was a brother of Constantine.

Jumbo — See *Trotter, Colonel Jumbo*.

Jumbo (*BM*) — One of the riding horses at the British legation in Azania. It is owned by Percy Legge.

"Jungle Venom" (*LO*) — The lotion Aimée Thanatogenos puts in her hair while preparing for a date.

Jungman, Mr. (*SKME*) — A gynaecologist from The Hague who attends the Bellorius celebration in Neutralia.

K

Kaiser (*LO*) — A tycoon who dominates the stonelesspeaches market. He had purchased a gravesite on the Lake Island of Innisfree in Whispering Glades.

Kakophilos, Dr. (*OD*) — A magician who enables Alastair Trumpington to dream that he is in the Middle Ages and helps Rip Van Winkle dream that he lives in London in the twenty-fifth century. The word kakophilos means in Greek "lover of evil."

Kanyi, Mme (*C, TMI, EB, SOH*) — A Jewish woman of Fiume married to a Hungarian engineer. In *EB, SOH* she is the principal spokesman for the refugees in Yugoslavia whom Guy Crouchback tries to help. She and her husband are eventually executed by Tito's partisans because they have allegedly collaborated improperly with the British. In *C, TMI* she seeks Major Gordon's help.

Kaprikis, Madame (*OG, SOH*) — A wealthy Greek woman whose home and hospitality were made available to X Commando in Alexandria.

Kätchen (*Sc*) — An attractive refugee girl (she looks like Elisabeth Bergner) with whom William Boot falls in love in Ishmaelia. She uses every ruse to obtain money from him and finally leaves Ishmaelia with the German she calls her "husband" although she has never been legally married. Her father was Russian, and her mother Polish.

Kätchen's "husband" (*Sc*) — A German adventurer who obtains gold ore in Ishmaelia. Although he has deserted his real wife in Germany, Kätchen is very much in love with him. The two of them flee Ishmaelia aboard William Boot's inflatable boat after selling the ore specimens to him. Later Kätchen sends a letter to William revealing that she and her "husband" are on a ship bound for Madagascar and asking him for more money.

Kemble (*MA, SOH*) — A town near Box-Bender's home in Gloucestershire.

Kemp, Sister (*WS*) — A baby nurse hired by Roger and Lucy Simmonds in the last week before Lucy's baby is due. She stays with Lucy during and after the birth, and they become very friendly.

Kempy (*WS*) — An affectionate nickname Lucy Simmonds uses for her nurse Sister Kemp.

Kent-Cumberland, Gervase Peregrine Mountjoy St. Eustace (*WTA*) — The older son, who triumphs in prestige, romance, etc., over his younger brother, Tom, because of his status as oldest son and his mother's favoritism. Kent and Cumberland are traditional titles of royal dukes.

Kent-Cumberland, Mrs. (*WTA*) — The main protagonist who makes certain that her older son, Gervase, gets every advantage at the expense of her younger son, Tom.

Kent-Cumberland, Thomas (*WTA*) — The second son, who is badly treated. Even his prospective moneyed bride is taken away from him and given to his older brother.

Kentish, Mr. (*IA*) — The assistant native commissioner in Azania. For a time he appears to be the romantic favorite of Prunella Brooks.

Kents (*Sc*) — The Duke and Duchess of Kent; the Duke (1902–42) was the younger son of King George V. They came to dinner at the home of Julia and Algernon Stitch.

Kenworthy, Dr. Wilbur (*LO*) — The money-oriented, death-is-happy founder and owner of Whispering Glades, frequently called "The Dreamer." He is modeled after Hubert Eaton, the founder of Forest Lawn cemetery, who was called "The Builder."

Kerr of Gellioch (*OG, SOH*) — The uncle of Angus Anstruther-Kerr.

Kerr-Stuart, Alastair (*VB*) — A mythical laird invented by Adam Symes for his "Chatterbox" gossip column.

Kew (*OGP*) — The town where Gilbert Pinfold's elderly mother lives.

Kilbannock, Lady Kerstie (*OG, EB, SOH*) — In *OG, SOH* the personable wife of Ian Kilbannock. In *EB*,

THE DICTIONARY

SOH she has left her position at the canteen of the Transit Camp to become a cipher clerk. She is a friend of Virginia Troy and tries to help Virginia obtain an abortion. She cannot understand why Guy Crouchback would agree to marry the pregnant Virginia and adopt her son.

Kilbannock, Lord Ian (*MA, OG, EB, SOH*) — In *MA, SOH* a former sports journalist and acquaintance of Guy Crouchback who becomes an air force officer. He had once been to Kenya and later wrote a gossip column. In *OG, SOH*, attached to Hostile Offensive Operations, he becomes liaison officer to the newspapers and is responsible for making Trimmer a hero in the mass media. In *EB, SOH* he runs a busy news service from London headquarters. He is given frequent promotions and is quite successful. When activities eventually slow down because of Allied victories and the war's end is in sight, he asks to be sent as a correspondent to Yugoslavia to cover the story of the partisans there. He wishes to establish himself as a popular journalist so that he can have a flourishing postwar career in that field. He also hopes to write books. He may be based on Waugh's friend Patrick Balfour, Lord Kinross.

Kilbannock, the Dowager Lady (*EB*) — Ian Kilbannock's mother, who entertained the Kilbannock children during school holidays at the ancestral home in Scotland during World War II.

Kilcartney, Charlie (*BR*) — A heavy drinker. His fiancée Sylvia makes it a condition of marriage that he should take the cure at a sanatorium in Zurich. After he stops drinking, Sylvia leaves him because he has become a bore.

King of Ruritania (*VB*) — The sad, deposed ruler of that country who stays at Lottie Crump's hotel. Most of his family have had bombs thrown at them, and his wife is in an insane asylum because she mistakenly thought that the cook was going to bomb her at a dinner party (he was in fact preparing a "bombe," a dessert). Ruritania is the name of the fictional Balkan kingdom invented by Anthony Hope in his popular novel *The Prisoner of Zenda* (1894). Such a setting supplied a scene for romantic adventure and court intrigue.

Kingsley-Wood (*Sc*) — A British government official mentioned in the book Wenlock Jakes is writing. See Glossary under *Sc*.

King's Thursday (*DF, BSRA*) — In *DF* the ancestral home of the Pastmasters in Hampshire. The original mansion had been an excellent example of Tudor architecture. Margot Beste-Chetwynde bought it from her brother-in-law, had it torn down, and then rebuilt it in a modern, factorylike mode. After Otto Silenus has thus "modernized" it, Margot plans to have it redone again. It is also mentioned in *BSRA*; Peter Pastmaster still lives there, but he also has a house in London.

Klugmann's Operation (*LAR*) — An operation for sterilization which sometimes results in the woman growing a thick beard. This happens to Clara, and yet she later becomes pregnant.

Knights of Malta (*SKME*) — Noblemen in Neutralia who belong to this organization and lounge about the Ritz Hotel. See Glossary under *SKME*.

Knode Hall (*BFGP*) — A country home in need of repair; it is near Fleacetown, Ireland.

Komstock, Colonel (*LO*) — Mrs. Komstock's son, who asks for Aimée Thanatogenos to arrange his mother's hair for her funeral at Whispering Glades.

Komstock, Mrs. (*LO*) — A customer of Aimée Thanatogenos when Aimée worked at the beauty parlor in the Beverly-Waldorf.

Kong (or **King Kong**) (*OG, SOH*) — The nickname of an instructor sent to the island of Mugg to teach cliff climbing. Actually this is a name adopted by the soldiers for Chatty Corner. See also *Corner, Chatty*.

Kramm, Mr. (*BR*) — A distracted and stiff official of Interastral Films and guest at the shipboard party arranged by Celia Ryder. He later breaks his arm during the storm.

Kremlin, The (*MK*) — A pseudo-Russian restaurant and nightclub in Paris managed by Boris, a military cadet who escaped from Russia after the Bolshevik Revolution.

Kronomim, Prince Fyodor (*BM*) — The manager of the Perroquet Hotel in Debra-Dowa.

Krump, Sophie Dalmeyer (*LO*) — A third-rate poet buried in Whispering Glades.

Kurt (*BR*) — Sebastian's injured German friend. He was in the Foreign Legion and shot off his toe to obtain a discharge. Sebastian took up with him in Tangier, and they went to French Morocco, where Sebastian enjoyed looking after him. Later, after Sebastian and Kurt go to Greece, Kurt is arrested and returned to Germany. There is he unwillingly placed in the storm troops, tries to desert, and is arrested and sent to a concentration camp. Sebastian learns later that Kurt had hanged himself in the camp.

Kut-al-Imara House (*MA, SOH*) — A preparatory school at Southsand-on-Sea, turned into a Halberdiers' training headquarters; both Guy Crouchback and Apthorpe spend considerable time in training there. Robert Murray Davis notes that the name of the school derived from a battle lost by a combined English and Indian military force in 1916; cf. Robert Murray Davis, *Evelyn Waugh, Writer* (Norman, Okla., 1981), p. 246. "Kut the bitter" is the translation of the Arabic.

L

Lady of Waybroke — See *Waybroke*.

Laird of Cockpen (*MA*) — The leader of the Cockpen clan who joins Prince Charles in a movie version of the Rising of 1745. The name comes from a comic Scottish song with that title.

Lake Island of Innisfree (*LO*) — An exclusive burial spot on an isle in the middle of a lake at Whispering Glades cemetery. It is a popular lovers' lane in *LO*. The island takes its title from William Butler Yeats's famous poem "The Lake Isle of Innisfree."

Laku (*Sc*) — A mythical Ishmaelian city existing only on the country's map. The word means "I don't know" in the native language. Dr. Benito arranges for the journalists to be sent there so that they will be out of the way when the revolution occurs in Jacksonburg.

Lamb and Flag (*DF*) — A pub at Camberwell Green which Philbrick claims to have owned.

Lance, James (*OGP*) — A friend of Gilbert Pinfold who also enjoys antique furniture. Lance sends an antique washstand to Pinfold. Pinfold's mind begins to play tricks on him, and he insists that the stand came with a copper tap. Lance, however, points out that it did not have the tap to begin with. Lance appears on the BBC broadcast with Jane Cumberleigh. He is a poet, artist, and broadcaster "who had let himself become popularized." He is based on poet John Betjeman, who in reality did send Waugh a washstand.

Lane-Foscote, Sir Roderick (*MCLO, MCO, MLLO*) — In *MLLO* a member of Parliament representing Lord and Lady Moping's district. He helps arrange the release of Loveday from the mental institution. He is also mentioned in *MCO, MCLO*.

Lang, Swithin (*TB*) — A student at Oxford, acquainted with Adam Doure.

Larkin, Sprat (*Sc*) — He accompanied General Cruttwell on a trip to Ishmaelia in 1897.

Larne (*MK*) — An expensive Paris restaurant where Boris has what might have been his last meal.

Larrigan, Alf (*DF*) — He is castrated through the machinations of Toby Crutwell because he has become involved with one of Toby's prostitutes.

Last, Agnes (*HD*) — The twelve-year-old daughter of Mr. and Mrs. Richard Last, the heirs of Hetton.

Last, John Andrew (*HD*) — The spoiled, brattish, outspoken, emotionally sensitive child of Brenda and Tony Last. He is killed when he is thrown from his pony and accidentally kicked in the head by another horse.

Last, Lady Brenda (née Rex) (*HD, BSR*) — In *HD* the chief feminine figure, who betrays her husband with John Beaver. Her character deficiency is best revealed in the famous scene when she learns that John has been killed and soon sighs with relief when she learns that it is her small son who is dead and not her shiftless lover. In *BSR*, Brenda is deserted by John Beaver and returns to Tony at Hetton. She becomes pregnant. She is unaware that Tony has made arrangements to take over her old flat in London. The same situation occurs in the "Alternative Ending" to *HD*.

Last, Mr. and Mrs. Richard (*HD*) — Tony Last's cousins, who inherit Hetton after Tony is officially declared dead. Although they are not well-to-do, they have a genuine regard for the estate. After Tony's "official" death, they inherit Hetton and, with their children, raise silver foxes.

Last, Molly (*HD*) — One of the daughters of Mr. and Mrs. Richard Last.

Last, Peter (*HD*) — One of the sons of Mr. and Mr. Richard Last; he attends Oxford.

Last, Teddy (*HD*) — One of the sons of Mr. and Mrs. Richard Last. He takes care of the silver foxes which they raise.

Last, Tony (*BSR, HD*) — In *HD* the decent and gentlemanly protagonist. He has an adequate amount of money, loves Hetton, and is devoted to his son and wife. He is shattered by Brenda's adultery and her demands for financial support. He goes off on a South American jungle expedition and becomes trapped by Mr. Todd's obsession with Dickens. In *BSR* and in the "Alternative Ending" to *HD*, Tony returns from travelling abroad and is reunited with Brenda, who returns to Hetton with him. Tony decides to keep the London flat that Brenda had used, although he doesn't tell Brenda this. He intends to use it to carry on romantic affairs.

"Last Latinist, The" (*SKME*) — An essay written by Scott-King to commemorate the tercentenary of Bellorius's death.

Latin-American Entertainment Co., Ltd (*DF*) — A chain of South American brothels run very profitably by Margot Beste-Chetwynde, who inherited it from her father.

La Touche, Miss Effie (*VB*) — An amateur actress who plays the lead role, Selina, Countess of Huntingdon, in a film about John Wesley.

Lawyer from Zagreb (*C, TMI, EB, SOH*) — In *EB, SOH* one of the Jewish refugees in Yugoslavia whom Guy Crouchback attempts to help. He appears in *TMI* and in *C*, where Major Gordon tries to assist.

League of Dumb Chums (*BM*) — A society for the prevention of cruelty to animals. Mildred Porch and Sarah Tin are members who unsuccessfully carry their campaign to Azania.

Lecce (*EB, SOH*) — The Italian town where the Jewish refugees are encamped after they are freed from Yugoslavia. It is there that Guy Crouchback learns that the innocent Madame Kanyi and her husband have been executed by the Communist partisans.

Legge, Mr. and Mrs. Percy (*BM*) — Members of the British legation group in Azania. Percy is the second secretary at the legation.

Legge, Mrs. (*WS*) — John Plant's landlady when he lived in an apartment on Ebury Street, London. She has caught Julia, in a moment of teenage infatuation, kissing John's razor.

Lennox, David (*DF, VB, POMF*) — In *DF* a society photographer and homosexual who attends a party at King's Thursday. In *VB* he is mentioned as a photographer. In *POMF* it is noted that he had been an interior decorator before World War II and painted several grisailles for Angela Lyne's home. He is criticized by Ambrose Silk in one of the *Ivory Tower* articles. It is generally agreed that Sir Cecil Beaton was the real-life model for Lennox.

Lennox, Sylvia (*ER*) — The girl friend of Simon Lent.

Lent, Simon (*ER*) — A young novelist who works for a time on a film version of *Hamlet*.

Leo (*LO*) — A famous film magnate who discovered Juanita del Pablo. His movie empire later collapsed, and he died in poverty at the Garden of Allah (Tents of Kedar in the American edition) Hotel. See Glossary under *LO*.

Leonard, Daisy (*MA, SOH*) — Jim Leonard's pregnant wife. She is a constant complainer and has no respect for Halberdier traditions. She wants her husband close to her at all times and does not wish to endure any inconvenience caused by war. She pressures and badgers her husband so persistently that he transfers to home-front duties.

Leonard, Jim (*MA, SOH*) — A Halberdier who trains with Guy Crouchback. He worked for an insurance company before the war and played regularly for a football club. He is sensible, likable, and the sort who would make a good Halberdier. His wife's nagging and selfishness, however, force him to transfer to a home-front training depot. Ironically, Leonard is later killed by a bomb during an air raid in England.

Lepperidges (*BM, IA*) — Friends of the Reppingtons. He is Commanding Officer of the native levy. He receives his appointment after Azania becomes a joint British-French protectorate of the League of Nations. He is also mentioned in *IA*, where Mrs. Lepperidge helps initiate Prunella Brooks into the social behavior and proprieties expected of members of the British colony in Azania.

***Le President Carnot*, S.S.** (*BM*) — The ship carrying Mildred Porch and Sarah Tin to Azania.

Lesser House (*EB, SOH*) — One of the buildings on the Broome estate of the Crouchbacks. It has been used for various purposes; the bailiff lived there at the time of Mr. Crouchback's funeral. It is called the "Little Hall" by the villagers.

Levy, Mr. (*DF*) — A member of the staff of Church and Gargoyle, an employment agency for teachers. He arranges for Pennyfeather to interview Dr. Fagan for the job at Llanabba School.

Licinianus (*H*) — The son of Constantia who is ultimately put to death for treason by Emperor Constantine.

Licinius (*H*) — A Roman leader and military figure. He is the husband of Constantia and at various times a rival and a friend of Constantine.

Lil (*BM*) — An English girl who is asked by her father and mother, since she is the family member most recently in school, where Azania is situated.

THE DICTIONARY

Lily (*VB*) — A young woman manicurist. Her father was opposed to her choice of a job because he felt that this occupation was merely an excuse to hold hands.

Little Bayton — See *Bayton*.

Littlejohn, Eddy (*VB*) — Better known as Ginger (because of his red hair), he is a friend of Nina Blount and Adam Fenwick-Symes. Nina and he played together as children, being reared in the same area. He was involved in military service in Ceylon before retiring and returning to London. He marries Nina. Although she proves unfaithful to him, he continues the marriage, persuading himself that her baby is his, although it is apparently Adam's. He has been called up for duty with his regiment, but eventually obtains a military post in the war office in Whitehall.

Llanabba School (*DF*) — A school in Wales, situated in a large house called Llanabba Castle, where Paul Pennyfeather teaches for a time. The school is owned and managed by Dr. Fagan.

Llandudno (*DF*) — The largest town near Llanabba School. Grimes and Dingy Fagan go shopping there to purchase materials for the annual sports day.

Lochiel (*MA*) — One of the clans which joins Prince Charles in a movie version of the Rising of 1745.

Loch Moidart (*MA*) — A Scottish lake.

Lockejaws (*PP*) — A socially prominent family.

Lockwood (*SKME*) — A former student of Scott-King's who serves in the British army in Palestine and recognizes his old teacher when the schoolmaster arrives there at an illicit immigrants' camp.

Lockwoods (*LITS*) — On their honeymoon they went to Morocco and were captured by brigands.

Loder, Colonel (*DF*) — A visitor to one of the sports days at Llanabba School.

Lola (*WS*) — A prostitute in Morocco.

Lollianus (*H*) — A Roman political leader.

London Despatch — See *Despatch*.

London Hercules (*DF*) — A publication in which Jack Spire writes about preserving the original Tudor style of King's Thursday. Waugh was apparently referring to the *London Mercury* and its editor Sir John Collings Squire.

London Library (*WS, OGP*) — A private subscription library. In *WS*, John Plant and Basil Seal belong to this institution. In *OGP*, Gilbert Pinfold and Algernon Clutton-Cornforth are also members. In a letter Waugh gave Lady Mary Lygon good advice about how to behave herself there; see *Letters*, p. 240.

Long, Mr. (*WS*) — An alias used by Arthur Atwater to reach John Plant by phone.

Longworth, Mr. Justice (*WS*) — The judge at the trial in which Arthur Atwater is acquitted of the death of John Plant's father.

Loot — See *Padfield, Lieutenant*.

Lord-Lieutenant of Somerset County (*EB, SOH*) — He attends the funeral of Guy Crouchback's father.

Lord Mayor of Bellacita (*SKME*) — A one-eyed, taciturn official in Neutralia.

Lorenzo (*WS*) — A maitre d' at the Ritz. He is on duty when John Plant gives his lunch for Lucy and Roger Simmonds.

Lost Chord, The (*OGP*) — A book by author Gilbert Pinfold taken from the *Caliban*'s library to be read by one of the passengers.

Love Among the Ruins — A novelette (1953) by Waugh depicting life in England in the future as a result of welfare-state ideas. The Department of Euthanasia is immensely popular, and the so-called enlightened ideas of the new progressive state cause unhappiness and disaster.

Loveday, Mr. (*MLLO*) — A seemingly gentle and sane inmate of the Country Home for Mental Defectives. He is released and then returned there after he commits another murder. He had strangled a young lady on a bicycle and spent thirty-five years in the asylum. Nevertheless he longs for another outing. Through the efforts of Angela Moping he is released, whereupon he strangles another young lady who is riding a bicycle.

Loved One, The — A novel (1948) in which Waugh satirizes Forest Lawn Memorial Park, a Hollywood pet mortuary, and other aspects of modern American life. The novel first appeared in *Horizon*, February, 1948, pp. 76–159.

"**Love in the Slump**" — A short story by Waugh about the honeymoon of Tom Watch and Angela Trench-Troubridge. Through a series of misadventures the honeymoon passes without consummation of the marriage. During the honeymoon period Angela becomes involved with an old school friend of Tom's and agrees to become his mistress. The story was published as "The Patriotic Honeymoon" in the London *Harper's Bazaar*, January, 1932, pp. 14–15, 86. It was first collected in *Mr. Loveday's Little Outing*

THE DICTIONARY

and Other Sad Stories (London and Boston, 1936) and renamed "Love in the Slump."

Lover's Seat, The (*LO*) — Also called "The Heart of the Bruce," a marble seat in Whispering Glades near the Wee Kirk o' Auld Lang Syne. A carved heart with an opening is provided, and the lovers kiss through the opening and swear their devotion to one another. It actually exists in Forest Lawn Memorial Park, Glendale, California.

Lower Chipping Manor (*MA, OG, SOH*) — The country home, near Tetbury, of Arthur and Angela Box-Bender. It is mentioned in *MA, SOH* but not by name. It is stated that the house is in Gloucestershire.

Lowndes Square (*MA, SOH*) — The location of Box-Bender's London home. It is closed during the war.

Lucas-Dockery, Sir Wilfred (*DF*) — The chief official of Blackstone Gaol, the prison to which Pennyfeather is sent. He is a former holder of the Chair of Sociology at an English university. He is obsessed with statistics and theories and totally impractical in prison matters. His lenient theories lead to Prendergast's death.

Ludovic, Corporal-Major (*OG, EB, SOH*) — In *OG, SOH*, a meditative, rather mysterious warrant officer assigned to Ivor Claire and then promoted to headquarters. He keeps a journal of his daily life. On Crete he tries to find a boat and leave the island without the approval of his unit. In the confusion there things ultimately turn out well for him. He joins Guy Crouchback and a group of soldiers in another boat, which sails across the Mediterranean to Egypt. He carries the delirious Guy ashore in Egypt, having survived the water ordeal in good physical condition (he had reported as a reservist when World War II began, but no one seemed to have information about his background). In *EB, SOH*, Ludovic is now a major in the Intelligence Corps; he had once had a homosexual relationship with Sir Ralph Brompton, both as his "valet" and as his "secretary" — now the two men are no longer in homosexual union. He wants to have some of his written material (called "Pensées") published in *Survival*, and he enjoys writing. He is assigned as commandant of a parachute training base. He avoids seeing Crouchback when Guy is sent to this camp because of guilt over Major Hound and his actions against a sapper in the boat in which he and Guy escaped from Crete. (In the "Synopsis of Preceding Volumes" at the beginning of *EB* it is suggested that Ludovic was involved in the murder of Major Hound and the killing of the sapper captain who commanded the escape boat.) Ludovic writes a romantic novel called *The Death Wish*, which becomes a best seller. Ludovic buys the Castello Crouchback and settles in Italy, along with Lieutenant Padfield, at the conclusion of the war.

Lumo (*BM*) — The overnight train stop on the line between Matodi and Debra-Dowa. The hotel proprietor there shares his profits with the president of the railroad.

Lumsden of Strathdrummond (*DF*) — An unruly undergraduate at Scone College, Oxford, who is one of the drunken members of the Bollinger Club responsible for debagging Paul Pennyfeather. The name indicates that he is a Scottish laird.

Lunt (*BR*) — Charles Ryder's servant ("scout") at Oxford. He is charmed by Sebastian Flyte.

"Lush Places" (*Sc*) — The name of the biweekly newspaper column on various aspects of nature and rural life that William Boot writes for the *Beast*.

Luxmore, Jean (*BR*) — A friend of Anthony Blanche. He had a pot dropped on his head during the General Strike of 1926.

Luxmore, Tony (*OG, EB, SOH*) — In *OG, SOH* he commands X Commando after Tommy Blackhouse's promotion. He was a member of the Coldstream Guards and comes from a well-to-do family. He is taken prisoner by the Germans during the campaign in Crete. In *EB, SOH* it is mentioned that he has escaped from the PW camp and eventually returned safely to England.

Lychpole (*OGP*) — A small village about one hundred miles from London where Gilbert Pinfold and his family have their home.

Lyne, Angela (*BM, POMF, BSRA*) — In *BM* the only child and heiress of a Scottish millionaire. Although she is married, she becomes the mistress of Basil Seal. She gives him money so that he can make a journey to Azania. She is stylish and impeccable in manner. Consequently, in *POMF* much surprise develops among the characters when it is discovered that when Basil begins to neglect her she starts to drink heavily in the privacy of her home. After her husband is killed in World War II, she and Basil agree (in *POMF*) that they should marry. In *BSRA* she and Basil visit a health spa. She is the mother of Barbara Seal.

THE DICTIONARY

Lyne, Cedric (*POMF, BSRA*) — In *POMF* the gentle, aesthetic husband of Angela Lyne. He builds attractive grottoes at their country estate. He has served for years in the army, and during World War II he becomes his battalion's intelligence officer. He is killed in the British campaign in Norway. His death is also mentioned in *BSRA*.

Lyne, Nigel (*POMF, BSRA*) — In *POMF* the young son of Cedric and Angela. He spends most of his time away at school. He is generally ignored by his mother. In *BSRA* it is mentioned that he received Angela's country estate on the occasion of his twenty-first birthday.

M

Mabel (*BM*) — One of the wives at the British legation in Azania.

MacAdder, Colonel (*DF*) — The predecessor of Lucas-Dockery as Governor of the prison to which Pennyfeather is sent. He was a strict disciplinarian whose philosophy was to "give hell" to the man immediately below one in rank, who will in turn pass that attitude down the chain of command.

Macarius (*H*) — The bishop of Aelia Capitolina (Jerusalem), who wishes to preserve the location of the Holy Sepulcher. He aids Helena in her quest.

Macassor, Mr. (*TB, IA*) — The shrewd proprietor of a London bookstore who pretends to be unaware of rare books in his shop.

Macdonald, Mrs. (*IA*) — The proprietor of a *pension* on the outskirts of Matodi.

MacDougal (*HD, POMF*) — In *HD* the barman at Brat's Club. In *POMF* he knows "secret" war information.

MacDougal, Bessie (*WTA*) — An Australian who marries Gervase Kent-Cumberland. Originally she had been engaged to Gervase's younger brother.

MacDougal, Mr. (*WTA*) — A wealthy Australian rancher whose daughter marries Gervase Kent-Cumberland.

Mackay, Father (*BR*) — An unsophisticated, congenial parish priest who comes to Brideshead to give Lord Marchmain the last sacraments.

Mackenzie (*TE*) — A doctor in a small Cornish village consulted separately by both John and Elizabeth Verney as they use him to support their alibis about the intended murders of each other.

Mackenzie, Mr. (*SKME*) — A friend of Mrs. Antonic's father.

Mackingtosh [American mispronunciation of Mackintosh] (*MA*) — A character in a movie about the Rising of 1745.

McKinney, Captain (*MA, SOH*) — The acting camp commandant who meets Guy when the latter arrives at Kut-al-Imara Preparatory School.

McMaster, Mr. James (*TMWLD*) — The son of an English missionary and a Shiriana mother. He lives in a remote Brazilian clearing. Unable to read but loving Charles Dickens's novels, he forces Barnabas Washington and later Paul Henty to read Dickens. He is the Mr. Todd of *HD*.

Macrae, Sir James (*ER*) — An extremely busy and protean film tycoon. He wants Simon Lent to write modern dialogue for *Hamlet*. As the scenario progresses, it is decided to blend *Hamlet* with *Macbeth*, and the film title is changed to *The White Lady of Dunsinane*. Finally the project is scrapped, and Macrae decides to return to Shakespeare's version of *Hamlet*. He is probably based on Sir Alexander Korda (1893–1956), with whom Waugh worked desultorily as scriptwriter.

McTavish (*OG, SOH*) — The Scottish name Trimmer uses when Guy Crouchback meets him on the island of Mugg. After leaving the Halberdiers, he goes to Scotland and joins a unit there, using (he claims) his mother's name, McTavish. See *Trimmer*.

Macushi (*HD*) — A South American Indian tribe that does not wish to have any contact with the Pie-wies. Members of the tribe escort Tony Last and Dr. Messinger deep into the jungle but are frightened by the mechanical mice and desert the explorers. Rosa is the most prominent of the Macushi.

Madame de Supplice — See *de Supplice*.

Madge (*Sc*) — The wife of newspaper correspondent Corker.

Maharajah of Pukkapore (*VB*) — A romantic acquaintance of Mary Mouse who attends Margot's party. He takes Mary back to India with him.

Mahmoud Pasha (*OG, SOH*) — A guest at one of Julia Stitch's parties in Egypt.

Mahmud el Khali bin Sai'ud (*BM*) — A member of the oldest family in Matodi. He appears to spend most of his time chewing khat.

Maiden, Caroline (*MA, SOH*) — A friend of the Box-

THE DICTIONARY

Bender family. She is reproved by a policeman in Stroud because she does not have her gas mask with her.

Mainwaring, Sir Joseph — See *Mannering, Sir Joseph*.

Maison Basque (*DF*) — A fashionable restaurant in London's Mayfair section. When Pennyfeather and Margot Beste-Chetwynde dine there, Philbrick is seated at the next table.

Majesty (*BM*) — One of the horses at the British legation in Azania kept for pleasure riding.

Major, the drunken (*VB*) — A heavy drinker who owes Adam 35,000 pounds because of a winning choice in a horse race. He keeps reappearing, promising to repay the loan. At the end of the novel he is a British general whom Adam meets on a battlefield on the Continent. We never learn his name.

"Major Intervenes, The" — See *"Compassion."*

Makepeace, Mr. (*DF*) — One of the new schoolmasters at Llanabba hired after Pennyfeather leaves. One of the boys claims that he has a glass eye.

Malfrey (*POMF, BSRA*) — In *POMF* the beautiful country estate of Freddy and Barbara Sothill. It is also the name of the adjoining village. In *BSRA* it has been taken over by the National Trust, and Barbara lives in a flat over the stables. Her niece, Barbara, stays with her for a time.

Malpractice, Hon Miles (*DF, VB, POMF*) — A son of Lady Throbbing and the late Lord Throbbing and younger brother of Edward, the present Lord Throbbing. In *DF*, Miles first appears as a homosexual who attends a party at King's Thursday. In *VB* he is also a partygoer and becomes Mr. Chatterbox when Adam Symes is fired. Near the novel's end he is forced to leave England for unspecified reasons. In *POMF* it is mentioned that he is a friend of Ambrose Silk. Malpractice may be based on the real-life Eddie Gathorne-Hardy. See also *Gaythorne-Brodie, Martin*. This name is used instead of Malpractice in the first English editions.

Maltby, Mr. (*TB*) — The director of the Maltby School of Art, in the London Quartier Latin (i.e., Chelsea).

Maltby, Mr. (*TB*) — Referred to as "the young Mr. Maltby," he works at his father's art studio.

Malt House, Grantley Green — See *Bride of Grantley Green*.

Malton, Lord (*BR*) — An acquaintance of Lord Marchmain.

Maltravers, Sir Humphrey (*DF*) — A Minister of Transportation; later he becomes Home Secretary and then Viscount Metroland and husband of Margot Beste-Chetwynde. Maltravers uses his influence to get Pennyfeather out of prison to induce Margot to marry him. After his marriage to Margot he becomes Viscount Metroland. See also *Metroland, Lord*.

"Manager of 'The Kremlin,' The" — A short story by Waugh (1930) which appeared in *John Bull*, February 15, 1930, pp. 22, 24. Boris, the protagonist, is a military cadet who escapes from Russia during the Bolshevik Revolution and after various vicissitudes becomes the manager of a Russian-style restaurant and nightclub in Paris. His success does not assuage his grief that he has been driven out of his homeland.

Manchu (*PP*) — Lady Amelia's cat.

Mannering, Sir Joseph (*BM, POMF, BSRA*) — An old family friend of the Seals and a rather pompous political figure who holds various government positions. In *BM*, Lady Seal discusses Basil's indiscretions with him and seeks his advice. In *POMF* he attempts, at the instigation of Lady Seal, to help Basil become properly placed in military service. In *BSRA* he is reminisced about. Basil by this time has joined the London club to which Mannering had belonged and often sits in Mannering's old chair behaving much as his self-appointed guardian used to. (In *POMF* Mannering's name is spelled Mainwaring, although the pronunciation is the same.)

"Man Who Liked Dickens, The" — A short story by Waugh (1933) which appeared in *Hearst's International Combined with Cosmopolitan* and in *Nash's Pall Mall Magazine*. It was reworked into the last section of *HD*.

"Man Who Read Dickens, The" — A short story by Waugh exactly the same as "The Man Who Liked Dickens."

Marchers (*BR*) — A short name for Marchmain House, the London home of the Marchmain family.

Marchmain (*BR*) — A town ten miles from Brideshead Castle.

Marchmain, Alex, Marquess of (*BR*) — The head of the Marchmain family. He is described as handsome and Byronic, wealthy and aristocratic. He converts to Roman Catholicism when he marries, but after serving in the British army in World War I, he leaves for Italy, where he lives with a mistress. His wife's religious attitudes repel him, and he cannot endure being near her. He does not attend her funeral but several years later returns to Brideshead Castle and dies there. The seventh Earl Beauchamp (1872–1938) apparently furnished the model for Lord Marchmain, but the death scene derived from the passing of Hubert Duggan.

Marchmain, Teresa, Marchioness of (*BR*) — The very civil, proper, and religious matriarch of the Marchmain family. Her piety disturbs most of the members of the family, causing her husband to live in Italy, and brings about Sebastian's heavy drinking. Improper family behavior causes her considerable suffering.

Marchmain Hounds (*BR*) — A fox-hunting group of which Brideshead is Joint Master with Walter Strickland-Venables.

Marchmain House (*BR, OG, SOH*) — In *BR* the impressive Saint James's, London, home of the Marchmains, one side of which overlooks Green Park. It is eventually sold by Lord Marchmain after his wife's death and converted into a block of stores and apartments. In *OG, SOH*, Guy Crouchback reports to Hazardous Offensive Operations Headquarters, which at that point of the war takes up three apartments there. Later H.O.O. is to expand beyond Marchmain House. Donald Greene identifies Devonshire House as the Marchmain House; see his "Reality into Art: Some Detective Notes on Waugh," *EWN*, Spring, 1986, p. 2.

Marchpole — See *Grace-Groundling-Marchpole*.

Marcias (*H*) — A learned slave, Helena's tutor in Britain. Later he settles on the Continent and becomes an important Gnostic philosopher.

Margaret (also called Meg, Mimi, and Peg; *OGP*) — A timid, rather compassionate character Pinfold hears speaking on the *Caliban*. She declares her love for him.

Margaret's mother (*OGP*) — A character whose voice Pinfold hears aboard the *Caliban*. She tries to encourage a love affair between Pinfold and her daughter.

Margot — See *Beste-Chetwynde, Margot*.

Maria Cristina (*VB*) — The wife of the deposed king of Ruritania. She is in an asylum suffering from bomb shock. She believes everyone is a bomb.

Marine Hotel (*MA, OG, EB, SOH*) — The hotel in Matchet where Guy Crouchback's father resides during World War II.

Marino, Captain (*VB*) — The ace racing-car driver who throws a wrench at the driver of car 13; later Marino's car is demolished by Agatha Runcible, who takes over driving car 13.

Marius (*H*) — A Roman political leader.

Marjorie — See Rex, Marjorie.

Mark (*H*) — A companion of the youthful Constantine.

Marmaduke, Lady — See *Transept, Lady*.

Marmaduke, Lord (*EB, SOH*) — A character in Ludovic's novel *The Death Wish*. His wife is mentioned in *SOH*. In *EB* she is called Lady Marmaduke Transept.

Marshal, the (*SKME*) — The dictatorial ruler of Neutralia. He is presumably based on General Francisco Franco of Spain.

Marx, Mr. (*BM*) — A European mechanic in the service of Emperor Seth. He deserts the emperor and Azania when it appears that the rebel forces of Prince Seyid will defeat Seth. Marx is in charge of Seth's only tank; however, the tank is useless in the hot sun, and General Connolly uses it as a punishment cell for disciplining his troops.

Marxville (*Sc*) — During the brief but unsuccessful Communist revolution in Ishmaelia this name was given to Jacksonburg.

Mary (*TB*) — A friend of Lady Rosemary Quest.

Massop, Mrs. (*HD*) — One of the Last family servants at Hetton.

Master, the (*DF*) — The head of Scone College, Oxford. He makes the decision to expel Pennyfeather from Oxford.

Matchet (*MA, OG, EB, SOH*) — An English resort town where Guy Crouchback's father lives after the estate at Broome is sold. For a time he teaches at Our Lady of Victory's Preparatory School there. He also dies there.

Matodi (*BM, IA*) — In *IA* a city in Azania, the scene of most of the action. In *BM* it is the chief seaport city. Based on Djibouti, on the Red Sea.

Matron (*VB*) — The woman in charge of the nursing home where Agatha Runcible is sent to recover from her racing-car accident.

Maureen, Aunt (*WS*) — The aunt of Lucy Simmonds.

Mavrocordato, Miss (*LO*) — For a time secretary to Francis Hinsley at Megalopolitan Studio. She is later transferred to the studio Catering Department.

Maxentius (*H*) — A Roman military leader and the brother of Fausta. He is drowned in the Tiber by order of Emperor Constantine.

THE DICTIONARY

Maximian (*H*) — The father of Fausta, a Roman general who is a rival of Constantius for power. He is one of Probus's chiefs of staff, and when Diocletian ascends the throne, he divides the Empire with Maximian, giving the latter charge of the West. Constantine ultimately has him murdered in Gaul.

Mayfield, Captain (*POMF*) — An officer in a British military unit training for World War II.

Mayfield, Ma (*BR*) — The proprietor of the seedy Old Hundredth Club. She is presumably based on the historical Mrs. Kate Meyrick. See *Old Hundredth*.

Meadowes, Lady Mary (Molly) (*POMF, BSRA*) — In *POMF* she is courted by and marries Peter Pastmaster. She serves in a fire brigade during World War II. In *BSRA* she is mentioned as still married to Peter, but her maiden name is spelled Meadows. Her mother is Emma, Countess, or Marchioness, of Granchester.

Meadows, Bill (*BR*) — The leader of a Defence Corps group during the General Strike of 1926. His unit was delegated to protect food deliveries to the more destitute areas of London. Charles Ryder joined this group.

Medical Officer (*DF*) — The prison doctor at Blackstone who fills out the required medical form for Pennyfeather and reads the prayers at the chapel service on the occasion of Prendergast's death.

Medici, Lorenzo (*LO*) — Sir Francis Hinsley's successor at Megalopolitan Studios.

Megalo (*LO*) — A short form for Megalopolitan Studios in Hollywood, where Sir Francis Hinsley and several other figures in the novel work. It is based on the Metro-Goldwyn-Mayer (MGM) studios in Culver City, Los Angeles, which engaged Waugh to write the script for a film version of *BR* in 1947 (never made). *Megalos* is Greek for "big."

Megalopolitan building (also called Copper House; see *Copper*; *Sc*) — The headquarters of the *Daily Beast* at 700–853 Fleet Street, London.

Meikeljohn, Muriel (*WS*) — A pallid singing student and close friend of Lucy Simmonds. She visits Lucy every Tuesday, and they spend the day together.

Melchior (*BR*) — A cousin of Charles Ryder's who got into debt and had to go to Australia before the mast; mentioned gleefully by Charles's father.

Melstead Carbury (*BR*) — The nearest town to Brideshead Castle that has a railroad station. It is also referred to as Melstead.

Membling, Father (*BR*) — A priest who has been bombed out of his lodging during the war and is given shelter by Julia at Brideshead Castle.

Men at Arms — The first novel (1952) of Waugh's World War II trilogy *Sword of Honour*. In *MA*, Guy Crouchback, the protagonist, a lonely thirty-five-year-old Roman Catholic whose wife has divorced him, joins the army. Crouchback undergoes training, experiences the ennui and vicissitudes of military life, takes part in a landing at Dakar, and is inadvertently responsible for the death of his friend Apthorpe.

Mendoza (*HD*) — One of Thérèse de Vitré's potential suitors in Trinidad.

Mendoza's wife, Senator (*SKME*) — She was tortured hideously by the bimetallists during the civil war in Neutralia.

Mentone (*TB*) — A country house.

Mercer (*CRS*) — One of the students at Spierpoint.

Mervyn, Uncle (*Sc*) — The name used for the Prime Minister by one of his secretaries to whom he is related. Mervyn gives the wrong Boot birthday honors.

Messinger, Dr. (*HD*) — A youthful explorer searching for a fabulous lost city in the South American jungle. He is joined by Tony Last on the expedition. He is killed in a waterfall accident deep in the jungle.

Metcalfe, Beverley (*EH*) — The principal figure in the story, a practical, upright businessman who retires to a pleasant home in the Cotswolds. Becoming a public benefactor, he saves the area from possible conversion into a factory site. In his honor the new building for the scouts is named the Metcalfe-Peabury Hall, and the local inn becomes the Metcalfe Arms.

Metcalfe, Sophie (*EH*) — Beverley Metcalfe's wife.

Methodist Monitor (*Sc*) — A correspondent from this publication covers the Ishmaelia crisis.

Metroland (*LO*) — The suburban area stretching out from London served by the Metropolitan Underground Railway.

Metroland, Lady — See *Beste-Chetwynde, Margot*.

Metroland, Lord (*DF, VB, OD, POMF, ER*) — In *DF* he is Minister of Transportation. Christened Humphrey Maltravers, he comes from an impoverished family, but through scholarships, talent, and hard work he has become Sir Humphrey. He wants to leave the House of Commons, however, and enter the House of Lords. He also wants to marry Margot Beste-Chetwynde, uniting political influence with wealth and social position. When Pennyfeather is arrested and given a long prison term, Maltravers marries Margot and is created Viscount Metroland and hence a member of the House of Lords. Through his political position as Home Secretary he is able to arrange to have Pennyfeather freed from prison. In *VB*, he continues as a high government official. He, Prime Minister Outrage, and Father Rothschild confer on more than one occasion. He is aware that his wife is carrying on an affair with Alastair Trumpington, but he does not interfere. In *OD* in 1933 he is present at one of his wife's parties, during which he chats with Rip Van Winkle and Alastair Trumpington. In *ER* he invites novelist Simon Lent to lunch. In *POMF* he is mentioned as "hard-boiled and rich" and as a friend of Angela Lyne's father.

Metropole — See *Hotel Metropole*.

Mhomala, Duchess of (*BM*) — A member of the nobility of Azania.

Michael (*VB*) — One of the poets mentioned in a conversation with Mr. Benfleet at Lady Metroland's party for Mrs. Ape.

Milbank Hospital (*OG, SOH*) — A hospital in London to which Ritchie-Hook is transferred after he is wounded during the Dakar expedtion.

Miles — See *Malpractice*.

Miles — See *Plastic, Miles*.

Miles (*BR*) — An acquaintance of the Ryders on the passenger liner from the United States to England.

Milly (*HD*) — A low-class prostitute. She becomes the companion of Tony Last on the seashore trip so that Tony can chivalrously take the blame for the divorce.

Miltiades, General (*OG*) — A Greek general who participates in the evacuation of Crete. It should be noted that the successful Greek military strategist and leader at the Battle of Marathon (490 B.C.) bore the same name. Waugh probably chose the name to ironically contrast the two battles.

Mimi (*OGP*) — A sympathetic character Pinfold hears speaking on the *Caliban*. She is the same character frequently called Margaret.

Minervina (*H*) — The first wife of Constantine and mother of Crispus.

Minister of Culture (*LAR*) — A prominent government official in the Coalition government.

Minister of the Interior (*C, TMI, EB, SOH*) — An old lawyer from Split who serves as a member of the Yugoslavian partisan "general staff." He also appears in *TMI* and *C*.

Minister of Popular Enlightenment (*SKME*) — A political manipulator who arranges for the Bellorius group to lay wreaths at the National Monument in Neutralia.

Minister of Rest and Culture (*LAR*) — A prominent government official in the Coalition government.

Minister of Rest and Culture (*SKME*) — A young, saturnine official in Neutralia. He has very few fingers because he played with a bomb during the revolution.

Minister of Welfare (*LAR*) — An important government official.

Ministry of Modernisation (*BM*) — The Azanian government department instituted by Emperor Seth and headed by Basil Seal. It is designed to initiate modern concepts and practices in Azania.

Mischief (*BM*) — The name of Prudence Courteney's pony, and an appropriate word for several of Prudence's activities.

"Miss Runcible's Sunday Morning" — A short story published as "The Tutor's Tale" in *The New Decameron, The Sixth Volume* (Oxford, 1929). It is a more condensed version of the episode in *VB* (chap. 4) where several of the Bright Young People have a party at the Prime Minister's house at 10 Downing Street.

"Mr. Crutwell's Little Outing" — See *Mr. Loveday's Little Outing*.

"Mr. Crutwell's Outing" — See *Mr. Loveday's Little Outing*.

"Mr. Loveday's Little Outing" — A short story about a mental patient in an asylum who for thirty-five years has been serving time for murder. Since he now appears mild and harmless, he is released and kills again. The story earlier appeared under the titles "Mr. Crutwell's Little Outing" and "Mr. Crutwell's Outing" before it was renamed and appeared in *Mr. Loveday's Little Outing and Other Sad Stories*.

Mr. Loveday's Little Outing and Other Sad Stories — A collection of Waugh's stories (London and Boston, 1936). The following stories were published in this collection: "Mr. Loveday's Little Outing," "By Special Request," "Cruise," "Period Piece," "On Guard," "Incident in Azania," "Out of Depth," "Excursion in Reality," "Love in the Slump," "Bella Fleace Gave a Party," and "Winner Takes All."

THE DICTIONARY

Mock House (*BFGP*) — An impressive country home near Fleacetown, Ireland; also called Mock Hall.

Mockstock, Lord and Lady (*BFGP*) — Wealthy landowners living near Bella Fleace who come uninvited to Bella's party. Bella, who has looked down upon the Mockstocks because Lady Mockstock is a draper's daughter, refuses to entertain them.

Mohamed Ali Club (*OG, SOH*) — A club in Alexandria frequented by British officers.

Moke (*Sc*) — The school nickname of Jack Bannister, British Vice-Consul in Ishmaelia. He is friendly with William Boot and gives him vital information on the political situation there. The word is English slang for "donkey."

Molly (*POMF*) — A pet kangaroo kept for a month by Sonia Digby-Vane-Trumpington.

Molly (*MA, SOH*) — Guy Crouchback writes to her asking if she will intercede with her husband to obtain a war service post for him.

Monastery of St. Mark the Evangelist (*BM*) — The center of Nestorian Christianity in Azania, ruled by an autocratic abbot. Achon has been imprisoned there. Among other relics it contains "the rib from which Eve had been created."

Monomark, Lord Rex (*VB, BM, HD, POMF, WS*) — In *VB* the owner of many newspapers, including the *Excess*. He presumably had an affair with Margot Beste-Chetwynde before her second marriage. He attends Margot's party for Mrs. Ape. In *BM* he refuses to send Basil Seal to Azania as a foreign correspondent. In *HD* he vacations on his yacht. In *POMF* we hear that Basil Seal served for a time in Monomark's personal entourage. He is also mentioned in the 1942 edition of *WS*. He is probably a version of Lord Beaverbrook, who began his career as a press lord with the acquisition of the *London Daily Express*, on which Waugh worked for a time. "Monomark" was the registered trade name of a commercial system for identifying valuable articles in case of theft.

"Monstrous regiment of gentlemen" (*MA, SOH*) — A searchlight battery group composed of fashionable aesthetes. "Monstrous regiment" is taken from the Scottish Calvinist reformer John Knox's famous tract denouncing the Catholic queens Mary of Scotland and Mary Tudor of England, *The First Blast of the Trumpet Against the Monstrous Regiment [Rule] of Women* (1558).

Montagu, Captain (*EB, SOH*) — An effigy in Westminster Abbey. See Glossary under *EB*.

Monte Rosa (*OG, EB, SOH*) — In *OG, SOH* a boarding house at Matchet taken over for quartering soldiers. In *EB, SOH* there is no longer a need for such rooms, and Monte Rosa is unoccupied.

Montesquieu, Miss (*Sc*) — A London socialite and friend of John Courteney Boot.

Montrose (*MA*) — One of the clans which joins Bonnie Prince Charlie in a movie version of the Rising of 1745.

"Monument to a Spartan" (*POMF*) — The principal contribution in *Ivory Tower*. It is Ambrose Silk's account of Hans, his former lover, who is drafted into the German army. Basil Seal suggests that several pages be omitted, and as a result the novella appears to glorify Hitler youth. Ambrose consequently is forced to flee England, and Basil takes over his apartment and belongings.

Mooney's Saloon (*LO*) — A watering hole in Hollywood in which Mr. Slump gives his last, fatal advice to Aimée Thanatogenos.

Moping, Angela (*MCLO, MCO, MLLO*) — In *MLLO* the tenderhearted daughter of Lord and Lady Moping. She is instrumental in obtaining Mr. Loveday's release from the asylum. In *MCLO, MCO*, earlier versions of the story, she performs the same function for Crutwell.

Moping, Lady (*MCLO, MCO, MLLO*) — In *MLLO* the pragmatic wife of the suicidal Lord Moping. She also appears in *MCLO, MCO*, earlier versions of the story.

Moping, Lord (*MCLO, MCO, MLLO*) — In *MLLO* an inmate of the Country Home for Mental Defectives. Moping tried to hang himself on the occasion of one of his wife's annual garden parties. Mr. Loveday serves as his secretary at the asylum. He also appears in *MCLO, MCO*, earlier versions of the story.

Morning Despatch — See *Despatch*.

Morning Post (*BR*) — A London newspaper.

Morris (*TB, VB, BR*) — An automobile manufactured in England. In *VB* the salesman who tries to sell Colonel Blount a vacuum cleaner drives a Morris. In the same novel Lily's "sugar daddy" drives a Morris Oxford saloon. The saloon was a four-door passenger car. William Morris started his automobile manufacturing business in the city of Oxford. In *BR* the Morris-Cowley model described is the open two-seater roadster that Sebastian "borrows" from Hardcastle, a fellow student at Oxford, to take Charles Ryder to Brideshead Castle for the first time. Hardcastle's car is also used in the drunken-driving episode after the visit to the Old Hundredth. A Morris auto is also mentioned in *TB*.

Morticians Journal (*LO*) — A periodical devoted to undertakers' news. The engagement of Joyboy and Aimée Thanatogenos is announced there.

Mortlake (*EB, SOH*) — A section in the southwestern suburbs of London near the Thames River. Peregrine Crouchback, Virginia Troy, and Mrs. Corner were buried there in the churchyard of Saint Mary Magdalen's Catholic Church after being killed by a buzz bomb.

Moshu (*BM*) — The principal city of the Wanda tribe in Azania. It is there that the body of Seth is burned on a pyre and a great funeral feast takes place. Prudence Courteney furnishes part of this meal, having been captured and cooked by the Wanda.

Mossop, Mrs. (*HD*) — One of the Last family's servants.

Mother Wales (*DF*) — A book on Wales, written by Dr. Fagan, which becomes very popular.

Mottram, Rex (*BR*) — A handsome Canadian who had served in World War I. He was a member of Parliament and moved in the world of high finances. He is the embodiment of "power and prosperity." He marries Julia Marchmain, but since he is divorced, they cannot marry in the Catholic Church. Their marriage is thus a squalid event. As time progresses, he and Julia do not get on well. He has a mistress and tolerates Julia's affair with Charles Ryder. He eventually becomes an important minister in the British cabinet during World War II. It has been suggested by several critics that Mottram is modeled on the British politician Brendan Bracken (who, however, was not Canadian). Another possible source is the Canadian Max Aitken, Lord Beaverbrook — a militant Protestant — who also held important posts in the wartime cabinet.

Moulay Abdullah (*WS*) — The section of Fez, Morocco, inhabited mainly by prostitutes. John Plant visits Fatima there.

Mountdragon, Ruth (*POMF*) — The pseudonym of Mrs. Parker, a popular novelist whose books are published by Rampole and Bentley. She writes charming stories about domestic happenings in various families. Rampole reads her novels in prison and finds them quite delightful. A possible model for her is the prolific and popular Angela Thirkell.

Mountjoy Castle (*LAR*) — A permissive, progressive prison. Miles Plastic, an arsonist and former inmate, eventually sets it on fire.

Mountrichard, Lady (*WS*) — A character in one of John Plant's mystery stories.

Mountrichard Castle (*WS*) — The scene of John Plant's latest detective story, *Murder at Mountrichard Castle*.

Mouse, Mrs. (*VB*) — A wealthy English matron, Mary's mother.

Mouse, Mary (*VB*) — One of the admirers and observers of the Bright Young People. She finances several of their parties. She ultimately leaves England to run off to India with the Maharajah of Pukkapore.

Mowbray, Father (*BR*) — The Jesuit who gives religious instruction to Rex Mottram and finds it a difficult job.

Mowbray, Montgomery (*Sc*) — General editor of the *Beast*.

Much Malcock (*EH*) — A pleasant, unspoiled Cotswold village, the scene of the story.

Much Malcock Hall (*EH*) — The pleasant rural home of Beverley Metcalfe threatened by the possibility that a factory will be built nearby.

Much Malcock House (*EH*) — The home of Lady Peabody, threatened by the possibility that a factory will be built nearby.

Muck (*OG, SOH*) — An island off the coast of Scotland, supposedly some distance from the fictional Mugg.

Mudge, Mr. and Mrs. (*POMF*) — A tough farming family who are able to endure the Connollies for only a short time.

Mudge, Willie (*POMF*) — A son of Mr. and Mrs. Mudge. He is bashful but romantically pursued by Doris Connolly.

Mudshore (*MA, SOH*) — The location of a rifle range near Kut-al-Imara.

Mugg (*OG, SOH*) — A short name used for Colonel Hector Campbell as Laird of the Isle of Mugg.

Mugg, Isle of (*OG, SOH*) — An island off Scotland, a Commando training base. No doubt modeled after the actual Scottish island of Muck.

Mulcaster, Viscount (Boy) (*BR*) — A student at Oxford who is acquainted with Sebastian Flyte and Charles Ryder. Although he comes from an upper-class background, his tastes are generally coarse and unrefined. He, Sebastian, and Ryder are arrested for intoxication after an outing at the Old Hundredth Club. His sister Celia marries Charles Ryder.

Mulligan, Joe (*OG, SOH*) — An American newsman in England during World War II. He interviews Trimmer.

Murder at Mountrichard Castle (*WS*) — The title of one of John Plant's detective stories.

Murdoch, Mr. (*OGP*) — A businessman, one of the passengers aboard the *Caliban*. He appears to be a mysterious, solitary figure but is in reality congenial though quiet. He leaves the *Caliban* with Pinfold, and they drive to Cairo together.

Muriel, Lady (*Cr*) — She has an affair with the father of the letter writer.

Musgrave (*MA, SOH*) — Sometimes called "Musgrave the Monster," he was the former owner of the Castello where the Wilmots live in Santa Dulcina delle Rocce, Italy. There are warrants for his arrest in England and America.

Muspratt, Admiral (*BR*) — Beryl's first husband. His hobby was collecting matchboxes. His death is also mentioned.

Muspratt, Mrs. Beryl (*BR*) — The middle-aged Catholic widow whom Brideshead marries.

Muthaiga Club (*MA, SOH*) — A club in Nairobi, Kenya, frequented by Guy and Virginia Crouchback when they lived in Africa. Waugh visited the club in January, 1931 (see his *Remote People* and *When the Going Was Good*).

Myers, Miss (*PP*) — The paid companion of Lady Amelia who specializes in reading novels to the elderly aristocrat.

N

Nailsworth (*OGP*) — A member of Bellamy's Club whose mother and wife, according to an eccentric earl at the club who gossiped constantly, were whores.

Nameless major — See *Grace-Groundling-Marchpole*.

Nannie (*OG, SOH*) — Guy Crouchback's nurse, whom he remembers from childhood.

Nanny (*EB, SOH*) — The attendant of the grandchildren of the elder Mr. and Mrs. Scrope-Weld.

Nanny (*HD*) — John Andrew Last's very proper and dedicated nanny. She particularly disapproves of Ben Hackett.

Nanny Hawkins — See *Hawkins*.

National Academy of Cinematographic Art (*VB*) — The actors' training school run by Mr. Isaacs.

National and Provincial Union Bank of England, Ltd. (*VB*) — The bank where the drunken major claims the money owed to Adam Symes is deposited. It merged in 1968 with the Westminster and District Bank to become the National Westminster Bank, now the largest commercial bank in Great Britain.

National Memorial (*SKME*) — A Neutralian monument which the Bellorius scholars decorate with wreaths. They have been tricked into thinking that it is a monument to the country or is related to the Bellorius celebration, when in fact it is a tribute to fifty supporters of the now-dominant political party who were killed by the opposition.

Necker, Mr. (*TMWLD*) — A biologist scheduled to take part in the Anderson expedition. At the last moment his mother refuses to allow him to experience the dangers of the Brazilian jungle. She takes him off the boat, leaving the expedition without a biologist.

Ned (*BR*) — The gentlemanly and chivalrous brother of Lady Marchmain; he was killed in France in World War I. Lady Marchmain has Mr. Samgrass prepare a privately printed memorial about him. She gives a copy to Charles Ryder.

Ned, Uncle (*Cr*) — A Friend of Lady Muriel.

Nepotianus (*H*) — Emperor Constantine's nephew who is allegedly engaged in a plot against his uncle.

Nestorian Metropolitan (*BM*) — Also referred to as the Nestorian Patriarch, he is head of the established church in Azania. As the Minister of Works he conspired with the American attaché on a half-commission basis to have the Azanians buy a steamroller. He is vehemently opposed to Emperor Seth's birth-control dicta. He joins the French ambassador and General Connolly in the plot to overthrow Seth. He crowns Achon the new Emperor.

Neutralia (*SKME*) — A totalitarian country (modeled mainly on Franco's Spain, which was neutral during World War II) visited by Scott-King.

New Castle (*OG, SOH*) — The name given to the large home of Colonel Hector Campbell on the Isle of Mugg.

New Destiny (*SKME*) — An American magazine. It has

published works by the poet who appears at the Bellorius celebration.

Newhill (*BFGP*) — A country estate near Fleacetown. Bella Fleace's mother was an O'Hara of Newhill.

New House (*BR*) — Another name used by old-timers for Brideshead Castle.

New Nation (*DF*) — A paper which publishes a favorable article on Sir Wilfred Lucas-Dockery's penal experiments. Modeled on the still influential leftist London weekly, the *New Statesman and Nation*.

Newport, Sylvia (*HD*) — One of the London social set, a friend of Mrs. Beaver.

Ngoma (*IA*) — The ship that brings Prunella Brooks and her father to Azania.

Ngumo, Earl of (*BM*) — The feudal overlord of a remote tribe in Azania. When his home in Debra-Dowa is appropriated by Seth for a museum, he joins in a revolt against the Emperor. He goes to the Nestorian monastery and makes arrangements to free Achon. He, Connolly, and the French achieve Seth's overthrow.

Nicagoras (*H*) — A soothsayer in Rome.

Nichols, Mr. (*BR*) — A cab driver in Oxford who returns Aloysius to Sebastian after the latter inadvertently left the teddy bear in Nichols's cab.

Nichols, Mary (*POMF*) — She once had a shipboard romance with Basil Seal. Basil is unable to remember her when she is mentioned by the bride of Grantley Green.

Norah (*OD*) — She brings Dr. Kakophilos to a party at Margot Metroland's.

Northcote, Mrs. (*HD*) — A fashionable London fortuneteller who tells fortunes by reading the soles of feet.

Norton (*WS*) — A pseudonym that Arthur Atwater uses at the Wimpole Club.

Nought, John (*Sc*) — An agent of the Credential Assurance Co.

November Handicap (*VB*) — A horse race at Manchester won by Indian Runner. Adam Symes, Nina Blount, and the drunk major attend this event. It is there that Adam first meets Eddy Littlejohn.

Nudge (*BSRA*) — Angela and Basil Seal's servant.

Number 4 Special Training Centre (*EB, SOH*) — The parachute training camp in Essex commanded by Ludovic. Guy Crouchback receives his parachute jumping injury there.

Number 6 Transit Camp, London District (*OG, EB, SOH*) — In *OG, SOH* a former hotel where troops are "in transit" from one unit to another (or to discharge, if they are found unemployable). Kerstie Kilbannock works there for a while in the canteen. In *EB, SOH*, Jumbo Trotter becomes commandant of this post.

Numerian (*H*) — A Roman leader and military figure.

O

Oakshott (*VB*) — The home of the Littlejohn family when Ginger was growing up.

Oates, Mr. (*EB, SOH*) — The civilian efficiency expert who works in the Royal Victorian Institute, where various military offices are located (part of Hazardous Offensive Operations).

Obbethwaite, Tom (*DF*) — A student at Scone College, Oxford. He is a friend of Alastair Digby-Vane-Trumpington.

Officers and Gentlemen — A novel by Waugh (1955) that continues the saga of Guy Crouchback in World War II and forms the second part of the *Sword of Honour* trilogy. Crouchback joins the recently organized Commandos and after training, sails to Egypt. Eventually his unit is sent to shore up the defense of Crete, which is being overwhelmed by the German attack. Chaos reigns on Crete, and several officers — most notably Ivor Claire and "Fido" Hound — desert their posts. On the day the British are to surrender, Crouchback, Ludovic, and a small group manage to escape capture by taking to the Mediterranean in a small boat. Both Crouchback and Ludovic reach Africa safely, but Guy needs a long period of recuperation. Guy has evidence of Ivor Claire's desertion, but Mrs. Stitch destroys it to protect Claire. Upon recovery Guy is sent back to England by ship.

Oglander, Mrs. Stuyvesant (*BR, OG, SOH*) — In *BR* a fashionable elderly American guest at the shipboard party Celia Ryder arranges. She also participates in the last-night shipboard party. Anthony Blanche calls her a frump. She disparages Charles Ryder's paintings of Latin America. In *OG, SOH* she is one of the women on the Atlantic passenger liner voyages whom Trimmer served as hairdresser.

Oglander, Senator Stuyvesant (*BR*) — Mrs. Oglander's husband, who is also a passenger on the passenger liner the Ryders take from America back to England.

O'Hara (*BFGP*) — Bella Fleace's mother had been an O'Hara of Newhill House.

Olafsen, Erik (*Sc*) — A Swedish newspaperman, surgeon, businessman, and vice-consul in Ishmaelia. He also ran a religious mission. Through his violence he is instrumental in helping overthrow Dr. Benito's rebel regime (at seventeen, while intoxicated, he had killed his grandfather; he had then left Sweden and settled in Jacksonburg, Ishmaelia).

Old Castle (*OG, SOH*) — The former home of Colonel Hector Campbell on Mugg. Chatty Corner and the Colonel's factor presently live there.

Old Crouchers (*EB, SOH*) — A nickname given to Peregrine Crouchback by his cousins the Scrope-Welds.

Old Crouchers (*OG, SOH*) — A nickname for Guy Crouchback's father used by the boys in his classics class at Our Lady of Victory's Preparatory School at Matchet.

Oldenshaw (*OG, SOH*) — A Halberdier Colour-Sergeant whose function is training and drilling the soldiers. One of his drill sessions concludes *OG*. He is also mentioned in *SOH*.

Old Fisticuffs (*OGP*) — One of the nicknames of Reginald Graves-Upton.

Old Hundredth (*HD, BR*) — A seedy London nightclub visited by Tony Last and Jock Grant-Menzies. In British editions of *HD* it is called the Old Hundredth and is situated at 100 Sink Street. In American editions it is called the Sixty-four and is situated at 64 Sink Street. In *BR*, Sebastian Flyte, Charles Ryder, and Boy Mulcaster visit it and shortly after leaving it, intoxicated, the three are arrested. In *BR* it is located at 100 Sink Street. Based on the notorious nightclub at 43 Gerrard Street, operated by Mrs. Kate Meyrick, which the authorities tried several times unsuccessfully to shut down (see Waugh's *A Little Learning*, p. 202). There is an effective account in Ronald Blythe's *The Age of Illusion*. "Old Hundredth" is the name of a famous old hymn tune, originally set to Psalm 100. Nowadays it is usually heard as the tune of the Doxology, "Praise God, from whom all blessings flow."

Old Mack (*TE*) — An affectionate nickname given to Dr. Mackenzie by his neighbors in the Cornish village where he practices.

Old Mill House, North Grappling (*POMF*) — The lovely, idyllic abode of Mr. and Mrs. Harkness. The Connollies cause havoc there.

Old Rectory (*BR*) — The country home of Celia and Charles Ryder. As part of the divorce settlement it is turned over to Celia, and she and her new husband, Robin, plan to live there.

Old Rectory, Adderford (*POMF*) — The attractive home of Mr. and Mrs. Grace, who billet the Connollies for two days.

Oliphant, Mr. (*HG*) — A friend of Ernest Vaughan's.

Olive (*POMF*) — A housemaid of the Sothills who leaves Malfrey to work in a wartime airplane factory.

Olivia (*DF*) — One of the guests at Margot's party at King's Thursday, apparently a lesbian friend of Pamela Popham.

O'Malley, Desmond (*CRS*) — An unpopular student at Spierpoint. He was appointed to the Settle and as head of the dormitory is very much resented.

Omega (*VB*) — Marino, the Italian ace driver in the car race, drives a red Omega, number 28. See Glossary under *VB*.

"On Guard" — A short story by Waugh (1934) about Millicent Blade, whose most appealing feature is a beguiling nose. Her boy friend goes off to Africa to make his fortune, leaving her pet dog to ward off other suitors. Her pseudo-fiancé does not prosper, and the dog continues to forestall potential suitors, ultimately biting off Millicent's nose. The story was first published in London's *Harper's Bazaar*, December, 1934, pp. 32–33, 84, 86, and appears in *Mr. Loveday's Little Outing and Other Sad Stories, Work Suspended and Other Stories Written Before the Second World War, Tactical Exercise*, and *Charles Ryder's Schooldays and Other Stories*.

Onslow Square (*DF*) — A square in fashionable Kensington, London. Paul Pennyfeather's guardian lived there.

Opalthorpe, Anne (*VB*) — A London socialite who lives in a house opposite Edward Throbbing's house.

Operation Popgun — See *Popgun*.

Operation Truslove (*MA*) — Guy Crouchback's private name — based on the fictional Captain Truslove — for the landing on the African coast in which he, Ritchie-Hook, and a few other British soldiers participated.

Orchid Room (*LO*) — The largest of the Slumber

Rooms at Whispering Glades. Sir Francis Hinsley's body is placed on view there.

Ordeal of Gilbert Pinfold, The — A novel (1957) by Waugh, heavily autobiographical, in which the protagonist suffers severe hallucinations while he is on a voyage to Ceylon.

Orme-Herrick, Gloria (*BR*) — A dreary student of the cello invited to dinner by Charles Ryder's father to discomfit Charles.

Orme-Herrick, Lady (*BR*) — The wife of Sir Cuthbert. She and her drab husband and daughter attend a dinner gathering given by Charles Ryder's father.

Orme-Herrick, Sir Cuthbert (*BR*) — A friend of Charles Ryder's father.

Orraway-Smith, Mrs. (*VB*) — A member of a Conservative association at Chesham Bois. She protests against the alleged wild party held at the Browns when Brown is Prime Minister.

Our Lady of Victory's Preparatory School (*OG, EB, SOH*) — The boys' prep school at Matchet where Mr. Crouchback teaches classics. It has been temporarily transferred to Matchet because of the war. Also spelled Our Lady of Victories.

"Out of Depth" — A short story by Waugh (1933) in which a wealthy forty-three-year-old socialite named Rip Van Winkle is transported in a dream to London of the twenty-fifth century. There he finds a return to primitivism and hopeless savagery, but the Catholic church has survived, and the Latin Mass is still being said. The story was first published in London's *Harper's Bazaar*, December, 1933, pp. 46–48, 106, and was included in *Mr. Loveday's Little Outing and Other Sad Stories* (London and Boston, 1936).

Outrage, The Right Honourable Walter (*VB, BM*) — In *VB* the former Prime Minister of England who is chosen for the office again after the scandal involving Sir James Brown (the gathering at his house where Agatha Runcible appears in Hawaiian costume). At cabinet meetings he is treated like a child, and he never understands what his ministers are talking about. In *BM* he is mentioned as the opposition leader in Parliament. Brown and Outrage probably stand for Stanley Baldwin (Conservative) and Ramsay MacDonald (Labour), who alternated as Prime Minister and Leader of the Opposition in the 1920s and 1930s.

Ozymandias (*TB*) — The pet cat Adam Doure alternately tormented and coaxed as a child. From Shelley's short poem with that title.

P

Packard (*VB*) — Mrs. Melrose Ape owned a much-traveled Packard, one of the most fashionable and expensive American car makes in the 1920s.

Padfield, Lieutenant (*EB, SOH*) — A mysterious American officer stationed in London during World War II. He attends all the fashionable parties and visits all the "right" people and seems to have no military function. He visits Italy and Yugoslavia. (Before the war he was a member of a Boston law firm. He presents Bert Troy with evidence of Virginia's unfaithfulness so that Troy can obtain a divorce. After the war he becomes Ludovic's general factotum in Italy. The British call him "the Loot," using the American pronunciation of "lieutenant" (the British pronunciation is "leftenant"). He is based on Sergeant Preston [see *The Diaries of Evelyn Waugh*, p. 549, and Peter Quennell, *The Wanton Chase* (New York, 1980), p. 47].

Paillard's (*BR*) — An expensive restaurant in Paris where Charles Ryder and Rex Mottram dine. The meal indicates Mottram's deficiencies as a judge of food and wine.

Paleologue (*Sc*) — The Ishmaelian servant to journalist Wenlock Jakes. He has two wives and many children and has previously worked for the British legation. He does side jobs, such as selling wastepaper left by the British to officials at rival legations. Paleologue is the name of a family which provided several emperors of Byzantium.

Panorama of Life (*BM*) — The title of the novel Prudence Courteney is trying to write.

Panrast, Mrs. (*VB*) — A divorcee and lesbian. She was formerly Eleanor, Countess of Balcairn, and is the mother of gossip columnist Lord Balcairn. Chastity goes out driving with her because she thinks Mrs. Panrast is a man.

Pappenhacker (*Sc, POMF*) — In *Sc* a youthful Communist correspondent in Ishmaelia for the *Daily Twopence* (which see). He often plays with a toy train which he carries about in his travels. He insults waiters and other proletarians so that they will become anticapitalistic. In *POMF* another journalist

THE DICTIONARY

with the same name represents the Hearst press and is investigating the story of a Polish submarine which has arrived in England. Since the Hearst press was anti-Communist, it had to be represented by another correspondent unless Pappenhacker had repudiated his earlier beliefs.

Paris Soir (*Sc*) — This newspaper has a correspondent in Ishmaelia to cover the crisis there.

Parker, Mrs. — See *Mountdragon, Ruth*.

Parks, Mr. (*LO*) — One of the younger morticians at Whispering Glades whom Mr. Joyboy reprimands because of his lack of special respect for his place of employment.

Parsnip (*POMF, LAR, EB, SOH, BSRA*) — In *POMF* a left-wing British poet who, like his close friend the poet Pimpernell, goes to the United States when World War II begins. Basil Seal facetiously remarks that Pimpernell is an alias for Parsnip and that the two poets are really one. In *BSRA* he is Dr. Parsnip, Professor of Dramatic Poetry at Minneapolis. He delivers the dinner speech at the banquet honoring Ambrose Silk. He is mentioned in *EB, SOH* as a pacifist expatriate who has written an essay for *Survival* on Kafka and Klee. In *LAR* he finally gets enough courage to be gassed by the Department of Euthanasia. He is based on the poet W. H. Auden. See also *Pimpernell*.

Parsons (*TB*) — A maid of the Doure family.

Parsons (*MA, OG, EB, SOH*) — A servant at Bellamy's Club.

Partridge (*BR*) — An Oxford student, one of Charles Ryder's first friends at college.

Partridge (*DF*) — An unpopular undergraduate at Scone College, Oxford, who owns a painting by Matisse. Some drunken Bollinger Club members tear his bed sheets and throw the painting into a water jug.

Partridge, Mr. (*HD*) — He is associated with running a shop. Tony Last speaks with him after a church service at Hetton.

Pastmaster, Bobby, Earl of (*DF*) — The brother-in-law of Margot Beste-Chetwynde. He does not get along with Chokey. He had sold King's Thursday to Margot. His death is reported in a newspaper Pennyfeather reads while being transferred from Blackstone to the Egdon Heath Penal Settlement. It is reported in the same paper that Margot's son Peter, then sixteen years old, has succeeded his uncle as the new Earl of Pastmaster.

Pastmaster, Molly, Countess of — See *Meadowes, Molly*.

Pastmaster, Peter, Earl of — See *Beste-Chetwynde, Peter*.

Pastmaster House (*VB, BM*) — Lady Metroland's impressive mansion in *VB* said to be on London's Hill Street; in *BM*, on Curzon Street. Both streets are in Mayfair.

Pat (*MA, SOH*) — Frank de Souza's mistress. Guy meets her and de Souza while he is on military leave in London. She has an apartment there, and de Souza stays with her when he is in London.

"Patriotic Honeymoon, The" — See *"Love in the Slump."*

Paul (*POMF*) — One of Ambrose Silk's acquaintances who in the year of the American stock-market crash attempted to enter a monastery.

Pauling, Mr. (*POMF*) — An official in the Ministry of Information. Eventually he is transferred to the Woodcuts and Weaving Department.

Paul's Literary Agency (*Sc*) — It attempts to interest William Boot in book and cinema rights as well as an autobiography after he becomes famous for his journalistic scoop. No doubt named for Waugh's own literary agent, A. D. Peters, always addressed by Waugh as "Peter."

Peabury, Lady (*EH*) — A snobbish and stuffy neighbor of the Metcalfes.

Peacock, Mr. (*CRS*) — He taught the classical upper-fifth group of boys at Spierpoint.

Pelecci, Giuseppe (*MA, OG, SOH*) — In *MA, SOH* the proprietor of the Garibaldi Restaurant at Southsand. Pelecci is a part-time spy for his homeland, but when he discovers that Guy Crouchback speaks Italian and has lived at Santa Dulcina, the two become friendly. In *OG, SOH* we learn that his restaurant has been closed and he has been arrested as a spy. He is sent by boat to Canada but is killed when the boat is torpedoed in the ocean. In *OG* and in the similar *OG* segment in *SOH*, the name is spelled Peleci.

Pelecci, Mrs. (*MA, SOH*) — The wife of the proprietor of the Garibaldi Restaurant.

Pendle-Garthwaite, Mr., Mrs., and Miss (*BR*) — They send a wedding present to Julia Flyte when she marries Rex Mottram.

Penfold, Miss (*POMF*) — A governess of the youthful Barbara and Basil Seal.

Penfold, Mr. G. (*OGP*) — The name under which Gilbert Pinfold is listed on the passenger sheet of the *Caliban*.

Penkirk (*MA, OG, EB, SOH*) — A farming region of Scotland, twenty miles from Edinburgh, which becomes a training base for the Halberdiers. It is there that Apthorpe receives command of Headquarters Company while Guy Crouchback becomes merely one of the platoon commanders in D Company.

Pennyfeather, Paul (*DF*) — The novel's protagonist, who begins and ends the story as a student at Oxford. He is an Anglican theological student who is expelled from college, becomes a teacher, and then Margot Beste-Chetwynde's prospective husband. He is jailed for "white slavery" and later spirited out of prison. He returns to Oxford pretending to be a cousin of the disgraced Pennyfeather.

Pennyfeather's guardian (*DF*) — The lawyer who supervises the terms of Pennyfeather's father's will and refuses to give Pennyfeather any money after he is sent down from Oxford.

"Pensées" (*OG, EB, SOH*) — A collection of thoughts and aphorisms by Ludovic rejected by book publishers but accepted by *Survival*. The title is also the title of Blaise Pascal's famous theological meditations (perhaps objected to by Waugh as too "Jansenist"); also it is the French word from which the English word "pansies" is derived (an allusion to Ludovic's sexual orientation).

Pension Dressler (*Sc*) — An unimposing, farmlike hotel in Jacksonburg, Ishmaelia. William Boot goes to stay there because he wearies of the overcrowded conditions at the Hotel Liberty. In Europe a *pension* is a boardinghouse.

Peppermint (*HD*) — A mule in the first World War who had died by drinking the entire rum ration of the troops, because mules, according to Ben Hacket, are unable to "cat" (vomit). Ben knew the mule during the war and tells the story to John Andrew Last.

Perdita, Lady (*EB, SOH*) — A society woman who becomes a London air-raid warden during World War II. She attends Everard Spruce's party. She is referred to as "the Smart Woman."

"Period Piece" — A story by Waugh (1936) in which Lady Amelia describes how Etty Cornphillip had an affair with one of her husband's relatives and conceived a child which her husband accepted as his own. The story appears in *Mr. Loveday's Little Outing and Other Sad Stories*, *Work Suspended and Other Stories Written Before the Second World War*, *Tactical Exercise*, and *Charles Ryder's Schooldays and Other Stories*.

Perroquet (*BM*) — The principal banquet hall in Debra-Dowa, Azania. Seth's victory ball is held there. The word is French for "parrot."

Perry, Uncle (*EB, SOH*) — The name used for Peregrine Crouchback by the grandchildren of the elder Mr. and Mrs. Scrope-Weld.

Peter (*BM*) — A member of the British legation staff in Azania.

Peter (*HG*) — A friend of Ernest Vaughan.

Peterborough, aunt at (*MA, SOH*) — Apthorpe claims to have an aunt at Peterborough, a city in east-central England. On his deathbed he admits to Guy Crouchback that this was a fabrication.

Peterfield (*DF*) — The doctor who castrates Alf Larrigan by order of Toby Cruttwell.

Philbrick (*HG*) — The proprietor of a London tailor shop.

Philbrick, Chick (*DF*) — The prizefighter father of Solomon Philbrick (the Philbrick at Llanabba School). He is noted for heavy drinking and beating up his wife. This account may, of course, be "made up."

Philbrick, Miss (*B*) — The conscientious secretary at the Maltby School of Art.

Philbrick, Solomon (Solly) (*DF*) — The butler at Llanabba School. He claims to be engaged to marry Diana Fagan, but this is probably one of his "tall tales." He tells three different stories to three different people about his background, claiming to be a retired burglar, a wealthy shipowner, and a novelist. Later he admits that the stories are false. Further on he is sought by the police for false pretences and impersonation and is imprisoned at Blackstone, where Pennyfeather again meets him. Near the end of the novel he is seen riding in the back of a Rolls Royce and invites Pennyfeather to come and see him at Skindles's (see Glossary under *DF*). In the original version of *DF* (London: Chapman and Hall, 1962) it is suggested that Philbrick is carrying on a sexual intrigue with Diana Fagan.

Philippa (*BR, CRS*) — Charles Ryder's aunt. She hopes to make a home with her brother and Charles, but her brother's eccentric antics eventually force her to leave. She goes abroad to Bordighera. In *CRS* she takes Charles to a restaurant and also to church services in London.

THE DICTIONARY

Phillips, Miss Mabel (*Cr*) — A woman passenger who chases after various men.

Philpotts, Henry, Bishop of Exeter (*VB*) — Represented by an actor in the film being based loosely on the life of John Wesley. Philpotts was a strong opponent of the evangelicalism preached by Wesley and George Whitefield, although he lived much later.

Phipps, Father (*BR*) — A Roman Catholic priest who lives in a monastery near Brideshead Castle. He comes to Brideshead to say Mass on Sundays. He is an easygoing man who is very much interested in cricket.

Pierre (*BM*) — An employee of the French legation at Azania. He is assigned to help interpret the code used in some British telegrams. In fact the terms are those of a chess game being played long distance.

Pie-wies (*HD*) — A South American Indian tribe living in a remote area between Brazil and Dutch Guiana. They are devoted to Mr. Todd and hence will not help Tony Last escape. Mr. Todd's mother was a Pie-wie.

Pigge (*Sc*) — One of the English newspaper correspondents in Ishmaelia.

Pigstanton (*HD*) — A fox-hunting "pack," as well as a town near Hetton.

Pilbury Steeple (*EH*) — The spire of a church near Much Malcock.

Pimpernell (*POMF, LAR, BSRA*) — In *POMF* a left-wing British poet who goes to the United States when World War II commences in England. He and Parsnip are close friends, and he is also friendly with Poppet Green. In *BSRA* he is Dr. Pimpernell, Professor of Poetic Drama at Saint Paul, Minnesota. He attends the dinner honoring Ambrose Silk. In *LAR* he volunteers and is killed by the Department of Euthanasia. His friend Parsnip later comes to the same end. Pimpernell is based on Christopher Isherwood. Auden and Isherwood lived together for a number of years and collaborated on various pieces of writing.

Pinfold, Gilbert (*OGP*) — The protagonist of the novel. Based on Waugh himself, he is a famous middle-aged novelist who suffers a series of frightening hallucinations while he is on a cruise to Ceylon.

Pinfold, Mrs. (*OGP*) — The widowed mother of Gilbert. She is eighty-two years old, and her mind is not as sharp as it might be. She lives at Kew with a maid, and her income is supplemented through Gilbert's generosity. He finds it a considerable effort to visit her and spend time in her company (as Evelyn Waugh did for his mother, Mrs. Arthur Waugh).

Pinfold, Mrs. Gilbert (*OGP*) — The wife of the protagonist. She is much younger than Pinfold and is actively engaged in farming. Without a doubt she represents Laura, Waugh's wife.

***Plangent*, H.M.S.** (*OG, SOH*) — The ship that lands Hookforce on Crete.

Plant, Andrew (*WS*) — John Plant's uncle, who handles all the funeral arrangements for John's father when John is in Morocco.

Plant, John (*WS*) — The protagonist of the unfinished novel, a successful thirty-four-year-old writer of detective novels. He falls in love with Lucy Simmonds although he does not declare his affection because she is happily married. During her pregnancy she and he spend much time together, especially looking for a suitable house for him to purchase. When he finally finds a suitable home, he never spends any time there because it is requisitioned for war use. During World War II he is active in regimental soldiering.

Plant's father (*WS*) — The father of John Plant, whose first name is never mentioned. Eccentric and very self-centered, he is a successful artist. He is killed when he is struck by a motor car driven by Arthur Atwater.

Plastic, Miles (*LAR*) — The arsonist protagonist of the novel who ironically symbolizes a triumph of the British governmental system of the future. He is sent to prison after committing arson at an air force station. After "rehabilitation" he is freed from the penal settlement (called Mountjoy Castle) and becomes a worker in the popular Department of Euthanasia. He falls in love for a time with a bearded ballet dancer named Clara. Eventually he returns to Mountjoy and burns down the building. He marries a Miss Flower and is sent on a lecture tour to extol the advantages of a new, rebuilt Mountjoy and the success of the government's prison rehabilitation system.

Plender (*BR*) — Lord Marchmain's valet. When his master returns to England, he shares chief authority at Brideshead Castle with Wilcox.

Plessington, Charles, Sir (or Lord) (*EB, SOH*) — A member of one of the old landed Roman Catholic recusant families.

THE DICTIONARY

Plessington, Domenica (*EB, SOH*) — The second wife of Guy Crouchback. She was for a time a nun and then worked on the family farm. In the first editions she and Guy have two boys of their own in addition to Trimmer's son. Later Waugh omits the two children. In *SOH* they have only Trimmer's boy.

Plessington, Eloise, Lady (*EB, SOH*) — A London society woman, the wife of Sir (or Lord) Charles Plessington. She is a convert to Roman Catholicism and becomes godmother of Virginia Troy's baby. She takes care of Trimmer's son for a while while Guy Crouchback is overseas. Her daughter also helps care for the child and marries Guy when the war is over.

Plum, Colonel (*POMF*) — The Assistant Deputy Director of Internal Security at the Ministry of Information, a fictitious office. Plum is a formidable figure about the same age as Basil Seal. Plum has met Basil at Djibouti and Prague and other places over the years, but Basil does not remember him. Plum offers Basil a position on the General Service List working for the War Office. When Ambrose Silk and the other alleged enemy agents escape, Basil tells the Director of Internal Security that Susie may have leaked the information of their imminent capture because of her intimacy with Colonel Plum. Susie is transferred to another office and becomes Basil's mistress. This incurs Colonel Plum's displeasure, and Basil ultimately decides to stop working under Plum and join a special elite corps that is being organized.

Plunket-Bowse (*VB*) — The racing car, number 13, which Agatha Runcible drives in the race. She smashes into Captain Marino's car, knocking him out of the competition. She drives the car off the track and eventually wrecks it by smashing into a large stone cross monument in a village square. See Glossary under *VB*.

Pobble (*BSRA*) — A sobriquet for Basil Seal in his later years, so given because of a limp owing to a World War II accident. The sobriquet is used by his daughter and her friends. The name comes from Edward Lear's poem about "the pobble who has no toes."

Podger's (*DF*) — One of the "houses" at Harrow, which Grimes attended as a boy.

Poet, the (*SKME*) — The egotistical and foolish dinner companion of Scott-King in Neutralia.

Pogson, Miss (*HG*) — An acquaintance of Ernest Vaughan's.

Pollock (*BR*) — A suburb of Glasgow, Scotland. It is the site of the army camp described at the beginning of the novel.

Ponsonby — See *Fitz Clarence*.

Popgun (*OG, SOH*) — Operation Popgun, a military exercise in which an unused lighthouse on a deserted island near the French coast is to be dynamited. The operation is designed to be used for publicity to build civilian morale. As a result of this episode the cowardly Trimmer becomes a national hero.

Popham, Pamela (*DF, VB*) — A fashionable London lesbian who attends a party at King's Thursday.

Popotakis (*Sc*) — The proprietor of a popular ping-pong parlor in Jacksonburg, Ishmaelia, frequented by Kätchen and William Boot.

Porch, Dame Mildred (*BM*) — A member of the Royal Society for the Prevention of Cruelty to Animals. She also belongs to the League of Dumb Chums. Her cause does not prosper in Azania. She and Sarah Tin suffer considerable inconvenience and witness much of the revolt against Emperor Seth. The RSPCA is real; the League of Dumb Chums is fictitious.

Porch, Stanley (*BM*) — A member of Parliament and husband of Mildred Porch, who dominates him.

Porson, Sir Adrian (*BR*) — A poet and close friend of Lady Marchmain.

Portuguese Count (*DF*) — A nobleman gambler shot in a duel with Philbrick after Philbrick returns his wife's emerald ring he has won from the Count in a baccarat game. Philbrick later admits that he made up this story.

Portuguese Countess (*DF*) — The wife of the Portuguese Count; she is delighted to regain the emerald ring her husband lost to Philbrick. She tries to date Philbrick after her husband's death.

Poski, Myra (*LO*) — An employee of the Happier Hunting Ground.

Posthumus (*H*) — A Roman political leader.

Postlethwaite, Mr. (*DF*) — The Domestic Bursar (i.e., financial manager) of Scone College, Oxford, who anticipates much destruction from the Bollinger Club so that Founder's port can be made available. He witnesses Pennyfeather's debagging.

Potts, Arthur (*DF*) — A friend of Paul Pennyfeather's at Oxford; later he works for the League of Nations and is responsible for having Pennyfeather arrested in connection with Margot's prostitution ring.

Prefect of Jerusalem (*H*) — The chief Roman government official.

Prendergast, Mr. (*DF*) — An Anglican clergyman who suffered "doubts" about why God bothered to make the world and decided to leave his parish. He teaches at Llanabba School. Later he becomes a "Modern Churchman," which requires no particular belief, and serves as a prison chaplain. He is murdered by a maniacal religious fanatic at the prison.

Prendergast's mother (*DF*) — She kept house for him when he was an Anglican clergyman.

Prentice, Colonel (*OG, SOH*) — One of the stern, dedicated officers in B Commando, a serious military professional. He is killed during the campaign on Crete. In *SOH* some references to him have been deleted, but his name is mentioned several times, and his death is announced.

Prentices (*MA, SOH*) — Neighbors of the Box-Benders in the Cotswolds.

Prettyman-Partridge, Mr. and Mrs. (*POMF*) — A family living at Malt House, Grantley Green, who might billet the Connollies. Basil Seal, however, learns that the husband has died and the wife has sold the house. The new owners are a very pretty young woman and her husband, Bill, who is away doing military training with the yeomanry. Basil carries on an affair with the wife until her husband returns several weeks later. The last name of the married couple and the first name of the girl are never mentioned.

Price, Nanny (*Sc*) — One of the Boot family nannies. Bedridden for many years, she gives money to the Chinese missions. Near the end of some British editions she is mistakenly confused with the card-playing Nannie Bloggs.

Prince de Portallon — See *de Portallon, Prince*.

Princes Risborough (*HD*) — The Richard Lasts lived there on a chicken farm before assuming control of Hetton after Tony Last's reputed death. In some passages in American editions Great Missenden is substituted as the location.

Principessa Fogliere — See *Fogliere*.

Pringle, Sergeant (*MA, SOH*) — The Halberdiers' physical-training instructor.

Probus (*H*) — A Roman military leader who becomes emperor. He is murdered in office.

Provna (*VB*) — A mythical Polish sculptor invented by Adam Symes for his "Chatterbox" column. As a result, alleged examples of his work are offered for sale.

Pseudo-consul of Ishmaelia (*Sc*) — He burns William Boot's passport issued by the rival political group. Although he is black, he claims to be pure Aryan.

Pug (*OGP*) — A nickname for Reginald Graves-Upton.

Put Out More Flags — A novel (1942) by Waugh depicting the period in England during the "Great Bore War." This was the era after war was declared between England and Germany but before it heated up into total conflict.

Puttock (*EB, SOH*) — The Kilbannocks' family physician. Virginia Troy visits him and learns that she is pregnant. He refuses to perform an abortion.

Pylades (*H*) — Helena's horse when she was a young woman in Britain.

Q

Quartering commandant (*BR*) — A sensitive, sympathetic reappointed lieutenant colonel who shows Charles Ryder the condition of Brideshead Castle when Ryder's military unit is assigned there and briefs him on its military use.

Queen of Arcady (*DF*) — A large, modern passenger liner Philbrick claims to have owned. He allegedly wagers it against the Portuguese Count's emerald in a baccarat game. He later admits the story was untrue.

Queen's Restaurant (*DF*) — A dining establishment in London's Sloane Square where Pennyfeather and Arthur Potts eat.

Quest, Charles (*TB*) — The well-to-do father of Imogen and Henry.

Quest, Henry (*TB*) — The snobbish brother of Imogen Quest, a student at Oxford. He and Adam Doure do not like each other.

Quest, Imogen (*TB*) — The young, fickle, rather brainless socialite who carries on a brief affair with Adam Doure until her mother sends her away from London. She next eagerly looks forward to meeting Ernest Vaughan, to whom she is attracted because he rarely bathes, is unkempt, and is generally drunk.

Quest, Lady Rosemary (*TB*) — A prominent socialite

and the mother of Imogen and Henry. She successfully terminates the romance between her daughter and Adam Doure.

Quest, Mrs. Andrew (Imogen) (*VB*)—A mythical woman who represented the ideal height of fashion; invented by Adam Symes for his "Chatterbox" gossip column.

Quintilius (*H*)—Constantius's uncle.

R

R, Lady—See *Quest, Lady Rosemary*.

R's maid, Lady (*VB*)—She sends in a news item for Mr. Chatterbox's gossip column.

Rab (*C, EB, TMI, SOH*)—In *EB, SOH* a Yugoslav island on which was located an Italian concentration camp. The Jewish refugees in Yugoslavia whom Guy Crouchback attempts to help came from there. In *TMI* and *C* Major Gordon tries to aid these refugees.

Raith, Mr. (*BM*)—The British bank manager at Debra-Dowa. He takes refuge at the British legation during the revolt that leads to Seth's overthrow.

Rampole, Mr. (*VB, POMF*)—In *POMF* the cranky and essentially book-hating partner of Geoffrey Bentley in the publishing firm of Rampole and Bentley. Through Basil Seal's skulduggery he is arrested and jailed for being involved in the publication of Ambrose Silk's *Ivory Tower*, which is regarded as fascist. In *VB* he is mentioned as a director and senior partner of a London publishing firm.

Randal (*BR*)—His entry in the pig contest wins first prize at an agricultural show, much to Cordelia Flyte's displeasure.

Randall (*BM*)—A London journalist.

Randalls (*LITS*)—On their honeymoon they were snowed in for ten days in Norway.

Ranieri's (*BR*)—The restaurant in Rome where Lord Marchmain dines with his son Brideshead and Beryl Muspratt.

Ratisbon (*H*)—A city in Bavaria, Germany, where Helena lives for a time while her husband is away on military and political activities. Now called Regensburg.

Rattery, Major (*HD*)—The slightly discredited officer who is the former husband of Mrs. Rattery.

Rattery, Mrs. (*BSR, HD*)—The "shameless blonde" who for a time is the mistress of Jock Grant-Menzies. She is wealthy and restless. She is a steadying influence for Tony Last at the time of John Andrew's death. She is pursued by John Beaver after he rejects Brenda. In *BSR* and in the "Alternative Ending" to *HD* she is mentioned as taking no interest in his romantic efforts.

Rawkes, Company Sergeant-Major (*MA, OG, SOH*)—A calm, experienced Halberdier who later fights in Crete.

Rector (*VB*)—The Anglican clergyman in Colonel Blount's parish. He owns a car and is much imposed upon by Blount to drive him and his friends at every opportunity. A showing of Blount's film in the Rector's home causes an electrical blackout there for the whole Christmas weekend.

Rector of Bellacita University (*SKME*)—A venerable official, the head of the university, who gives a long speech of welcome to the delegates attending the Bellorius Tercentenary Celebration in Neutralia.

Rector's wife (*VB*)—The sociable wife of the clergyman in Colonel Blount's parish.

Reggie (*HD*)—He does not appear for a luncheon party, so John Beaver takes his place.

Regional Director (*LAR*)—The official-in-chief of Satellite City.

Rendall, Jimmie (*WS*)—One of the fellows in the old John Plant–Roger Simmonds social set. He is now employed by Lord Monomark. He is referred to only in the 1942 edition.

Rending, Lord (*DF*)—An undergraduate at Scone College, Oxford, who collects china. The drunken Bollinger club members break his china and grind his cigars into the carpet. Misprinted as Reading in some early editions.

Reppington, Mr. (*BM, IA*)—The new district magistrate after Azania becomes a joint British-French protectorate of the League of Nations.

Reppington, Mrs. (*BM, IA*)—The wife of the district magistrate. In *IA* she helps initiate Prunella Brooks into the social behavior and proprieties expected of the British colony in Azania.

Reverend Mother at the Convent (*MA, SOH*)—Guy Crouchback visits her at Santa Dulcina delle Rocce, Italy, before he leaves to serve in World War II.

Rex, Lady Marjorie (*BSR, HD*)—Brenda Last's sister, married to a man whose first name is Allan (his last name is never mentioned). In *HD* it is noted that, although married, Marjorie had once carried on an affair with Robin Beaseley. The same information is given in *BSR* and in the "Alternative Ending" to *HD*. In *BSR* the spelling Beasley is used.

Rex sisters (*HD*) — Refers to Brenda (Tony Last's wife) and her younger sister, Marjorie. Rex is their family name.

Riley (*BFGP*) — Bella Fleace's devoted butler, who helps arrange her disastrous party.

Riley (*VB*) — One of the cars participating in the race. The Riley, an English car first built in 1898, had a very successful record of race victories in the 1920s and 1930s.

Ripon, Miss (*HD*) — A young, inept horse rider whose unruly steed, frightened by a bus's backfire, knocks John Andrew Last off his pony and accidentally kicks him to death.

Ritchie-Hook, Ben (*MA, OG, EB, SOH*) — A famous one-eyed Halberdier commander in World War I, a legend of daring and bravery. At the beginning of *MA, SOH* he is a Lieutenant-Colonel; he then becomes a Brigadier. He is scheduled to be sent to France as a leader of a battalion with Colonel Tickeridge second-in-command. That operation is canceled, however, and during the trip to the French African coast Ritchie-Hook goes ashore without orders and is wounded. He is sent back to England under a cloud. In *OG, SOH* he is restored to active service owing to Churchill's intervention. Recovering from his wounds at Dakar, he takes over as commander of Hookforce. On his way to the Middle East his airplane is lost in Africa. He turns up in Abyssinia leading a group of natives. Authorities manage to get him to Khartoum, and he is scheduled to rejoin the Halberdiers in Cairo. Upon arriving in Egypt, he leads the First Battalion in various attacks in North Africa. In *EB, SOH* he is now Major General of the Halberdiers but is relegated to noncombat duty. He quarrels with General Montgomery and seeks a new post. Thus he is sent to Yugoslavia as an observer. When the Yugoslavian partisans are to attack a blockhouse held by collaborators, he alone dashes forward to attack and is killed. In real life there were several English military figures, such as General Adrian Carton de Wiart and Orde Wingate, who had affinities with the character of Ritchie-Hook. Michael Davie (*Diaries*, p. 461 n. 3) identifies him with Waugh's first Brigade Commander, Brigadier St. Clair Morford. Waugh undoubtedly took the second element in his name from the pirate Captain Hook in James Barrie's *Peter Pan*, who, like the one-eyed Ritchie-Hook, had part of his anatomy missing — a hand, for which an iron hook had been substituted.

Ritz (*DF, VB, HD, OD, POMF, WS, BSRA*) — The fashionable and expensive London hotel on Piccadilly where, in *POMF*, Margot Metroland lives after she closes her house. In *DF*, Paul Pennyfeather prepares there for his wedding to Margot Beste-Chetwynde, and it is in the hotel's restaurant where he is arrested on the white slavery charge. This hotel is also mentioned in *VB, HD, WS, BR*, and *OD*. Margot Metroland is still living there in *BSRA*, and the banquet honoring Ambrose Silk is held there.

Ritz (*SKME*) — The most luxurious and important hotel in Neutralia, officially called the Hotel 22nd March. There are expensive real Ritz Hotels in various large cities of the world, named after the hotelier César Ritz, (1850–1918), who founded the first one in Paris in 1898. See also *DF*, Chap. 8, ". . . any Ritz hotel from New York to Budapest."

Robert (*Cr*) — A passenger who dates various girls on the cruise and for a time is engaged to the young lady letter writer.

Roberts, Mrs. (*DF*) — She runs a bar in a village near Llanabba School. It is the tavern where Grimes does most of his drinking.

Robin (*BR*) — A young admirer of Celia Ryder who marries her after her divorce from Charles.

Rochfort-Doyle-Fleace, Miss Annabel (*BFGP*) — The full name of Bella Fleace.

Roderick (*MA, SOH*) — One of the older Halberdiers. He had been a rubber planter in Malay in civilian life.

Roger, Sir (*BR*) — An ancestor of the Marchmain family.

Roger of Waybrooke (*MA, OG, EB, SOH*) — An English knight who on his way to Palestine during the Second Crusade was shipwrecked on the Italian coast. He died fighting in a battle for a local Italian count and was buried in Santa Dulcina delle Rocce.

Rolls Royce (*DF, VB, BR*) — Near the end of *DF*, Philbrick is observed riding in this most prestigious British car. In *VB*, Mrs. Mouse owns a Rolls Royce, and so does Mrs. Panrast. Chastity goes for a ride with Mrs. Panrast in it. In *BR* the Marchmains also own a Rolls.

Ron (*EB, SOH*) — The first name of a British sentry at the base for Adriatic Liberation in Italy.

Roots, Captain (*OG, SOH*) — The Staff Captain of B Commando. He is expected to return with a rations group to his Commando unit on Crete, but he does not reappear.

Rosa (*HD*) — A Macushi woman who speaks broken English to Dr. Messenger and Tony Last while they are exploring the South American jungle. She is obsessed with obtaining cigarettes.

Rosenbaum, Mrs. (*DF*) — The proprietor of a London house of prostitution. A girl interviewed for a job by Margot had worked there.

Ross (*PP*) — Lady Amelia's butler.

Rosscommon, Lady Fanny (*BR*) — The sister-in-law of Lady Marchmain. She always believed that Lady Marchmain had brought up her children badly. Julia stays with her for a while at a villa on Cap Ferrat.

Rothschild, Father (*VB*) — The wily, mysterious, know-it-all, motorcycle-riding Jesuit who is a member of the fabulously wealthy Rothschild family.

Round, Mrs. (*DF*) — The mother of Mrs. Bundle. She was a very good church-goer in Mr. Prendergast's parish while he was an Anglican minister.

Royal George (*VB*) — A third-rate hotel in the town where the auto race is held. Adam, Archie Schwert, Miles Malpractice, and Agatha Runcible spend most of the night there but are so inconvenienced and uncomfortable that they leave without paying.

Royal George Hotel, Chagford (*LITS*) — Tom Watch spends a night there when he gets separated from his bride on their honeymoon. Waugh wrote many of his novels at the Easton Court Hotel, Chagford, Devonshire.

Ruben (*EB, SOH*) — The owner and the name of a very elegant London restaurant.

Ruby (*EB, SOH*) — An elderly, well-to-do London socialite visited by Lieutenant Padfield. She is a talented though forgetful storyteller about the old days. She lived at the Dorchester Hotel. Her husband had been in Asquith's cabinet. She is based on the real-life Emerald Cunard. See glossary under *LO, Maud*.

Rum (*OG, SOH*) — An island off the coast of Scotland near Mugg.

Runcible, the Honourable Agatha (*VB*) — The daughter of Lord and Lady Chasm, a wild society girl who behaves outrageously. One of the Bright Young Things of the 1920s, she drives a racing car, and after a serious crash and a period of hospitalization she dies from her injuries. The name comes from the nonsense word in Edward Lear's "The Owl and the Pussy Cat," who ate honey with a "runcible spoon."

Rupert (*CHR*) — A man of about twenty-five who bets on a losing horse, tries to kill Tom, and then does kill a policeman. He is taken prisoner and hanged.

Ryder, Charles (*BR, CRS*) — The protagonist of *BR*. His devotion to Sebastian Flyte at Oxford eventually leads him to love Sebastian's sister Julia. Ryder has a successful career as an artist; marries Celia, the sister of Boy Mulcaster; and later divorces her to marry Julia. When she refuses to marry him, Ryder is left a middle-aged, loveless captain in the British army in World War II. He becomes a convert to Roman Catholicism.

Ryder, Edward (*BR, CRS*) — Charles Ryder's father. As a result of his wife's death he lives in a world of his own. He has a home in London and collects antiques. He is clever and eccentric and conducts a battle of wits with his son. It is maintained that Evelyn drew on some aspects of his own father, Arthur Waugh, for this portrait.

Ryder, Lady Celia (*BR*) — Charles Ryder's very social-minded and outgoing wife.

Ryder, mother of Charles (*BR, CRS*) — She went to Serbia with the Red Cross in World War I and was killed there. In *CRS* it is noted that she was killed in Bosnia by a German shell.

"Ryder by Gaslight" (*CRS*) — The title of the first and only chapter of *CRS*.

Rylands, Betty (*VB*) — She is more or less engaged to a young man named Anderson who sells radios.

S

Sackville-Strutt, Sally (*EB, SOH*) — She is mentioned as having a daughter attending the convent school at Broome.

St. Augustine's (*MA, SOH*) — A Roman Catholic church in Southsand attended by Guy Crouchback while he is training there at Kut-at-Imara House.

St. Christopher Social Club (*VB*) — A cheap drinking spot in London. On the night Adam, Agatha, Nina, and Ginger visit it, the club is serving no liquor because the police have telephoned and said they will soon raid the place.

THE DICTIONARY

St. Cloud, Lady (Countess or Marchioness of) (*HD*) — The rather pompous, aloof, stiff mother of Brenda Last. She does not feel that Brenda's adultery is really wrong.

St. Cloud, Lord (*HD*) — The deceased father of Lady Brenda Rex, the wife of Tony Last.

St. Cloud, Reggie, Lord (Earl or Marquess of) (*HD, BSR*) — In *HD* the older brother of Brenda Last. Archaeology is his hobby. He is pompous and unfeeling and acts as Brenda's representative in the divorce arrangements, for which he asks unreasonable alimony. In *BSR* and in the "Alternative Ending" to *HD* it is mentioned that he managed to keep John Beaver out of Brown's club.

St. Dulcina (*MA, SOH*) — The patron saint of Santa Dulcina delle Rocce, Italy. She was reputedly a martyr during the reign of Diocletian.

"St. Helena Meets Constantius: a legend retold" — A short story by Waugh which appeared in the *Tablet*, December 22, 1945, pp. 299–302. It contains material that was later developed in *H*.

St. Jean de Luz (*POMF*) — A French resort town near the Spanish Basque border, the location of the Basquebar.

St. Margaret's, Westminster (*DF, LITS, EB, SOH, BSRA*) — The fashionable London church where, in *DF*, Margot Beste-Chetwynde and Paul Pennyfeather were to have been married. In *BSRA*, Angela and Cedric Lyne are married there. In *LITS*, Tom Watch and Angela Trench-Troubridge also were married there. This church is also mentioned in *EB, SOH* (where Ludovic's handsome appearance in uniform in the guard of honor at a fashionable wedding attracts Sir Ralph Brompton) and in *BSRA*.

St. Olaf's (*MA, SOH*) — A prep school. As a youth Apthorpe played goal for Staplehurst against St. Olaf's.

Sakayu (*BM, IA*) — One of the principal tribes of Azania, eventually conquered by Amurath. In *IA* Sakuyu is mentioned as delivering a note from Prunella Brooks to her father. Joab, the leader of the brigands, is a Sakuyu. The word is based on "Kikuyu," one of the principal tribes of Kenya (see Waugh's *Remote People*).

Sally (*CHR*) — The horse which Rupert rode and bet on and which lost.

Salter, Mr. (*Sc*) — The foreign editor of Lord Copper's newspaper, the *Beast*. Presented as a mild, somewhat inept newsman, he is easily confused and has some peculiar notions of rural life. At the end of the novel he becomes Art Editor of the Home Knitting section, much to his relief.

Salter, Mrs. (*Sc*) — The wife of the *Beast's* foreign editor. She, like her husband, enjoys a regular, tranquil life.

Sam (*EB, SOH*) — The senior sergeant in the group at Hazardous Offensive Operations Headquarters that built model replicas of European beaches.

Sam (*LO*) — The director of publicity at Megalopolitan Pictures. He suggests that his wife's cousin take over Francis Hinsley's job.

Sam (*MA, SOH*) — Apparently a government minister. Guy Crouchback writes to him seeking a war service position.

Sambo (*LO*) — Mrs. Joyboy's pet parrot. She claims that the bird talks to her when Joyboy is out of the house. Sambo eventually dies, and Mrs. Joyboy gets a new parrot.

Samgrass, Mr. (*BR*) — A young Oxford history don at All Souls College, Oxford, hired to arrange a memorial book about Lady Marchmain's brother Ned. A scheming sycophant, he becomes a kind of warder over Sebastian because of Lady Marchmain's influence. He goes on a tour of the Levant paid for by the Marchmains. He is supposed to accompany Sebastian and prevent him from drinking excessively, but Sebastian manages to give him the slip. He then pretends that Sebastian is still with him. When the truth finally comes out, he is dismissed by the family. Later he becomes a reporter for Lord Copper's *Daily Beast*. His portrait is said to have been based on the real-life Oxford don Maurice Bowra (who was nevertheless a good friend of Waugh's). Others have suggested A. L. Rowse, who was a fellow of All Souls, whereas Bowra was at Wadham College. Moreover, Rowse was in history, whereas Bowra was in classics. Bowra's memoir, though giving a friendly portrait of Waugh, does not mention the identification.

Sampson, Sister (*Sc*) — The retired second nurse to old Mrs. Boot.

Samson, Mr. (*DF*) — A member of the staff of Church and Gargoyle, an employment agency through which Pennyfeather obtains his job at Llanabba School.

Samson, Mrs. (*PP*) — Lady Amelia's cook.

Sanders (*BM*) — A newspaper employee of Lord Monomark.

THE DICTIONARY

Sanders (*DF*) — An undergraduate at Scone College, Oxford, who once went to dinner with Ramsay MacDonald.

Sanders (*ER*) — The butler of Sir James Macrae.

Sanders, Captain (*MA, SOH*) — An officer of the Halberdiers who, among other activities, plays golf with Apthorpe. Once in *MA* (in the housey-housey game segment) he is mistakenly referred to as Captain Sanderson. Since the bingo game section has been omitted from *SOH*, the name Sanderson does not appear, but Sanders does.

Santa Dulcina delle Rocce (*MA, OG, EB, SOH*) — The town in Italy where Guy Crouchback's home is located.

Santa Maria (*SKME*) — The seaport from which Scott-King, disguised as an Ursuline nun, is smuggled out of Neutralia by the Underground.

Sarah (*VB*) — The daughter of the proprietor of the Royal George. She snores excessively.

Sarah, Lady — See *Flintshire's daughter*.

Sarum-Smith (*MA, OG, EB, SOH*) — In *MA, SOH* a Halberdier and a friend of Trimmer. He is a careless and unreliable soldier. In *OG, SOH* he is among the Halberdiers fighting in Crete. In *EB* it is stated that he was killed in the war. This fact is not mentioned in *SOH*.

Satellite City (*LAR*) — A Population Centre in the New Britain of the future. Miles Plastic is sent there to work in the Department of Euthanasia.

Saunderson, Kevin (*DF*) — One of the partygoers at Margot's King's Thursday. In later editions his name was changed to Lord Parakeet to avoid resemblance to Gavin Henderson, the name of the real-life figure on whom the character was based.

Savoy (*OG, SOH*) — An elegant London hotel and restaurant where the three American journalists interview Trimmer after Operation Popgun.

Savoy-Carlton Hotel (*BR*) — A New York City hotel where Charles and Celia Ryder stay after his return from South America.

Savoy Chapel (*BR*) — An Anglican chapel in London where Julia Flyte and Rex Mottram are married.

Sayle, Mr. (*TB*) — A well-to-do student at Merton College, Oxford.

Scarfield, Mr. and Mrs. (*OGP*) — Passengers on the *Caliban*. Mr. Scarfield is engaged in the timber trade in Burma. Both the Scarfields are friendly, and Mrs. Scarfield is extremely pretty.

Schlum, Bum (*OG, SOH*) — An American newsman in England during World War II; he interviews Trimmer.

Schonbaum, Mr. (*BM*) — The American minister to Azania. He had retired from business after becoming extremely wealthy ("had subscribed largely to a successful Presidential campaign") and felt that diplomacy was a romantic profession. (The British, French, and American senior diplomatic representatives in Azania have the lower rank of minister, not the higher one of ambassador — no doubt because Azania is such an unimportant country.)

Schonbaum, Mrs. (*BM*) — The wife of the American minister to Azania.

Schoolmaster (*DF*) — The prison official in charge of educating the inmates at Blackstone. The books he dispenses are horribly out of date and inappropriate.

Schultz, Mr. (*LO*) — The pragmatic owner of the Happier Hunting Ground, a pet cemetery. He is primarily interested in the financial returns from his business.

Schwert, Archie (*VB*) — He gives a party attended by many of the Bright Young People. He pals around with Adam Fenwick-Symes, Agatha Runcible, and others. He attends the auto race at which Agatha takes over the driving of car number 13. When the war begins, he is placed in prison as an undesirable alien.

Scone College, Oxford (*DF*) — The college from which Paul Pennyfeather is expelled for "indecent behavior." At the end of *DF* he returns there pretending to be a distant cousin of the disgraced Pennyfeather.

Scoop — A novel by Waugh (1938) describing the adventures of William Boot, who is suddenly thrust into the role of foreign correspondent in the remote African country of Ishmaelia. Through a series of improbable occurrences Boot manages to acquire a "scoop" and returns to England as a famous figure.

Scope, Miss (*Sc*) — The governess of Lady Anne Trilby.

Scott, Henry (*HG*) — An acquaintance of Ernest Vaughan.

Scottie (*OG, SOH*) — A nickname for Trimmer, who had changed his name to McTavish and joined a Scottish regiment, no doubt wearing a Scottish uniform. Kerstie Kilbannock and the other ladies at the war canteen used this nickname for him.

Scottie (old Scottie) (*SKME*) — A nickname given to Scott-King by the boys at Granchester.

Scott-King (*SKME*) — The gentle, middle-aged classical schoolmaster at Granchester who is the protagonist of the novel. He visits Neutralia to participate in the Bellorius celebration, but after the festivities he is unable to find a way to get out of Neutralia. Finally he agrees to pay the underground to leave. He is disguised as an Ursuline nun and shipped to an illicit immigrants' camp in Palestine.

Scott-King's Modern Europe—A novel by Waugh (1947) in which a classical schoolmaster travels to Neutralia to participate in a scholarly celebration. There he is involved in several of the horrors and discomforts of a modern totalitarian state. It was published in book form in England in 1947 and in the United States in 1949. It had first appeared in a magazine under the title "A Sojourn in Neutralia," which see.

Scroggs, Bill (*Co*)—A heavy drinker who ultimately becomes a member of Parliament and casts the deciding vote in favor of a war.

Scrope-Weld, Francis (*EB, SOH*)—One of the young grandchildren of the elder Mr. and Mrs. Scrope-Weld. He is tired of having Peregrine Crouchback visit each Christmas. Scrope and Weld are actual names of old English Roman Catholic families.

Scrope-Weld, Mr. and Mrs. (*EB, SOH*)—Distant cousins of Peregrine Crouchback with whom he generally spent the Christmas holidays.

Scrope-Weld, Mrs. (*EB, SOH*)—The daughter-in-law of the elder Mr. and Mrs. Scrope-Weld.

Scrunch, Mr. and Mrs. Leicester (*LO*)—Friends of Mr. and Mrs. Walter Heinkel. The Heinkels are dining with the Scrunches when news arrives that the Heinkels' pet dog, Arthur, has been run over and killed.

Seal, Angela—See *Lyne, Angela.* In *BSRA* she and Basil live in London in a large house on Hill Street. She married Basil after the death of her first husband, Cedric Lyne.

Seal, Barbara (*BSRA*)—The frivolous, partygoing eighteen-year-old daughter of Basil and Angela Seal. She hopes to marry Charles Albright, whom she met at Oxford while she was studying history there. Through trickery Basil persuades her that Albright is actually her brother and therefore she cannot marry him.

Seal, Basil (*BM, POMF, WS, BSRA*)—Although he comes from a moneyed upper-class family, Basil is rude, unreliable, undisciplined, and caddish. He attended Balliol. Born in 1903 (the same year as Waugh), he is twenty-eight years old at the beginning of *BM*. Plagued by financial problems, disappointed with politics, and bored with England, he travels to Azania. He knew Emperor Seth slightly when Seth was an undergraduate at Oxford, and he now joins Seth's campaign to modernize Azania. In Seth's government he is the High Commissioner and Comptroller General in the Ministry of Modernisation. He quarrels with General Connolly over the issue of boots for the army, has a love affair with Prudence Courteney, and, when Seth is overthrown, flees disguised as a Sakuyu merchant. He hopes to return the Emperor to power, but Seth is murdered. He sees to Seth's funeral, delivers the eulogy, and then returns to England. In *WS* we are told that Basil had stood unsuccessfully for Parliament, had a girl friend named Trixie for a while, was an acquaintance of John Plant and Lucy and Roger Simmonds, and was a member of the London Library. He was also searching for a wealthy heiress to marry.

In *POMF* we hear that, besides his adventures in Azania, he once lived in La Paz during a dangerous period there, worked as a journalist and gun runner in Spain, wrote leaders (i.e., editorials) for the *Daily Beast*, sold champagne, and created dialogue for movies. He was in Djibouti in 1936, in Saint Jean de Luz in 1937, and in Prague the following year. At the beginning of *POMF*, Basil is thirty-six years old. We observe the close attachment between him and his sister Barbara. While waiting for a suitable easy military post, he lives at Barbara's rural home and handles the billeting of the Connollies. Later he works for the War Office and finally volunteers for a new hazardous special services unit then forming. For some time he has been the lover of Angela Lyne. We learn that Basil had gone to Balliol and then studied at Oxford in the mid-1920s and that after his first scandal his father, the soul of upright propriety, had disinherited him, leaving any family financial support to come from Basil's mother. When news of the death of Angela Lyne's husband in the army's campaign in Norway arrives, Basil and Angela agree that they should marry.

Basil had been left a considerable sum of money by his aunt but wasted it on an expedition to Afghanistan. Always receiving ample allowances, he had constantly overspent and his mother had had to pay his debts on numerous occasions. A job had

THE DICTIONARY

been reserved for him at a bank in Brazil but he had never reported for work.

In *BSRA*, Basil is fifty-eight years old. As a commando in World War II he had lost the toes on one foot while demonstrating an explosive he had invented to destroy bridges. He had then been discharged from the army and had married Angela Lyne. For many years thereafter he had lived as a country gentleman, and then he and Angela had traveled about, living in various homes and apartments owned by his wife. In *BSRA*, feeling old and ponderous, Basil enrolls, with his wife, in a health spa and by a clever ruse prevents his daughter Barbara from marrying her disreputable boy friend, Charles Albright.

Basil is based on Peter Rodd and Basil Murray, although several critics have noted similarities to Waugh himself.

Seal, Edward (*POMF*) — Lady Seal's brother, who had an undistinguished career as a brigadier in World War I.

Seal, Lady Cynthia (*BM, POMF*) — Basil's mother. She first appears in *BM* where she continuously makes plans for Basil to settle down and become successful. She is a wealthy grande dame who has often helped her son financially in his nefarious career. In *POMF* she fancies that he may become a dashing World War II warrior. She is thrilled when Basil finally joins a commando unit.

Seal, Sir Christopher (*BM, POMF*) — Chief Conservative Whip in Parliament for twenty-five years, a paragon of responsibility and propriety, the father of Basil Seal. He died shortly after the first of Basil's several disgraces. He disinherited Basil before his death.

Seal, Tony (*BM, POMF, BSRA*) — The respectable brother of Basil Seal. In *POMF* it is noted that he had a promising career in diplomacy ahead of him. In *BSRA* we learn that he served as a British diplomat until retirement.

Second-in-command (*BR*) — A member of the brigade in which Charles Ryder is a captain.

Second-in-command (*C*) — A member of Major Gordon's regiment. He is negative and misanthropic.

Second-in-command (*C, TMI, EB, SOH*) — A member of the partisan "general staff" in Yugoslavia.

Selina — See under *Huntingdon*.

Sergeant-instructor (*MA, SOH*) — One of the Halberdiers' instructors of trainees.

Sergeant-major (*BR*) — The sensible and supportive senior warrant officer of the company of which Charles Ryder is captain.

Sessorian Palace (*H*) — Helena's home in Rome.

Seth (*BM*) — The emperor of Azania. A graduate of Oxford, Seth survives an attempt to overthrow his rule. He then, with the aid of Basil Seal, attempts various changes and reforms in the name of progress and the New Age. His changes cause a new revolt, in which he is dethroned and soon murdered.

Settringham, Lord and Lady (*WS*) — Diners at the Ritz. To Roger Simmonds they look like a drab couple from the American Midwest.

Seyid, Prince (*BM*) — Seth's father and the leader of an unsuccessful rebellion against his son's rule as Emperor. He is captured and eaten by a cannibal tribe.

Shanks, Halberdier (*MA, OG, SOH*) — A member of Guy Crouchback's company. In *MA, SOH* he unsuccessfully requests leave to participate in a dance contest. In *OG, SOH* he is wounded by a mortar on Crete.

Shaw, Mrs. (*ER*) — She performs domestic services for Simon Lent.

Shepheard's (*VB*) — A London hotel at the corner of Dover Street and Hay Hill. It is run by Lottie Crump. It is modeled on the Cavendish Hotel on Jermyn Street. The Cavendish was managed by Rosa Lewis. The name here comes from the famous Shepheard's Hotel in Cairo. The Cairo Shepheard's is mentioned in *OG, SOH*.

Shiriana Indians (*TMWLD*) — A Brazilian tribe. In *HD* they are called Pie-wie.

Shock, Silas (*Sc*) — A journalist for the *New York Guardian*.

Shrub, Sheila (*HD*) — The girl friend of Billy Angmering.

Shumble (*Sc*) — A special correspondent for the *London Echo*. He cabled a story that a Russian agent had arrived in Ishmaelia. Dr. Benito, the minister of foreign affairs and propaganda, denied the story, and so did the other correspondents; thus Shumble's news was repudiated.

Shutter, Mrs. (*HD*) — A London interior decorator who is an aggressive business competitor of Mrs. Beaver's. Mrs. Beaver regards her as a "ghoul."

Sickly Child (*BR*) — The nickname of one of the party girls at the Old Hundredth Club. She joins Charles, Sebastian, and Mulcaster at their table.

Sidebotham, Colonel (*DF*) — One of the guests at the

Llanabba Sports Day. The drunken Prendergast tries to engage him in conversation about "bounders." Sidebotham recalls how the Fuzzy-Wuzzies in the Soudan would cut the tent ropes of British soldiers and knife them through the canvas.

Sidi Bisha (*OG, SOH*) — The site of British "Hookforce" desert camp in Egypt.

Silenus, Otto Friedrich (*DF*) — The eccentric young German architect hired by Margot Beste-Chetwynde to rebuild King's Thursday. He believes that architecture should be very modernistic and prefers factories to domestic architecture. He calls himself Professor Silenus. He is perhaps modeled on Walter Gropius. See Glossary under *DF*, *Bauhaus at Dessau*.

Silk, Ambrose (*POMF, BSRA*) — In *POMF* he is introduced as an author, an aesthete, and an intellectual. He has had many male lovers and becomes distressed over an abortive affair with a young German named Hans. He is eventually put in charge of atheism in the Religious Department of the Ministry of Information. He writes the first issue of his magazine, *Ivory Tower*, but owing to Basil Seal's machinations, he is accused of being a Fascist. He flees to Ireland and settles briefly in a remote area planning to write, but he moves from one location to another, continuing to be peripatetic. In *BSRA* he is invested with the Order of Merit on the occasion of his sixtieth birthday. In conjunction with these events he is honored at a public banquet in London. According to Dr. Parsnip's speech, Ambrose had lived — after Ireland — in Tangier, Telaviv, Ischia, Portugal, and then England and had written no books since the 1930s. Waugh once asserted that Silk was modeled on Brian Howard. Howard (1905–1958) was an Oxford aesthete and notorious homosexual who did some writing and much traveling before his death from a drug overdose.

Simmonds, Dr. (*TMWLD*) — An anthropologist on the Anderson expedition who is arrested by a revolutionary garrison in Brazil. The largest part of the expedition's supplies, over which he has charge, are confiscated. He decides, after being imprisoned for a time, to protest the matter to the central government in Rio, thus leaving the expedition.

Simmonds, Lucy (*WS*) — Roger Simmonds' unaffected, pleasant, and very wealthy wife. Lucy is an orphan (her mother dying when she was born) and has been brought up by her aunt. She is interested in politics and writing because Roger is. She shares Roger's Marxist sympathies, so she and John Plant do not talk to each other about politics. She is serious by nature and thinks her husband a great writer. John Plant falls in love with her, but she looks upon him only as a friend. She enjoys his company, which helps occupy her time when she is pregnant. Her child, a boy, is born on August 25, 1939. There is a suggestion that she is based on Diana Mitford (then Mrs. Bryan Guinness and later Lady Mosley, Sir Oswald's wife). See the correspondence between her and Waugh in *Letters*, pp. 638–39. *VB* is dedicated to Bryan and Diana Guinness.

Simmonds, Roger (*WS*) — A writer friend of John Plant. Simmonds went to Oxford with John and coedited a paper with him there. He wrote books of humor and worked for various newspapers and wrote several films, but in the late 1930s he became a Socialist, and his chief interest then centered on politics. He had disturbed his publisher by writing an avant-garde play. He married Lucy, who was very wealthy and very much in love with him. During World War II he worked in the office of Political Warfare. His wife has their baby near the end of *WS*.

Simon (*BR*) — One of Lady Marchmain's brothers. He attended Oxford and was killed in World War I.

Simon (*PP*) — Lady Amelia's nephew, who tells Billy Cornphillip's son that he is illegitimate, being the actual child of a liaison between Etty Cornphillip and Ralph Bland.

Simon (*VB*) — A man who has been hospitalized after falling out of an airplane. He is in the same sanitarium as Agatha Runcible. The nurses refer to him as Simple Simon.

Simona (*SKME*) — A city in Neutralia where Bellorius's statue is unveiled.

Simona University (*SKME*) — The scene of the celebration in Neutralia to honor Bellorius.

Simpleforth, Fanny (*DF*) — A wealthy British socialite.

Sink Street — See *Sixty-four, The*, and *Old Hundredth*.

Sitwell, Sir Osbert (*OGP*) — An actual English author, mentioned as an acquaintance of Pinfold. See Glossary under *OGP*.

Siwa (*MA*) — An oasis in upper Egypt visited by General Alexander. Siwa is west of Alexandria in the Libyan desert.

Sixty-four (*HD*) — A seedy London nightclub at 64

Sink Street visited by the tipsy Tony Last and Jock Grant-Menzies. It is at the Sixty-four that Tony meets Milly and Babs. In British editions it is called the Old Hundredth and is at 100 Sink Street.

Skimp, Judge (*VB*) — A white-haired American who drinks heavily as a guest at Lottie Crump's hotel. He is very generous about lending money. He eventually falls asleep with his hair in an ashtray. Flossie (Florence Ducane) swings to her death on the chandelier in his suite.

Skylark (*MA, SOH*) — The boat that carries Guy Crouchback and other members of the small patrol for the raid on the North African shore.

Sligger (*VB, EB, SOH*) — An acquaintance of Guy Crouchback's at Oxford; he is mentioned by Joe Cattermole in *EB, SOH*. It was the familiar nickname of F. F. Urquhart, Dean of Balliol College, frequently mentioned in Waugh's life of Ronald Knox and also referred to in *A Little Learning*. Although Urquhart was a Roman Catholic, Waugh distrusted him. In *VB* it is mentioned that Adam Fenwick-Symes lunched with him and Father Rothschild.

Maurice Bowra, in his *Memoirs*, p. 119, says that Sligger's nickname was Oxford slang for "the sleek [American 'slick'] one." Peter Quennell, in *Evelyn Waugh and His World* (Boston, 1973), p. 37, reports that Waugh as an undergraduate used to go around outside Balliol shouting, "The Dean of Balliol sleeps with men!" At Oxford (except at Christ Church) "Deans" are not the heads of their colleges but disciplinary officers. The head of Balliol is the "Master."

Slimbridge, Captain (*OG, SOH*) — The signals commander of B Commando. He accompanies Captain Roots and the rations group on Crete but never returns to his commando unit.

Slump, Mr. (*LO*) — One of the two newspaper correspondents who write the Guru Brahmin column. He is a heavy drinker, and Aimée's letters vacillating on a choice between Dennis Barlow and Joyboy annoy him. After he is fired from the newspaper, Aimée phones him at a bar; during their conversation he advises her to commit suicide.

Smallwood, Mr. (*POMF*) — The platoon commander of Alastair Digby-Vane-Trumpington's unit.

Smart Woman (*EB, SOH*) — A nickname given to Lady Perdita because of her suavity and aristocratic background. Ludovic was part of the honor guard at her first wedding.

Smerdyakev (*Sc*) — A mysterious Russian who comes to Ishmaelia; he stays with Dr. Benito and tries to put the Russians in control of the country by setting up a Soviet state.

Smethers (*MA, SOH*) — Apthorpe mistakenly calls a Halberdier duty servant named Crock by this name.

Smethwick, Constantia (*BR*) — A dull guest at the dinner given by Charles Ryder's father. She is chosen as one of the guests in an effort to drive Charles out of the house and cause him to live elsewhere.

Smiley, Sergeant (*OG, SOH*) — A member of the Hookforce unit. He is involved in the action on Crete. His name is omitted from *SOH*.

Smith, Miss (*HD*) — The pseudonym used by Tony Last for Winnie on the hotel register at Brighton. Winnie, Milly's young daughter, accompanies her mother, much against Tony's wishes, on the divorce-evidence excursion.

Smudge, Horace (*SKME*) — An uncooperative British consulate official in Neutralia. He is not particularly helpful when Scott-King tries to leave the country after the Bellorius celebration.

Sneiffel, Mr. (*EB, SOH*) — General Spitz's personal photographer. He takes pictures of Ritchie-Hook's attack on the blockhouse in Yugoslavia and the brigadier's subsequent death.

Sniggs, Mr. (*DF*) — The Junior Dean of Scone College, Oxford, who anticipates much destruction from the Bollinger Club's party so that the founder's port can be made available. He witnesses Pennyfeather's debagging.

Soames, Sergeant (*MA, SOH*) — Guy Crouchback's platoon sergeant. He is crude and difficult. Guy recommends him for officer candidate school so that the platoon can get rid of him.

Soapy (*LAR*) — Formerly a burglar who becomes an inmate at Mountjoy prison during the time Miles Plastic is incarcerated there. His experience as a cat burglar enables him to escape from the burning institution after Miles later returns and sets it on fire.

Sojourn in Neutralia, A — Scott-King's Modern Europe was so titled in *Hearst's International Combined with Cosmopolitan* 123 (November, 1947): 67ff.

Sonia (*HD*) — Trumpington, perhaps? John Beaver

serves as a last-minute replacement for her male partner at a luncheon.

Sopater (*H*) — A soothsayer in Rome.

Sothill, Barbara (*BM*, *POMF*, *BSRA*) — Basil Seal's sister, who is married to Freddy Sothill and lives at Malfrey. She is first mentioned in *BM*. In *POMF* she has a much larger role. She is the billeting officer of the Malfrey district, and Basil manages to relieve her of the burden of the Connollies. Despite Basil's unruly life, she is extremely fond of him — there is a strong hint of incestuous feeling (a theme repeated in *BSRA*) — and they can be childlike and playful when they are together. She fancies him becoming a World War II hero. In *BSRA* she still lives at Malfrey, which is now under the National Trust.

Sothill, Freddy (*BM*, *POMF*, *BSRA*) — The pompous husband of Barbara, Basil Seal's sister. He is mentioned in *BM*. In *POMF* he is in military training as a member of the British yeomanry at the beginning of World War II. In *BSRA* we learn that he has been killed in the war.

Soum, Smiles (*Sc*) — He had only a bit of the Jackson family lineage since he was a grandson of Samuel Smiles Jackson through the female line. Unhappy with his lowly post as assistant director of public morals, he starts a revolution against the Jacksons called the White Shirt Movement and proclaims a nationalist government. The Germans, hoping to use him as a puppet, furnish him with money to help them gain ascendancy over the Russians. He is outwitted by Dr. Benito's group and flees to the Soudan.

Southsand and Mudshore Yacht Squadron (*MA*, *OG*, *SOH*) — A club which Guy Crouchback and Apthorpe join while they are stationed with the Halberdiers at Kut-al-Imara House, Southsand-on-Sea. In *OG*, *SOH*, Guy stays there for a while while waiting for Chatty Corner to get in touch with him.

South Twining (*BR*) — Sebastian spends much of his time on the day of the fox hunt drinking in a hotel bar there.

Sparks (*OGP*) — The *Caliban*'s radio operator. Sparks is the traditional nickname for a wireless operator aboard ship.

Sparrow, Mrs. (*MA*, *SOH*) — An elderly woman who broke both legs falling out of an apple loft. She was an acquaintance of the Box-Benders and lived near them in Gloucestershire.

Sparrow, Mrs. (*VB*) — The cook at 10 Downing Street for Prime Minister Sir James Brown's family.

Speit, General — See *Spitz, General*.

Spierpoint (*CRS*) — The private school attended by Charles Ryder. It is based on the school Waugh attended, Lancing College.

Spire, Jack (*DF*) — A journalist who supported the preservation of King's Thursday. He was interested in preserving old aspects of England. He is no doubt modeled on Sir John Squire (1884–1958), minor poet, "man of letters," and editor of the *London Mercury* (see Glossary under *LO*).

Spitz, General (*EB*, *SOH*) — An American officer sent as an observer of the partisans in Yugoslavia. He witnesses the "battle" in which Ritchie-Hook is killed. In *SOH* he is named General Speit.

Spot (*VB*) — A cranky fox terrier owned by the matron of the nursing home where Agatha Runcible is treated after her racing-car accident.

Sprat (*OG*, *EB*, *SOH*) — A nickname for Major-General Whale. A sprat is a very small fish, by contrast with "whale."

Spratt (*CRS*) — A student at Spierpoint. He is a platoon commander in the Officers' Training Corps.

Sproggin, Colonel (*POMF*) — An officer in Freddy Sothill's army unit.

Spruce, Everard (*EB*, *SOH*) — The pompous, self-important founder and editor of the magazine *Survival*. He was formerly one of a coterie of Socialist writers, and during the war, then in his middle thirties, he was aided by the Ministry of Information in producing *Survival*. He lives in an impressive house in Cheyne Walk and is tended by four secretaries. He publishes Ludovic's *Pensées* in *Survival*. At one point in *EB* he is by error referred to as Jack by Sir Ralph Brompton, but that is corrected to Everard in *US* and *SOH*. The portrait is based to a degree on literary critic Cyril Connolly and the magazine *Horizon*.

Spruce's veiled ladies (*EB*, *SOH*) — The secretaries, like Coney and Frankie, who are devoted to Everard Spruce and his monthly review *Survival*.

Squadron Leader (*C*, *TMI*, *EB*, *SOH*) — The British officer in charge of air traffic at the Allied base in Yugoslavian partisan territory. In the RAF the rank of squadron leader corresponds to that of major in the army.

Squib, Huckleberry (*POMF*) — A nom de plume of

THE DICTIONARY

Ambrose Silk, who signs one of the articles in his *Ivory Tower* with this name.

Staplehurst House (*MA, SOH*) — A school attended by Apthorpe as a youth. He did not have a very distinguished record there. At one time Ambrose Goodall taught there.

Star (*BR*) — One of the London newspapers that carry the story of Sebastian Flyte, Boy Mulcaster, and Charles Ryder being arrested for public intoxication.

State Meteorological Institute (*LAR*) — A state department in the England of the future which was designed to control the climate. Despite election promises, it had failed.

Station Hotel (*VB*) — A hotel in the town where the car race is held. Adam Symes, Miles Malpractice, Archie Schwert, and Agatha Runcible try vainly to obtain rooms there for the night. Station hotels in many British cities, being close to the noise of the railway, are of only moderate status.

Station master (*BM*) — He deserts Azania when it appears that Seth will be overthrown by Prince Seyid. Later he returns and resumes his function on the railroad between Matodi and Debra-Dowa.

Stayle (*HG*) — A village in the story. Also a short form for the Marquess of Stayle.

Stayle, Andrew, Duke of (*DF, VB, BM, BSRA*) — A wealthy English nobleman. In *BM* he attends Lady Seal's party with the duchess. In *BSRA* he is the father of Lady Betty Albright and the grandfather of Clarence Albright.

Stayle, Duchess of (*DF, VB, BM, Sc, POMF*) — A wealthy socialite of London. The Stayles are mentioned in *DF*. In *VB* the duchess is mentioned as one of the guests at Lady Metroland's party during which Mrs. Ape entertains. She and her husband appear at one of Lady Seal's parties in *BM*. She gives a fashionable London ball in *Sc* and attends Peter Pastmaster's wedding in *POMF*.

Stayle, Marquess of (*HG*) — The eighteen-year-old grandson and heir of the Duke of Vanburgh; his Christian name is George Theodore Verney. He is deemed insane by his elderly relatives when in reality it is they who are insane.

Stayles' daughter (*VB*) — Lady Urusula, the oldest daughter of the Duke and Duchess of Stayle who, after pressure by her mother, becomes engaged to Edward Throbbing.

Stebbing, Major (*CRS*) — A schoolmaster at Spierpoint.

Stebbing, Sam (*IA*) — An Englishman who works in the immigration office at Matodi. He believes that the "kidnapped" Prunella Brooks's messages are written in cipher code. He suffers a breakdown while interpreting this alleged code and has to be shipped back to England. He is finally sent to a nursing home, where he works out hidden messages in the railway guide.

Steerforth, Captain (*OGP*) — The civil, efficient master of the S.S. *Caliban*. During his illness Pinfold suspects the captain of being hostile and villainous, but these suspicions are invalid. He is named after the attractive but sinister Byronic character in Dickens's *David Copperfield*.

Sterne, Sir Lionel (*WS*) — A youthful millionaire who purchases a large painting by John Plant's father.

Stevenson, Mr. (*TB*) — A book lover who at the last minute cannot bring himself to sell his books to Macassor's Bookshop.

Steyle, Marjorie (*WS*) — Her son is mentioned as a seller of haberdashery.

Stiggins (*DF*) — An Oxford undergraduate who reads a paper on "Sexual Repression and Religious Experience" at the Oxford S.C.U. Potts mentions him in a letter to Pennyfeather.

Stillingfleet, Roger (*OGP*) — A writer friend of Gilbert Pinfold. The character was based on Christopher Sykes, who became Waugh's "official" biographer.

Stitch, Algernon (Algie) (*Sc, OG, EB, SOH*) — The husband of Julia Stitch. In *Sc* he is Minister of the Department of Imperial Defence. Then, in *OG, SOH*, he is in the diplomatic service, assigned to keep watch over the activities of the Egyptian king. In some passages in *OG* he is called Reginald or Reggie Stitch, while in other passages he is called Algie. In the British edition of *OG* only Algernon and Algie are used. In *SOH*, Waugh corrected the Reginald (Reggie) error, and Mr. Stitch is called Algernon or Algie. In *EB, SOH* he and his wife are mentioned as living in Algiers, where Mr. Stitch has a position in the British government. He is obviously based on Lady Diana Cooper's husband, Alfred Duff Cooper, the late Viscount Norwich, who held several high cabinet and diplomatic posts. Waugh disliked him.

Stitch, Josephine (*Sc*) — The bright but somewhat un-

THE DICTIONARY

disciplined eight-year-old daughter of Julia and Algernon Stitch. As a joke she enjoys kicking John Boot. She was perhaps modeled on the Coopers' allegedly somewhat spoiled only child, John Julius, Viscount Norwich.

Stitch, Julia (*POMF, WS, OG, EB, SOH*) — The wife of Algernon Stitch, a beautiful, fashionable, intelligent, flamboyant English socialite. Among her activities is to pursue, in her small car, a man she wants to chat with down the steps to a lavatory. In *Sc* she is a friend of John Courteney Boot and has many political and social connections in high places. She is mentioned in *POMF*, and in *WS* she buys one of John Plant's father's paintings. In *OG, SOH* her yacht is used by the military in World War II. She is also a friend of Ivor Claire. She is in Egypt when X Commando arrives there, and she entertains several of the military. Her appearance in the hospital revives Guy Crouchback from his stupor while he is recovering from his escape by boat from Crete. She has him transferred to her home so that he can convalesce in pleasanter surroundings. Through her influential contacts she has Ivor Claire transferred to India. When she learns that Ritchie-Hook is coming to Egypt, she makes certain that Guy is immediately sent to England since she is afraid that Guy might bring Ivor Claire's desertion to the brigadier's attention and Claire might be court-martialed for treason. In *EB, SOH* it is noted that she and her husband are now living in Algiers. Mrs. Stitch is based on Lady Diana Cooper.

Stop (*HD*) — The name of a stuffed spaniel in the bathroom of an elderly gentleman's house where Tony Last boarded for a summer in France. Probably the Frenchman's error for "Spot."

Strapper, Colonel (*HD*) — A fellow passenger of Tony Last and Dr. Messinger on the cruise from England to South America.

Strapper, General (*VB*) — Agitated by a news item in a gossip column referring to his daughter, he carries a whip to the newspaper office to punish the person responsible.

Strickland-Venables, Jean (*BR*) — An acquaintance of Cordelia Flyte who falls in the mud while fox-hunting near Brideshead.

Strickland-Venables, Sir Walter (*BR*) — The joint master of a fox-hunting group called the Marchmain Hounds. Lord Brideshead shares the master's role with Sir Walter.

Stroud (*MA, SOH*) — A town near Box-Bender's home in Gloucestershire. The nearest large town to Waugh's home, Piers Court, Dursley.

Stuart-Kerr, Captain Angus (*VB*) — A mythical big-game hunter; invented by Adam Symes for his Chatterbox gossip column.

Stubbs (*DF*) — A serious-minded theological student at Oxford who becomes a close friend of Paul Pennyfeather when Paul returns to college after his alleged death.

Sugdon (*CRS*) — A former student at Spierpoint.

Sunningdale (*BR*) — The location of the home of a stockbroker friend of Rex Mottram. Rex spends a weekend there (with Brenda Champion also as a guest) while being engaged to Julia Flyte.

Suora Tomasina — See *Tomasina*.

Sub-Deputy (*LAR*) — A penology official.

Surgeon, the (*DF*) — The alcoholic doctor who signs the death certificate of Pennyfeather while the latter is in Dr. Fagan's nursing home.

Survival (*EB, SOH*) — An intellectual journal managed by Everard Spruce. It is generally believed to be based on Cyril Connolly's *Horizon*.

Susie (*EB, SOH*) — The nickname of an RAF sergeant attached to an arts-and-crafts unit which makes replicas of the beaches of Europe for military purposes. He has curly gold hair and is a homosexual. He is also a member of the Communist party and is closely associated with Sir Ralph Brompton.

Susie (*POMF*) — A beautiful lance corporal attached to Colonel Plum's office for a time. In addition to her military duties she serves as Plum's mistress. Later she becomes Basil Seal's paramour.

Sussex Gardens (*HD*) — A street in Bayswater, London. John Beaver and his mother live there.

Sveningen, Miss Irma (*SKME*) — A leggy, Amazon-like Scandinavian who comes to Neutralia to attend a physical-training congress. For a time she is accidentally involved with the Bellorius celebration group. She is an eager boxer and manages to beat up several policemen.

Swallow (*DF*) — A steam yacht allegedly owned by Philbrick. He claims to wager it in the baccarat game with the Portuguese count. He later admits the story is untrue.

Sweat, Mr. (*LAR*) — Miles Plastic's next-door neighbor in Mountjoy prison. He escapes from the institution when Miles returns and sets the building on fire.

Swedish Consulate, Surgery, Bible and Tea Shop

(*Sc*) — The establishment in Ishmaelia presided over by Erik Olafsen. When taxi drivers cannot understand their passengers' instructions, they automatically drive to Olafsen's place.

Swindon (*BR*) — An important railway junction and industrial town in Wiltshire. It is there that Sebastian turns the car off the main road and eventually finds a bucolic spot where he and Charles picnic on wine and strawberries.

Sword of Honour — The revised version of Waugh's *Men at Arms*, *Officers and Gentlemen*, and *The End of the Battle* (*Unconditional Surrender*). This one volume recension was published in England in 1965 and in the United States in 1966.

Sword of Stalingrad (*EB, SOH*) — An impressive, artistically crafted sword conceived by King George VI and displayed in various parts of England as a tribute to the Russian defenders at Stalingrad.

Sybil — See *Anderson, Sybil*.

Sybil, "old" (*HD, BSR*) — A gossipy London society woman, a friend of Polly Cockpurse, also mentioned in the "Alternative Ending" to *HD*. She declines to act as Tony's partner in the "adultery" needed for Brenda's divorce case because "there's a certain person who might hear about it and take it wrong." The "certain person" with whom Sybil is apparently having a liaison is probably modeled on the Prince of Wales, later Edward VIII and Duke of Windsor. In real life two of the Prince's earlier mistresses, before Wallis Simpson, were Freda Dudley Ward and Thelma, Viscountess Furness. The most famous Sybil on the social scene at the time was Sybil, Lady Colefax, a celebrated hostess, who moved in the Prince's circle.

Syd (*OG, SOH*) — One of the British soldiers on Crete. Ludovic persuades him to give his tin of food to Major Hound.

Sylvester, Pope (*H*) — The reigning pope when Helena arrives in Rome. Sylvester and Helena establish a friendly respect for each other. Pope Sylvester I reigned from A.D. 314 to 355.

Sylvia (*BR*) — She is engaged to the heavy-drinking Charlie Kilcartney; she leaves him when he stops drinking because he has become dull.

Symes (*VB*) — Short for Adam Fenwick-Symes; see Fenwick-Symes above, p. 147.

Symonds (*CRS*) — The most prominent student at Spierpoint. He edits the magazine and leads the debating society.

"Sympathetic Passenger, The" — A short story by Waugh which appeared in the London *Daily Mail* on May 4, 1939, p. 4. The protagonist, Mr. James, who hates radio programs, picks up a hitchhiker who also hates radios. The hitchhiker turns out to be an escaped lunatic who almost kills James.

T

"Tactical Exercise" — A short story by Waugh about a bored married couple, each of whom plots to kill the other using sleepwalking and an accidental fall as the means of extinction. The story appeared in the *Strand*, March, 1947, pp. 45–54; and in *Good Housekeeping*, March, 1947, pp. 22ff. It was the title story in the collection *Tactical Exercise* (Boston, 1954).

Tactical Exercise — This collection by Waugh (Boston, 1954) contains "The Curse of the Horse Race," "Cruise," "Bella Fleace Gave a Party," "On Guard," "Period Piece," "Excursion in Reality," "Mr. Loveday's Little Outing," "Winner Takes All," "An Englishman's Home," "Work Suspended," "Tactical Exercise," and "Love Among the Ruins."

Tampen, Count (*VB*) — A Liberal minister in Ruritania who stole the gold fountain pen of the king of Ruritania.

Tamplin (*CRS*) — A friend of Charles Ryder's at Spierpoint.

Tangent, Lord (*DF*) — The courtesy title of the oldest son and heir of the Earl and Countess of Circumference. A student at Llanabba School, he is accidentally shot in the foot by the drunken Prendergast on Sports Day. Eventually he dies from the wound. Waugh puns cleverly on the names: in geometry a tangent is an offshoot of the circumference of a circle.

Tarquin (*H*) — Another name for Helena's grandson Crispus.

Tatton, Private (*POMF*) — A British soldier who loses his gas mask during military training.

Taunton (*Sc, EB, SOH*) — The county town (capital) of Somerset. In *Sc*, William Boot goes to the cinema there. It was also the location of a railroad branch line. In *EB, SOH* a special coach is added on this line for those who wish to attend the funeral of Guy Crouchback's father. Guy's father's lawyer is from

THE DICTIONARY

Taunton. Waugh lived at Combe Florey, near Taunton, from 1956 until his death in 1966 and is buried at Combe Florey.

Ted (*WTA*) — The uncle of the Kent-Cumberland boys.

Temperance (*VB*) — One of evangelist Mrs. Melrose Ape's "angels."

Tendril, Miss Ada (*HD*) — The dignified sister of the vicar of Hetton.

Tendril, Reverend Mr. (*HD*) — The elderly vicar of the Anglican church at Hetton. He still preaches the sermons he gave in India when he was stationed there as a chaplain.

Tennyson (*BR*) — A very talented cricket player mentioned by Father Phipps.

Tetricus (*H*) — A military official in Gaul who gave Marcias as a slave to Helena's father. Later his troops fight against Aurelian and Constantius and lose, and he is taken prisoner.

Thame (*BR*) — A town near Oxford. Anthony Blanche takes Charles Ryder to dinner at a hotel there and comments memorably about the Marchmain family.

Thanatogenos, Aimée (*LO*) — A cosmetician at Whispering Glades and the principal woman in the novel. She is chosen to be trained as the first female embalmer at Whispering Glades. She is torn between love for Joyboy and love for Dennis Barlow and finally commits suicide by injecting herself with poison, on the advice of Guru Brahmin. Aimée, in French, means the "loved one" (feminine). Thanatogenos, in Greek, means "born of (or for) death."

Thatch (*TB*) — The country home of the Hay family near Oxford.

Theodora (*H*) — The daughter of Maximian and the second wife of Constantius.

Thimble (*OG, SOH*) — Ivor Claire's talented show horse.

Thingummy (*VB*) — The name Lottie Crump uses for a person whose name she cannot remember. At one point she calls Adam Symes Lord Thingummy; later she calls Judge Skimp Judge Thingummy. On a third occasion she calls Ginger Littlejohn Mr. Thingummy, and still later she refers to Adam as Young Thingummy. Familiar variants are "thingamajig" and "thingamabob."

"This Quota Stuff: Positive Proof That the British Can Make Good Films" — A short story by Waugh later entitled "Excursion in Reality," which see.

Thorne, Cedric (*OGP*) — An actor who commits suicide before a scheduled BBC interview.

Throbbing, Lady Fanny (*VB*) — The mother of Miles Malpractice and Edward, Lord Throbbing. Her daughter worked in Buenos Aires for Lady Metroland's prostitution ring but is presently associated with a "touring company." Fanny is the twin sister of Kitty Blackwater. She is an old, gossiping busybody, a relic of the free-and-easy days of Edward VII, and is obsessed with sexual topics.

Throbbing, Lord Edward (*VB*) — The brother of Miles Malpractice. He supposedly retires to a log shanty in Canada but actually is doing government work in Ottawa. He returns to England midway through the novel and eventually becomes engaged to the Duchess of Stayle's daughter, Lady Ursula.

Thunder-box — See *Bush Thunder-box*.

Thunderclap (*HD*) — John Andrew Last's pony.

Thurston, Mr. (*WS*) — One of the pseudonyms used by Arthur Atwater, who drives the car that hits and kills John Plant's father. He uses the pseudonym so that he can be certain John Plant will see him.

Tickeridge, Jenifer (*MA, OG, EB, SOH*) — The young daughter of Major and Mrs. Tickeridge. In *EB* Mrs. Tickeridge moves away from Matchet to be near a school for Jenifer.

Tickeridge, Major (*MA, OG, EB, SOH*) — A friend of Guy Crouchback's father, he enables Guy to join the Royal Corp of Halberdiers. He later becomes one of Guy's superiors and is promoted to lieutenant colonel. He is agreeable, sensible, and capable. In *OG, SOH*, as a colonel, he is a leader of the Halberdiers on Crete. After the evacuation he dines with Guy at Julia Stitch's home in Egypt. In *EB, SOH* it is mentioned that he is now the brigadier of the Halberdiers.

Tickeridge, Mrs. Vi (*MA, OG, EB, SOH*) — The likable wife of Major Tickeridge and a friend of Guy Crouchback's father.

Tim (*EB, SOH*) — The younger brother of Virginia Troy is killed in World War II.

Time & Tide (*EB, SOH*) — A popular leftist British magazine. Ludovic unsuccessfully submits a poem on the Sword of Stalingrad to this periodical.

Tin, Sarah (*BM*) — A member of (presumably) the Royal Society for the Prevention of Cruelty to Animals and of the fictional League of Dumb Chums. She arrives in Azania and encounters much difficulty because of indifference to her cause and the revolt against Seth. She and Mildred Porch view much of the coup from the roof of Youkouman's hostel. She ultimately takes refuge in the British embassy.

Tinkerbell (*BR*) — The horse Sebastian Flyte rides on the fox hunt near Flyte St. Mary. He uses the hunt as an excuse to get away to drink at a local bar. The horse is named after the fairy in Sir James Barrie's *Peter Pan*.

Tipping, Lady (*HD*) — A society matron who gives a last-minute meal invitation to John Beaver when an additional man is needed to balance the number of guests.

Titchcock, Mr. (*VB*) — A guest at a low-class provincial hotel, he is inconvenienced when Adam Fenwick-Symes, Miles Malpractice, Agatha Runcible, and Archie Schwert stay the night to attend the car race.

Titmuss, John (*Sc*) — A journalist for the *News Chronicle*.

Titus Carpicius (*H*) — A sculptor who works on Emperor Constantine's triumphal arch in Rome.

Todd, Mr. James (*HD*) — The son of a Barbadian missionary and a Pie-wie Indian woman. He is an elderly, unbalanced Dickens fanatic who speaks English but cannot read. He keeps Tony Last a prisoner in his South American jungle home, forcing him to read Dickens's novels aloud. He thwarts Tony's would-be rescuers, convincing the outside world that Tony is dead. Waugh admitted that Todd was based on a man named Christie whom he met while traveling in the South American jungles. See his travel book *Ninety-two Days* (1934).

Todhunter, Mr. (*POMF*) — An astute billeting officer who takes over the management of the Connollies from Basil Seal.

Tom (*BR*) — A homosexual acquaintance of Anthony Blanche at the Blue Grotto Club. He asks Charles Ryder to dance the rhumba with him.

Tom (*CHR*) — A character who does not have money enough to bet on a horse. After Rupert tries to kill him and does kill a policeman, Tom manages to capture Rupert and turn him over to the authorities.

Tom (*POMF*) — A left-wing friend of Poppet Green who does not wish to serve in World War II. He cannot become a conscientious objector because he has no conscience.

Tomasina, Suora (*MA, SOH*) — A teaching nun in the school at Santa Dulcina delle Rocce, Italy. *Suora* is Italian for "Sister."

Tomb (*WTA*) — The village near the Kent-Cumberlands' estate.

Tomb Park (*WTA*) — The country home of the Kent-Cumberlands.

Tony (*TMWLD*) — The captain in the Coldstream Guards with whom Mrs. Paul Henty carries on an adulterous affair.

Tony (*VB*) — One of the poets mentioned in a conversation with Mr. Benfleet at Lady Metroland's party for Mrs. Ape.

"Too Much Tolerance" — A short story by Waugh which appeared in *John Bull*, May 21, 1932, pp. 22, 24, satirizing a person for being too tolerant. The narrator meets an unnamed middle-aged British commercial agent waiting for a ship at a Red Sea port. The salesman has been a partner in a successful business, but the business has failed because of the partner's treachery. He still helps support his parasitic twenty-seven-year-old son, who wants to be an actor. He is lonely, for his wife has left him for another man. Nevertheless, he does not blame any of these people for their conduct, since he is tolerant.

Tour de Force (*TB*) — An expensive London restaurant at which Adam Doure and Imogen Quest dine.

Transept, Lady Marmaduke (*EB, SOH*) — Lord Marmaduke Transept's second wife, the heroine of Ludovic's novel *The Death Wish*. In *SOH* this character is called simply Lady Marmaduke.

Travellers (*BR*) — A Paris club where Rex Mottram wins a considerable amount of money gambling.

Travellers Club (*BM, POMF*) — A London club (founded 1819) to which in *BM*, Sir Joseph Mannering belongs. In *POMF* it is the scene of a luncheon attended by Basil Seal, Sir Joseph Mainwaring, and a lieutenant colonel of the Bombardiers.

Trehearne, Mr. (*TB*) — A student at Oxford and a friend of Henry Quest.

Trench, Major (*MA, SOH*) — An officer in the Halberdiers.

Trench, William (*BM*) — In some editions this name is used instead of William Bland.

Trench-Troubridge, Angela (*LITS*) — A London society girl who marries Tom Watch. After her honeymoon is interrupted, she takes up with an old school friend of Tom's who is a bachelor. She visits this friend from time to time though continuing to live with Tom.

Trench-Troubridge, Colonel (*LITS*) — The father of Angela Trench-Troubridge. Known as a sportsman, he ran several times for Parliament as a member of the Conservative party.

Trench-Troubridge, Mrs. (*LITS*) — The mother of Angela Trench-Troubridge.

Trenchard, Sergeant (*OG, SOH*) — An efficient, matronly woman assigned to Hazardous Offensive Operations Headquarters in London.

Tresham (*EB, SOH*) — A member of a recusant Catholic family who attends the funeral of Guy Crouchback's father.

Trèves (*H*) — The French name for Trier, a city in Germany near the Luxembourg border, where Helena lives for a time after her husband divorces her.

Trilby, Lady (*Sc*) — A widow, she is William Boot's great-Aunt Anne, the older sister of William's father. She owns the only car in the family. It has an old-fashioned horn which stentoriously announces her coming when she makes her weekly trip to church. In some British editions she is called Agnes instead of Anne.

Trimmer (*MA, OG, EB, SOH*) — A careless, undisciplined, and irresponsible member of the Halberdiers. Very immature, in *MA, SOH* he is removed from the temporary officer commission list when Ritchie-Hook takes command of the brigade. In *OG, SOH* he is stationed on Mugg. He goes to Glasgow on leave and has a brief affair with Virginia Troy. (Before the war he was a hairdresser on the *Aquitania* and served Virginia there. Of course, "Trimmer" refers to that occupation, though as a hairdresser he was known as Gustave.) On leave in Glasgow he lies to his second-in-command, and to avoid punishment he transfers himself (illegally) to Tommy Blackhouse's Commando group. He is put in charge of a demolition squad. Later he is sent on a public relations military mission to a small island off the coast, but his unit accidentally lands on the coast of France. He shows fear and cowardice, but journalist-publicist Ian Kilbannock writes him up as a hero. He is promoted to colonel and is sent around England as a "common man hero" to boost civilian morale. He insists that Virginia Troy be sent with him, and this is arranged. In *EB, SOH* he is sent to America on his public relations mission. Virginia has wearied of him and refused to go along. He is not aware that he has made her pregnant. After the War his whereabouts are unknown. There is a rumor that he jumped ship in South Africa.

Trinovantes (*H*) — The British tribe of whom Helena's father, Coel, was the head.

Trixie (*WS*) — A onetime girl friend of Roger Simmonds. Basil Seal had passed Trixie on to Roger. She exudes an air of disdain and superiority and is not liked.

Trooper (*EB, SOH*) — A large dog mentioned by Ludovic. Enlisted men in the cavalry are "troopers," as those in the artillery are "gunners," in the engineers "sappers," and in the infantry "privates."

Trotter, Colonel Jumbo (*OG, EB, SOH*) — He delivers a military message to Guy Crouchback. He retired in 1936 with the rank of full colonel. When World War II is declared, he appears at the Halberdiers' headquarters, but because of his age he is given no post. He possesses "sublime imperturbability." As a result of Guy's suggestion he becomes a valuable administrative officer under Tommy Blackhouse on the Isle of Mugg. He is not allowed to travel with Hookforce because of his age and is most disappointed. In *EG, SOH* he is Commandant of Number 6 Transit Camp, London District, after Hookforce service overseas is refused. He "rescues" Guy from the emergency ward after the latter's accident in the parachute training camp.

Trotter, Mr. (*HD*) — A former history teacher of Tony Last at prep school.

Troutbeck (*Sc*) — A servant of the Boot family.

Troy, Bert (*MA, SOH, OG*) — One of the husbands of Guy Crouchback's first wife, Virginia. Troy, an American, has been deserted by Virginia. He wins a divorce decree from her on the basis of her numerous infidelities. In *MA, SOH* he is called Bert Troy on one occasion and Hector Troy in another passage. Usually he is referred to as Mr. Troy.

Troy, Hector — See *Troy, Bert*.

Troy, Virginia (*MA, OG, EB, SOH*) — A vivacious, fashionable young woman who marries Guy Crouchback. She later falls in love with Tommy Blackhouse and divorces Guy. She eventually divorces Blackhouse and marries an American named Troy. She has numerous lovers, but when Guy later attempts to have sexual relations with her (on the grounds that in the Roman Catholic church the divorces are of no effect), she indignantly rejects him. In *OG*, *SOH* she does canteen work in London and then works at Hazardous Offensive Operations Headquarters. She has had a brief affair with Trimmer in Glasgow, and Trimmer wants to renew the affair with her now that he is a public relations hero. She does not wish to have a further dalliance with him, but she is finally persuaded by Ian Kilbannock to join Trimmer on his morale-building tour throughout England. In *SOH* she learns that she is pregnant by Trimmer. After failing to find an abortionist, she ingratiates herself with Guy and explains her plight to him. He marries her to give her child a name. After the baby is born, she shows little interest in it, and Angela Box-Bender takes it to the country. Virginia is killed in London by a German buzz bomb.

Troyte (*EB, SOH*) — A family mentioned by Peregrine Crouchback.

Trudie, Aunt (*Sc*) — A relative of a journalist.

Trumpery, Sarah (*LITS*) — A kleptomaniac who attends the wedding of Tom Watch and Angela Trench-Troubridge. She pinches a clock from the wedding presents.

Trumpington, Alastair — See *Digby-Vane-Trumpington, Alastair*.

Trumpington, Robin (*BSRA*) — The son of Alastair and Sonia Digby-Vane-Trumpington, he is a young man about town who shares a flat with his mother. He is properly called Sir Robin Digby-Vane-Trumpington, Bt. since his late father was a baronet, and he is presumably the only son (conceived in *POMF*), he inherits the "sir."

Trumpington, Sonia — See *Digby-Vane-Trumpington, Sonia*.

Truslove, Captain (*MA*) — A fictional British war hero of Guy Crouchback's boyhood reading.

Tunbridge Wells, aunt at (*MA, SOH*) — Apthorpe's aunt at Tunbridge Wells, a health resort in Kent. Apparently his only living relative she was a "High Church" Anglican.

Turf Club (*OG, SOH*) — A socializing spot in Cairo for Major Hound and other British officers stationed there.

Turtle's Club (*OG, EB, SOH*) — A London social club bombed in World War II. Fictional name of Boodle's Club (founded 1762) located on St. James's Street.

Tyler, Bert (*Sc*) — An inept young countryman without a driver's license who is scheduled to drive Mr. Salter to Boot Magna in a truck. His inexperience results in an accident which causes him serious injury.

Tyngate (*BR*) — A student at Oxford, the secretary of the College Essay Society. He shares rooms with Collins.

U

Ukaka, Duke and Duchess of (*BM*) — A title of nobility granted by Emperor Seth to General Connolly and his wife after Connolly and his troops defeat Seyid's rebel forces. Connolly's wife is especially delighted with her title.

Ukaka Pass (*BM*) — The scene of a great battle in Azania where Seth's supporters under General Connolly defeat the Sakuyu rebels. After the victory Emperor Seth awards Connolly and his wife the title Duke and Duchess of Ukaka.

Uncle (*MA, OG, EB, SOH*) — A nickname applied to both Apthorpe and Guy Crouchback because they are a good bit older than the other recruits.

Unconditional Surrender — See *End of the Battle, The*.

Under the Ermine (*Sc*) — The title of a book about some of his journalistic experiences which Wenlock Jakes is writing while serving as a correspondent in Ishmaelia. On official occasions members of the British royalty and nobility wear gowns trimmed with ermine fur. Hence Jakes's book is probably one of scandalous revelations about high society.

Union Bar (*OG, SOH*) — A drinking spot for British officers in Alexandria. Guy Crouchback visits the bar on more than one occasion. He and Tommy Blackhouse dine there before the trip to Crete.

Union Club (*IA*) — A social club at Matodi, Azania, for the British after Azania becomes a joint protectorate. The French are honorary members of the club.

Unknown Major — See *Grace-Groundling-Marchpole*.

Upper Mewling (*OGP*) — Reginald Graves-Upton's niece and nephew live there, and The Box is there.

Utteridge, Lord (*DF*) — In one of Philbrick's fantastic stories, a wealthy industrialist who lives in Utteridge House in London. His young son is kidnapped by Jimmy Drage. Delighted to be rid of his troublesome son, he refuses to pay ransom for his return.

THE DICTIONARY

V

Van Atrobus, Mrs. (*POMF*) — A London socialite who hopes her daughter will marry Peter Pastmaster.

Vanbrugh, Lady (*DF*) — A wealthy noblewoman who disapproves of the rebuilt King's Thursday.

Vanbrughs (*BR*) — A stuffy but fashionable husband and wife. They stay away from Julia Flyte's wedding to Rex Mottram.

Vanburgh (*HG*) — A town about four miles from the Duke of Vanburgh's estate. It contains the nearest railroad station.

Vanburgh, Duke of (*HG*) — He overprotects his grandson, the Marquess of Stayle, then plans for him to travel abroad but, upon reflection, changes his mind and tells the young marquess to return home.

Vanburgh, Lady Emily (*HG*) — A sister of the Duke of Vanburgh.

Vanburgh, Lady Gertrude (*HG*) — A sister of the Duke of Vanburgh.

Vanburgh, Lord (Marquess of Vanburgh) (*VB*) — The youthful gossip writer for the *London Morning Despatch* and one of the guests of Lady Metroland's party during which Mrs. Ape entertains. He is referred to by his friends as Van. In at least one early edition of *VB* his name is misprinted Vaughan. *Cyril Connolly: Journal and Memoir*, ed. David Pryce-Jones (New York, 1984), notes a similarity between the real-life gossip writing Marquis of Donegall (1904–75) and Vanburgh.

Vanburgh, Lord George (*WS*) — Mentioned as being found decapitated but actually killed by other means in John Plant's *Death in the Dukeries*. The reference to Vanburgh appears only in the 1942 edition of *WS*.

Van Gluck, Mr. (*LO*) — The Transportation Captain at Megalopolitan Pictures.

Van Halt, Bertha (*BR*) — The godmother of Charles and Celia Ryder's daughter, Caroline.

Van Winkle, Rip (*OD*) — A wealthy forty-three-year-old man about the world of New York and the more American parts of Europe. He is in a car accident in 1933 and through the efforts of a magician is transported to the London of the twenty-fifth century. In a state of savagery he finds the familiarity of a Roman Catholic priest saying Mass. He regains consciousness to find himself back in 1933 London.

Vascari, Cardinal (*WS*) — He dies under mysterious circumstances while saying a rosary that has a missing decade. He is a character in John Plant's *Vengeance at the Vatican* but is referred to only in the 1942 edition of *WS*.

Vaughan, Ernest (*TB*, *HG*) — An undisciplined, unkempt, heavy-drinking student at Oxford and an acquaintance of Adam Doure. In *TB* both drink excessively, and Ernest tries to drive a car and crashes. Imogen Quest hears about him and desires to make his acquaintance. Some time later, in *HG* he is hired as a tutor and traveling companion for the young Marquess of Stayle. After a few days in London with the marquess Vaughan is discharged when the family changes its mind about allowing the marquess to become acquainted with the outside world. Vaughan appears to be the prototype of Basil Seal.

Vaughan, Hugh (*HG*) — An uncle of Ernest Vaughan.

Vavasour, Miss (*MA*, *OG*, *EB*, *SOH*) — In *MA*, *SOH* an elderly, good-intentioned resident of the Marine Hotel in Matchet and a devoted friend of Guy Crouchback's father. In *OG*, *SOH* she becomes very agitated when the quartering commandant Grigshawe tries to evict Mr. Crouchback from the hotel. She brings the issue to the attention of Jumbo Trotter. In *EB*, *SOH* she is still living at the Marine Hotel. After Mr. Crouchback's funeral she asks for his tobacco jar as a memento. Guy readily agrees to her request.

Venables, Walter (*BR*) — An old friend and neighbor of Lord Marchmain. He had been Marchmain's commanding officer in World War I.

Vengeance at the Vatican (*WS*) — The title of one of John Plant's detective stories. Mentioned only in the 1942 edition.

Verney, Elizabeth (*TE*) — The wife of John Verney. She is a linguist who works for the Foreign Office. She plots, apparently successfully, to kill her husband. She and her husband accuse each other of sleep walking; she uses this as an eventual excuse to drug and then push the victim through a broken area of a balcony overlooking a Cornish cliff.

Verney, John (*TE*) — A British company commander during World War II; after the war he plots to murder his wife, but she manages to outwit him and kill him instead.

Verney's Aunt and Uncle (*TE*) — John and Elizabeth Verney live in the Hampstead home of Elizabeth's parents, who, since John and Elizabeth are cousins, are John's aunt and uncle.

Veronica (*HD*) — A member of the amoral, gossipy London social set friendly with Brenda Last and Polly Cockpurse.

Via Dolorosa (*LO*) — Mr. and Mrs. Walter Heinkel live at 207 Via Dolorosa in the wealthy Bel Air section of Los Angeles. Their dog dies, and the funeral arrangements are handled by the Happier Hunting Ground. The phrase means in Latin "Road of Sorrow" and refers to the route over which Christ carried his cross to Calvary.

Vicar (*PP*) — A middle-aged friend of Lady Amelia's who believes Major Etheridge is persecuting him by putting water in his gas tank and paying the choir boys to sing out of tune.

Vicar of Llanabba (*DF*) — He attends Sports Day at Llanabba school.

Vice-Consul (*MA, SOH*) — A British official in Italy mentioned by Guy Crouchback.

Victoria (*H*) — A Roman political leader.

Victorinus (*H*) — A Roman political leader.

Vile Bodies — A novel by Waugh (1930) describing the activities and mores of the "Bright Young People" of the English 1920s, a scene comparable in many respects to F. Scott Fitzgerald's depiction of life in America among the upper classes during the same "roaring twenties" era. Waugh insisted that he never read Fitzgerald until late in life and that his early inspiration was rather Hemingway, chiefly *The Sun Also Rises* (called *Fiesta* in England). See Waugh, *Diaries*, pp. 782, 787.

Villa Hermione (*MA, SOH*) — The original name of the Castello Crouchback, the home of Gervase and Hermione Crouchback in Santa Dulcina delle Rocce, Italy.

Vizier (*BM*) — One of the horses at the British legation in Azania kept for pleasure riding.

Vogel, Mr. (*LO*) — An assistant to Mr. Joyboy at Whispering Glades Cemetery.

von Gluck, Gräfin (*MA, SOH*) — A neighbor of Guy Crouchback in Santa Dulcina delle Rocce, Italy. She lives in open concubinage with her butler. "Gräfin" is the German equivalent of "countess."

von Weich (*EB, SOH*) — The leader of the German military forces in Yugoslavia.

W

Wagstaff (*Sc*) — The secretary of newspaper magnate Lord Copper.

Walker, Mr. (*BM*) — The secretary at the American legation in Azania. He delivers the news to the British that Emperor Seth's side has won the war. He also serves as the American commercial attaché, representing Stetson cars and the Cosmopolitan Oil Trust.

Walsh, Captain (*BM*) — The Oriental secretary at the British legation in Azania. Even though he suffers from recurrent malaria and beats his wife, he is kept at the legation because he is the only one there who can speak the Sakuyu language. He learns of possible trouble, warns Sir Samson, and is given permission to take his wife to the coast by train. Later he arranges for planes to fly from Aden and rescue the British stationed at the legation.

Walton (*DF*) — An Oxford student who participates in an O.S.C.U. debate on "Sex Repression and Religious Experience." He emphasizes the mystical element and so presumably will disagree with Stiggins; mentioned by Arthur Potts in a letter to Pennyfeather.

Wanda (*BM*) — One of the principal tribes of Azania. Amurath has become their leader and under his rule they have become the dominant group. Seth is a member of this tribe. Jeffrey Heath, in his book *The Picturesque Prison: Evelyn Waugh and His Writing*, p. 297, suggests that this name may owe its origin to the unconventional antics of Wanda Baillie-Hamilton. Mrs. Baille-Hamilton was an upperclass gadabout who, among other idiosyncrasies, received male visitors in her bathroom while she bathed.

Wandering Jew (*H*) — A legendary figure who appears to Helena in a dream and indicates the location of the True Cross.

Warder, the (*DF*) — The prison guard who receives Pennyfeather upon incarceration and censures him for being a white slaver.

Warder, the Chief (*DF*) — The principal official next to Lucas-Dockery at Blackstone Prison.

Warren (*HD*) — A London nightclub mentioned.

Warringtons (*DF*) — A family whose son attends Llanabba School.

Warwick, Gilbert (*WS*) — A fictional British novelist.

He writes essentially the same letter over and over to his admirers. He is possibly a combination of Sir Gilbert Parker and Warwick Deeping, popular novelists of the 1920s and 1930s.

Washington, Barnabas (*HD, TMWLD*) — In *TMWLD*, Mr. McMaster's first reader of Dickens's novels. Washington is from Georgetown and wants to return to civilization, but he dies reading Dickens and is buried in Mr. McMaster's encampment. In *HD*, where McMaster's name is changed to Todd, Washington meets the same fate. Tony Last later succeeds Washington as Todd's reader.

Waste of Time (*Sc*) — The most recent book by author John Courteney Boot, a travelogue about life among the Patagonian Indians.

Watch, Captain Peter (*LITS*) — A member of the Coldstream Guards who serves as best man at his brother Tom's wedding.

Watch, Hon. Wilfrid (*LITS*) — The father of Tom Watch.

Watch, Mrs. (*LITS*) — Tom Watch's mother.

Watch, Tom (*LITS*) — An accountant who marries Angela Trench-Troubridge but never achieves a honeymoon with his bride.

Watkins, Major (*Sc*) — A neighbor of the Boots; Priscilla Boot wants to borrow his trailer to take her horse to the Caldicotes.

Watson (*IA*) — An Englishman who works for the bank at Matodi.

Watts, Sister (*Sc*) — The retired first nurse to old Mrs. Boot.

Waurupang (*HD*) — The Machushi Indians' name for the various rivers in the Amazon system.

Waybroke, Lady of (*MA, SOH*) — Roger de Waybroke's wife.

Waybroke, Roger of — See *Roger of Waybrook*.

Waybrook (*MA, SOH*) — The newer form of the name Waybroke, a town near London. Sir Roger of Waybroke comes from there.

Wee Kirk o' Auld Lang Syne (*LO*) — One of the churches in Whispering Glades; nearby is the Lover's Seat.

Weld, Canon (*EB, SOH*) — The Catholic priest who instructs Virginia for reception into the Roman Catholic church.

Welterweight (*Sc*) — The former welterweight champion of the Adventist University of Alabama. He works for Dr. Benito to help establish the new Soviet state. He is butted severely by Frau Dressler's vicious goat.

Welwyn Garden City (*Sc*) — The London suburb where Mr. and Mrs. Salter live. Mr. Salter is the Foreign Editor of the *Beast* when William Boot first meets him.

Wendover (*VB*) — A village in Buckinghamshire near Aylesbury.

Westmacott, Mr. (*HD*) — The purchaser of John Andrew Last's pony after the boy is killed in a riding accident.

Westmacott, Mr. and Mrs. (*EH*) — A farming family, neighbors of Beverly Metcalfe. They sell their land, which precipitates a crisis among their neighbors when it appears that the property will be used for a factorylike laboratory.

Westmacott, Reverend Father (*OGP*) — A Roman Catholic priest who is a friend of the Pinfolds. He is consulted by Mrs. Pinfold during her husband's illness. He dispels the notion that groups like the Gestapo or the Existentialists could have invented a new advanced type of "Box."

Westminster, Duke of (*SKME*) — Garcia had once seen the impressive Duke and speaks of all the London property the Duke owned. The real estate holdings of the Grosvenors, Dukes of Westminster, in central London are immense. Engineer Garcia mistakenly uses "propriety" for "property." Waugh is probably taking a slap at the contemporary second Duke, who viciously persecuted his brother-in-law, Lord Beauchamp, the father of Waugh's Lygon friends, for homosexuality but in his own life was hardly "a man of great propriety."

Weybridge, Captain (*HD*) — The ostensible owner of the shady Old Hundredth nightclub. In American editions he is called Mr. Charles Weybridge.

Whale, General (*OG, EB, SOH*) — The director of land forces at Hazardous Offensive Operations Headquarters in London. See *Brides-in-the-Bath, Sprat*.

Whale, Mrs. (*EB, SOH*) — The general's wife. She is in charge of the restaurant in the officers' club at Hazardous Operations Headquarters and is very officious and domineering and attempts to seclude attractive women by raising steam from the coffee urn.

Wheatley (*CRS*) — One of the students at Spierpoint who is disappointed when he is not appointed to the Settle.

Whelan, Father (*MA, SOH*) — A Roman Catholic parish priest in the area where the Halberdiers train. The Catholics attend Mass at his church, and he is concerned about receiving payment from the War Office since there is no regular Catholic chaplain assigned to the Halberdiers.

Whelper (*Sc*) — A special news correspondent.

Whembley (*TB*) — A country house.

Whiskey-soda (*WS*) — An arrogant Sudanese prostitute in Morocco.

Whispering Glades Memorial Park (*LO*) — A cemetery modeled on Forest Lawn, in California.

Whispers from the Glades (*LO*) — The house publication of Whispering Glades Cemetery. Almost a complete issue is devoted to Joyboy's engagement to Aimée Thanatogenos.

Whitefield, George (*VB*) — English clergyman (1714–70), joint founder of Methodism with John Wesley, though they later disagreed over theology. An actor plays him in the film about John Wesley. In the movie version he wounds Wesley in a duel.

Whitemaid (*SKME*) — An Oxford University Professor of Roman law who attends the Bellorius celebration in Neutralia. He knows nothing of Bellorius; he simply likes to travel.

Widow Twankey (*OG*) — A derisive nickname given by X Commando to Ritchie-Hook.

Wilbur K. Lutit Memorial Block (*LO*) — The section of Megalopolitan Studios where Francis Hinsley worked. The name may be based on "Louis B. Mayer."

Wilcox (*BR*) — The principal servant of the Marchmain family at Brideshead Castle. When Lord Brideshead returns from Italy, the problem of who is to have more authority (Wilcox or Plender) is solved by their discussion with Cordelia, who apportions their different responsibilities, and as a result they become Joint Grooms of the Chambers.

Wilcox and Bredworth (*OGP*) — A British pharmacy mentioned by the voices.

William (*VB*) — One of the poets mentioned in a conversation with Mr. Benfleet at Lady Metroland's party for Mrs. Ape.

Wilmots (*MA, SOH*) — Neighbors of Guy Crouchback in Santa Dulcina delle Rocce, Italy.

Wimperis, Father (*CRS*) — An Anglican clergyman in a London parish noted for his preaching and rather theatrical religious services. Charles Ryder and his aunt Philippa attend one of his Sunday services. Probably a reference to the Reverend Basil Bourchier (Waugh, *Diaries*, p. 4).

Wimpole (*WS*) — A second-rate London club visited by John Plant and Arthur Atwater.

Wimpole Street (*VB*) — The site of the nursing home where Agatha Runcible is sent after her racing-car accident. Many medical offices are on this street and on Wigmore Street in west-central London.

"Winner Takes All" — A short story by Waugh (1936) in which a younger son is disadvantaged in every way by his mother's partiality for the older son. He must even give up his desirable and wealthy fiancée to his older brother because of the mother's machinations and the inherent favoritism shown to the older son by the English social system. This story first appeared in the *Strand* (March, 1936), pp. 530–39. It was first collected in *Mr. Loveday's Little Outing and Other Sad Stories Written Before the Second World War*. It appears in *Tactical Exercise* and in *Charles Ryder's Schooldays and Other Stories*.

Winnie (*HD*) — Milly's obnoxious, pesty eight-year-old daughter who accompanies her and Tony Last to Brighton so that Tony's divorce can be carried out. She wants to go bathing in very cold weather and causes a commotion about Tony's two breakfasts.

"Wish, The" (*TE*) — Another title for Waugh's short story "Tactical Exercise."

Witches (*H*) — Two witches from Egypt, one old, the other young, who are in cahoots with Fausta. The younger one recites a poem indicating British treachery. Both witches are killed by Constantine's order.

Wodehouse-Bonner, Bertie (*Sc*) — A mutual acquaintance of Uncle Theodore Boot and a man who sits next to him at the banquet given by Lord Copper for Boot of the *Beast*. This character's name was changed to Bertie Booth-Bryce in most editions after the first, probably because the reference to novelist P. G. Wodehouse and one of his chief characters, Bertie Wooster, was too obvious.

Wonderfilm Company of Great Britain (*VB*) — Mr. Isaac's company, which produces the film about John Wesley on Colonel Blount's estate.

Worcester Herald (*VB*) — This newspaper contains an obituary for Colonel Blount's friend Chatterbox.

Work Suspended — An unfinished novel by Waugh (1942) in which the protagonist falls in love with a friend's wife and is fascinated by her pregnancy.

THE DICTIONARY

Since the woman is totally devoted to her husband, the hero never declares his passion.

Work Suspended and Other Stories Written Before the Second World War — This collection of Waugh's stories (London, 1949) contains "Mr. Loveday's Little Outing," "Cruise," "Period Piece," "On Guard," "An Englishman's Home," "Excursion in Reality," "Bella Fleace Gave a Party," "Winner Takes All," and "Work Suspended." This version of the unfinished novel *Work Suspended* has several changes from the 1942 version.

Worthing (*DF*) — A well-to-do suburb of the resort town of Brighton, Sussex, where Mr. Prendergast was pastor of an Anglican church until his doubts commenced.

Wrottman of Garesby (*MA, EB, SOH*) — An ancient English Roman Catholic family presumably in Guy Crouchback's ancestral line. It is spelled Wrothman in *EB, SOH*.

Wrottman of Speke (*MA*) — An ancestral English family mentioned by Ambrose Goodall.

Wykham-Blake (*CRS*) — A student in the Under-School at Spierpoint.

Y

Yercombe, Mrs. (*OGP*) — The housekeeper who tends Gilbert Pinfold's elderly mother.

Yorke, Quartermaster-Sergeant (*MA, SOH*) — A calm, experienced Halberdier.

Yoshiwara, Baroness (*VB*) — Japanese diplomat's wife who meets Prime Minister Outrage for an assignation, but they are both baffled about making the first move, and their sexual union is never accomplished. She awaits his direct approach and is baffled by his aloofness. Eventually she and her husband leave for Washington, D.C., his new diplomatic post.

Youkoumian, Krikor (*BM, IA*) — The wily Armenian proprietor of the Amurath Café and Universal Stores in Azania. In *BM* he becomes financial secretary to Basil Seal in his post in the Ministry of Modernisation. Later he becomes the director of the Ministry of Fine Arts and First Lord of the Treasury. He always has financial deals in progress and survives all the political vicissitudes of Azania. His business skulduggery in obtaining boots for army use ultimately leads to a dispute between Basil Seal and General Connolly, which causes the overthrow and death of Emperor Seth. At the end of the novel he is running a café at Matodi and pursuing his financially profitable manipulations. In *IA* he helps Prunella Brooks and her lover stage a fake kidnapping so that they can acquire enough money to return to England and marry. Youkoumian gets a percentage of the ransom money for his help.

Youkoumian, Madame (*BM*) — The wife of Krikor Youkoumian. She is constantly mistreated and victimized by her husband. At one point he refuses to unbind her until he has caught up on his sleep.

Z

Zenobia (*H*) — Aurelian's wife (concubine).

Zero (*HD*) — A race horse on which Ben Hacket once won a bet.

Zinc, Lord (*Sc*) — The owner of the *Brute*, a newspaper competing with Lord Copper's *Beast*. When William Boot first comes to London to discuss great-crested grebes, the concierge at the *Beast* suggests that he go across Fleet Street and bother Lord Zinc.

Zingerman (*HD*) — A businessman acquainted with Dr. Messinger. He once lived in Agadir selling ammunition but now lives in Mogador and runs a restaurant. Spelled Zingermaun in British editions.

Zita (*OG, EB, SOH*) — A friend of Kerstie Kilbannock. She worked with Kerstie in a London canteen. She stays with the Kilbannocks for a time during the war.

APPENDICES

Appendix 1

FREQUENT ABBREVIATIONS USED IN WAUGH'S FICTION

ADC — Aide-de-camp; an officer who acts as a special assistant to a senior officer.
BBC — British Broadcasting Corporation.
CO — Commanding Officer.
DSO — Distinguished Service Order, an award to British commissioned officers for meritorious service in battle.
ESO — Embarkation Staff Officer.
JCR — Junior Common Room, the common social room for undergraduates of a college.
MC — Military Cross; a decoration awarded to British officers for bravery.
MO — Medical Officer.
NAAFI — Navy, Army, and Air Force Institutes, equivalent to the American Armed Services PX's (post exchanges). Printed as "Naafi" in *BR*.
OCTU — Officer Cadet Training Unit, students who did military drill and studied the science of warfare in preparation for a commission.
QM — Quartermaster.
RAF — Royal Air Force.
RTO — Rail Transport Officer.
SMO — Senior Medical Officer.
VC — Victoria Cross, a decoration given for conspicuous bravery to members of the British armed forces. It was instituted by Queen Victoria in 1856.

Appendix 2

COMMON REFERENCES IN WAUGH'S FICTION

Balliol — One of the colleges at Oxford.

Boxing Day — A holiday in England, the first weekday after Christmas, when traditionally gifts are given to servants and public employees such as postmen.

Bumf — Bureaucratic paperwork, supposed to be derived from "bum fodder," i.e., toilet paper.

Cockney — The London working-class dialect, perhaps made most famous by Liza Doolittle in George Bernard Shaw's play *Pygmalion* (1912).

Dial — A sleeping pill.

Digs — Lodgings off campus.

Dotheboys Hall — The harsh, brutal boarding school in Charles Dickens's novel *Nicholas Nickleby* (1838–39).

Girl Guides — Girl scouts.

Gong — A medal or decoration, not necessarily military. Ambrose Silk's Order of Merit, a civilian honor is referred to in *BSRA* as a gong.

Lloyd George — David Lloyd George (1863–1945), a Welsh political figure who was prime minister of England from 1916 to 1922. Many of his policies angered the Conservative party and his former Liberal associates. His greatest enemy was Asquith, the Liberal party leader, whom Lloyd George replaced as prime minister in 1916.

Matins — The service of morning prayer in the Church of England.

Orangery — A conservatory or large greenhouse where flowers, plants, and even orange trees can be grown.

Plus fours — Baggy trousers strapped just below the knee, with the material overhanging the knee by about four inches. They were commonly worn when the wearer was playing golf but were also worn on other occasions.

Quid — One pound, whether a pound note, a pound in silver, or a check for a pound.

Rum — Strange, odd, peculiar.

Sam Browne — A leather belt worn by officers in the British army. It had an attached strap that went over the right shoulder. It was named after General Sir Samuel Browne (1824–1901). In some editions of both *MA* and *EB* it is incorrectly spelled without the final *e*.

Sapper — A soldier in the Corps of Royal Engineers, whose duties include building fortifications and blowing up installations.

Scout — A male college servant at Oxford.

Shemozzle — A fight or a loud fuss. It is also spelled "schemozzle." In *IA* it appears incorrectly as *shimozzle*.

Appendix 3

EVELYN WAUGH'S HOLLYWOOD
By Donald Greene

As one who has lived for many years equidistant from the site of Sir Francis Hinsley's suicide and the ornate entrance to Whispering Glades, I continue to marvel at how well Evelyn Waugh came to know the topography of Hollywood and its environs during the six weeks or so (February 6 to late March, 1947) that he lived there. Of course we know from his travel books that he had an immense talent for detailed and accu-

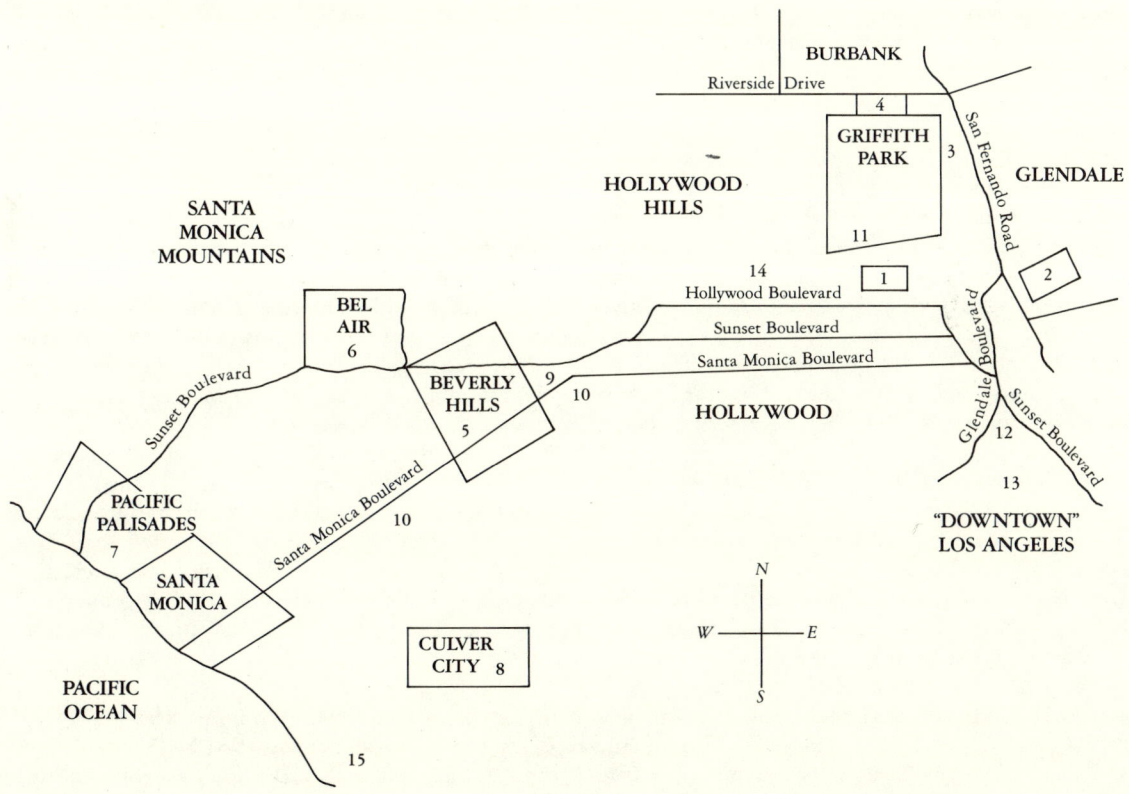

APPENDIX 3

rate observation. His lifelong addiction to moviegoing (and moviemaking) must have given him a good deal of familiarity with the Hollywood scene even before his visit. As well, he had just spent six years in the British Army, sometimes as an intelligence officer, experience that would have made him a skilled map reader (see his hilarious satire of incompetent military map reading in *Put Out More Flags*, chap 2, p. 10).

It is easy to superimpose the movements of the characters of *The Loved One* on a map of Hollywood and its vicinity. Only the sketch on page 209 is possible in the space available here, but it represents not too inaccurately the orientation of the places mentioned and the distances involved. Nowadays the map would be overlaid by the elaborate pattern of the Los Angeles freeway system, but that was rudimentary in Waugh's time.

Some general information for those unfamiliar with this part of the world: The sketch shows only a section, though the best-known section, of Los Angeles County, a huge tract with a population of nearly eight million. The county contains about eighty different incorporated municipalities, of which the largest is the *city* of Los Angeles (population around three million). Los Angeles City includes many "districts," some of which, like Hollywood, were once separate entities but were later absorbed by the city. Bel Air and Pacific Palisades, also shown on the map, are likewise part of the city of Los Angeles. But there are many other communities contiguous to, or even surrounded by, Los Angeles City, which remain independent—on the map note the cities of Beverly Hills, Santa Monica, Culver City, Burbank, and Glendale.

The numbers on the map indicate the localities mentioned in *The Loved One* (and a few others visited by Waugh during his stay). They are described below:

1. The setting of the opening of the novel—Sir Francis Hinsley's decayed residence. In the 1920s "this neglected district was the centre of fashion," and Sir Francis's swimming pool "had once flashed like an aquarium with the limbs of long-departed beauties." But the pool is "empty now, and cracked and overgrowth with weed," a "dry watering-hole."

The locality can only be the fascinating enclave in east Hollywood bounded (for the benefit of any who may want to visit it) by Los Feliz and Franklin boulevards and Edgemont and Western avenues. It has no special name, but it is dominated by its "main street," De Mille Drive, itself dominated by the palace reared by the great Cecil B. De Mille himself. It had been Charlie Chaplin's home in 1918; De Mille later bought it and extended it enormously. Across the road, at 2015 De Mille Drive, lived W. C. Fields, before his death on Christmas Day, 1946 (only a month before Waugh's arrival—perhaps the event drew Waugh's attention to the area). Although some of its mansions display cracked stucco and neglected landscaping, to enter it still puts one in a world exotically different even from that of the surrounding affluent upper-middle-class suburban homes ("the neighbouring native huts" with their "ever-present pulse of music"). The clincher of the identification: when Sir Ambrose Abercrombie left Sir Francis's house, his car "receded towards Hollywood Boulevard." No other former "centre of fashion" of moviedom is near Hollywood Boulevard.

2. "Whispering Glades"—Forest Lawn Memorial Park in Glendale (there are two more recent Forest Lawn subsidiaries, but neither has the glamour and mystique of the original). The close correspondence of Waugh's creation to the actual Forest Lawn has often been recounted: "the Wee Kirk o' Auld Lang Syne" is the Wee Kirk o' the Heather, and so on. The great wrought-iron gates are close to the junction of Glendale Boulevard and San Fernando Road; Dennis Barlow passes by them as he drives from Sir Francis's home (east on Hollywood Boulevard or a parallel street to Glendale Boulevard, then north on San Fernando) to his "place of business."

3. "The Happier Hunting Ground," the pets' mortuary (half a dozen are still listed in the Los Angeles yellow pages, one devoting itself exclusively to the disposal of the ashes of the loved one from an airplane, though none now apparently in this particular vicinity). To reach it, Dennis drives "towards Burbank... almost to the extremity of the city." Though Waugh perhaps meant only that such suburbs as Burbank and Glendale, then more sparsely populated than now, were hardly to be described as "city," it is interesting that a narrow tongue of Los Angeles City proper does project up between San Fernando Road and Griffith Park.

4. The playing field of the "Cricket Club," the haunt of the British movieland émigrés. The Hollywood Cricket Club was founded in 1931 by (Sir) C. Aubrey Smith, often thought to be the original of Sir Ambrose Abercrombie. Shortly afterward it acquired the area

shown on the map just north of Griffith Park as its playing ground. "Turf," as Waugh writes, "does not prosper in southern California," and Sir Aubrey imported grass seed of the proper kind from England to improve it. The field survived until 1981, when, after considerable wrangling, it was absorbed by a new "Equestrian Center." But passersby on Riverside Drive can still see a patch of withered brownish grass where presumably cricket once flourished. During its heyday it was used by such émigré stars as H. B. Warner, Basil Rathbone, and Nigel Bruce ("the actor who plays Dr. Watson," as Waugh noted in his diary for February 13, after meeting him). I cannot find that the field ever possessed a "pavilion" such as that in which the club's members convened to receive Sir Ambrose's instructions: their convivial gathering spot seems to have been the nearby Old Trail Inn, now a Mexican restaurant.

5. Beverly Hills.

6. Bel Air.

7. Pacific Palisades. The more fashionable areas in which Sir Ambrose successively relocated. During the Waughs' visit, they stayed first at the Bel Air Hotel (701 Stone Canyon Road, Bel Air) and then at the Beverly Hills Hotel (9641 Sunset Boulevard). The "Beverly-Waldorf," where Aimée's work as coiffeuse to Mrs. Komstock proved to be her entree to Whispering Glades, is no doubt the Beverly-Wilshire (9500 Wilshire Boulevard, Beverly Hills). All three hotels retain their elegance; the Bel Air retains its exotic setting, reminiscent, Waugh thought, of Addis Ababa.

8. Culver City, whose principal landmark is the great Metro-Goldwyn-Mayer (Megalopolitan) studio, the scene of Sir Francis's days of glory and his later debacle. Waugh visited it often in connection with the abortive filming of *Brideshead Revisited* and commented acidly on it in his diaries (in Gore Vidal's novel *Myron* the hero finds himself indefinitely entrapped, by a time warp, in the same MGM studio complex of the 1940s).

9. The famous Garden of Allah Hotel (in American editions called the Tents of Kedar, no doubt for fear of a suit for damages), where "poor Leo," " fallen from great heights," died with his bill unpaid. At least two books recounting its history have been published, one by Sheilah Graham, mistress of F. Scott Fitzgerald, who was among its many movie-connected habitués. The hotel was founded by the actress Alla Nazimova in the 1920s and finally collapsed in the 1950s. Its site, 8150 Sunset Boulevard, is occupied by a branch of the Great Western Savings and Loan Association, which preserves a somewhat dilapidated model of its raffish predecessor.

10. Either of the two locations so marked could be the site of the unprepossessing home of Mr. Joyboy and his Mom. "They travelled a long way down Santa Monica Boulevard" before reaching the "building estate" — in American, "development" — where it was situated. Obviously this could not have been in the section of Santa Monica Boulevard that runs through Beverly Hills, but it might have been on either side of it. Both areas are nowadays well built up and prosperous, but, as Waugh reports, the Los Angeles of 1947 was "full of vacant lots and filling stations and nondescript buildings." Here and there on Santa Monica Boulevard can still be seen a few remnants of the track of the streetcar on which Aimée returned to her apartment near Whispering Glades, unescorted by the ungallant Mr. Joyboy.

11. Griffith Park Observatory, site of the Planetarium where Miss Poski, Dennis's colleague at the Happier Hunting Ground, has a date on the day we first meet her and where, later, exhausted by the search for an appropriate poem to present to the finicky Aimée, Dennis takes her. It is still a popular locale for inexpensive dating.

12. Angelus Temple, of the Four Square Gospel Church (1100 Glendale Boulevard), raised to prominence by its first pastor, the Reverend Aimée Semple Macpherson (perhaps the model for Mrs. Ape in *Vile Bodies*), after whom Aimée Thanatogenos was named. It was here that her father "lost his money in religion." It flourished until recently under the aegis of the Reverend Aimée's son.

13. "Downtown" — the business center of Los Angeles. The editorial offices of the local newspapers are here; in one of them worked Mr. Slump and his colleague, who jointly constituted the Guru Brahmin, the agent of Aimée's downfall. He succeeded "Aunt Lydia" (the *Los Angeles Times* nowadays prints "Dear Abby," and the *Herald-Examiner* "Ann Landers").

It is testimony to Waugh's topographical expertise that twice (pp. 119, 127, in the Little, Brown edition) he gets the distance of the Guru's office to Aimée's cosmetic room at Whispering Glades exactly right — five miles. Only once, I think, does Waugh's map reading slip; even on today's freeways, Dennis could

APPENDIX 3

hardly have got from his place of work near Burbank to the Heinkels' residence on Via Dolorosa, Bel Air, in so short a time as half an hour. There are, incidentally, more than five hundred streets in Los Angeles County named "Via," though none apparently in Bel Air, and none, it may be said to the credit of Los Angeles, with so blasphemous an addition as "Dolorosa"—the Via Dolorosa was the route over which Christ bore his cross. Another note on street nomenclature: Dennis proposes to carry on his new occupation of nonsectarian clergyman ("Funerals a speciality") at 1154 Arbuckle Avenue. There is an Arbuckle Avenue in the far reaches of the San Fernando Valley, but the actual site of the Fatty Arbuckle affair of the 1920s, still the greatest sex-and-death scandal ever to hit Hollywood, is quite close to Sir Francis Hinsley's residence.

Some may be a little bothered by the geography of the Cricket Club, where, at the end of Sir Ambrose Abercrombie's report on the demise of Sir Francis Hinsley, "the sun sank below the bushy western hillside. The sky was still bright but a shadow crept over the tough and ragged grass of the cricket field, bringing with it a sharp chill" (a fine burlesque of that favorite Victorian trope, the pathetic fallacy). The bushy hillside of Griffith Park is south rather than west of the grounds of the Hollywood Cricket Club. But in winter, the season of Waugh's visit, and, presumably, of Sir Francis's suicide, sunset would in fact take place toward the southwest, over the Hollywood Hills. Waugh was evidently familiar with the "Mediterranean" climate of Los Angeles, as well as its topography. *The Loved One* opens during the "dry season," in August or September, when the heat is "barely supportable" until the sea breeze arises in the late afternoon, and "the dry sounds of summer . . . the grating cicadas" are heard. Then "weeks passed, the rains came," and for the rest of the story we are in the "rainy season," from around November to March.

For those interested in Waugh's own movements during his visit, 14 is the location of Immaculate Heart High School, probably the "fine convent school in the hills" where he lunched on 11 February (though it might also have been Marymount High School, 10643 Sunset Boulevard, Bel Air), and 15 is the location of Loyola University, which he visited the same evening.

Author's Postscript: Professor James Durbin, a colleague of Donald Greene's at the University of Southern California, adds the following:

> The De Mille house is actually two houses. Charlie Chaplin used to be D.M.'s next-door neighbor, and when the Chaplins moved farther west to keep up with the fashion, Cecil B. bought their place. He connected the two with a roofed arcade and used the former Chaplin mansion as his office. A secretary still puts a fresh rose on his desk every morning (a neat Waugh touch) and one wall is entirely covered by a life-size painting of Victor Mature as Samson in *Samson and Delilah*. Some of De Mille's Oscars stand, badly in need of polish, on a very rickety table just by the back door.

Appendix 4

MAP OF AZANIA

The Azanian Empire plays a significant role in *Black Mischief* and in the short story "Incident in Azania." For certain editions of *Black Mischief*, Waugh supplied a map of this island empire.

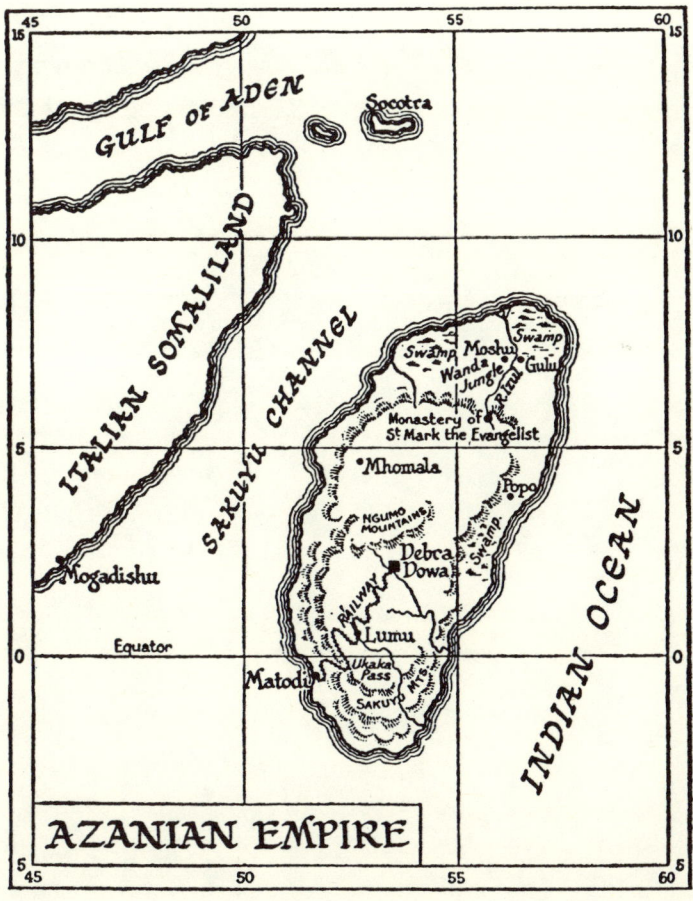

BIBLIOGRAPHY

I. Works by Waugh

"The Balance," in *Georgian Stories*. London: Chapman and Hall, 1926.
Basil Seal Rides Again. Boston: Little, Brown, 1963.
Black Mischief. London: Chapman and Hall, 1932.
Brideshead Revisited. Boston: Little, Brown, 1945.
Charles Ryder's Schooldays and Other Stories. Boston: Little, Brown, 1982.
"Compassion," *Month*, NS, 2 August 1949, 79–98.
"Consequences," *Manchester Guardian*, 4 April 1929, 18.
"The Curse of the Horse Race," in *Little Innocents: Childhood Reminiscences*. London: Cobden Sanderson, 1932.
Decline and Fall. London: Chapman and Hall, 1928.
The Diaries of Evelyn Waugh, ed. Michael Davie. Boston: Little, Brown, 1976.
The End of the Battle. Boston: Little Brown, 1961. Entitled *Unconditional Surrender*. London: Chapman and Hall, 1961.
The Essays, Articles and Reviews of Evelyn Waugh, ed. Donat Gallagher. Boston: Little, Brown, 1984.
Evelyn Waugh: Apprentice, ed. Robert Murray Davis. Norman, OK: Pilgrim Books, 1985.
"A Flat in London," *Harper's Bazaar* (New York), June–October 1934, in five installments.
A Handful of Dust. London: Chapman and Hall, 1934.
Helena. Boston: Little, Brown, 1950.
"A House of Gentlefolks," in *The New Decameron: The Fifth Day*, ed. Hugh Chesterman. Oxford: Basil Blackwell, 1927.
The Letters of Evelyn Waugh, ed. Mark Amory. New Haven and New York: Ticknor and Fields, 1980.
A Little Learning. Boston: Chapman and Hall, 1964.
Love Among the Ruins. London: Chapman and Hall, 1953.
The Loved One. Boston: Little, Brown, 1948.
"The Man Who Liked Dickens" in *Hearst's International Combined with Cosmopolitan*, September 1933, 54–57ff.
"The Manager of The Kremlin," *John Bull*, 15 February 1930, 22, 24.
"The Major Intervenes," *Atlantic Monthly*, July 1949, 34–41.
Men at Arms. Boston: Little, Brown, 1952.
"Mr. Crutwell's Little Outing," *Harper's Bazaar* (New York), March 1935, 61ff.
"Mr. Crutwell's Outing," *Nash's Pall Mall Magazine*, May 1935, 30–32ff.
Mr. Loveday's Little Outing and Other Sad Stories. Boston: Little, Brown, 1936.
Monsignor Ronald Knox. Boston: Little, Brown, 1959.
Ninety-Two Days. New York: Farrar & Rinehart, 1934.
Officers and Gentlemen. Boston: Little, Brown, 1955.
The Ordeal of Gilbert Pinfold. Boston: Little, Brown, 1957.
Put Out More Flags. Boston: Little, Brown, 1942.
Remote People. London: Duckworth, 1931.
Robbery Under Law: The Mexican Object Lesson. London: Chapman and Hall, 1939.
Scoop. Boston: Little, Brown, 1938.
"A Sojourn in Neutralia," in *Hearst's International Combined with Cosmopolitan*, November 1947, 67–70ff.
Sword of Honour. Boston: Little, Brown, 1966.
Tactical Exercise. Boston: Little, Brown, 1954.
"This Quota Stuff: Positive Proof That the British Can Make Good Films," *Harper's Bazaar* (London), August 1932, 10–11ff.
Vile Bodies. London: Chapman and Hall, 1930.
When the Going Was Good. London: Little, Brown, 1946.
Work Suspended and Other Stories Written Before the Second World War. London: Chapman and Hall 1948.

II. Works about Waugh

A Bibliography of Evelyn Waugh, eds. Robert Murray Davis, Paul A. Doyle, Donat Gallagher, Charles E. Linck, Winnifred M. Bogaards. Troy, N.Y.: Whitston, 1986.
Acton, Harold, *Memoirs of an Aesthete 1939–1969*. New York: Viking, 1971.
Balfour, Patrick, *Society Racket*. London: John Long, 1933.
Blythe, Ronald, *The Age of Illusion*. Boston: Houghton Mifflin, 1964.

BIBLIOGRAPHY

Bowra, Maurice, *Memories 1898–1939*. Cambridge: Harvard University Press, 1967.

Cyril Connolly: Journal and Memoirs, ed. David Pryce-Jones. New York: Ticknor and Fields, 1984.

Davis, Robert Murray, *Evelyn Waugh, Writer*. Norman, Okla.: Pilgrim Books, 1981.

———, "*Vile Bodies* in Typescript," *EWN*, Winter 1977, pp. 7–8.

Doyle, Paul A., "That Poem in *The Loved One*," *EWN*, Winter 1981, pp. 6–7.

Fielding, Daphne, *The Duchess of Jermyn Street*. Boston: Little, Brown, 1964.

Greene, Donald, "Another Waugh Identification: Mrs. Beaver," *EWN*, Spring 1987, pp. 1–2.

———, "Reality into Art: Some Detective Notes on Waugh," *EWN*, Spring 1986, pp. 1–5.

———, "Real-life counterparts of Ritchie-Hook and Rex Mottram," *EWN*, Autumn 1975, pp. 7–9.

———, "Sir Ralph Brompton — An Identification," *EWN*, Winter 1974, pp. 1–3.

Gribble, Thomas A., "The Nature of a Trimmer," *EWN*, Autumn 1981, pp. 1–3.

Hazen, Allen T. and W. S. Lewis, *A Catalogue of Horace Walpole's Library*, 3 vols. New Haven: Yale University Press, 1969.

Heath, Jeffrey, *The Picturesque Prison: Evelyn Waugh and His Writings*. Kingston and Montreal: McGill-Queens University Press, 1982.

Lynch, James J., "An Allusion to Dante in *Men at Arms*," *EWN*, Winter 1984, p. 7.

Martin, W. R. "Misdated Crouchback Entry," *EWN*, Spring 1975, p. 7.

McAleer, Edward C., "*Decline and Fall* as Imitation," *EWN*, Winter 1973, pp. 1–4.

Mitford, Nancy, *Love in a Cold Climate*. London: Hamilton, 1949.

Mosley, Diana, *A Life of Contrasts*. London: Hamilton, 1977.

Quennell, Peter, "A Kingdom of Cokayne," in *Evelyn Waugh and His World*, ed. David Pryce-Jones. Boston: Little, Brown, 1973, pp. 23–38.

———, *Customs and Characters*. Boston: Little, Brown, 1982.

———, *The Wanton Chase*. New York: Atheneum, 1980.

Scheideman, J. W., "'In Rich Milwaukee Accents,'" *EWN*, Autumn 1983, p. 3.

St. John, John, *To the War with Waugh*. London: Whittington Press, 1973.

Sykes, Christopher, *Evelyn Waugh: A Biography*. Boston: Little Brown, 1975.

Waugh, Alec, *My Brother Evelyn and Other Portraits*. New York: Farrar, Straus and Giroux, 1967.

Wykes, David, "Evelyn Waugh's Sword of Volgograd," *DQR*, 1977, pp. 82–99.

INDEX TO THE GLOSSARY

A

A.A., 15, 83
abattoirs, 23
A.B.C., 27
A.B.C. shop, 111
Abdul El Krim, 47
"Abou Ben Adhem," 106
above stairs, 3
Absolution, 95
Academy, 43
Accidenti! Porca miseria, 83
Achilles statue, 3
A.C.I.G.S., 83
ack, 73
Ack-Ack, 73
Acre, 15, 47
across the river, 3
Actium, 67
Act of Emancipation, 95
Adam room, 47
ADDIS, 35
Aden, 95
ADS, 83
Aelia Capitolina, 67
Aeneas, 67
Aeons, 67
affection for the horse, 95
Afridi, 83
A.F.V.'s, 35
A.G., 83
Agadir, 27
Agamemnon, 61
agape, 67
Agincourt, 15, 47, 73
Ah, chère madame, 83
Ahriman, 67
"Aimée, thy beauty is to me . . . ," 61
Aintree, 27

Aitkin, William Maxwell, 53, 86
Aladdin's treasury, 47
Alban, 67
Albert I, 73
Albert Hall, 91
Alcazar, 59
Alcestis, 61
Alcibiades, 35
ALCs, 83
Aleppo, 47
Alex, 83
Alexander, General, 95
Alexander's visit to Siwa, 73
Alhambra, 43
Ali Baba's lamp, 83
alienist, 109
Allectus, 67
All Souls, 47, 95
All Soul's Day, 83
Alma Tadema, Laurence, 109
Almanak de Gotha, 15
almoner, 95
Alpes-Maritimes, 83
Alsatian, 83
Altar of the Repose, 73
Altmark, 73
ambulatory, 23
American slump, 105
AMGOT, 83
amphoras, 27
Ampleforth, 47
Anabaptists, 61
Analogies, 27
Andersen, Hans, 95
the immortal Anderson couple, 61
Andromeda-like, 108
And two pence for the cheque, 15
Angelus, 23
Anglais . . . Par-là, 83

Anglo-Catholics, 47
Anglo-Sephardi, 95
angst, 91
animal snap, 23
Annamese, 3, 23
annexation of the Baltic republics, 83
A.N. Other, 95
Antic Hay, 47
Anti-Comintern pact, 83
Antigone, 61
Antioch, 67
Anzac, 73
Anzio, 95
A.O., 95
apaches, 47, 108
Aphrodite of Melos, 35
Apollo, 61
Apostolic Claims of the Church of Abyssinia, 3
Apuleius's ass, 35
Apulia, 95
Arbuckle Avenue, 61
Arcady, 3
Arciprete, 73
Arianizer, 67
Aristotle, Works of (illustrated), 15
Arius, 67
Arlen, Mr., 3, 23
Arlenish, 15
Armageddon, 83
Armistice Day, 15
Army class, 59
Army Class B, 106
A.R.P., 35, 83
Arrivederci, 31, 43, 95
Ars longa, 35
artificial poppies, 15
art nouveau, 3

217

INDEX TO THE GLOSSARY

Arundel prints, 43, 47
Ascot, 3, 35
Ashmolean Museum, 47
Ash Wednesday, 73
askar, 23
Asquith, 35, 95
Astarte, 67
A.T., 83, 95
À tes beaux yeux, 35
Athenaeum Club, 3, 43
Athenia, 35
Atlas, 47
Atlas caids, 27
ATM, 73
At Philippi, 79
A.T.S., 35
Attention, je vous en prie, 31
at the Bar, 3
at the shop, 3
Attic, 61
Attlee Brigade, 111
A/Ty, 95
Auchinleck, Sir Claude, 95
Augustus, 67
Aurelian, 67
Ave atque vale, 67
Ave Imperatrix Immortalis..., 110
"Aves," 73
Avez-vous les jeunes filles de Madame Beste-Chetwynde?, 3
awful cloud on Sinai, 95
Aylesbury, 15
Ayrshire, 83

B

Bacchic, 3
Bach, 110
back-benchers, 83
Babylonian captivity, 3
Badajos, 111
badders, 27
Bad hats every one of them, 15, 105
Bakerloo railway, 35
Balaclava, 47, 95
Baldachino at St. Peter's, 47
Baldwin, 47
ballata station, 27
Balliol, 96
balls up, 73
Banja, 31
Bannockburn, 47

Banquo, 96
Barbizon, 47
Barchester Towers, 23
Barham, 73
Bari...bones of St. Nicholas, 111
Barnardo case, 27
Barren Fig Tree, 23
Barrie, Sir James, 96
Bart., 16, 109
Bartolozzi prints, 43
Basque district, the, 3
Bassett-Lowkes, 35
batman, 35, 73
battels, 4, 47
Battle in the West where Arthur fell, 47
Battle of Britain, 83
Battle of Malplaquet, 73
Battle Schools, 73
Batum, 47
Bauhaus at Dessau, 4
Bayswater, 48
Beach, Sylvia, 96
beak, 43, 81
beano, 4, 67
Beardsley, Aubrey, 35, 41
Beatific Vision, 48
Beaverbrook, Lord, 53, 86
Bechuanaland, 73
Bechuana tummy, 73
beaucoup, 31
beaver, the, 4
Beckley, 4
Beddoes, Thomas L., 35
Bedfordshire for you, 74
Bedivere, 4, 27
Beds and Herts or the Black Watch, 74
Beerbohm, Max, 43
béguin, 35
being fly, 83
Bel Air, 61
Belgian Futurist, 48
Belgrave Square, 4
Belgravia, 74
Belisha crossing, 43
Bell, Clive, 43, 48
belle époque, 105
bell for Hall, 106
Bellini, Giovanni, 48, 105
"Bells of Heaven, The," 106
Benares, 4, 96
Benares trays, 31

Bench, 35
Benedictus, 96
Benediteme padre,..., 74
Benghazi, 83
Bennett, Arnold, 4, 61
Berber, 43
Bergner, Elisabeth, 31
Bessie Cotter, 109
bêtise, 48
Bevan-Eden coalition, 81
Bevis, 27
BGS, 83
Biarritz, 27
bibelots, 96
biffing, 74
Bilbao, 61
bimetallism, 27
bimetallists, 59
birds, 81
Bisley, 83
Bithynia, 4, 67
Black and Tans, 23
Black Birds, 48
blackleg, 59
black-shirt, 74
blackwater, 23
Blakewell, 31
Blackwell's, 48
Blanco, 74
blaspheming against the beauties..., 4
Blast, 16
Blessed Sacrament, 48
blighter, 106
blind, 110
blood, 74
bloods, 96
Bloody Mary, 4
Bloomsbury, 4
blot your copy book, 74, 96
blow-out, a, 67
Blücher, Gebhard von, 35
Bluebell, 96
Blue Books, 16
blue funk, 74
blue jobs, 84
Blues, 74, 96
Blunden, Edmund, 61
B.M., 74, 84
BNC, 48
Boadicea, 67
Boar's Hill, 4, 48
boater hat, 61

INDEX TO THE GLOSSARY

bob, 4, 48, 74
bobby, 4
Boccaccio, Giovanni, 105
Boche, 74
Bodleian, 4
Boeotian, 61
Boer farms, 108
Boeuf sur le Toit, 48
Bohemia, 74
boiled, 84
boil out, 74
Boller blind, 4
Bollinger Club, 4
bolshie, 106
bondieuserie, 48
Bond Street, 16
Bond Street and Park Lane, 4
bone-setting, 27
bonhommous, 4
bonnet, 16, 84
Bonnie Prince Charlie, 84
boodle, 23
books . . . . in my list, 16
Boots subscriber, 61
Bordighera, 48, 96
Borghese Gardens, 84, 96
Bosch, Jerome, 84
bosh, 48
Botany Bay, 35
both Archbishops, 16
bottles under the board, 16
Boucher, François, 91
Bouchers, 74
Boulanger, 4
Boulestin, 84
Boulestin's *Conduct of Kitchen*, 4
Boulle, André, 74
boundaries inclusive and exclusive, 36
bowler, 96
Box, The, 91
box-wallah, 74
Boxer rising, 4
Bracken, Brendan, 84
Brahms, Caryl, 85
Brancusi, Constantin, 36, 48
Brand from the Burning, A, 16
Brazzaville, 84
Brendan's, 84
Bren gun, 36, 74
Bricktop's and the Bal Nègre, 48
Brigade tie, 91
Briggs as Brolly, 4

Bright Young People, 16
Brindisi, 105
Brinkman ma., 74
British Council, 59
British warm, 96
Broadmoor, 4
broke his Lenten fast, 84
Bronzino Venus, 110
brook Kedron, 23
Brooke, Rupert, 36, 61, 84
Brother Grandee, 48
Broughton, 106
Brown, Ford Madox, 43
Brown House, 36
Brown Shirt, 36
Brummel, Beau, 16, 73
Brutus, 67
"Bubbles," 48
Buda-Pesth, 4, 105
Bude, 16
Bühl, Charles, 105
Bulldog Drummond, 36
Bullingdon, 48, 109, 110
bulrushes, the burning bush . . . , 96
bum-boats, 67
bunked, 48
Burberry, 16
burgee, 74
Burke, 16
Burton's stucco tent, 96
"Bury the great Knight . . . ," 61
buskers, 48
Butcher Cumberland, 16
bye-term, 106
Byron, 48
Bystander, 106

C

Ça, 59
Ça c'est le hoquet, 59
cachet Faivre, 16
caid, 27
Caine, Sir Hall, 96
Cain's wife, 4
Calais, 74
called out the marker, 74
Ça madame, c'est génial, 84
came out, 96, 109
campaigns on the Afghan frontier, 5
Canadians . . . Dieppe, 96
Canea, 84

Canning, 48, 110
Canning Town, 16
Canon, 74
canon, 74
canty, 61
Canvey Island, 96
Cape Town, 84
Cap Ferrat, 48
capitation grant, 74
capitulations, 31, 43
Captain Morvin's Riding Academy, 48
"captains and the kings depart, The," 96
Cardiff, 5
Career, The . . . , 67
Carinus, 67
Carlton, 48
Carlton House Terrace, 5
Caroline, 96
Carpaccio, 36
Carpentier, Georges, 48
Carthusian tie, 106
Cartier, 5
Carus, Marcus Aurelius, 67
Casanova Hotel, 16
cassava, 27
Castellane, Boni de, 96
cat, to, 27
Catalan refugees, 84
catechism, 48
catechumen, 67
Cathedral, 96
Catherine, 67
Cavafy, Constantine, 84
cave, 91
Cavour, Camillo, 96
censed, 96
certificates, 5, 106
Cervantes, 36
Cesare armato, 74
C'è scappata la mucca, 84
C'è scappato il capitano, 84
Cézanne, Paul, 36, 43, 48
Chadband, Mr., 91
chaffing, 74
Challoner, Richard, 84, 98
Châlons, 67
Chamberlain, Neville, 48, 74
Champs Elysées, 5
chancery, 23
Chanel diamonds, 5

INDEX TO THE GLOSSARY

"Change and decay in all around I see," 31
chantry, 27
charabancs, 27
"Charge of the Light Brigade, The," 48
Charing Cross Road, 5
Charles I, 36
"Charlie copped it," 84
Charlus, 48
Chartreuse de Parme, 84
Charvet, 5
chassés, 74
Chatham, 48, 110
Chelsea, 5
Cheltenham Spa, 5
chemist, 23
Chère madame, quel . . ., 84
Chesham Bois, 16
Cheyne Walk, 5
Chiang, 96
Chief Conservative Whip, 23, 36
Chief Constable, 16
Childermas, 97
Chindits, 97
Chippendale, Thomas, 48
Chipps, the Carpenter's daughter, Miss, 25
XP, 68
chits, 84, 109
chloral, 16
Chlorus, 67
"Choice, The," 106
Choral Communion, 106
chotá pegs, 23, 31, 74
Christ Church Grind, 36, 109
Christie's, 16
chucked, 27
Chums, 27, 36
Churchill . . . Sphinx, 96
churchings, 5
church-warden, 31
C.I.G.S., 84
C-in-C, 84
Cincinnatus, 16
Cin no Djinñ how?, 27
Circe, 84
circus factions, 27
City, the, 74, 111
Ciudad Bolivar, 27
clap, 74
Claudius, 67
Clausewitz, Karl von, 97

clear as the horn of Roland, 84
cleft staff, 23
cleft sticks, 31, 105
Clive, Robert, 48
clock golf, 23
Clos de Bère, 48
Clovis's army, 48
coat, 31
cobs, 109
Cochran, Charles Blake, 36
Cock-a-hoop, 59
Cocktail Party, The, 91
Cocteau, Jean, 36, 49
Coimbra, 97
Cointreau, 110
Coldstream blazer, 61
Coldstream Guards, 27, 74
Collections papers, 49, 110
Colleoni, Bartolomeo, 49
Colombo, 16
combinations, 5
come a cropper, 49
Comic Muse, 59
Coming to the Graves?, 106
coming up, 49
Commander-in-Chief, 84
comme ça, 31
Commem., 49
Comment dit-on en français 'hiccup'?, 59
Comment dit-on humidor?, 31
commissionaire, 108
commoner's gown, 5
Common Room, 5
company schemes, 75
comprenez, 31
Compton-Burnett, Ivy, 61
Concorso Ippico, 84
Condamine, Robin de la, 64
Condominium, 109
Confiteor, 97
conform, 84
congress at Teheran, 97
Connolly, Cyril, 62
consecration of Archbishop Parker, the, 5
consequences, 23
constituency, 24, 27
construe, 84
Convents in the Manuelo style, 44
Coo, 17, 24, 110
Cook's offices, 28, 49
cop it, 91
cop it hot, 5

cop one, 97
copper, 43
coprophagists, 24
Coptic elder, 67
Corbusier, 5
Cor chase my Aunt Fanny, 36
Cor . . . dekko, 97
Corfu, 5
Corinthian tie, 107
corner turned up, 5
Corporate Communion, 49
Corybantes, 91
cosseted, 75
Côte d'Azur, 31, 97
Cottesmore, 28
cotton famine, 5
Country House Rag, 5
county families, 5
Courantyne, 28
Court of St. James's, 59
covered lines, 75
cow-cake, 109
Cowes, 97
CP oblique RX . . . , 84
cracking form, 97
Craig, Edward G., 85
Crane, Walter, 107
"Cras, Hora septem," 97
crazy pavements, 31
Creative Endeavour, 17
Crécy, 36
crêpe de chine, 5
Cressid, 49
Crick, the, 5
cribs, 81
Crillon, 105
crimson of a monsignor, 97
Cripps's Fund, Lady, 99
Crisis years, 109
crocodile, 49
crofters, 85
Crosse and Blackwell's regiment, 36
crossing the Red Sea, 97
Crown Derby, 81, 105
Croydon, 5, 24
cruiser Fiji was torpedoed, 75
Crump's, Lottie, 25
C.S.M., 75, 85
Ctesiphon, 68
cubbing, 31
Cunarder, 24, 62
curate's wife, 5
Curzon, Lord and Elinor Glyn, 97

INDEX TO THE GLOSSARY

cushy, 5
cut, 5
cutting, 17
Cymbeline, 68
cypher book, 24

D

dado, 28
Daily News, 5
Dakar, 75
Dakota, 97, 111
Dali, 36
Dalmatia, 68, 97
Dante's *Purgatorio*, 17
Danzig, 59
Darby and Joan, 97
Dardanelles, 5
Dar-es-Salaam, 36
Darling, Grace, 49
Dartmouth, 75, 107
Daumier, Honoré, 49, 107
Daumier's law courts, 59
Davy Jones' locker, 6
day Churchill became Prime Minister, 75
D.B.S., 24
dead ground, 75
deal, 36
Dean Stanley's *Eastern Church*, 6
death duties, 28, 111
Deaths of the Persecutors, 68
debate with Jesus, 6
Debrett, 17, 49
Decameron, 105
de Castellane, Boni, 96
Dedlock, Leicester, 28
Defence Corps, 49
D.4.12, 6
DeGaulle, General Charles, 75
Deirdre, 62
dekko, 75, 85
Delacroix, Eugène, 49
Demerara, 28
Demiurge, 68
demobilized, 28
Deposition, 85
De Profundis, 97
Derby day, 17
désoeuvré, 59
Deuxième service, 49
Diaghilev, 36, 49

Diary of a Nobody, The, 49
dibs, 107
dicky, 17
Dies Irae, 97
Diocletian, 68
dippy, 5
Dispersal, 97
Disraeli, 36
Dissent, 75
Distressed Area, 31
d'Italie, 107
Divine Discontent, 17
Dizzy, 31
D.L.F., 85
do down, 31
"dog it was that died, The," 36, 97
doings, the, 5
Dolce far niente, 91
Domestic Bursar, 5
domestic Tudor, 6
Domine non sum dignus, 75
Dominican, 49, 109
Dominican . . . Advent, 97
Donatus, 68
done in, 81
done out, 43
dons, 24, 43
Don't Mr. Disraeli, 85
doppelganger, 75
Doric temple, 49
Dositheus, 68
dotty, 6
douanier, 32
Double Greek, 107
Doubting Hall, 17
douceur de vivre, 97
Douro, 49
Dover Street, 6
dower house, 68, 111
Downside, 75, 85
Dowson, Ernest, 62
doyen, 24
D.P.S., 85
D.Q.M.G., 85
drabs, 97
Dracula, Major, 97
dragoman, 32
Drake, Francis Sir, 49
Dreparium, 68
dressed up to the nines, 6
Dreyfus' innocence, 24, 43
Drummond, Bulldog, 36
dryclinkers, 24

D.S.D., 85
D.S.O., 85
D.T.'s, 6, 97
ducal house, 105
Duchess of Malfi, 49
ducks, 36
ducks and drakes, 75
Du Côté de Chez Beaver, 28
Du Côté De Chez Todd, 28
Duke of Wellington at St. Paul's, 75
Duke of York Steps, 85
du Maurier, George, 109
dumb crambo, 43
dun, 17
Dunkirk, 75
Durban, 24, 85
dust up, 24
d.v., 108
dye the carnation for his buttonhole, 17

E

Earl of Essex, 75
"earth is the Lord's . . . , The," 85
East Finchley, 32
Easter duties, 85
Eaton Terrace, 97
eau de Nil, 17
Ebionites, 6
Ecce ancilla Domini . . . , 24
Ecco ci siamo, signori, 49
Edgware Road, 6
Edmonton, 6
Edward of Carnarvon, 6
Edwardian era, 17
Edward Prince of Wales, 6
Egdon Heath Penal Settlement, 6
Ego te absolvo in nomine Patris, 49
18B, 91
1800 hours, 75
Eights week, 49, 111
Eisteddfod, 6
Elaine, 28
electric brougham, 6
1130, 97
Elgin marble, 32
Elizabeth, Princess, 19
Elizabeth to her Archbishop, Queen, 64
Elliott, Ebenezer, 89
Ellis, Havelock, 6

INDEX TO THE GLOSSARY

emblazoned with the Royal Arms, 6
Eminent Victorians, 49
"empress... Christian slave," 6
en brosse, 75
enfant terrible, 75
Eno's, 24
Ensa, 75
entail, 49
Entrate e s'accomode, 97
epergne, 49
Ephesus, 49
episcopal lawn sleeves, 17
Erchman, 36
Eritrea, 24
Eros, 109
Esperanto, 24
Ethelred the Unready, 32, 109
Et in Arcadia Ego, 50
Eton, 37
Eton-cropped, 17
Eton Rambler tie, 62
Eton suits, 6
Et pour, 85
Et uxor tua?, 98
E.V., 110
Evensong, 6
Evian, 24
Évidemment, 59
Excusez-moi, mon père, 85
ex-Emperor of Germany, 17
Expressionismus, 110
extension night, an, 108
Exultet, 85

F

Facilius loqui latine, 98
factor, 85
factotum, 98
fags, 107
F.A.N.Y., 98
Farewell to Arms, A, 28
Farm Street, 50, 75
farouche, 37
fast, 6
Father Brown, 50
Father Christmas, 50
Father Rank, 75
fatigue du Nord, la, 50
F.D.L.'s, 37
F.E., 50
Februato Juno, 75

fender, 85
fête champêtre, 50
fifth form, 6
Fiji, 75
filbert, 91
"Fine Flower of the Nation," 85
Firbank, Ronald, 50
First Ashanti War, 75
first Crusade, the, 6
fist in Barcelona, 81
Fitzgerald, Scott, 98
five and sixpence, 6
Five per cent of ninety pounds, 7
fives, 111
five-to-two, 62
fixative, 110
fixed lines, 75
fizzer, 76
flag day, 7
flageolet, 17
Flanders, 7
flap, 50, 76
Flavian family, 68
Flaxman Greeks, 37, 43, 98
flea in the ear, 105
Flecker, James E., 62
Fleet Street, 85
Flint and Denbigh Herald, 7
floater, 32, 98
Floreat Azania, 24
Florentine Quattrocento, 50
Floribus Austrum, 32
fly, 107
Flying Scotsman, The, 50
F.O., 24
Foggia, 98
footer, 50, 76
"For East is East and West is West," 17
formation of the Coalition, the, 7
Forster... *Guide*, 85
Forsyte Saga, 7
Fortitude, 107
forty aces and two-fifty for the rubber, 17
Founder's port, 7
Four Last Things, 17, 50
four months' solitary, 7
Four Square Gospel, 62
"43," 109
fou rire, 43
1415, 76
Fowler, Henry, 98

Fox, 17
Fragonard, Jean, 91, 98
Français, 85
Français de Dakar, 76
Franco, Francisco, 50, 98
freehold, 43
Free State, 106
Freetown, 76
French novels of the second empire, 50
F.R.G.S., 32
Freud, Sigmund, 62
frightful wax, 76
frisson, 7
Fritsch, Werner von, 37
Frith, 43
froggy, 76
frogs, 108
Fry, Roger, 50
Fuseli, Henry, 98
Fuzzy-Wuzzy in the Soudan, 7, 108

G

gaffes raisonnées, 76
Gaius, 68
Galahad, 28
Galerius, 68
Galla, 24
Galleface in Colombo, 91
Gallic, 68
Gallienus, 68
Gallipoli, 50, 85
game leg, 7
Gamp, Mrs., 98
Garbo, 32
garconnière, 50
Garden of Gethsemane, 68
Garden of the Soul, 98
Garge, 32
Garibaldi, 98
Garnett, David, 52
Garsington, 50
gated, 50
Gauguin, Paul, 43, 50
Gaul, 68
gave him the raspberry, 108
Gawaine, 28
gazetted, 98
gear, 76
gêne, 28
general dogsbody, 76

INDEX TO THE GLOSSARY

General Strike, 7, 37
Geneva, 7
gentleman's relish, 17
George, 50
Georges, 50
George IV, 37
Georgetown, 28
Georgian Poetry, 50, 107
German Uhlans, 76
Gestapo, 85, 98
Gethsemane, 51
gets gay, 7
get sniffy, 7
geyser, 37
G.H.Q.M.E., 85
Gib, 85
Gide, André, 51
Gilbert and Sullivan, 7, 51
Gioconda, La, 51
give him socks, 98
given a dose, 51
gives me the pip, 7
Gladstone, William E., 98
Glencoe, 87
Gnostic, 68
Goan, 24, 76, 109
G.O.C.s, 85
"God gave all men all earth to love...," 105
God of Kipling's "Recessional," 76
"God set her brave eyes wide apart," 62
"God's in His heaven...," 7
Goebbels, 37, 51
Goering, 37, 51
goggling, 76
going to Brighton, 76
Golden Bough, The, 7
Golden Treasury, The, 107
Golgotha, 68
golliwog, 28
General? Regan...Cornwall, 91
Goodwood week, 37
Gorbals, 51, 85
Gordian, 68
Gordon, General, 7, 37, 110
gorge of Roncesvalles, 55, 85
Gosse, Edmund Sir, 62
Gosse, Philip Henry, 91
Got the push, 7
Gothic revival, 107
gouache, 92
Government Front Bench, 92

Government House at Ottawa, 17
Goya, Francisco, 76
Grace Darling, 49
"Grace of God is in courtesy," 98
Grand chemin de Fer d'Azanie, 24
grand couturier, 85
Grand Hotel in Rome, 98
grandmother's steps, 51, 68
Grand Sanhedrin, 62
gratia plena, 24
Gratias, 98
Gratias tibi, 98
grazier, 92
grease-caked Channel swimmer, 7
greased, 107
Great North Road, 17
Great Panjandrum, 24
Greats, 43, 51
great sucks, 51
great tattoo of Aldershot, 24
Great Western, 28
Great West Road, 85
Green Jackets, 85
"green thought in a green place, a," 37
Grenadiers, 51, 62
Greswold major, 85
Gretna Green Romances, 105
Grid, 51
Grimm, Jacob and Wilhelm, 98
Grinling Gibbons, 37
grip, 76
grog tray, 28
Grosvenor Square, 37
GSO1, 85
G.S.O.2, 76, 98
GSO2(Q), 76
G1098, 76
G2, 76, 98
G.2 Training, 76
Guards tie, 92
guichet, 62
Guinevere, 28
gymkhana, 17, 24, 109
Gyppy, 85

H

Habsburg Empire, 98
"Had he not moved unseen...?," 8
ha-ha, 105
Halberdiers, 76

Halfpenny, William, 44
Halifax, Edward F.L.W., 51
Hall, 107
halma, 24, 51
Halte-la! Qui vive?, 76
Hamburg, 8
Hamilton-Grand, 86
Handel, George F., 62
handkerchief at Downside, 76
Hanover Terrace, 62
Hansard, 17, 51
Hanse ghetto, 8
ha'p'orth, 105
Happy families, 25, 76
hard cheese, 28, 106
Hardy, Thomas, 8
Harley Street, 17, 76
Haroun al-Raschid, 25
"Has he given all to his daughters?," 17
Hassall's *History*, 107
hatchment, 98
Hatton Garden, 51
Hawkins, John Sir, 51
Hawksmoor, 32
Hay, Ian, 76
Hay, Mr. Will, 59
Head's House, the, 107
he and an American sang..., 17
Heart of the Bruce, the, 61
Heart of the Matter, The, 76
heart-to-hearter, 98
Hegel, Georg W.F., 51
He had made a desert..., 81
H.I.M., 25
Helen and Menelaus, 86
Helena, 68
Helena's isle, 68
Heliogabalus, 32
heliograph, 77
Hellas, 62
Hemingway...Bret, 98
Henley, William E., 62, 108
Henley Regatta, 51
Henrietta Street, 18
Henry's speech on St. Crispin's Day, 51
Hera in the arms of Zeus, 77
Here, my dear Watson, 86
Hertford, 8
her twin brethren, 68
Hesperides, 62
High, the, 8, 109

INDEX TO THE GLOSSARY

high church, 77
High Commissioner, 18
high fender of diamonds, 18
Hindu Love-song, 62
Hinsley, Cardinal, 98
Hinsley, Francis, 65
"His Aunt Jobiska made him drink...," 105
historic Liberal campaign of 1906, the, 8
History Previous, 51
Hittite tablets, 77
HLI, 86
HMG, 92
Hoare, Sir Samuel, 51
Hogarthian, 37, 51
hogmanay, 62
holding the sponge, 8
Holman Hunt's "The Awakened Conscience," 51
Holy Saturday, 86
Holy Week, 77
Holywell, 51
Holywell Press, the, 8
Home Office, 109
Home Secretary, 18, 51
"Home they brought her warrior dead," 52
Homoiousion, 68
H.O.O., 86
Hopkins, Gerard Manley, 62
Hoppner, John, 111
Horace, 37
Hore-Belisha, Leslie, 37, 77
Horizon, 63, 81
horologium, 69
Horthy, Miklos, 52
hosier, 108
Host, the, 77
hot and strong, as nice as Mother makes it, 18
hotted, 52
House, 8, 52, 98
house-captain, 107
House colours, 111
House of Savoy, The, 98
House Room, 107
Housewives' Union, 81
Housey-housey...Kelly's eye, 52, 77
Ho visitato Sicilia, poi, 98
How support batteries, 37
H.R.H., 105
hubble-bubble, 25, 86

Hudor. Hydro. Dipsa, 86
huîtres, 8
Humber Snipe, 37, 77
Humboldt's Gibbon, 44
Hunt, William Holman, 51
Hussar, 86
Huxdane-Halley bomb, 18
Huxley, Sir Julian, 18
Hyde-Jekyll, 107
Hyde Park, 8
Hydriotaphia, 110
hymeneal, 81
Hypatia, 37, 86
hypostatic, 69

I

"I can do it in Greek," 86
I.C.I., 44, 59
Idaea, 69
idée fixe, 77
Il faut en finir, 37
Il faut manger, 32
Iliad, 69
Ilium, 69
Illyrians, 69
"I'm coming...," 86
immortal Anderson couple, 61
Imperator Immortalis, 25
Imperial Government, 111
incense, 8
Independent Labour Party, 18
in extremis, 52
in full ball rig, 63
Ingemisco, tanquam reus, 99
Ingres, Jean Auguste, 52
In memoria aeterna, 99
"In Memoriam," 37
Inns of Court, 18, 25
International Brigade, 99
in the box, 8
in the soup, 8
"In Thy courts no more are needed," 8, 32
Invention of the Cross, 69
I.O., 77
Irish Guards, 77
Irish Sweepstake, 32
ironmongery, 37
Ironside, General, 77
Ischia, 105
Isis, 52

"I smote the Philistine," 8
Ite, missa est, 109
"I told him what was the matter with her," 8
"I wither...," 63
"It is an evil thing...," 37
"It's a mad world, my masters," 99
It was a sign in Israel, 8
I Zingari ribbon, 63

J

jackal, 32
Jacobite, 44
James, Henry, 63, 99
James II, 77
Janissary, 81
J.C.R., 8
J.D., 77
Je crois bien, 86
Jelalabad, 28
Jellyby, Mrs., 28
J'en ai affreusement, 59
Je ne sais quoi, 8
Jenkins's ear, 92
Jeroboam, 8
Jerries, the, 37, 86
Jesuitical, 52
jeune premier, 8
Je veux me confesser, 86
Jimmy-o-goblins, 28
jobbery, 32
jockeys, 28
Jocks, 86
John, Augustus, 37, 47
Johnson, Dr., 8, 18
Joignez-vous, 77
Jones, Inigo, 52
Joyce, James, 63
Joynson-Hicks, Sir William, 37
jugged, 8
Jugs, 99
juju, 25
jumble sale, 105
junker, 77, 81
Juno copped it, 86

K

Kafka, Franz, 63
Kaiser, 52, 77

INDEX TO THE GLOSSARY

Kandy, shrine of, 92
Karonga, 77
Kasanga, 77
Kauffer, McNight, 52
Kauffmann, Angelica, 35
K.C.B.'s, 32
Keatings, 25
Keble, 52
Kedgeree, 25
Kelly's eye, 52, 77
Kemal's army, 52
Kensington Gardens, 44
Kenya Game Reserves, 25
kept *cave*, 77
Khartoum . . . Kitchener, 86
khat, 25
Kierkegaard, Sören, 63
Killiecrankie, 18
King-in-Exile, 99
Kingsley, Charles, 93
Kingsley Wood, 32
King's Proctor, 28
King's Regulations, 77
Kipling's *Light That Failed*, 44
Kitchener, Lord, 37
Klee, Paul, 99
Knife and Fork Club, 63
Knight of Malta, 44, 52, 99
Knightsbridge or Windsor, 86
Knights Templar, 38
knocking shops, 52
"Know that death is common . . . ," 63
"Know you her secret none can utter," 110
knuckle dusters, 38
knut, 92
Kolchak, 111
Krafft-Ebing, 25
Krak-des-chevaliers, 52
kulak, 44
Kümmel, 38
Kurds, 52
Kyrie, 99

L

Labarum, 69
Labour fellows, 28
Lactantius, 69
Lady Cripps's Fund, 99
Lady Day, 92
Lady Hamilton, 18
Lady into Fox, 52
la fatigue du Nord, 50
lag, 81
laissez-passer, 18
Lake Isle of Innisfree, 63
Lancelot, 28
Landseer, 52
Langley, Batty, 38, 44
Lares et Penates, 38
larger honours came with the Georges, 50
Lascar, 28, 92
Last Post, 77, 92
Last Trump, 18, 52, 86
Last Viceroy, the, 81
Lateran treaty, 99
Latin alcaics, 32
latrine wallah, 26
Lauder, Harry, 63
Laudian, 63
Laurels, The, 18
Laurencin eyes, 18
"La vache souterraine?," 86
La veuve, 86
La Vie Parisienne, 18
lawner, 109
Lawrence, Gertie, 51
Lawrence, T. E., 32, 38, 105
League of Nations, 8
League of Nations Committee, 8
League of Nations Union, 7, 52
Lear, Kent, Fool, 52
Lear on the heath, 52
Lecky, William, 18
Leech, 38
Lee-Enfield rifles, 25
Left Book Club, 81
Léger, Fernand, 99
legitimist, 52
Lely, Peter, 44
leman, 92
Le Nôtre, 59
Lent, 77
Leonardo, 38
Lepanto, 38, 52
Levant, 52
Leviticus, 25
levy, 25
Ley, Doctor, 36
Liberty's new building, 9
Lido, 33, 52, 86
life preserver, 44
lifts, 33
lighter, a, 86
"Like a beautiful and ineffectual angel . . . ," 99
"Like the immortal private of the Buffs . . . ," 59
Lillehammer, 77
Limbo, 38, 53
Limerick, 77
limeys, 63
Lincoln's Inn, 77
lingua franca, 77
link arms, 107
"Lion Has Wings, The," 38
lip, 107
Lì per me . . . , 99
Little Lord Fauntleroy, 18
live, as Jehovah was said to have done . . . , 18
Livy, 86
Lloyd George, 38
Lloyd George creation, 63
Lloyd *Trestino*, 105
LMG, 77
Loamshires, 38, 77
locum refrigerii, lucis et pacis, 99
L of C, 53, 86
Locust years, 99
London Mercury, 63
Longfellow, Henry W., 9
Longinus, 69
loofah, 33
loopy, 9
Loos, 77
Lord's, 60
Lotti, 18, 53
louche, 53
Louis Seize, 110
Lourdes, 77
Lovat-Fraser, 38, 63
Lovat tweed, 107
Lover's Seat, The, 63
Low Church, 9
Luna, 53
Luna Park, 9
Lyonnesse, 53
Lytton report, 38

M

MacDonald, Ramsay, 9, 38
Mackenzie, Compton, 36

INDEX TO THE GLOSSARY

MacMillan, Harold, 86
made his recce, 77
made one big bomb, 18
Maenad, 63
Maeterlinck, Maurice, 53
Mag, 18
Magdalen, 53
Maginot Line, 38, 77
Maginot or the Siegfried Line, 77
magistras, 99
Magnasco, Alessandro, 92
Magyar, 53
Maida Vale, 38
Maisky, Mrs., 86
Maison Japonaise, 53
Malory, 28
mal soigné, 9
man who used to dress as an Arab, 38
Manáos, 28
Manchester school utilitarian, 9
Mangelwurzels, 33
Mannerheim, Carl, 77
mantle of Lear, 63
Manuelo style, 44
Mapin and Webb of London, Messrs., 25
Marat, Jean Paul, 63
Marathon, 53
marchese, 53, 99
march tactically, 38
Mare Nostrum, 53
Marie Therese thalers, 25
Marinetti's Futurist Manifesto, 18
Maritain, Jacques, 53
market cross, 18
mark of the Plague..., 105
Maronites, 53
marriage dot, 44
Marseilles, 9
Martin, John, 86
Marylebone, 19
Mary Selena Wilmark of Britain, the, 34
Mary Tudor, 78
matelots, 38
Matisse, Henri, 9
Matto Grosso, 28, 78
Maud, Alice, 63
Maundy Thursday, 53, 78, 86
Maureen, 64
Maurier, George du, 57
mauvais poisson, 33

Max, 53, 86
Maximian, 69
Mayfair, 9
"May his soul...," 86
Maynooth, 78
M.E., 86
mealies, 78
Medici, Lorenzo, 63
Medici Press, 53, 107
M.E.F., 86
Mein Kampf, 38
Mekka, 25
Memento, homo, 78
memento mori, 38, 64
Mende...Swahili, 78
Mendelssohn, 9
Men of Harlech, 9
Merc, 19
Merci, Monsieur! Gardez bien votre chapeau, 9
Mercury, 53
Merlin, 28
Merton, 53
Mesopotamia, 9, 53
Metroland, 64
Metropolitan, 25
Meuse, 78
mewses, 9, 108
Michaelmas, 25, 92
Michaelmas term, 53
middle-day dinner, 19
Midnight Orgies at No. 10, 19
Mihajlovic, 100
Mikkeli Marshes, 78
Miles Anglicus sum, 100
Millais, John E., 19, 44
Mills, Florence, 53
Milton, John, 38
Milton-on-his-blindness, 107
Milvian Bridge, 69
Milwaukee accents, 78
"Mine eyes have seen the glory...," 25
M.I.9, 38
Minotaur, 64
minute, 78
missal, 100
Mitford, Miss, 53
Mithras, 69
Mithraum, 69
MLC, 86
M.M., 86, 100
Moabite, 9

Modern Churchman, 9
Modern Greats, 53
Modern Side, 107
Modern Upper, 107
Mods, 44
Moesia, 69
Moesian connection, 69
Mogador, 29
moke, 64
Molotov pact, the, 87
Mombasa, 109
Mon bon homme...il vous fait, 25
money for old rope, 39
monkey-puzzler, 109
Monmouth, Lord, 39
Monro, Harold, 64
monstrance, 78
Montagu, Captain, 100
Monte, 9
Montenegrin, 100
Montessori, 25
Montparnasse in Belgravia, 19
Monty, 100
moonstone, 92
Moor, on the, 81
Moore at Corunna, Sir John, 78
Mordred, 28
More birthdayers, 33
Morgan le Fay, 29
Morris stuffs, 44, 53
Morris, William, 9, 39
Mortlake, 100
mosky, 87
Mosley, 39, 92
mostica, 53
Mother Wales, 9
mot juste, 78
Moulay Abdullah, 44
M.T., 78
Mudies, 25
Muezzin, 25
mug, 53
Mumm, 9
Munera, 33
muniment-rooms, 53
Museum, 106
Mussolini, Benito, 78, 100
my heart just stood still, 9
Mystical Body, 100

N

Nacktkultur, 25
Nancy, 19

INDEX TO THE GLOSSARY

Napoleon III, 9
National Art Treasures, 78
National Gallery, 110
National Service, 53, 78
National Trust, 105
"Nature I loved, and next to Nature, Art," 39
nautch, 64
navvies, 25
"Nay not so much as out of bed?," 33
N.B.G., 19, 100
N.C.O.'s, 53
Nebi Daniel, 87
Nelson, Horatio, Lord, 39, 53
Ne pas dépasser deux, 109
Nestorian, 25
New College, 100
New College Essay Society, 44
Newdigate Prize Poem, 9
Newman Club, 54
Newman's day, 54
Newmarket, 9
Newport, 100
New Statesman, 19, 107
New Writing, 81
Nicaea, 69
"Night and day," 87, 100
Nightingale, Florence, 100
nineteen stone, 81
1920 Committee, 54
nipper, 81
Nish, 69
Nissen hut, 54, 64, 81, 100
No capitano oggi, signora, Tenente, 87
no catch, 78
nocturnes, 39
Nollekens, 39
no longer *persona grata*, 100
Nomen, 100
"None but my foe...," 69
Nones of May, 69
Non es partisan, 100
No Orchids for Miss Blandish, 87, 100
Nor iron bars a cage, 9
not on the end of a barge pole, 9
Notre condition professionnelle, 33
Notre Dame, 19
"Now sleeps the crimson petal...," 64
nuit de Noël, 19
Numerian, 69
numéro mille soixante dix-huit, 19

O

Oberammergau, 19
obliques of 'Badger,' 87
O.C., 26, 109
OC D Coy to OC 2 pl, 78
O.C. Transit Camp, 87
O.C. Troops, 100
Odi profanum vulgus et arceo, 69
Oedipus, 26
off collar, 78
off-colour, 78
Office of Works, 10
0500 hrs, 87
0830, 78
Oggi, sempre, 78
"O God our help in ages past," 9
O group, 39
"Oh, death, where is thy sting-a-ling-a-ling?," 10
"Oh for the Wings of the Dove," 19, 64
"Oh God, make me good, but not yet," 54
Old Bailey, 10
Old Bill, 39
old Etonian, 92
old Greats, 60
Old Man, 87
Old Marston, 10
Old's House, 107
oleograph of the Sacred Heart, 54
Olivet, 70
Omega, 19
Omega workshops, 54
one-and-six, 10
0930 hours, 92
one-over-the-eight, 10
0900 hours, 87
0915 hours, 54
1098 stores, 41
On such a night as this, 81
on the rocks, 100
on the start line
"On thy midnight pallet lying," 64
Oona, 64
Oppenheim, 10
Oran, 87
Oratory, 78
Order of St. John of Jerusalem, 100
order of St. Michael and St. George, 19
Oremus, 70

Ormazd, 70
O.R.'s, 78
Oscar and Aubrey—see Wilde and Beardsley, 39
O.S.C.U., 10, 54
0700, 78
0700 hours, 54
0730, 78
0610 hrs., 87
0615 hours, 87
ostlers, 29, 108
OTC, 107, 111
other House, the, 10
Other Ranks, 100
other two advantages, the, 10
0312 hours, 92
O.U.D.S., 54
Ouida, 64
Our Lady of Lourdes, 78
Outrage has It, Mr., 19
outré, 100
Overlord, 100
oxer, 29
Oxford Book of English Verse, 64
Oxford Movement, 107
Oxford Union, 26
OZNA, 111
Ozymandias, 110

P

packet, 87
packets, 26
P.A.D., 78, 100
padlocked, 78
Palace, 87
palais de Danse, 39
Palatine, 70
Palazzo, pronto, 54
Palladian, 19, 54, 111
pallium, 70
Palmerston—see Pam, 54
Pam, 33
panatrope, 10
P and O, 26, 33, 54
Pan-Slavism, 100
Pantelleria, 54
panto, 19
Paolos and Francescas, 64
paper games, 29, 110
Papistry, 78
Para, 29

227

INDEX TO THE GLOSSARY

Parks, 54
Parlez anglais?, 19
Parsee, 33, 92
Parsee death house, 26
Partagas, 54
partition of Poland, the, 87
Paschendael, 78
pas-devant, 44
Pass of Glencoe, 87
passes of Thessaly, 87
Paternoster, 100
Pathans, 78
Pathetic Fallacy, 54
Paton, Noel, 87
Pavlova, Anna, 100
Peachum, Polly, 54
peckish, 39
Pecksniff, Mr., 29
Peckwater, 54
Peerage, 106
Pegity, 26
peg out, 54
Peke, 54
PEN Club, 106
penal times, 100
penal years, 78
Penelope, 54
penitential psalms, 19
penny at the church door, a, 54
penny dreadfuls, 44
People's Army, 100
Per, 100
Perceval, 29
per Christum Dominum nostrum, 10, 70
Pericles, 60
Pernod, 33
Pervigilium Veneris, 10
Pétain, 39
Pétainist, 60
Peter Pan, 100
Petronius, 110
Peut-être, 33
Pharaoh and Moses, 87
Philippi, at, 79
Philoctetes, 87
Phoenix, 64
piacere, 33
piano nobile, 54
Picabia, Francis, 54
Picasso, Pablo, 87
picket, 26
Pict, 70
picture house, 10

pied à terre, 33
Piedmontese usurpation, 100
Pierrots, 39
pigeon, 87
Pig Scheme, 29
pig-skin Gladstone, 87
piling arms, 79
pinching, 87
Pindar's Orphism, 54
Pine's *Horace*, 101
Pinfold, 92
pips, 79, 87
Piranesi, Giovanni, 54, 109
Pitt, William, 19
place . . . coolness, light and peace, 101
Plaît-il, mon professeur?, 60
platoon schemes and company schemes, 39
play boxes, 10
plenary indulgences, 54
Plunket-Bowse, 19
Podesta, 79
Podger's, 10
Poems of Today, 64
Pompeian sentry, 10
Pompeian, 39, 54
Pompeii, 10
pongoes, 87
Pont Street, 54, 111
Pontifex Maximus, 70
Pontus, 54
Pooter at the Mansion House, Mr., 92
Pope Pius IX, 79
popped it, 10
poppet, 54
Pop. Sci., 107
Popular Front, 79
Portsmouth, 87
Poseidon, 60
Posillipo, 101
post coitum tristis, 81
poste restante, 33
potin, 54
pounding the square, 79
Poussin, Nicholas, 110
praesente cadavere, 101
Praesidium, 101
Praetorian, 70
Praxiteles, 70
prefects, 10
Prep, 10

Pre-Raphaelitism, 54
presbytery, 101
presence of Royalty, the, 19
presented to a living, 10
Priam, 70
prie-dieu, 39, 101
priest hole, 10
Priestley, J. B., 39, 60
Priestley's novels, J. B., 26, 79
Prime Minister is nuts on rural England, the, 33
Probus, 70
proctors, 55
procureuse, 19
prosciutto, 55
Proust, Marcel, 10, 50
Provence, 10
Providence, 79, 101
P.T., 39
public or secondary?, 10
public-school man, 10
Puginesque, 101
"Pull for the shore," 92
Punch, 19
Punch-and-Judy, 33
purgatory, 101
purposeless obstruction of stone, 81
'Pussy' Gresham, 32
putative parentage, 55
put down, 81
put down smoke, 39
put it over on one of his girls, 10
put the kybosh on it, 29
putting you on the square, 87

Q

Q fellows, 87
QMG, 87
Q side, the, 79
quad, 11
Quadragesimo Anno, 39
Quantocks, 79
Quantum mutatus ab illo Hectore, 107
quartier toléré, 44
Quattrocento, 55
Quebec, 55
Queen Alexandra's Day, 55
Queen Alexandra's nurses, 101
"Queen Elizabeth said . . .," 64
Queen Empress, 29

INDEX TO THE GLOSSARY

Qui diligit Deum diligit et fratrem suum, 107
Quiller-Couch, Arthur, 110
Quintilius, 70
Quis, 55
Quisling, Vidkun, 92, 101
quiversful of boys, 81
Quominus and *Quin*, 11
Quomodo sedet sola civitas, 55

R

R.A.C., 19, 33
racé, 79
racket, 26
rag, 92
rag is brewing, 101
Raj, 91
R.A.M.C., 79, 87, 101
Randal, Cantuar, 11
Rank, Father, 75
R.A.P., 39
Rape of the Sabines, 110
Rape, Right Honourable, 20
Raphael, 55
RASC, 87, 101
rat-catcher, 29
Ratisbon, 70
Raven, 70
Ravenna, 55
R.C., 55
R.C.H., 101
R.D.F., 39, 87
Reach-me-downs, 33
reading History, 55
real aristocracy . . . , 19
reason she left you, the, 11
Récamier, Madame, 55
Red Flag, 87
Red Square, 39
Reigate, 11
Reign of Terror, 11
Reinhart nun, 55
remittance man, 55
requiem, 79, 101
Reservation in the Lady Chapel, 11
resources of the Ukraine, 87
R.G.S., 29
Rhinebeck, 92
Rhodes, 33
Rhodes trust, 110

Rhyme Sheets from the Poetry Bookshop, 55
Ribbentrop, Joachim von, 39, 55, 101
ribbon of the Garter, 19
Richelieu, 79
rien ne va plus, 106
rifles pulled through, 40
Rift Valley, 87
Rimbaud, Jean, 55
ring contour, 40
rip, a, 11
Rising of '45, the, 79
Risorgimento, 101
R.N.V.R., 79
Robin de la Condamine, 64
rocket, 40, 70
Rock, The, 92
Rodin, F. Auguste, 64
Rodin's Burghers, 79
Roget, Peter, 101
Roland, 85
"Roll up the map . . . ," 29
Roman candles, 101
Romano's, 33
Rommel, Erwin, 87
Romneys, 111
Roncevalles, 55, 85
rood screen, 11
rosary, 88
Rossetti, Dante Gabriel, 101
Rosslyn Park, 79
Rotarian, 64
Rothschild, 20
Rouault, Georges, 92
Rousseau, 33
Row, 106
Royalist officers, 101
RSM, 88
RT, 79
Rubenses, 44
Ruby, 101
Rupert's horse, 55
Ruskin, 54, 55, 79
Ruskin School of Art, 55
Ryder, 108

S

Sacred Heart, 101
sacring bell, 11
sacring place, 101

Saint James's Palace, 33
Saint Roger of Waybroke defend us, 88
Saladin, 40
Salamanca, 108
Salerno, 101
Sales Boches!, 88
Salisbury, 11
saloons, 20
saltire, 33
sal volatile, 20
Sam Browne belt, 40
Samothrace, 56
Sanctuary, 109
Sandhurst, 88, 101, 108
sang-froid, 101
"Santo Inglese," 79
Saphist, 110
Sappers-demonstration, 56
Sartre, Jean Paul, 64
Sassanian lounge, 33
Sassoon, Siegfried, 40
sat . . . for Smalls and Matriculation, 11
Saturnalia, 40
sauve qui peut, 88
Savings your cloth, Rothschild, 20
savoir faire, 11
Sayers, Dorothy, 101
Scamander, 70
scamped, 79
Scapa, 40
Scapa Flow, 88
Schleswig-Holstein, 40
schools, 11, 56
Scobie, 79
Scone College, 11
Scottsboro trials, 40
scrape, 79
scratch, 79
scrimshankers, 56
Scrubs, 81
scupper, 56
sea-girt Kranae, 70
Sebastian contra mundum, 56
Second Coming, 11
Second Evening, 108
Sedobrol, 29
Seleucia, 70
Semon, Larry, 110
send in my papers, 79
Senegalese, 44
"Senior, the," 88

INDEX TO THE GLOSSARY

Serpentine, 106
Seth, 26
Settle, 108
sent down, 56, 110
Seven Dolours, 56
1700, 79
Severn, 79
Sèvres, 56, 79
Shaftesbury Avenue, 11
shakedown, 44
"Shall I compare thee to a summer's day?," 64
sham-Augustan, 79
shari, 26
shari of all the Wanda and Sakuyu chiefs, a, 26
Shaw, 26
Shaw's *Alphabets*, 108
sheepish house, 20
Shelley, Percy B., 64, 110
shingle, 29
shingled, 110
shirty, 20
shooting a line, 80
shooting a stick, 56
shrine of Kandy, 92
Shropshire Lad, A, 56
Sia lodate Gesu Cristo, 80
Siciliano Lei?, 101
Siddons, Mrs., 40
sidesmen, 108
Sidney, Philip, 40
Si la jeunesse savait . . ., 20
Silchester, 70
Simon, S. J., 85
Simonstown, 88
simpatico, 80
Simpson, Mrs., 56
Sinister Street, 56
Sir Bedivere, 4
sirens, 109
si, si, subito, signori, 56
Sitrep, 88, 92
sitter, 60
Sitwell, Osbert, 92
643202, 80
S.J., 20
slag, 33
slap-up, 29
Sloane number, 29
Sloane Square, 11
slosh, 101
Slovene royalists, 60

sluicing, 108
Slump, 29, 40, 109
small pieces of coal in his dripping, 11
small public school of ecclesiastical temper . . . , 11
Smiles' *Self-Help*, 12
Smith, Logan Pearsall, 99
snaffle, 70
Snap, 80
SNO, 88
snubs to her, 56
Soanesque, 56
Soapy Sponge, 40
sock, 29
Socrates, 40
S.O.E., 92
soft, 110
soldier manqué, 40
Somaliland, 80
Soma, The, 88
Song of Solomon, 44
Sono più abituato, 101
Souls, 70
"sound of lyres and flutes, the," 56
Southgate, 12
South Kensington, 12
South Wind, 56
sowars, 26
Spahi capes, 33
Spahi officers, 45
spanner, 20
sparklers, 81
Spartans, 41
Spectator, 106
Speed Kings, 20
Spender, Stephen, 81
Spezia, 56
Sphakia, 88
Spierpoint Down, 108
Spion Cop, 88
spliced, 12
Split, 101
Spode, 45
spoilt priest, 40
Spread Eagle at Thame, 40
Spruce's veiled ladies, 102
Spy, 20
Squadron Lawn at Cowes, 40
squiffy, 33
St. Anthony of Padua, 55
St. Bride's, 33
St. Edward the Confessor, 101

St. James's, 11
St. John's Wood, 44
St. Margaret's, 101
St. Mark's, 56
St. Nichodemus of Thyatira, 56
St. Nicholas' Day, 101
St. Omers records, 88
St. Peter and St. Paul in prison, 11
St. Peter-in-Chains, 101
St. Sepulchre's, 11
St. Vincent de Paul Society, 80
stabularia, 70
Stalin, 102
stand down, 26
standing on the Clydeside, 29
Standing Orders, 12
Stanhope gate, 45
Stanley, Arthur, 6
"start all over again from your beginnings . . . ," 80
Stein, Gertrude, 40, 64
Sten, 102
Stilton, 40
stinkeries, 29
Stoke-on-Trent, 12
stolen queen, 70
stone, 80
stone, the, 56
"Stone Walls Do Not a Prison Make," 12
stony, 80
Stonyhurst, 56
Stopes, Marie, 26
Storm, Iris, 99
Strand, 88
Strasbourg, 70
strawberry leaves, 20, 56
Strongbow, Richard
Stuart, Charles Edward, 79
stubborn Jew, 20
Stukas, 88
stumer, 56
stylographic pen, 20
subaltern, 40, 56
subfusc, 56, 102, 108
sub judice, 80
Subs, 45
subscription, 102
sub specie aeternitatis, 88, 93
sucking up, 80
Sucks to you, 40
Suda, 88
Sunday Express, 12

230

INDEX TO THE GLOSSARY

Sunday Mail, 12
sundowner, 26
super, 20, 108
suppedaneum, 70
Surrealism, 26
surréaliste, 40
Surtees, Robert Smith, 40
Swabian, 40, 70
Swiss firm, a, 12
Sword of Stalingrad, 102
syce, 26, 109
syndicates, 80

T

Tablet, 80
table-turning, 64
tabulae exsecrationum, 29
Taisez-vous, officier,..., 26
Takutu, 29
tale of Mithras, 69
Tales from the Mist, 20
Tanks for Russia Week, 88
tarboosh, 109
tart, 20
Tatler, 56, 110
taurobolium, 70
Tea-cake, 108
tea-train, 93
tea was "off," 88
Te Deums, 70, 102
tell your beads, 41
temperance hotels, 20
Teneat Bene Beste-Chetwynde, 12
Tenebrae, 56
1045 hours, 56
1000 hours, 87
1000 to 1100 hours, 87
1098 stores, 41
Tennyson, Lionel, 56
Tents of Kedar Hotel, 64
Teucer, 70
TEWTS, 80
that morning's new fire, 88
That's an odd thing to ask..., 12
"That's the King with the beard...," 20
theosophy, 20
"There's a special Providence...," 102
"There swimmeth One...," 108
Thermopylae, 41, 70

"They also served...," 102
"They told me, Francis Hinsley...," 65, 88
"they were lighting a candle that day...," 60
Thiers, 29
thimble and pen men, 20
third E in Bee Garden, 41
Third Evening, 108
Third in History, 109
1300, 80
"This scepter'd isle, this earth of majesty...," 20
Thornton, 41
three line whip, 29
"Three little maids from school are we," 26
Three Miles (Open), 12
tick, 93
tiffin gun, 33
Tiger Tim, 109
"Till a' the Seas Gang Dry My Dear...," 65
till Tom stops ringing, 56
Tilsit...Tolstoi, 88
Tintoretto, 56
Tipu Sultan's musket, 88
"'Tis Invercauld comes yonder," 80
Titian, 56
Tito, 102
Titus, 70
Tobruk, 88
Toad in *The Wind in the Willows*, Mr., 80
toff, 12
Tolpuddle martyrs, 60
ΤΟΥΤΩ ΝΙΚΑ, 70
Tom-all-alone's, 29
Tomasina, Suora, 80
tombola, 29, 56
Tom Quad, 56
ton, 12
took him to Dr. Peterfield, 12
topee, 26
toper, 21
Torres Vedras, 111
tosh, 102
toties quoties, 88
Toulon, 41
Toulouse-Lautrec, Henri, 102
Toulouse-Lautrec odalisque, 56
Tours, 29
Tous sont des effets, 33

tout-de-suite, 33
track junction, 41
Trafalgar, 57
Trajan, 71
Tranby Croft cut, 12
transmontane pietists, 106
Travancore, 93
Travellers', 57
Trebizond, 57
Trent, 57
Trèves, 71
Trevi, 60
tricoteuse of the Terror, 60
Trilby, 57
Trinity, 57
Trinovantes, 71
Triple Crown, the, 110
Tristram, 29
Trollope's *Can You Forgive Her?*, 102
Trotskyism, 41
Trotskyites, 60
Troubles, 41
Troy, 80
trunk calls, 12
Trust House, 41
Tsarkoe Seloe, 89
tube stations, 108
Tuis enim fidelibus, 102
tukals and fanes, 102
Turf in London, the, 41
Turkish delight, 12
Turner, Joseph M. W., 89
Tussaud's, Madame, 86
Tutankhamen, 34
Tweedledum, 45
Twelfth Night, 71
twelve hundred hours, 80
20/6/41, 89
twenty-firster, 106
24 Comprimés narcotiques, hypnotiques, 109
2300 hours, 41
2315 hours, 57
twig, 41
two Generals Gordon, 110
two men with bowler hats, 21
two minutes silence at eleven o'clock, 21
T/y, 89
Tyre, 71

U

Ulysses, 102
U.N., 34

INDEX TO THE GLOSSARY

Uncle George, 108
Uncle Joe, 102
undergraduate "rags," 21
Underground, 21
under-school table, 108
"Under the wide and starry sky," 108
unfrocked priest, 102
Union, 57, 102
un peu, 89
U.N.R.R.A., 102, 111
Up Jenkins, 12, 93
Upper Dormitory, 108
Upper House, 21
Upsala, 60
Uraricuera, 29
using an instrument, 57
Ustashi, 111
Ut exultat in coitu elephas..., 110
Utrillo, Maurice, 41

V

V.A.D. (VADs), 21, 80
Vale, 80
Valerian, 71
valet-de-chambre, 21
Valse, 80
Vanburgh, John, 29
Van Gogh's "Sunflowers," 57
"Vanity of vanities," 57
vaporetto, 57
veil of Cryphius, 71
Veniam day, 108
veronal, 12
"Very flat Norfolk...," 89
vestal virgin, 65
vet them, 111
vetted, 34
Vicar Apostolic, 26
Vichy French, the, 89
Vickers, 41
Vie Parisienne, La, 109
village post office, 12
ville lumière, 89
Vincent de Paul Society, 80
vin d'honneur, 102
vin triste, 110
Virgil, 41, 71
Vitruvian, 71
Viva! Arriba! Heil!, 71
Viveash, Mrs., 102
von Fritsch, 37

Von Hügel, 12
von Weichs, 102
vox humana, 12

W

W.A.A.F., 102
Wagner, Richard, 65
waits, 21
walked across the hall, 108
walk out, 30, 108
Wallace Collection, 80
Wallah, 26, 109
Walpole, Horace, 110
Walpole, Sir Hugh, 102
Wal-Wal, 60
Wandering Jew, 57
War Memorial Fund, 13
"Warning Shadows," 57
War Office, 80
Waste Land, The, 57, 102
Waterloo, 41
Watt's *Physical Energy*, 30
"Wearing of the Green, The," 65
W.C., 26
W.D., 41
Wee Kirk o' Auld Lang Syne, 65
Weichs, Maximillian, 102
Wellington, 41
Wendover, 21
Wesleyan, 21, 102
West End, 108
Westward Ho!, 93
wet, 93
wettest fellows, 80
"What a sell!," 41
What did Dr. Johnson say about fortitude?, 13
Whatman H. P. drawing paper, 57
"What have I done for you, England, my England...?," 108
What price the coon?, 13
what sucks, 71
Whembley, Mentmore and Thatch, 111
when I was up, 13
When we got over 1098, 41
"When wilt thou save the people?," 89
"Where is the best place to hide a leaf?," 80
Where the Rainbow Ends, 65

Whistlerian, 45
Whitaker, 21
white-aproned as Mrs. Noah, 13
white ducks, 36
White Fathers, 26
white feathers, 41
Whitehall, 21, 81
White Man's Grave, 80
whore of Babylon, 13
Widow Twankey, the, 89
Wilde, Oscar, 41
William and Mary, 13
Willis's rooms, 34
Wilmarch, 34
Wilson, General, 106
Wilson, 'Scottie,' 65
Wind in the Willows, The, 13
windy, 102
"wings in vain," 102
winkle the mortar out, 89
Winn, Godfrey, 41
Winston, 102
Winterhalter, Franz, 45
"Wipers," 30, 80
Wisdom of Father Brown, The, 57
Wiseman Club, 102
"Without shedding of blood...," 21
wogs, 26, 89
Wolf Cub account, 105
Wolfe, James, 41
"woman's only a woman, A," 103
Woolf, Virginia, 13
Works, the, 65
"Would you like to sin...," 80
W/T, 89
Wykehamist, 57

X

Xanthus-side, 57
Xenophon, 41, 80

Y

Yarmouth Castle, 30
Yashmak, 30
Yellow Book, 41
York Minster, 13

INDEX TO THE GLOSSARY

Young Visiters, The, 30
your standard, 13
You want either a first or a fourth, 57
Yseult, 30
Yuan Tse tsung, 41

Z

Zeitgeist, 103
zero hour, 41
zero plus fifty-two, 89

zero plus sixty, 89
Zion, 103
Zionist, 80, 103
"Zivio...," 71
Zola, 65
Zululand, 80
Zurbarán ascetic, 103